The North Carolina Experience

The North Carolina Experience
An Interpretive and Documentary History

Edited by Lindley S. Butler
and Alan D. Watson

The University of North Carolina Press

Chapel Hill and London

© 1984 The University of North Carolina Press

Manufactured in the United States of America

98   8   7   6   5

Library of Congress Cataloging in Publication Data
Main entry under title:

The North Carolina Experience.

  Includes index.
    1. North Carolina—History—Addresses, essays,
lectures. 2. North Carolina—History—Sources.
I. Butler, Lindley S., 1939–   II. Watson, Alan D., 1942–
F254.5.N67   1984   975.6   83-27357
ISBN 0-8078-1609-4
ISBN 0-8078-4124-2 pbk.

Contents

Preface

The North Carolina Experience: An Interpretive and Documentary History is designed to introduce the reader to the process of history. Simply stated, history is the recorded past interpreted, and this work presents to the reader brief interpretive essays and primary sources on specific topics. In this encounter with historians and their sources of history, one should grow to understand that history is no simple formula but a complex discipline that often raises more questions than are answered.

Although conceived as a supplementary reader for the teaching of North Carolina history on the college level, this work will serve well as a basic text in brief survey courses or as a source book for teachers on the elementary, secondary, or postsecondary level. The efforts of nineteen scholars have been combined to present in topical form the state's history from discovery to the present. The structure of the work provides a midpoint at 1835, which is the traditional date dividing year-long courses in North Carolina history. The editors realize that there are obvious gaps and that not every reader will agree with their choice of subjects, but they chose topics or issues that could provide a general framework for a broad look at the state's past and illuminate some of the key issues or turning points in our history.

The format was planned with flexibility in mind to enable the teacher to select the classroom approach that best satisfies his needs and goals. In order to present the widest possible coverage of the topics as well as to develop an entrée into the field, each chapter consists of an introductory essay, supportive documents, and a list of suggested readings. The authors bring their own expertise to their essays and have produced well-rounded, interpretive surveys of specific segments of the state's history. Following each essay is a collection of documents emphasizing the major points of the discussion and offering a brief foray into the primary sources for the students. The documents not only illuminate the past from the viewpoint of the contemporaries but in conjunction with the essay may also be a springboard for extended discussion on the topic or for further research. Each author has proposed readings to acquaint the student with readily available pertinent secondary literature and published sources.

Despite the specific educational purpose for which this work was planned, it beckons to all who profess an interest in the Tar Heel State. Broad coverage of various facets of North Carolina's past, coupled with the widest latitude granted to the authors in order to encourage their speculations, has produced an undertaking both historical and relevant to the present. The general tenor of the work provides insight for all with the fascinating history of a unique southern state. If this volume kindles an interest in significant aspects of the Tar Heel heritage and contributes to an understanding of North Carolinians, then it has fulfilled its purpose.

Lindley S. Butler
Alan D. Watson

The North Carolina Experience

CHAPTER I

The Tragedy of the
North Carolina Indians
Herbert R. Paschal

Old Man of Pomeiock, by John White, 1585, engraving by Theodore De Bry,
1590 (Courtesy of the Division of Archives and History, Raleigh, N.C.)

The study of the American Indian in North Carolina has proceeded at two levels. One of these has had as its principal goal the description of the Indians' origins and culture, social and political organizations, and manner of life at the time of their first encounter with Europeans. The second level of study has centered upon the interaction between the Indians and the Old World intruders.

The confrontation between Indians and Europeans holds out to the historian many possible topics for exploration, but there is one that transcends all others—the rapid disintegration of the Indians' way of life and their virtual disappearance from North Carolina after the arrival of the European settlers. Loss, therefore, is the central theme of North Carolina Indian history. The astonishing rate of attrition suffered by the Indians of North Carolina dwarfs all other aspects of their history. Only a clear understanding of the tragic details of this story can lead to a full appreciation of the Indians' role in North Carolina history. Before turning to explore this theme, however, we need briefly to note the origins of the first inhabitants of the American continent and to describe the Indians in North Carolina at the time of permanent European settlement.

The Indians who peopled North America were descendants of the Asian hunters who gradually pushed westward from Siberia over the Bering land bridge into Alaska probably between twenty-eight thousand and twenty thousand years ago. By 9000 to 8500 B.C. the aborigines had reached and begun to settle in small numbers in the region that would someday be North Carolina. These earliest arrivals belong to the Late Paleo–Indian period. They were nomadic hunters who moved about in small bands hunting the giant bison, mastodons, mammoths, and other great mammals, using spears tipped with a distinctive stone point known as the Clovis Fluted.

Upon the appearance of the Archaic period, dated 7000 to 6000 B.C., the economy of the Paleo-Indian peoples of this region changed noticeably. They gradually came to depend on small game, fish and shellfish, and wild plants for their food sources. Although the variety of tools increased, the spear continued to be the chief weapon of the hunters, but it was now used with a spear thrower or *atlatl* to give it greater distance. Altogether, the Archaic period can be viewed in the words of Peter Farb as "a long period of time during which local environments were skillfully exploited in a multitude of ways."

Sometime about 700 to 500 B.C. the Woodland period evolved. This period was characterized by the appearance and development of pottery, the beginnings and growth of agriculture, and the replacement of the spear by the bow and arrow as the chief weapon of the hunter. The Woodland period passed through a number of increasingly complex stages, and by historical times well-developed and highly diversified societies were occupying the land that would become North Carolina.

The Indians in North Carolina entered the historical period early in the sixteenth century with the arrival of European explorers along the coast. The earliest visitors to North Carolina found the Indian a fascinating element in the New World scene and were soon sending reports describing these people and their physical characteristics, dwellings, villages, manner of life, religion, government, and society back to an entranced Europe. As European discovery and exploration gave way to European settlements, descriptions of the Indians and comments upon them came more and more to express two sharply divergent views about the Indians' nature and character.

To many observers the Indian was a noble savage living without guile or the conceits of more advanced societies and finding in the forces of nature and the wilderness about him spiritual strength and direction. Others saw the Indians as brutal and bloodthirsty, devoid of even the most limited attributes of civilization, and unwilling or unable to master them. Obviously the truth lies somewhere between these two extremes, but which point of view is to be given the greater credence is difficult to determine. Recent scholarship has leaned heavily toward the concept of the Indian as nature's child while assigning his European protagonist the role of the brutal interloper.

The first permanent settlers of North Carolina found nearly thirty Indian tribes living within its borders. They ranged in size from a few hundred persons to several thousand. Although each tribe spoke a different language, each of the languages belonged to one of three linguistic groups. That is, each tribe spoke a tongue that belonged to either the Algonquian, Iroquoian, or Siouan linguistic families.

The Algonquians in the mid-seventeenth century were represented in North Carolina by nine to ten tribes. They lived in an area extending from the Virginia border southward to about Bogue Inlet and from the Outer Banks westward to an imaginary line running along the west side of the Chowan River through present-day Plymouth, Washington, and New Bern, and on to the ocean near Bogue Inlet. The tribes living in this area in the mid-seventeenth century were the Pasquotank, Yeopim, Poteskeet, Chowanoc, Machapunga, Bay or Bear River, Pamptico, Hatteras, Neusioc, and possibly the Coree. These tribes were the most southerly of all the Algonquian linguistic groups. Tribes speaking an Algonquian-related tongue occupied the entire Atlantic seaboard from coastal North Carolina northward into Canada.

Archaeological research in North Carolina has identified cultural materials produced by the Algonquians as beginning about A.D. 800 to 900.

The region that would become North Carolina lay within the gray zone between the northeastern and southeastern cultural areas, so it is not strange that the culture of the Algonquian tribes and most other North Carolina tribes contained elements from both regions. The impact of southeastern culture traits was, however, less obvious upon the Algonquians than upon any other groups in North Carolina.

The Algonquian tribes, with the exception of the Siouan Cape Fear Indians, were the only tribes in North Carolina to have any sustained contact with the European intruders in the sixteenth century. (Document 1.1) Contact that began in the 1520s reached a climax in the 1580s, when English colonists sent out by Sir Walter Raleigh made several efforts to establish themselves on Roanoke Island. The abortive settlements on Roanoke Island were productive of several accounts of the coastal Algonquian as well as watercolor studies of these Indians and their way of life by the artist John White.

The Algonquian tribes lived in villages of about ten to thirty houses. Some of the villages were palisaded, and some were clusters of houses surrounded by open fields. The houses were rectangular, usually thirty-six to forty-eight feet in length, with barrel roofs, which early explorers likened to an English arbor. The basic frame was formed by saplings lashed together and covered by bark or reed mats.

Corn was the principal agricultural crop of the Algonquians although pumpkins, beans, and other crops were grown. Fishing and shellfishing were of major importance, as is clearly indicated by temporary fishing campsites and vast piles of oyster shells. The Indians concentrated upon those pursuits primarily in the spring, before corn could be harvested. Hunting with bow and arrow and gathering nuts and berries were also crucial to the Algonquian diet.

The scarcity of stone in the coastal area limited its use among the Algonquians, who relied chiefly on wood, bone, and shell for their tools and utensils. Coils of clay were shaped into pots and fired to make them hard. The basal portion of these pots was typically globular in form.

Religion was important to the Algonquians, who worshiped a large number of gods and spirits, many of them found in the forces of nature. They erected anthropomorphic idols to represent their gods and believed in an afterlife for all.

The three Iroquoian-speaking Indian tribes living in whole or in part in North Carolina at the time of European settlement were the Cherokee, Tuscarora, and Meherrin. The Cherokee occupied both sides of the southern Appalachian chain and claimed a hunting range of forty thousand square miles of wilderness, a vast region that included the entire mountain area of North Carolina. Their towns were located in three different geographical areas, and the inhabitants of each area spoke a different one of the three principal dialects of the Cherokee language. These three groupings of the Cherokee villages were known as the Lower Towns, the Middle Towns, and the Overhill or Western Towns. The Middle Towns were located along the rivers of western North Carolina and spoke the Kituwah dialect.

The Cherokee, according to linguistic analysis, broke away from the original north Iroquoian center about thirty-five hundred to thirty-eight hundred years ago. Although there is no proof that they moved into the southern Appalachian region at this time, archaeological evidence discovered over the past quarter of a century has increasingly indicated that there has been a long and unbroken occupation of that area by the Cherokee. The period of Cherokee occupancy of the southern Appalachians, which can be supported by archaeological evidence, has been variously estimated at one to two thousand years.

Earliest Cherokee population figures date from the first decades of the eighteenth century and vary widely. The most likely estimates fall between sixteen and twenty thousand persons living in sixty to sixty-four towns and villages. Located in the river valleys of their mountainous land, the towns were often strung along bottom lands of the rivers for miles with the dwelling houses scattered among the fields of corn, squash, pumpkins, and beans. Houses were square or rectangular in shape and composed of a framework of poles covered with bark or woven siding. The roofs were made of bark or wood. Clay or earth was often tamped into the sides of the houses in a wattle-and-daub construction.

Many of the Cherokee towns had a flat-topped earthen mound near their center on which a ceremonial or town house was built. This house was constructed by the town and was usually larger than the ordinary dwelling. Its roof was thatched with rushes. Here guests were entertained, council meetings were held, and ceremonial events were carried out. (Document 1.2) The Cherokees were excellent farmers, although like all North Carolina Indians they relied heavily upon game for their food. The gathering of roots, nuts, and berries and fishing added to their diet.

The Tuscarora, who derived from the same Iroquoian linguistic center to the northward as did the Cherokee, are estimated on the basis of linguistics to have broken away from the main northern trunk from nineteen hundred to twenty-four hundred years ago. When precisely they thrust themselves into the North Carolina coastal plain is not known. The events and circumstances of the historical period indicate a surprisingly close relationship between the Tuscarora and the most important

Iroquoian group to the northward, the Five Nations of New York. At the same time, relations between the Tuscarora and the Cherokee were always bitterly hostile.

Although accurate early population figures are lacking, the Tuscarora apparently numbered about five thousand persons in the seventeenth century and lived in about fifteen villages lying chiefly between the Tar and Neuse rivers, especially along Contentnea Creek and its tributaries. The warlike character of these people was early noted by explorers and affirmed by their Indian neighbors. The emphasis on village autonomy that characterized their political organization has led some writers to insist that the Tuscarora nation was a confederation of tribes, but recent studies have shown that this was not the case.

The villages of the Tuscarora fall into two general categories. The most common was the rural village or plantation, which was composed of several clusters of three or four cabins surrounded by cultivated fields and scattered over an area of several miles. The other form of village consisted of a number of habitations surrounded by a palisade made of upright logs. The houses were bark-covered and circular in design, resembling beehives, though the rectangular barrel roof structures made familiar by the Algonquians were also used by the Tuscarora. Agriculture was important to the Tuscarora, although hunting and gathering remained an essential part of the tribe's life.

The Meherrin Indians lived principally in Virginia along the river of that name and were tributary to that government, but they asserted control over some lands on the North Carolina side of the border. In the eighteenth century, under pressure from the Virginia government and settlers, the main body of the tribe moved southward into the less populated area of Carolina below the border. In 1669 they were reported to have fifty fighting men in two villages.

The Siouan-speaking tribes of North Carolina held the piedmont region between the Tuscarora and the Cherokee and occupied the Cape Fear River valley to the sea. Linguistically the North Carolina Sioux were related not only to the Siouan tribes of the Virginia piedmont and South Carolina but also to the powerful Sioux of the Dakotas and the Great Plains. Because of the migratory habits of many of the piedmont Siouan tribes, it is difficult to determine whether certain of these tribes ever settled permanently in North Carolina. At least some of the villages of the following Siouan tribes were located in North Carolina at one time or another: Cape Fear, Catawba, Keyauwee, Saponi, Eno, Tutelo, Sissipahaw, Occaneechi, Shakori, Sugeree, Waccamaw, Woccon, Waxhaw, Saura or Cheraw, and Adshusheer.

Except for the Catawba, who numbered about five to six thousand, most of these tribes were small. The villages of the Sioux consisted of round, domed houses all of which were encircled by a palisade. There was a heavy reliance upon hunting and gathering, although crops of corn, beans, and squash added considerably to their diet. (Document 1.3) When Europeans began to enter the Siouan country they found these tribes living in great anxiety and fear because they were being subjected to constant raids by war parties from the Five Nations of New York. In an effort to avoid these fierce raiders from the north the Sioux began to move about and shift their village locations so that they could be less easily located.

The frantic movements of the Sioux as they sought to avoid destruction were portents of the future for the nearly thirty tribes of North Carolina. Forces more powerful than the dreaded Iroquoian raiding parties confronted all of the tribes as European settlers began to push southward from Virginia. As a result, the Indian all but vanished from the borders of North Carolina.

Warfare between Indians and settlers and between one group of Indians and another sharply reduced and, on occasion, virtually destroyed a number of tribes in North Carolina. Although the losses sustained in pitched battle were debilitating to the tribes, of at least equal importance was the destruction of their supplies, villages, and crops. Because each tribe lived almost entirely upon its own resources, the destruction of its food and instruments of production could lead to starvation and death. The prominence of agriculture among the North Carolina tribes made them even more vulnerable because the increased availability of foodstuffs had led to a population growth that could not be sustained by hunting and gathering alone. Unlike the settlers, the Indians had no system of credit or avenues of trade by which they could replenish a destroyed food supply.

The first significant conflict between Indians and settlers in North Carolina pitted the Chowanoc against the Albemarle settlers in a two-year war that ended in 1677 with the defeat of the Indians. Thereafter relative peace reigned for three decades, though the numerous Tuscarora and smaller tribes were sufficiently powerful to restrict white settlement to the eastern coastal area from the Albemarle to Pamlico Sound.

Early in the eighteenth century white expansionist efforts, represented particularly by the New Bern settlement of 1710, the enslavement of Indians, and continued "sharp" trading practices by settlers provoked the Tuscarora and their allied tribes to a full-scale assault upon North Carolina settlements. The Tuscarora War would have been devastating but for the timely assistance rendered by two South Carolina expeditions, led by John Barnwell and James Moore respectively, which resulted in the complete defeat of the Indians by 1715. Most of the Tuscarora subsequently migrated northward to join the Iroquois in New York;

the remainder settled upon a reservation laid out for them in present-day Bertie County. (Document 1.4)

With the decline of the coastal tribes only the Cherokee in the west stood in the path of white expansion in North Carolina. Coinciding with the French and Indian War in the 1750s was the appearance of white settlers in the foothills of the Appalachians, and the French seized upon Cherokee apprehensions to gain the Indians' support in the conflict against England. The Cherokee War, lasting from 1759 to 1761, was concluded by the combined efforts of the colonists and British regulars. Although the Lower and Middle towns had been devastated, the Overhill remained virtually untouched. The Cherokee had been defeated but not broken, as attested by events during the American Revolution. (Document 1.5)

A decade and a half later the colonials sought independence from Britain. Fearing an Anglo-Indian alliance during the war with England, the Americans took preventive measures early in the conflict. In the summer of 1776, Griffith Rutherford with approximately twenty-four hundred men, including forces from Virginia and South Carolina, marched into Cherokee country to destroy thirty-six towns and vast stores of supplies. With the signing of the Treaty of Long Island on Holston in 1777, the Cherokee War of 1776 officially ended. But hostilities had not concluded. Upon the appearance of British troops in the South in 1779–80, American fear of an alliance between the enemy and the Indians prompted another invasion of the Cherokee country in 1780. A second Treaty of Long Island in 1781 terminated that conflict, leaving the Cherokee nation divided, impoverished, and virtually at the mercy of the land-hungry whites. As James H. O'Donnell has suggested, the "Trail of Tears" in many ways originated during the revolutionary era.

Not only war but man's age-old enemy, disease, was at times a terrible scourge to the North Carolina tribes. Especially devastating were smallpox and other diseases introduced by the European invaders and hitherto unknown to the Indians. Even before the advent of the permanent settlement of the North American coast the ravage of disease brought by early explorers had taken its toll. The tribes of the New England coast were almost destroyed before the arrival of the *Mayflower* on that coast in 1619.

Similarly, the Carolina Algonquians in the vicinity of Albemarle Sound apparently suffered heavy losses from disease between the arrival of the Raleigh colonists on Roanoke Island in the 1580s and the coming of permanent settlers in the 1650s. Thomas Harriot in his *Brief and True Report* notes one Algonquian tribe destroyed by an epidemic of measles. The once proud Pamlico tribe was decimated by smallpox in the 1690s and reduced to one village of fifteen fighting men. In 1738 and 1739 epidemics of smallpox swept both the Catawba and the Cherokee villages. The Cherokee lost about half of their population. The disease was particularly severe in the Middle towns. The high death toll from such European diseases as smallpox was in part the result of the totally inappropriate treatment with which the Indians sought to cure themselves as well as the absence of any immunity to the alien maladies.

Although designed in part to assure the continued peaceful existence of the Indian on at least a portion of his tribal land, reservations in the end also played a major role in his disappearance from North Carolina. Reservations were tracts of land set aside by the colonial government and later by the state and federal governments for the exclusive use of Indian tribes. The lands were generally granted in perpetuity and could not be sold or alienated in any way by the tribes who lived upon them.

Carolinians resorted to reservations early in the Albemarle. In 1677, following the Chowanoc Indian War, that tribe was assigned a twelve-mile-square reservation south of Bennetts Creek in present Gates County. (Document 1.6) Before the end of the century reservations for the Yeopim, Poteskeet, and Pasquotank had been established in the Albemarle. The Tuscarora Indian War of 1711–15 led to the establishment of a reservation for the Tuscarora on the north bank of the Roanoke and another for the Machapunga on the south shore of Lake Mattamuskeet. Later the Croatan and other small tribes were located on this last reservation. Today none of these tribes can be found on their old reservation lands.

The Indians were not purposely destroyed but were assimilated into the dominant European culture about them. As early as 1686, John Archdale, a Lord Proprietor and later governor, noted that this process of acculturation was well under way. He observed that some of the Indians near him were beginning to keep livestock. Others found that the reservation Indians handled English "tolerably well" and wore English clothing. Although the Cherokee adapted themselves to the dominant European culture to a remarkable degree, they did not lose their identity as a tribe and as an Indian people.

The disappearance of the Indians from this region was partly the result of the removal of a number of tribes to lands beyond the borders of North Carolina. Their removal was in part voluntary and in part involuntary. Some tribes, particularly the Sioux, suffering constant attack by the warriors of the Five Nations, moved into South Carolina and eventually took refuge among the Catawba, who had consolidated their villages south of the North Carolina border. Other Siouan tribes such as the Eno and Tutelo moved to New York, where they placed themselves under the protection of their enemies, the Five Nations, and assumed the humiliating role of dependent nations.

Following their defeat in the Tuscarora War, most of the Tuscarora moved northward to New York, where they ultimately joined the league of the Five Nations, which henceforth was known as the Six Nations. About eight hundred Indians under the leadership of chieftain Tom Blount remained. They found reservation life intolerable. Confinement, enticement by other Indians, and insults from white neighbors resulted in the rapid decline of the Tuscarora. In 1803, at the behest of Tuscarora in New York, the aging, dwindling remnant of the tribe in North Carolina left their North Carolina reservation to join their brethren in the North.

The most famous departure of a tribe from North Carolina took place in the 1830s, when the Cherokee were forced against their will to leave their beloved southern mountains and move to a large reservation in Oklahoma. In 1830 Congress passed the Indian Removal Act, which had as its purpose the removal of all Indian tribes living east of the Mississippi to reservations west of that river. Because of the treaties of Hopewell and Holston the Cherokee hoped to avoid removal, but in 1835 the federal government was able to persuade a group of Cherokees to sign the Treaty of New Echota, which set aside the earlier treaties and opened the way for their forced removal by the U.S. Army in 1838. (Document 1.7) It is estimated that nearly one-fourth of the Cherokee died on the "Trail of Tears" westward. About a thousand North Carolina Cherokees hid out in the mountains and escaped being transported. They were eventually granted permission to remain and subsequently became the Eastern Band of the Cherokee Nation and were assigned the Qualla Reservation in parts of present Swain and Jackson counties. (Document 1.8) Although the Cherokee are the only Indian tribe in the state today that retains a knowledge of their history, culture, language, and identity, remnants of acculturated Indian groups survive in eastern North Carolina to be recognized in the present century as the Lumbee, Coharie, and Waccamaw.

Warfare, disease, and migration played a major role in the rapid decline and virtual disappearance of the Indians from North Carolina, but many additional elements were also present. Strong drink, the Indian trade, and the enslavement of the Indians also help to explain the central theme of North Carolina Indian history. (Document 1.9)

DOCUMENT 1.1

Thomas Harriot Describes the Algonquian Indians

They are a people clothed with loose mantles made of Deere skins, & aprons of the same rounde about their middles; all els naked; of such a difference of statures only as wee in England; having no edge tooles or weapons of yron or steele to offend us withall, neither know they how to make any: those weapons that they have, are onlie bowes made of Witch hazle, & arrowes of reeds; flat edged truncheons also of wood about a yard long, neither have they anything to defend themselves but targets made of barks; and some armours made of stickes wickered together with thread.

Their townes are but small, & neere the sea coast but few, some containing but 10. or 12. houses: some 20. the greatest that we have seene have bene but of 30. houses: if they be walled it is only done with barks of trees made fast to stakes, or els with poles onely fixed upright and close one by another.

Their houses are made of small poles made fast at the tops in rounde forme after the maner as is used in many arbories in our gardens of England, in most townes covered with barkes, and in some with artificiall mattes made of long rushes; from the tops of the houses downe to the ground. The length of them is commonly double to the breadth, in some places they are but 12. and 16. yardes long, and in other some wee have seene of foure and twentie.

In some places of the countrey one onely towne belongeth to the government of a Wiróans or chiefe Lorde; in other some two or three, in some sixe, eight, & more; the greatest Wiróans that yet we had dealing with had but eighteene townes in his government, and able to make not above seven or eight hundred fighting men at the most: The language of every government is different from any other, and the farther they are distant the greater is the difference.

Their maner of warres amongst themselves is either by sudden surprising one an other most cōmonly about the dawning of the day, or moone light; or els by ambushes, or some suttle devices: Set battels are very rare, except it fall out where there are many trees, where eyther part may have some hope of defence, after the deliverie of every arrow, in leaping behind some or other.

If there fall out any warres between us & them, what their fight is likely to bee, we having advantages against them so many maner of waies, as by our discipline, our strange weapons and devices els; especially by ordinances great and small, it may be easily imagined; by the experience we have had in some places, the turning up of their heeles against us in running away was their best defence.

In respect of us they are a people poore, and for want of skill and judgement in the knowledge and use of our things, doe esteeme our trifles before thinges of greater value.

Thomas Hariot, A Brief and True Report of the New Found Land of Virginia *(1588; reprint, New York: History Book Club, 1951), p. E2.*

DOCUMENT 1.2

The First Englishmen Reach and Describe the Cherokee in 1673

At ye end of fiftteen dayes from Sitteree they arive at ye Tomahitans river, being ye 6th river from ye mountains. this river att ye Tomahitans towne seemes to run more westerly than ye other five. This river they past in connoos ye town being seated in ye other side about foure hundred paces broad above ye town, within sight, ye horse they had left waded only a small channell swam, they were very kindly entertained by them, even to addoration in their cerrimonies of courtesies and a stake was sett up in ye middle of ye towne to fasten ye horse to, and aboundance of corne and all manner of pulse with fish, flesh and beares oyle for ye horse to feed upon and scaffold sett up before day for my two men and Appomattocke Indian that theire people might stand and gaze at them and not offend them by theire throng. This towne is seated on ye river side, haveing ye clefts of ye river on ye one side being very high for its defence, the other three sides trees of two foot over, pitched on end, twelve foot high, and on ye topps scafolds placed with parrapits to defend the walls and offend theire enemies which men stand on to fight, many nations of Indians inhabitt downe this river, which runes west upon ye salts which they are att warre withe and to that end keepe one hundred and fifty cannoes under ye command of theire forte. ye leaste of them will carry twenty men, and made sharpe at both ends like a wherry for swiftness, this forte is foure square; 300: paces over and ye houses sett in streets, many hornes like bulls hornes lye upon theire dunghills, store of fish they have, one sort they have like unto stocke—fish cured after that manner. Eight dayes jorny down this river lives a white people which have long beardes and whiskers and weares clothing, and on some of ye other rivers lives a hairey people, not many yeares since ye Tomahittans sent twenty men laden with beavor to ye white people, they killed tenn of them and put ye other tenn in irons, two of which tenn escaped and one of them came with one of my men to my plantation as you will understand after a small time of rest one of my men returnes with his horse, ye Appomatock Indian and 12 Tomhittans, eight men and foure women, one of those eight is hee which hath been a prisoner with ye white people, my other man remains with them untill ye next returne to learne ye language. the 10th of September my man with his horse and ye twelve Indians arived at my house praise bee to God, ye Tomahitans have a bout sixty gunnes, not such locks as oures bee, the steeles are long and channelld where ye flints strike.

Letter of Abraham Wood to John Richards, 22 August 1674, in Clarence Walworth Alvord and Lee Bidgood, The First Exploration of the Trans-Alleghaney Region by the Virginians, 1650–1674 *(Cleveland: Arthur H. Clark Co., 1912), pp. 212–14.*

DOCUMENT 1.3

John Lawson Describes the Siouan Tribes

Next Morning, it proving delicate Weather, three of us separated our-selves from the Horses, and the rest of the Company, and went directly for *Sapona* Town. That day, we pass'd through a delicious Country, (none that I ever saw exceeds it.) We saw fine bladed Grass, six Foot high, along the Banks of these pleasant Rivulets: We pass'd by the Sepul-chres of several slain *Indians.* Coming, that day, about 30 Miles we reach'd the fertile and pleasant Banks of *Sapona* [Yadkin] River, whereon stands the *Indian* Town and Fort. Nor could all *Europe* afford a pleas-anter Stream, were it inhabited by *Christians*, and cultivated by ingenious Hands, These *Indians* live in a clear Field, about a Mile square, which they would have sold me; because I talked sometimes of coming into those Parts to live. This most pleasant River may be something broader than the *Thames at Kingston*, keeping a continual pleasant warbling Noise, with its reverberating on the bright Marble Rocks. . . .

The *Saponas* had (about 10 days before we came thither) taken Five Prisoners of the *Sinnagers or Jennitos*, a Sort of People that range several thousands of Miles, making all Prey they lay their Hands on. These are fear'd by all the savage Nations I ever was among, the Westward *Indians* dreading their Approach. They are all forted in, and keep continual Spies and Out-Guards for their better Security. Those Captives they did intend to burn, few Prisoners of War escaping that Punishment. . . .

The *Toteros*, a neighbouring Nation, came down from the Westward Mountains, to the *Saponas*, desiring them to give them those Prisoners into their Hands, to the Intent they might send them back into their own Nation, being bound in Gratitude to be serviceable to the *Sinnagers*, since not long ago, those Northern-*Indians* had taken some of the *Toteros* Prisoners, and done them no Harm, but treated them civilly whilst among them, sending them, with Safety, back to their own People, and affirming, that it would be the best Method to preserve Peace on all Sides. At that time, these *Toteros*, *Saponas*, and the *Keyauwees*, 3 small Nations, were going to live together, by which they thought they should strengthen themselves, and become formidable to their Enemies. The Reasons offer'd by the *Toteros* being heard, the *Sapona* King, with the Consent of his Counsellors, deliver'd the *Sinnagers* up to the *Toteros*, to conduct them home. . . .

Five Miles from this River [Uwharrie], to the N.W. stands the *Keyauwees* Town. They are fortify'd in, with wooden Puncheons, like *Sapona*, being a People much of the same Number. Nature hath so fortify'd this Town, with Mountains, that were it a Seat of War, it might easily be made impregnable; having large Corn-Fields joining to their Cabins, and a *Savanna* near the Town, at the Foot of these Mountains, that is capable of keeping some hundred Heads of Cattle. And all this environ'd round with very high Mountains, so that no hard Wind ever troubles these Inhabitants. . . .

We being six in Company, divided ourselves into Two Parties; and it was my Lot to be at the House of *Keyauwees Jack*, who is King of that People. He is a *Congeree-Indian*, and ran away when he was a Boy. He got this Government by Marriage with the Queen; the Female Issue carrying the Heritage, for fear of Imposters; the Savages well knowing, how much Frailty possesses the *Indian* Women, betwixt the Garters and the Girdle.

John Lawson, A New Voyage to Carolina, *ed. Hugh T. Lefler (Chapel Hill: University of North Carolina Press, 1962), pp. 52–53, 56–57.*

DOCUMENT 1.4

Christopher Gale's Account of the Tuscarora War, 1711–1713

Much more time, and a hand more skilful, would be requisite to give you a view of the calamities and miseries of so fine a country laid waste and desolate by the most barbarous enemies: I mean the Corees and Tuscarora Indians. . . .

I shall, therefore, inform your honors, that on Saturday the 22d of September last, was perpetrated the grossest piece of villainy that was ever heard of in English America. One hundred and thirty people massacred at the head of the Nuse, and on the south side of Pamptaco rivers, in the space of two hours; butchered after the most barbarous manner that can be expressed, and their dead bodies used with all the scorn and indignity imaginable; their houses plundered of considerable riches (being generally traders), then burned, and their growing and hopeful crops destroyed. What spectacle can strike a man with more horror and stir up more to revenge, than to see so much barbarity practised in so little a time and so unexpectedly. And what makes it the more surprising, that nefarious villainy was committed by such Indians as were esteemed as members of the several families where the mischiefs were done, and that with smiles in their countenances, when their intent was to destroy. . . .

I shall not trouble you with a particular relation of all their butcheries, but shall relate to you some of them, by which you may suppose the rest. The family of one Mr. Nevill was treated after this manner: the old gentleman himself, after being shot, was laid on the house-floor, with his stockings turned over his shoes, and his body covered all over with new linen. His wife was set upon her knees, and her hands lifted up as if she was at prayers, leaning against a chair in the chimney corner, and her coats turned up over her head. A son of his was laid out in the yard, with a pillow laid under his head and a bunch of rosemary laid to his nose. A negro had his right hand cut off and left dead. The master of the next house was shot and his body laid flat upon his wife's grave. Women were laid on their house-floors and great stakes run up through their bodies. Others big with child, the infants were ripped out and hung upon trees. In short, their manner of butchery has been so various and unaccountable, that it would be beyond credit to relate them. This blow was so hotly followed by the hellish crew, that we could not bury our dead; so that they were left for prey to the dogs, and wolves, and vultures, whilst our care was to strengthen our garrison to secure the living.

William L. Saunders, ed., The Colonial Records of North Carolina, *10 vols. (Raleigh: State of North Carolina, 1886–90), 1:826–28.*

Christopher Von Graffenried's Account

There were about five hundred fighting men collected together, partly Tuscaroras, although the principal villages of this nation were not involved with them. The other Indians, the Marmuskits, those of Bay River, Weetock, Pamtego, Neuse, and Core began this massacring and plundering at the same time. Divided into small platoons these barbarians plundered and massacred the poor people at Pamtego, Neuse, and Trent. A few days after, these murderers came back loaded with their booty. Oh what a sad sight to see this and the poor women and children captives. My heart almost broke. To be sure I could speak with them, but very guardedly. The first came from Pamtego, the others from Neuse and Trent. The very same Indian with whom I lodged brought a young boy with him, one of my tenants, and many garments and house utensils that I recognized. Oh how it went through my heart like a knife thrust, in the fear that my colony was all gone, and especially when I asked the little fellow what had happened and taken place. Weeping bitterly he told me that his father, mother, brother, yes, the whole family had been massacred by the very same Indian above mentioned.

Vincent H. Todd, ed., Christopher Von Graffenried's Account of the Founding of New Bern *(Raleigh: North Carolina Historical Commission, 1920), pp. 270–71.*

DOCUMENT 1.5

Destruction of Home and Food during the Cherokee War, 1761

Thursday 11th June

When we built our Wigwams of the materials of the Houses. This morning Mr. Monroe dyed on the march & was buryed in the Evening in one of the Houses, which was afterward burn'd over him, that the Indians might not know where he was lay'd as they would take him up to scalp him.

Friday 12th June

Halted, which we wanted very much as the head of the Army had been 28 Hours under Arms, & most of the Time without eating. This Day all the Troops off Duty were sent with their Arms to destroy the Corn around about the Town which they did very effectualy. Papon & I burn'd two of their Houses & a Pow-wow House. . . .

About 500 Men . . . march'd over the Mountains, a round about way towards Ayoree, three Miles & having surrounded it we supris'd about 12 Indians in it, one of which we scalp'd and took an old Squa Prisoner [the rest escaped] we march'd by the way of Watogui, two miles from our camp where we arriv'd afout Six at night finding we could get no Intelligence from our Prisoner. We gave her some provisions, and convey'd her privately out of camp lest she should be scalp'd by our Indians who wanted much to do it, soon after another poor old Sqwa was brought into camp, & the savages having got hold of her soon kill'd & scalp'd her, they then threw her Body into the River, it is to be obeserv'd that the Sqwa we brought to Camp Smil'd at us even when she must have expected to be put to Death every Instant. We march'd [in our going out] over some of the highest mountain I ever saw, & which even being [compartively] almost perpendicular, this occasion'd it to be very fatiguing though not above Twelve Miles back and forward.

Saturday 13th June

This Day Parties were sent to destroy the Corn & co. which was executed, & one of them burn'd two new settled Villages call'd Neowee and Canuga.

Sunday 14 June

General at six. The Army march'd about 1/2 past Eight & reach'd a place call'd Watogui, three miles, here we halted pull'd up all the Corn, cut down the fruit Trees, & burn'd the Houses, in number about Fifty. We then continued our march to Ayoree, 1 mile, where we encamp'd & began to destroy the Corn immediatly; Here we found the old Sqwa we had taken prisoner before, who it seems did not choose to leave her habitation, 'though at the risk of her Life.

Monday 15th June

Halted. Several Parties sent to destroy Corn.

Tuesday 16th June

General at six, march'd about Eight, & at 1/2 past Ten reach'd Cowhee, about three Miles. This is pleasantly situated upon the River. We halted & destroy'd a great quantity of Corn, & cut down fruit Trees. We then cross'd the River [which was very deep] & reach'd Ussanah about two Miles. This is a small village, & by much the worst we had yet seen. One of the Catawbas [the same who kill'd the old Sqwa at Noukassi] kill'd our Sqwa for the Sake of her Scalp.

Captain Christopher French, "Journal of an Expedition to South Carolina," Journal of Cherokee Studies *(1977):284–85.*

DOCUMENT 1.6

Adjusting to the Reservation, The Chowanoc

Upon Petition of Jno Hoyter on behalfe of himselfe and the rest of ye Chowan Indyans therin setting forth that ye Said Indyans had granted to them in the Administration of Govr Archdale for their settlmt a tract of Land on ye Eastern side of Bennets Creek including Meherins Neck of Twelve Miles Square which not being laid out according to ye directions of ye Order of Councill they aply'd themselves to ye Honble President Glover & ye Councill then being to have ye same laid out upon wch it was ordered that a tract of six miles square within those bound should be laid out for their setlemt wch yet hath not been done and further that most of ye said Indyans have been upon Eight Expiditions agt the Indyan Enemy of this province and during the time they were in ye Countys Service they Suffered Considerable loss in their plantations & Stocks loosing Seaventy five head of hoggs a Mare & Colt their Corne destroy'd by horses & Cattle their fences burnt & fruit trees destroy'd by all wch & ye wearing out of their clothes they are reduced to very great poverty and pray's that their Land may be laid out according to ye intent of ye Grant and that they may have some allowance made for their services & Losses, &c and this board haveing Considered the whole matter.

It is ordered that Coll Wm Maule doe Examine in the former Survey Made by Coll Moseley and Doe see whether ye same be made pursuant to former order of ye Councill & Whether it Conteyns ye Quantity & Make report therof to this Board. . . .

North Carlin,

To the onerable Councel the humble Petison of John Hiter Engen for that your piteser understand that by order of his Ecelc and Onerabell Councell he had 6 mil Square granted him of Land to which it was not Sorvaid accorden to ordr for which Resen your petisener prays order It may be Sorvaid again and that he may have his Land Layd out acorden to ouder or other wese ther It can not Subsist for he is soo Upprest with Catell and hogs of other mens and the Ground is soe pore that Ite cannot make Corne to keep him was Sorved upon a nara neke of pinny Land that will not bar Corn and further yor ptinr prays he may be considered that he is not a stranger nor a foriner but is his one Nativ ples and therfor prays he may have ground to work upon therfor I Rest and pray that your petisner may find favor In yor presence and as in duty bound your petesner Shall pray.

John Hiter.

[Chief of the Chowanoc Tribe]

To the Honrble President & Councill The Humble Petition of John Hoyter & Rest of ye Chowan Indians in all Humble Maner Complaines Shewing

That whereas upon ye Humble Petition of ye sd Indians to this Honrble Board in the time when the Honble Henderson Walker Esqr was President of ye Councill an Order was past that Ye Surveyr Genll or Deputy should Lay out a tract of Land for ye sd Indians of Six Miles Square And allso another Order in ye Name of the Honble Landgrave Robt. Daniel Esqr pursuant to ye former Order.

In pursuance of ye afrsd Order ye Depty Surveyr vizt: Capt Luten Came & Undertook ye sd Services & by Various Courses Did Lay out a tract of Land for ye sd Indians but wholy Contrary to ye Intent & Meaneing of ye sd Order for ye petitionrs are very Confident that ye Intent of ye Councill was that such Land should be Layd out for them as would produce Corn for their Support & the petitionrs Do Say & are ready to Averr that no part or parcell of ye sd Land in ye sd tract Layd out will produce Corn being all pines & Sands & Desserts so that they have not their Land according to ye Intent & Meaning of the Honable Board neither for quality nor quantity it being not near Six Miles Square.

Wherefore your Humble Petitionrs Do humbly Pray your Honrs to take our Distressd Condition into yr Serious Consideration that your Petitionr may have Releife in ye Premises least we perish for Bread. And your Petitioners shall Ever Pray &c.

his

John X Hoyter

mark

In behalfe of himselfe & Rest of ye Nation.

Saunders, ed., Colonial Records, *2:140–41;* North Carolina Historical and Genealogical Register *3 (1903):75–76.*

DOCUMENT 1.7

Treaty of New Echota of 1835 between the Cherokee Nation and the United States

Articles of a treaty, concluded at New Echota in the State of Georgia on the 29th day of Decr. 1835 by General William Carroll and John F. Schermerhorn commissioners on the part of the United States and the Chiefs Head Men and People of the Cherokee tribe of Indians.

WHEREAS the Cherokees are anxious to make some arrangements with the Government of the United States whereby the difficulties they have experienced by a residence within the settled parts of the United States under the jurisdiction and laws of the State Governments may be terminated and adjusted; and with a view to reuniting their people in one body and securing a permanent home for themselves and their posterity in the country selected by their forefathers without the territorial limits of the State sovereignties, and where they can establish and enjoy a government of their choice and perpetuate such a state of society as may be most consonant with their views, habits and condition; and as may tend to their individual comfort and their advancement in civilization. . . .

And whereas Genl William Carroll and John F. Schermerhorn were appointed commissioners on the part of the United States, with full power and authority to conclude a treaty with the Cherokees east and were directed by the President to convene the people of the nation in general council at New Echota and to submit said propositions to them with power and authority to vary the same so as to meet the views of the Cherokees in reference to its details.

And whereas the said commissioners did appoint and notify a general council of the nation to convene at New Echota on the 21st day of December 1835; and informed them that the commissioners would be prepared to make a treaty with the Cherokee people who should assemble there and those who did not come they should conclude gave their assent and sanction to whatever should be transacted at this council and the people having met in council according to said notice.

Therefore the following articles of a treaty are agreed upon and concluded between William Carroll and John F. Schermerhorn commissioners on the part of the United States and the chiefs and head men and people of the Cherokee nation in general council assembled this 29th day of Decr 1835.

ARTICLE 1. The Cherokee nation hereby cede relinquish and convey to the United States all the lands owned claimed or possessed by them east of the Mississippi river, and hereby release all their claims upon the United States for spoliations of every kind for and in consideration of the sum of five millions of dollars to be expended paid and invested in the manner stipulated and agreed upon in the following articles. . . .

ARTICLE 2. Whereas . . . the United States guarantied and secured to be conveyed by patent, to the Cherokee nation of Indians the following tract of country "Beginning at a point on the old western territorial line of Arkansas Territory . . . to said due west line will make seven millions of acres within the whole described boundaries. In addition to the seven millions of acres of land thus provided for and bounded, the United States further guaranty to the Cherokee nation a perpetual outlet west,

and a free and unmolested use of all the country west of western boundary of said seven millions of acres, as far west as the sovereignty of the
United States and their right of soil extend. . . .

And whereas it is apprehended by the Cherokees that in the above
cession there is not contained a sufficient quantity of land for the accommodation of the whole nation on their removal west of the Mississippi
the United States in consideration of the sum of five hundred thousand
dollars . . . convey to the said Indians . . . the following additional tract
of land. . . .

ARTICLE 3. The United States also agree that the lands above ceded
. . . shall all be included in one patent executed to the Cherokee nation of
Indians by the President of the United States. . . .

ARTICLE 4. The United States also stipulate and agree to extinguish
for the benefit of the Cherokees the titles to the reservations within their
country made in the Osage treaty of 1825 to certain half-breeds. . . .

ARTICLE 5. The United States hereby covenant and agree that the
lands ceded to the Cherokee nation in the forgoing article shall, in no
future time without their consent, be included within the territorial limits
or jurisdiction of any State or Territory. But they shall secure to the
Cherokee nation the right by their national councils to make and carry
into effect all such laws as they may deem necessary for the government
and protection of the persons and property within their own country
belonging to their people or such persons as have connected themselves
with them: provided always that they shall not be inconsistent with the
constitution of the United States and such acts of Congress as have been
or may be passed regulating trade and intercourse with the Indians; and
also, that they shall not be considered as extending to such citizens and
army of the United States as may travel or reside in the Indian country by
permission according to the laws and regulations established by the Government of the same.

ARTICLE 6. Perpetual peace and friendship shall exist between the citizens of the United States and the Cherokee Indians. . . . It is stipulated
that they shall be entitled to a delegate in the House of Representatives of
the United States whenever Congress shall make provision for the same.

ARTICLE 8. The United States also agree and stipulate to remove the
Cherokees to their new homes and to subsist them one year after their
arrival there and that a sufficient number of steamboats and baggage-
wagons shall be furnished to remove them comfortably, and so as not to
endanger their health, and that a physician well supplied with medicines
shall accompany each detachment of emigrants removed by the Government. Such persons and families as in the opinion of the emigrating agent
are capable of subsisting and removing themselves shall be permitted to
do so. . . .

ARTICLE 9. The United States agree to appoint suitable agents who shall make a just and fair valuation of all such improvements now in the possession of the Cherokees as add any value to the lands. . . .

ARTICLE 10. The President of the United States shall invest in some safe and most productive public stocks of the country for the benefit of the whole Cherokee nation. . . .

ARTICLE 12. Those individuals and families of the Cherokee nation that are averse to a removal to the Cherokee country west of the Mississippi and are desirous to become citizens of the States where they reside and such as are qualified to take care of themselves and their property shall be entitled to receive their due portion of all the personal benefits accruing under this treaty for their claims, improvements and *per capita*; as soon as an appropriation is made for this treaty. . . .

ARTICLE 16. It is hereby stipulated and agreed by the Cherokees that they shall remove to their new homes within two years from the ratification of this treaty and that during such time the United States shall protect and defend them in their possessions and property and free use and occupation of the same.

Charles J. Kappler, ed., Indian Treaties, 1778–1883 *(New York: Interland Publishing, 1972), pp. 439–49.*

DOCUMENT 1.8

The Cherokees who Remained

I am an old man, and have counted the snows of almost eighty winters. My hair, which is now very white, was once like the raven's wing. I can remember when the white man had not seen the smoke of our cabins westward of the Blue Ridge, and I have watched the establishment of all his settlements, even to the Father of Waters. The march of the white is still towards the setting sun, and I know that he will never be satisfied until he reaches the shore of the great water. It is foolish in you to tell me that the whites will not trouble the poor Cherokee in the Western country. The white man's nature and the Indian's fate tell a different story. Sooner or later one Government must cover the whole continent, and the red people, if not scattered among the autumn leaves, will become a part of the American nation. As to the white man's promises of protection, they have been too often broken; they are like the reeds in yonder river—

they are all lies. North Carolina had acknowledged our title to these lands, and the United States had guarantied that title; but all this did not prevent the Government from taking away our lands by force; and, not only that, but sold the very cow of the poor Indian and his gun, so as to compel him to leave his country. Is this what the white man calls justise and protection? No, we will not go to the West. We wanted to become the children of North Carolina, and she has received us as such, and passed a law for our protection, and we will continue to raise our corn in this very land. The people of Carolina have always been very kind to us, and we know they will never oppress us. You say the land in the West is much better than it is here. That very fact is an argument on our side. The white man must have rich land to do his great business, but the Indian can be happy with poorer land. The white man must have a flat country for his plough to run easy, but we can get along even among the rocks on the mountains. We never shall do what you want us to do. I don't like you for your pretended kindness. I always advise my people to keep their backs for ever turned towards the setting sun, and never to leave the land of their fathers. I tell them they must live like good citizens; never forget the kindness of North Carolina, and always be ready to help her in time of war. I have nothing more to say.

Charles Lannman, Letters from the Alleghany Mountains *(New York: George P. Putnam, 1849), pp. 109–10.*

DOCUMENT 1.9

Demon Rum and the Indian

Most of the Savages are much addicted to Drunkennes, a Vice they never were acquainted with, till the Christians came amongst them. Some of them refrain drinking strong Liquors, but very few of that sort are found amongst them. The chief Liquor is Rum, without any Mixture. This the *English* bring amongst them, and buy Skins, Furs, Slaves and other of their Commodities therewith. They never are contented with a little, but when once begun, they must make themselves quite drunk; otherwise they will never rest, but sell all they have in the World, rather than not have their full Dose. In these drunken Frolicks, (which are always carried on in the Night) they sometimes murder one another, fall into the Fire, fall down Precipices, and break their Necks, with several other Misfortunes which this drinking of Rum brings upon them; and tho' they are sensible of it, yet they have no Power to refrain this Enemy. About five years ago, when *Landgrave* [Robert] *Daniel* was Governour, he summon'd in all the Indian Kings and Rulers to meet, and in a full Meeting of the Government and Council, with those *Indians,* they agreed upon a firm Peace, and the *Indian* Rulers desired no Rum might be sold to them, which was granted, and a Law made, that inflicted a Penalty on those that sold Rum to the Heathens; but it was never strictly observ'd, and besides, the young *Indians* were so disgusted at that Article, that they threatened to kill the *Indians* that made it, unless it was laid aside, and they might have Rum sold them, when they went to the *Englishmens* Houses to buy it.

Lawson, A New Voyage to Carolina, *pp. 211–12.*

SUGGESTED READINGS

Blu, Karen I. *The Lumbee Problem: The Making of an American Indian People.* Cambridge: Cambridge University Press, 1980.

Brown, Douglas S. *The Catawba Indians: The People of the River.* Columbia: University of South Carolina Press, 1966.

Coe, Joffre L. *The Formative Cultures of the Carolina Piedmont. Transactions of the American Philosophical Society* 54, pt. 5. Philadelphia: American Philosophical Society, 1964.

Dickens, Roy S., Jr. *Cherokee Prehistory: The Pisgah Phase in the Applachian Summit Region.* Knoxville: University of Tennessee Press, 1976.

Farb, Peter. *Man's Rise to Civilization as Shown by the Indians of North America from Primeval Times to the Coming of the Industrial State.* New York: E. P. Dutton & Company, 1968.

Garrow, Patrick H. *The Mattamuskeet Documents: A Study in Social History.* Raleigh: Archaeology Section, Division of Archives and History, 1975.

Johnson, F. Roy. *The Algonquians.* 2 vols. Murfreesboro, N.C.: Johnson Publishing Co., 1972.

_____. *The Tuscarora.* 2 vols. Murfreesboro, N.C.: Johnson Publishing Co., 1967, 1968.

King, Duane H. *The Cherokee Indian Nation: A Troubled History.* Knoxville: University of Tennessee Press, 1979.

Lee, E. Lawrence. *Indian Wars in North Carolina, 1663–1763.* Raleigh: Carolina Charter Tercentenary Commission, 1963.

Milling, Chapman, Jr. *Red Carolinians.* Chapel Hill: University of North Carolina Press, 1940.

O'Donnell, James H. *The Cherokees of North Carolina in the American Revolution.* Raleigh: Department of Cultural Resources, 1976.
Parramore, Thomas C. "The Tuscarora Ascendency." *North Carolina Historical Review* 59(1982):307–26.
Rights, Douglas L. *The American Indian in North Carolina.* Durham: Duke University Press, 1947.
South, Stanley A. *Indians in North Carolina.* Raleigh: State Department of Archives and History, 1959.
Wetmore, Ruth Y. *First on the Land: The North Carolina Indian.* Winston-Salem: John F. Blair, 1975.

CHAPTER 2

An Elizabethan Experiment

William S. Powell

Sir Walter Raleigh, engraving by R. Cooper, after Houbraken, published 1 July 1830 (Courtesy of the Division of Archives and History, Raleigh, N.C.)

England did not follow up the late fifteenth-century explorations of John Cabot with settlement because she lacked adequate resources and was occupied with internal dissensions. It was Cabot's voyage, however, that gave her a firm claim to North America. During the reign of Queen Elizabeth the English briefly planted settlements on Roanoke Island that established the pattern for future overseas colonizing activity. Documents composed for a government far removed from London, careful instructions issued to cover a variety of contingencies, and the colonizing experience provided excellent precedents for the seventeenth century. Although at the time the activity between 1584 and 1590 appeared fruitless, it actually was a learning experience, and England soon began to build on the foundations laid then.

In the meantime France and Spain made early but sporadic attempts to explore and colonize various parts of the continent along the Atlantic coast. Giovanni da Verrazzano visited Cape Fear in 1524, sailed leisurely up the coast with stops along the way, and reported what he saw in some detail to his patron, Francis I of France. French Protestants, Jean Ribaut and René de Laudonnière in 1562 and 1565, respectively, unsuccessfully attempted to plant colonies on the coast of present South Carolina. A Spanish colony of men and women, including some black people, under the leadership of Luis Vasquez de Ayllon settled briefly near the mouth of the Cape Fear River in 1526, but illness and the loss of supplies in a shipwreck forced them to leave. Hernando de Soto in 1540 and Juan Pardo and Hernando Boyano in 1566–67 carried out extensive explorations in the mountains in a fruitless search for gold. Concluding that the Carolina region was unpromising, Spain withdrew but did not renounce claim to the territory. In the middle of the eighteenth century, during the course of some of the wars involving countries of Europe, Spanish forces landed along the North Carolina coast and wrought havoc, but subsequently Spain never bothered the colony.

English interest in the New World was sparked by the capture of Spanish ships returning from America with cargoes of gold, silver, lumber, and other treasures. Spain and England were old enemies in politics, religion, and commerce. The situation in England by the last quarter of the sixteenth century was stable enough that a challenge to Spain in the New World was feasible. Elizabeth—a Protestant, a daughter of Henry VIII, and a person in whom her subjects had the greatest trust—came to the throne in 1558. Alert, well-educated, a skillful manager of men, and anxious for the well-being and security of her subjects, she sought ways to restrict the wealth and influence of her enemy, Philip of Spain.

Jean Ribaut went to England in 1563 direct from his colony in present South Carolina, and a book, *True and Last Discovery of Florida*, which he published in London that year enabled Englishmen to read in their own language about an inviting part of America. English "sea dogs" such as John Hawkins, Richard Grenville, and Francis Drake seized Spanish ships on the high seas, thus enabling many Englishmen to sample useful and valuable New World products. The thirst for more was contagious. Ambitious men dreamed of an English empire in America, and they approached the queen with various schemes. Their ideas and hers meshed ideally, but the initiative was theirs. She would remain in the background and thus immune from blame in case of failure or excessive expense.

Sir Humphrey Gilbert was the first to gain her attention, and in 1578 Queen Elizabeth granted him a charter to discover and settle land overseas. (Document 2.1) Instead of confronting Spain directly in or near one of her colonies, Gilbert was directed to find a site not yet settled. His colonists were guaranteed the same rights and privileges in their new home as those enjoyed by natives of England; this was a grant of considerable freedom repeated many times afterward in colonial charters, and it was cited by American colonists with greater frequency as the American Revolution approached. In August 1583, Gilbert arrived near the present St. John, Newfoundland, with a small colony, but it was soon determined that the site was not a very good one. After about a month Gilbert and his colonists sailed for home, but en route the ship on which Gilbert was sailing was lost in a storm.

Undaunted and anxious to succeed with Gilbert's plan, which in reality was intended to establish a base from which Spanish ships and colonies could be more successfully harassed, Queen Elizabeth renewed the charter in the name of his half-brother, Walter Raleigh. Soon to be knighted for his efforts, Raleigh was destined to plan and direct the Elizabethan experiment that demonstrated to England the practicality of colonies in America. It was a cruel blow of fate that his experiment was not entirely successful—the threat of the Spanish Armada in 1588 was fatal to the English plan. Ultimately, however, Spain suffered not only the loss of the Armada but also her claims to parts of North America. England eventually was the victor when out of the experience of Raleigh and his backers came a permanent English colony in America. Elizabeth died four years before this notable event. Raleigh lived for nearly a dozen years afterward, yet he was denied any glory for it by her successor, the suspicious James I.

Acting quickly, Raleigh had a reconnaissance expedition ready to sail just one month and two days after receiving his charter. Young captains, Philip Amadas and Arthur Barlowe, were hired along with an experienced pilot, Simon Fernandez, born in the Portuguese Azores but now an English subject and married to an English wife. On 4 July 1584 they sighted land and soon entered the sound back of Ocracoke Inlet, made their way up to Roanoke Island, and established a base from which they explored, collected specimens, and made notes for their employer. Barlowe's account of events has survived, and it gave Raleigh the glowing report he undoubtedly expected, the basis for extended effort, the promise of profit that would bring investors, and samples and specimens that would set people to talking. (Document 2.2) Not least among the objects displayed in England from America were two young Indian men, Manteo and Wanchese. Crowds gathered wherever they appeared, and people talked enthusiastically about Sir Walter's plans.

Raleigh was correct in thinking that solid information and assurances of profits to be made from an overseas colony would bring him support for furthering his plans. The queen provided a ship; from Ireland she called a member of her household staff, Ralph Lane, and placed him in Raleigh's service while she continued his pay. The secretary of state, not to be outdone by Her Majesty, also provided a ship, and many individuals subscribed money and offered supplies for the anticipated second expedition.

In April 1585, a colony of 108 men sailed from the West Country port of Plymouth for Roanoke Island. Sir Richard Grenville commanded the fleet; Lane was to become governor upon arrival. (Document 2.3) Philip Amadas, now designated admiral of Virginia, returned. Among the settlers were John White, an excellent watercolor artist; Thomas Harriot, astronomer, mathematician, and scientist and one of England's most versatile men (he had already learned some of the language of the Indians from Manteo and Wanchese); Thomas Cavendish, who later circumnavigated the globe; and others with assorted special abilities. Reaching Roanoke Island by mid-August, the colony, organized by Raleigh along strict military lines, constructed Fort Raleigh and built small houses such as they had known at home. For nearly a year Governor Lane commanded his men in organizing numerous exploratory expeditions that set out in all directions. A great deal of new information was gathered about the country and its resources as well as about the Indians. An expedition to the north concluded that a site along the Chesapeake Bay offered better advantages than Roanoke Island. The harbor there could accommodate larger ships, and the idea surely was considered that from such a point Spanish ships could more easily be captured.

Having arrived too late to plant crops, Lane expected a shipment of supplies to arrive in due course. Winter came on, Christmas passed, Easter followed, and still no supplies came. On 1 June 1586, Sir Francis Drake stopped by to look in on his countrymen. He had been in the West Indies attacking Spanish settlements and capturing their ships. With him were many English seamen as well as some Moorish prisoners and black slaves taken from the Spanish. He offered to leave adequate supplies at

Roanoke to tide the colony over for a time, and he would also leave some of his men with a ship to be used for further coastal exploration. Lane was inclined to accept this offer when a sudden severe storm frightened him into changing his mind. He decided to take his colony home with Drake's fleet. To make room for the passengers, Drake apparently put the blacks ashore; there is no further mention of them in the records. In his haste to be away, Lane departed without waiting for the return of an exploring party, but he did take Manteo back to England. In ferrying possessions from Fort Raleigh to the large vessels riding at anchor in the Atlantic, sailors were obliged to cast many items overboard to prevent the heavily laden boats from being swamped by the high waves. (Document 2.4)

Very soon after the departure of Drake and Lane, Grenville arrived with the anticipated supplies. Finding the colony gone, he left fifteen men with supplies for two years to hold the site for England. Had Lane been only a little more confident, he surely would have succeeded in establishing England's first permanent American colony. Instead he merely demonstrated that the land was hospitable for Englishmen, and he added to the knowledge and understanding of the region. John White's watercolor drawings, Lane's narrative, and Harriot's lengthy report, however, were valuable products of the colony.

With his personal resources nearly depleted, Raleigh felt some urgency in pursuing his goal. He set about once again to obtain assistance, and this time found nineteen merchants and more than a dozen "gentlemen of London" willing to invest. Abandoning a military organization, Raleigh planned a civil government for his new colony with John White as governor and a dozen assistants. At sailing time in early May 1587, there were 113 people who would remain with the colony in Virginia, including seventeen women and nine children. With Simon Fernandez as pilot, the colonizers were directed to sail to the West Indies for fresh water, to collect certain plants to try in Virginia, and to round up stray livestock left by the Spanish on an abandoned island. They were then to go by Roanoke Island to pick up the men left by Lane and Grenville and on to establish themselves on Chesapeake Bay. Upon reaching Roanoke Island, however, Fernandez refused to take the party any farther because he was anxious to get back into the shipping lanes to try to capture some treasure for himself. An advance party reached the fort and learned from evidence at the site and from friendly Indians that the men left by Grenville had been promptly murdered by unfriendly Indians from the mainland.

Making the best of a distressing situation, Governor White and the men began repairing the houses left by Lane and building new ones. In accordance with Raleigh's instructions, Manteo, who had returned with the colony, was baptized and created Lord of Roanoke. On 18 August a daughter was born to Eleanor White Dare and her husband, Ananias, one of the assistants to the governor. This child, the first of English parentage born in the New World and granddaughter of Governor White, was christened Virginia on the twenty-fourth. Another couple, Dyonis and Margery Harvie, became the parents of a child a few days later.

Like the Ralph Lane colony, the colony under Governor White discovered that it had arrived too late to plant crops, and it did not have enough supplies to last until the next harvest. The Indians had little that could be spared. The governor's assistants prevailed upon White to return to England to expedite the shipment, and after making careful arrangements for the protection of his personal property and for leaving proper guides to its location should the colony remove from Roanoke Island, White returned home with the fleet at the end of the month. (Document 2.5)

Upon arriving in England, White discovered the entire country deeply concerned over a pending attack by Spain. A great Spanish Armada was poised to conquer England, and Queen Elizabeth decreed that no ship suitable in any way to protect England could sail. The English in America could fend for themselves while England prepared to defend herself. Even so, White somehow secured two tiny ships in the spring of 1588, and with supplies and a few more colonists he sailed for Roanoke Island. Alas, the captains were untrustworthy and could not resist the temptation to try their hand at piracy. Instead of capturing, however, they were captured. A French pirate took all of their supplies, and they were forced to return home.

Although the Armada was destroyed by a storm in late July and early August, there are no records to tell what efforts Raleigh and White made in 1589. In 1590, however, Governor White at last returned to Roanoke Island. He found the site of his colony deserted, overgrown with weeds, and with deer roaming in and out of the houses. He discovered the letters CROATOAN and CRO carved on a tree and a post. There was no cross above, which would have indicated that the people left in distress. The clues seemed promising. He believed the settlers had gone peacefully to the place where Manteo's people lived on the Outer Banks. With the growing dark, a heavy storm blew up, and the little party returned to the ship hoping to continue the search next day. The storm grew more intense, and it was finally agreed to sail to the West Indies and spend the winter. They expected to return in the spring and reunite Governor White with his family and friends, but the storm proved to be so destructive and the winds so strong that new plans were made. Badly damaged and blown into the north Atlantic, the ship could barely return to England. (Document 2.6)

Raleigh's fortune was now spent. The queen was growing old. Spain was no longer a threat to England. The experiment in America was a failure, and there was neither incentive nor resources to continue it. White retired to one of Raleigh's estates in Ireland and after a few years was heard of no more.

But was the experiment a failure?

In 1606 King James I approved a charter for the Virginia Company of London only after being assured by ten men who had supported Raleigh that Virginia was indeed a promising place for Englishmen. The permanent settlement they founded was on the Chesapeake Bay, where Raleigh had instructed Governor White to plant his colony in 1587. Clearly, the Jamestown colony in 1607 was based on the experiment at Roanoke Island.

Although Raleigh did not succeed in his ambition to establish the first permanent English colony in America, the idea certainly was conceived in his mind. It was his efforts that set the stage for the momentous event that occurred in 1607, nearly a dozen years before his untimely death. The publicity resulting from the presence of American Indians in England, the samples of New World products, the watercolors of John White, and the maps, engravings, and books resulting from Raleigh's efforts all helped to convince Englishmen that they could flourish in America. Less than two weeks after the granting of a charter to the Virginia Company under which Jamestown was to be established, Michael Drayton wrote a poem recalling the promise of America from Raleigh's time and urging his countrymen to persist in occupying the earthly paradise across the Atlantic. His poem celebrated the birth of America. (Document 2.7)

DOCUMENT 2.1

Queen Elizabeth's Charter to Sir Humphrey Gilbert of 11 June 1578

Elizabeth, by the grace of God, etc. To all people to whom these presents shall come, greeting:

Know ye, that, of our especial grace, certain science, and mere motion, we have given and granted . . . to our trusty and well-beloved servant, Sir Humfrey Gilberte . . . free liberty and licence . . . to discover, search, find out, and view such remote heathen and barbarous lands, Countries, and territories, not actually possessed of any Christian Prince or people. . . .

And further, that he . . . shall have, hold, occupy, and enjoy . . . all the soil of all such lands, Countries, and Territories so to be discovered or possessed as aforesaid; . . . with the rights, royalties, and jurisdictions, as well marine as other, within the said lands or Countries, or the Seas thereunto adjoining; to be had or used with full power to dispose thereof . . . in fee simple or otherwise, according to the laws of England, as near as the same conveniently may be, at his . . . will and pleasure, to any person then being, or that shall remain, within the allegiance of us, our heirs and successors; reserving always, to us, our heirs and successors, for all services, duties, and demands, the fifth part of all the ore of gold and silver that, from time to time, and at all times, after such discovery, subduing, and possessing, shall be there gotten. . . .

And, for uniting in more perfect league and amity of such Countries, lands, and Territories, so to be possessed and inhabited as aforesaid, with our Realms of England and Ireland, and for the better encouragement of men to this enterprise, we do, by these presents, grant and declare that all such Countries, so hereafter to be possessed and inhabited as aforesaid, from thenceforth shall be of the allegiance of us, our heirs and successors; and we do grant to the said Sir Humfrey . . . and to all and every other person and persons being of our allegiance, whose names shall be noted or entered in some of our Courts of record within this our Realm of England, and that, with the assent of the said Sir Humfrey, his heirs or Assigns, shall now in this journey for discovery, or in the second journey for conquest, hereafter, travel to such lands, Countries, and territories as aforesaid . . . being either born within our said Realms of England or Ireland, or in any other place within our allegiance, and which hereafter shall be inhabiting within any the lands . . . shall and may have and enjoy all the privileges of free denizens and persons native of England and within our allegiance; in such like ample manner and form as if they were born and personally resident within our said Realm of England; Any law, custom, or usage to the contrary notwithstanding.

And forasmuch as, upon the finding out, discovering, and inhabiting of such remote lands, Countries, and Territories as aforesaid, it shall be necessary, for the safety of all men that shall adventure themselves in those journeys or voyages, to determine to live together in Christian Peace and Civil quietness, each with other, whereby every one may, with more pleasure and profit, enjoy that whereunto they shall attain with great pain and peril, we, for us, our heirs and successors, are likewise pleased and contented, and, by these presents, do give and grant to the said Sir Humfrey . . . full and mere power and authority to correct, punish, pardon, govern, and rule, by . . . good discretions and policies, as well in causes Capital or criminal as civil, both marine and other, all such, our subjects and others, as shall, from time to time hereafter, adventure themselves in the said journeys or voyages, habitative or possessive, or that shall, at any time hereafter, inhabit any such lands . . . or that shall abide within two hundred leagues of any the said place or places where the said Sir Humfrey. . . or any of his or their Associates or companies, shall inhabit within six years next ensuing the date here of, according to such statutes, laws, and ordinances as shall be . . . devised or established for the better government of the said people, as aforesaid;

So always, that the said statutes, laws, and ordinances may be, as near as conveniently may, agreeable to the form of the laws and policy of England;

And also, so as they be not against the true Christian faith or religion, now professed in the Church of England; nor in any wise to withdraw any of the subjects or people of those lands or places from the allegiance of us, our heirs or successors, as their immediate sovereigns under God.

Mattie Erma Edwards Parker, ed., North Carolina Charters and Constitutions, 1578–1698 *(Raleigh: Carolina Charter Tercentenary Commission, 1963), pp. 5–10.*

DOCUMENT 2.2

A Model Reconnaissance Report: Arthur Barlowe to Walter Raleigh

The twenty-seventh day of April, in the year of our redemption 1584, we departed the west of England with two barks well furnished with men and victuals, having received our last and perfect directions by your letters, confirming the former instructions and commandments delivered by yourself at our leaving the river of Thames. . . .

The second of July we found shoal water, which smelt so sweetly and was so strong a smell as if we had been in the midst of some delicate garden, abounding with all kind of odoriferous flowers, by which we were assured that the land could not be far distant. And keeping good watch and bearing but slack sail the fourth of the same month, we arrived upon the coast, which we supposed to be a continent and firm land, and we sailed along the same 120 English miles before we could find any entrance or river issuing into the sea. The first that appeared unto us we entered, though not without some difficulty, and cast anchor about three harquebus shot within the haven's mouth on the left hand of the same. And after thanks given to God for our safe arrival thither we manned our boats and went to view the land next adjoining and to "take possession of the same in the right of the Queen's Most Excellent Majesty as rightful Queen and Princess of the same"; and after delivered the same over to your use, according to Her Majesty's grant. . . . Which being performed according to the ceremonies used in such enterprises, we viewed the land about us, being whereas we first landed very sandy and low towards the waterside, but so full of grapes as the very beating and surge of the sea overflowed them, of which we found such plenty, as well there as in all places else, both on the sand and on the green soil on the hills as in the plains, as well on every little shrub as also climbing towards the tops of the high cedars, that I think in all the world the like abundance is not to be found. . . .

We passed from the sea-side towards the tops of those hills next adjoining, being but of mean height, and from thence we beheld the sea on both sides to the north and to the south, finding no end any of both ways. This land lay stretching itself to the west, which after we found to be but an island of twenty leagues long and not above six miles broad. Under the bank or hill whereon we stood we beheld the valleys replenished with goodly cedar trees and, having discharged our harquebus shot, such a flock of cranes (the most part white) arose under us, with such a cry redoubled by many echoes, as if an army of men had shouted all together.

This island had many goodly woods full of deer, conies, hares, and fowl, even in the midst of summer, in incredible abundance . . . the highest and reddest cedars of the world. . . .

We remained by the side of this island two whole days before we saw any people of the country. The third day we espied one small boat rowing towards us, having in it three persons. This boat came to the land's side, four harquebus shot from our ships, and there, two of the people remaining, the third came along the shore-side towards us and, we being then all within-board, he walked up and down upon the point of the land next unto us. Then the master and the pilot of the admiral, Simon Ferdinando, and the Captain, Philip Amadas, myself, and others rowed to the land, whose coming this fellow attended, never making any show of fear or doubt.

And after he had spoken of many things not understood by us, we brought him with his own good liking aboard the ships and gave him a shirt, a hat, and some other things and made him taste of our wine and our meat, which he liked very well. And after having viewed both barks he departed and went to his own boat again, which he had left in a little cove or creek adjoining. As soon as he was two bowshots into the water, he fell to fishing, and in less than half an hour he had laden his boat as deep as it could swim, with which he came again to the point of the land, and there he divided his fish into two parts, pointing one part to the ship and the other to the pinnace, which, after he had (as much as he might) requited the former benefits received, he departed out of our sight. . . .

When we first had sight of this country, some thought the first land we saw to be the continent, but after we entered into the haven we saw before us another mighty long sea, for there lieth along the coast a tract of islands two hundred miles in length, adjoining to the ocean sea, and between the islands two or three entrances. When you are entered between them (these islands being very narrow for the most part, as in most places six miles broad, in some places less, in few more) then there appeareth another great sea, containing in breadth in some places forty, and in some fifty, in some twenty miles over, before you come unto the continent, and in this enclosed sea there are about a hundred islands of divers bigness, whereof one is sixteen miles long, at which we were, finding it to be a most pleasant and fertile ground, replenished with goodly cedars and divers other sweet woods full of currants, of flax, and many other notable commodities, which we at that time had no leisure to view. Besides this island, there are many, as I have said, some of two, of three, of four, or five miles, some more, some less, most beautiful and pleasant to behold, replenished with deer, conies, hares, and divers beasts, and about them the goodliest and best fish in the world and in greatest abundance.

Thus, sir, we have acquainted you with the particulars of our discovery, made this present voyage, as far north as the shortness of the time we there continued would afford us to take view of. And so contenting ourselves with this service at this time, which we hope hereafter to enlarge as occasion and assistance shall be given, we resolved to leave the country and to apply ourselves to return for England, which we did accordingly and arrived safely in the west of England about the midst of September.

Louis B. Wright, ed., The Elizabethans' America *(Cambridge, Mass.: Harvard University Press, 1965), pp. 103–13. The spelling has been modernized in this source.*

DOCUMENT 2.3

"The Goodliest Soile Under the Cope of Heaven": Ralph Lane, 1585

In the meane while you shall understand that since sir Richard Greenvils departure from us, as also before, we have discovered the maine to bee the goodliest soile under the cope of heaven, so abounding with sweete trees, that bring such sundry rich and most pleasant gummes, grapes of such greatnes, yet wild, as France, Spaine nor Italy hath no greater, so many sortes of Apothecarie drugs, such severall kindes of flaxe, and one kind like silke, the same gathered of a grasse, as common there as grasse is here. And now within these few dayes we have found here a Guinie wheate, whose care yeeldeth corne for bread, 400. upon one eare, and the Cane maketh very good and perfect suger. . . . Besides that, it is the goodliest and most pleasing territorie of the world (for the soile is of an huge unknowen greatnesse, and very wel peopled and towned, though savagelie) and the climate so wholesome, that we have not had one sicke, since we touched land here. To conclude, if Virginia had but Horses and Kine in some reasonable proportion, I dare assure my selfe being inhabited with English, no realme in Christendome were comparable to it. For this alreadie we find, that what commodities soever Spaine, France, Italy, or the East parts do yeeld unto us in wines of all sortes, in oiles, in flaxe, in rosens, pitch, frankensence, currans, sugers, & such like, these parts do abound with the growth of them all, but being Savages that possesse the land, they know no use of the same. And sundry other rich commodities, that no parts of the world, be they West or East Indies, have, here we finde great abundance of. The people naturally most curteous, & very desirous to have clothes, but especially of course cloth rather than silke, course canvas they also like wel of, but copper carieth the price of all, so it be made red. Thus good Master Hakluyt and master H. I have joyned you both in one letter of remembrance, as two that I love dearely well, and commending me most hartily to you both, I commit you to the tuition of the almighty. From the new Fort in Virginia, this 3. September 1585.

David B. Quinn, ed., The Roanoke Voyages, 1584–1590, 2 vols. *(London: Hakluyt Society, 1955), 1:207–10.*

DOCUMENT 2.4

A Colony Fails: Ralph Lane to Walter Raleigh

[On the eighth of June 1586, there] came advertisement to me from captaine Stafford, lying at my lord Admirals Island, that he had discovered a great Fleete of 23. sailes: but whether they were friends or foes, he could not yet discerne, he advised me to stand upon as good gard as I could.

The 9. of the said moneth, he himself came unto me, having that night before, and that same day travelled by land 20. miles, and I must truly report of him from the first to the last, he was the gentleman that never spared labour or perill either by land or water, faire weather or fowle, to performe any service committed unto him.

He brought me a letter from the Generall sir Francis Drake, with a most bountifull and honourable offer for the supplie of our necessities to the performance of the action, we were entered into, and that not onely of victuals, munition and clothing, but also of barkes, pinnaces and boates, they also by him to be victualled, manned, and furnished to my contention. . . .

With such thanks unto him and his captaines for his care both of us and of our action, not as the matter deserved, but as I could both for my companie and my selfe, I (being aforehand) prepared what I would desire, craved at his hands that it would please him to take with him into England a number of weake, and unfit men for my good action, which I would deliver to him, and in place of them to supply me of his company, with oare men, artificers, and others.

That he would leave us so much shipping and victuall, as about August then next followyng, would cary me and all my companie into England, when we had discovered somwhat that for lacke of needfull provision in time left with us as yet remained undone.

That it would please him withall to leave some sufficient masters not onely to cary us into England, when time should be, but also to search the coast for some better harborow if there were any, and especially to helpe us to some small boats and oare men.

Also for a supplie of calievers, handweapons, match and lead, tooles, apparell, and such like.

He having received these my requests according to his usuall commendable maner of governement (as it was told me) calling his captaines to counsell, the resolution was that I should send such of my officers of my companie, as I used in such matters, with their notes to goe aboord with him, which were the master of the victuals, the keeper of the store, and the Vice-treasurer, to whom he appointed foorthwith for me the Francis, being a very proper barke of 70. tunnes, and tooke present order for bringing of victuall aboord her for 100. men for foure moneths withall my other demaunds whatsoever, to the uttermost. . . .

While these things were in hand . . . there arose such an unwonted storme, and continued foure dayes that had like to have driven all on shore, if the Lord had not held his holy hand over them, and the generall very providently foreseene the worst himselfe, then about my dispatch putting himselfe aboord: but in the ende having driven sundry of the Fleete to put to sea the Francis also with all my provisions, my two masters, and my companie aboord, shee was seene to be free from the same, and to put cleare to sea.

This storme having continued from the 13. to the 16. of the moneth, and thus my barke put away as aforesayd, the Generall comming a shore, made a new proffer to me, which was a shippe of 170. tunnes, called the Barke Bonner, with a sufficient master and guide to tarie with mee the time appointed, and victualled sufficiently to carie mee and my companie into England with all provisions as before: but hee tolde mee that hee would not for any thing undertake to have her brought into our harbour, and therefore hee was to leave her in the roade, and to leave the care of the rest unto my selfe, and advised mee to consider with my companie of our case, and to deliver presently unto him in writing, what I would require him to doe for us: which being within his power, hee did assure me as well for his Captaines, as for himselfe should be most willingly performed.

Hereupon calling such Captaines and Gentlemen of my companie as then were at hand, who were all as privie as my selfe to the Generals offer, their whole request was to mee, that considering the case that we stood in, the weaknesse of our companie, the small number of the same, the carying away of our first appointed barke, . . . with our principall provisions in the same, by the very hand of God as it seemed, stretched out to take us from thence: considering also, that his second offer, though most honourable of his part, yet of ours not to be taken, insomuch as there was no possibilitie for her with any safetie to be brought into the harbour: Seeing furthermore our hope for supplie with sir Richard Greenvill so undoubtedly promised us before Easter, not yet come, neither then likely to come this yeere considering the doings in England for Flaunders, and also for America, that therefore I would resolve my selfe, with my companie to goe into England and in that Fleete, and accordingly to make request to the Generall in all our names, that he would bee pleased to give us present passage with him. Which request of ours by my selfe delivered unto him, hee most readily assented unto, and so hee sending immediately his pinnaces unto our Island for the fetching away of fewe that there were left with our baggage, the weather was so boysterous, and the pinnaces so often on ground, that the most of all wee had, with all our Cardes, Bookes and writings, were by the Saylers cast over boord, the greater number of the Fleete being much agrieved with their long and daungerous abode in that miserable road.

From whence the Generall in the name of the Almightie, waying his ankers (having bestowed us among his Fleete) for the reliefe of whome hee had in that storme sustained more perill of wracke then in all his former most honourable actions against the Spaniards, with praises unto God for all, set saile the 19. of June, 1586. and arrived in Portesmouth, the 27. of Julie the same yeere.

David B. Quinn and Alison M. Quinn, eds., Virginia Voyages from Hakluyt *(London: Oxford University Press, 1973), pp. 42–45.*

DOCUMENT 2.5

The Lost Colony: John White's Journal

Julie . . . .
About the 16. of July, we fell with the maine of Virginia, which Simon Fernando tooke to be the Island of Croatoan, where we came to an anker, and rode there two or three daies: but finding himselfe deceaved, he waied, and bare along the coast, where in the night, had not Captaine Stafforde bene more carefull in looking out, then our Simon Fernando, wee had beene all cast away upon the breache, called the Cape of Feare, for wee were come within two cables length upon it: such was the care-lesnes, and ignorance of our Master.

The two and twentieth of Julie, we arrived safe at Hatoraske, where out shippe and pinnesse ankered: the Governour went aboord the pin-nesse, accompanied with fortie of his best men, intending to passe up to Roanoke foorthwith, hoping there to finde those fifteene Englishmen, which Sir Richard Greenvill had left there the yeere before, with whome he meant to have conference, concerning the state of the Countrey, and Savages, meaning after he had so done, to returne againe to the fleete, and passe along the coast, to the Baye of Chesepick, where we intended to make our seate and forte, according to the charge given us among other directions in writing, under the hande of Sir Walter Ralegh: but assoone as we were put with our pinnesse from the shippe, a Gentleman by the meanes of Fernando, who was appointed to returne for England, called to the sailers in the pinnesse, charging them not to bring any of the planters backe againe, but leave them in the Island, except the Governour, and two or three such as he approoved, saying that the Summer was farre spent, wherefore hee would land all the planters in no other place. Unto this were all the sailers, both in the pinnesse, and shippe, perswaded by the Master, wherefore it booted not the Governour to contend with them, but passed to Roanoke, and the same night, at Sunne set, went aland on the Island, in the place where our fifteene men were left, but we found none of them, nor any signe, that they had bene there, saving onely we found the bones of one of those fifteene, which the Savages had slaine long before.

The 23. of July, the Governour, with divers of his companie, walked to the North ende of the Island, where Master Ralfe Lane had his forte, with sundry necessarie and decent dwelling houses, made by his men about it the yeere before, where wee hoped to finde some signes, or certaine knowledge of our fifteene men. When we came thither, wee found the forte rased downe, but all the houses standing unhurt, saving the neather roomes of them, and also of the forte, were overgrowen with Melons of divers sortes, and Deere within them, feeding on those Mellons: so we returned to our companie, without hope of ever seeing any of the fifteene men living.

The same day order was given, that every man should be imploied for the repairing of those houses, which we found standing, and also to make other newe Cottages, for such as should neede. . . .

The eight and twentieth, George Howe, one of our twelve Assistants was slaine by divers Savages, which were come over to Roanoke, either of purpose to espie our companie, and what number we were, or els to hunt Deere, whereof were many in the Island. These Savages beeing secretly hidden among high reedes, where oftentimes they finde the Deere asleepe, and so kill them, espied our man wading in the water alone, almost naked, without any weapon, save onely a smal forked sticke, catching Crabs therewithall, and also being strayed two miles from his companie, shotte at him in the water, where they gave him sixteene wounds with their arrowes: and after they had slaine him with their woodden swordes, beat his head in peeces, and fled over the water to the maine.

On the thirtieth of Julie, Master Stafford, and twentie of our men, passed by water to the Island of Croatoan, with Manteo, who had his mother, and many of his kindred, dwelling in that Island, of whome we hoped to understande some newes of our fifteene men, but especially to learne the disposition of the people of the Countrey towards us, and to renew our olde friendshippe with them. At our first landing, they seemed as though they would fight with us: but perceaving us begin to marche with our shot towards them, they turned their backes, and fled. Then Manteo their countreyman, called to them in their owne language, whom, assoone as they heard, they returned, and threwe away their bowes, and arrowes, and some of them came unto us, embracing and entertaining us friendly, desiring us not to gather or spill any of their corne, for that they had but little. We answered them, that neither their corne, nor any other thing of theirs, should be diminished by any of us, and that our comming was onely to renew the olde love, that was between us, and them, at the first, and to live with them as brethren, and friendes: which answere seemed to please them well, wherefore they requested us to walke up to their Towne, who there feasted us after their manner, and desired us earnestly, that there might be some token or badge given them of us, whereby we might know them to be our friendes, when we met them any where out of the Town or Island. They tolde us, further, that for want of some such badge, divers of them were hurt the yeere before, beeing founde out of the Island by Master Lane his companie, whereof they shewed us one, which at that very instant laye lame, and had lien of that hurt ever since: but they said, they knew our men mistooke them, and hurt them in steade of Winginoes men, wherefore they held us excused.

August.

The next day, we had conference further with them, concerning the people of Secota, Aquascogoc, & Pomiock, willing them of Croatoan, to certifie the people of those townes, that if they would acccpt our friendship, we would willingly receave them againe, and that all unfriendly dealings past on both partes, should be utterly forgiven, and forgotten. To this the chiefe men of Croatoan answered, that they would gladly doe the best they could, and within seven daies, bring the Weroances and chiefe Governours of those townes with them, to our Governour at Roanoak, or their answere. We also understoode of the men of Croatoan, that our man Master Howe, was slaine by the remnant of Winginoes men, dwelling then at Dasamongueponke, with whom Winchese kept companie: and also we understood by them of Croatoan, how that the 15. Englishmen left at Roanoak the yeere before, by Sir Richard Greenvill, were suddenly set upon, by 30 of the men of Secota, Aquascogoc, and Dasamonqueponke. . . .

Having nowe sufficiently dispatched our busines at Croatoan, the same day wee departed friendly, taking our leave, and came aboord the fleete at Hatoraske. . . .

The 13. of August, our Savage Manteo, by the commandement of Sir Walter Ralegh, was christened in Roanoak, and called Lord therof, and of Dasamongueponke, in reward of his faithfull service.

The 18. Eleanora, daughter to the Governour, and wife to Ananias Dare, one of the Assistants, was delivered of a daughter in Roanoak, and the same was christened there the Sunday following, and because this childe was the first Christian borne in Virginia, she was named Virginia. By this time our shippes had unlanded the goods and victuals of the planters, and began to take in wood, and fresh water, and to newe calke and trimme them for England: the planters also prepared their letters, and tokens, to send backe into England.

Our two shippes, the Lyon, and the Flieboate, almost ready to depart the 21. of August, there arose such a tempest at northeast, that our Admirall then riding out of the harbour, was forced to cut his cables, and put to Sea, where he laye beating off and on, sixe days before hee coulde come to us againe, so that wee feared hee had beene cast away, and the rather, for that at the tyme that the storme tooke them, the moste, and best of their Saylers, were left aland. . . .

The 22. of August, the whole companie, both of the Assistants, and planters, came to the Governour, and with one voice requested him to returne himselfe into England, for the better and sooner obtaining of supplies, and other necessaries for them: but he refused it, and alleaged many sufficient causes, why he would not: the one way, that he could not so suddenly retune back againe, without his great discredite, leaving the action, and so many, whome he partly had procured through his perswasions, to leave their native Countrey, and undertake that voyage, and that some enemies to him, and the action at his returne into England, would not spare to slander falsely both him, and the action, by saying he went to Virginia, but politikely, and to no other ende, but to leade so many into a Countrey, in which he never meant to stay himselfe, and there to leave them behind him. Also he alleaged, that seing they intended to remove 50. miles further up into the maine presently, he being then absent, his stuffe and goods, might be both spoiled, and most of it pilfered away in the carriage, so that at his returne, hee should be either forced to provide himselfe of all such things againe, or els at his comming againe to Virginia, finde himselfe utterly unfurnished, whereof already he had found some proofe, beeing but once from them but three daies. Wherefore he concluded, that he would not goe himselfe.

The next day, not onley the Assistants, but divers others, as well women, as men, beganne to renewe their requests to the Governour againe, to take uppon him to returne into England for the supplie, and dispatch of all such thinges, as there were to be done, promising to make him their bonde under all their handes, and seales, for the safe preserving of all his goods for him at his returne to Virginia, so that if any part thereof were spoiled, or lost, they would see it restored to him, or his Assignes, whensoever the same should be missed, and demanded: which bonde, with a testimonie under their handes, and seales, they foorthwith made, and delivered into his hands. . . .

The Governour beeing at the last, through their extreame intreating, constrayned to returne into England, having then but halfe a daies respit to prepare him selfe for the same, departed from Roanoake, the seven and twentieth of August in the morning: and the same daye about midnight, came aboord the Flie boate, who already had waied anker, and rode without the barre, the Admirall riding by them, who but the same morning was newly come thither againe. The same day, both the shippes waied anker, and sette saile for England.

Quinn, ed., Roanoke Voyages, *2:515–38.*

DOCUMENT 2.6

A Futile Search: John White's Journal, 1590

The 15 of August towards Evening we came to an anker at Hatorask, in 36 degr. and on third, in five fadom water, three leagues from the shore, At our first comming to anker on this shore we saw a great smoke rise in the Ile Roanoak neere the place where I left our Colony in the yeere 1587, which smoake put us in good hope that some of the Colony were there expecting my returne out of England.

The 16 and next morning our 2 boates went a shore, & Captaine Cooke, & Captain Spicer, & their company with me, with intent to passe to the place at Raonoak where our countremen were left. At our putting from the ship we commanded our Master gunner to make readie 2 Minions and a Falkon well loden, and to shoot them off with reasonable space betweene every shot, to the ende that their reportes might bee heard to the place where wee hoped to finde some of our people. This was accordingly performed, & our twoe boats put off unto the shore, in the Admirals boat we sounded all the way . . . : but before we were halfe way betweene our ships and the shore we saw another great smoke to the Southwest of Kindrikers mountes: we therefore thought good to goe to that second smoke first: but it was much further from the harbour where we landed, then we supposed it to be, so that we were very sore tired before wee came to the smoke. But that which grieved us more was that when we came to the smoke, we found no man nor signe that any had bene there lately, nor yet any fresh water in all this way to drinke. Being thus wearied with this journey we returned to the harbour where we left our boates, who in our absence had brought their caske a shore for fresh water, so we deferred our going to Roanoak untill the next morning, and caused some of those saylers to digge in those sandie hilles for fresh water whereof we found very sufficient. That night wee retunred aboord with our boates and our whole company in safety. . . . Our boates and all things fitted againe, we put off from Hatorask, being the number of 19 persons in both boates: but before we could get to the place, where our planters were left, it was so exceeding darke, that we overshot the place a quarter of a mile: there we espied towards the North end of the Iland ye light of a great fire thorow the woods, to the which we presently rowed: when wee came right over against it, we let fall our Grapnel neere the shore, & sounded with a trumpet a Call, & afterwardes many familiar English tunes of Songs, and called to them friendly; but we had no answere, we therefore landed at day-breake, and comming to the fire, we found the grasse & sundry rotten trees burning about the place. From hence we went thorow the woods to that part of the Iland directly over against Dasamongwepeuk, & from thence we returned by the water side, round about the Northpoint of the Iland, untill we came to the place where I left our Colony in the yeere 1586. In all this way we saw in the sand the print of the Salvages feet of 2 or 3 sorts troaden that night and as we entred up the sandy banke upon a tree, in the very browe thereof were curiously carved these faire Romane letters CRO: which letters presently we knew to signifie the place, where I should find the planters seated, according to a secret token agreed upon betweene them & me at my last departure from them, which was, that in any wayes they should not faile to write or carve on the trees or posts of the dores the name of the place where they should be seated; for at my comming away they were prepared to remove from Roanoak 50 miles into the maine. Therefore at my departure from them in Anno 1587 I willed them, that if they should happen to be distressed in any of those places, that then they should carve over the letters or name, a Crosse in this forme, but we found no such signe of distresse. And having well considered of this, we passed toward the place where they were left in sundry houses, but we found the houses taken downe, and the place very strongly enclosed with a high palisado of great trees, with cortynes and flankers very Fort-like, and one of the chiefe trees or postes at the right side of the entrance had the barke taken off, and 5 foote from the ground in fayre Capitall letters was graven CROATOAN without any crosse or signe of distresse; this done, we entred into the palisado, where we found many barres of Iron, two pigges of Lead, foure yron fowlers, Iron sacker-shotte, and such like heavie things, throwen here and there, almost overgrowen with grasse and weedes. From thence wee went along by the water side, towards the poynt of the Creeke to see if we could find any of their botes or Pinnisse, but we could perceive no signe of them, nor any of the last Falkons and small Ordinance which were left with them, at my departure from them. At our returne from the Creeke, some of our Saylers meeting us, tolde us that they had found where divers chests had bene hidden, and long sithence digged up againe and broken up, and much of the goods in them spoyled and scattered about, but nothing left, of such things as the Savages knew any use of, undefaced. Presently Captaine Cooke and I went to the place, which was in the ende of an olde trench, made two yeers past by Captaine Amadas: wheere wee found five Chests, that had been carefully hidden of the Planters, and of the same chests three were my owne, and about the place many of my things spoyled and broken, and my bookes torne from the covers, the frames of some of my pictures and Mappes rotten and spoyled with rayne, and my armour almost eaten through with rust; this could bee no other but the deede of the Savages our enemies at Dasamongwepeuk, who had watched the departure of our men to Croatoan; and assoone as they were departed, digged up every place where they suspected any thing to be buried: but although it must grieved me to see such spoyle of my goods, yet on the other side I greatly joyed that I had safely found a certain token of their safe being at Croatoan, which is the place where Manteo was borne, and the Savages of the Iland our friends.

When we had seene in this place so much as we could, we returned to our Boates, and departed from the shoare towards our Shippes, with as much speede as we could: For the weather beganne to overcast, and very likely that a foule and stormie night would ensue. . . .

The next Morning it was agreed by the Captaine and my selfe, with the Master and others, to wey anchor, and goe for the place at Croatoan, where our planters were: for that then the winde was good for that place. . . .

On the 28. the winde changed, and it was sette on foule weather every way: but this storme brought the winde West and Northwest, and blewe so forcibly, that wee were able to beare no sayle, but our fore-course halfe mast high, wherewith wee ranne upon the winde perforce, the due course for England, for that wee were dryven to change our first determination for Trynidad.

Quinn, ed., Roanoke Voyages, 2:598–622.

DOCUMENT 2.7

A Transition to Jamestown: America Is Born

TO THE VIRGINIAN VOYAGE

You braue Heroique Minds,
  Worthy your Countries Name,
  That Honour still pursue,
  Goe, and subdue,
Whils loyt'ring Hinds
Lurke here at home, with shame.

Britans, you stay too long,
Quickly aboord bestow you,
  And with a merry Gale
  Swell your stretch'd Sayle,
With Vowes as strong,
As the Winds that blow you.

Your Course securely steere,
West and by South forth Keepe,
  Rocks, Lee-shores, nor Sholes,
  When EOLVS scowles,
You need not feare,
So absolute the Deepe.

And cheerefully at Sea,
Success you still intice,
  To get the Pearle and Gold,
  And ours to hold,
VIRGINIA,
Earth's onely Paradise.

Poems: by Michael Drayton, Esquire (London, [1619]), pp. 295–96. For a discussion of the significance of this poem, see Richard F. Hardin, Michael Drayton and the Passing of Elizabethan England *(Lawrence: University of Kansas Press, 1973), pp. 3–6, 124–25.*

SUGGESTED READINGS

Durant, David N. *Ralegh's Lost Colony.* New York: Atheneum, 1981.
Foss, Michael. *Undreamed Shores: England's Wasted Empire in America.* New York: Charles Scribner's Sons, 1974.
McIntyre, Ruth A. "William Sanderson: Elizabethan Financier of Discovery." *William and Mary Quarterly* 3d ser., 13(1956):184–201.
Morison, Samuel Eliot. *The European Discovery of America: The Northern Voyages, A.D. 500–1600.* New York: Oxford University Press, 1971.
Porter, Charles W., III. *Fort Raleigh National Historic Site, North Carolina.* Washington, D.C.: National Park Service, 1956.
Powell, William S. "Roanoke Colonists and Explorers: An Attempt at Identification." *North Carolina Historical Review* 34(1957):202–26.
Quinn, David B. "The Failure of Raleigh's American Colonies." In H. A. Cronne, T. W. Moody, and David B. Quinn, eds., *Essays in British and Irish History in Honour of James Eadie Todd.* London: Frederick Muller, 1949.

_____. "Preparations for the 1585 Virginia Voyage." *William and Mary Quarterly* 3d ser., 6(1949):208–36.

_____. *Raleigh and the British Empire.* New York: Collier Books, 1962.

_____, ed., *The Roanoke Voyages, 1584–1590.* 2 vols. London: Hakluyt Society, 1955.

Rowse, A. L. *The Elizabethans and America.* New York: Harper & Brothers, 1959.

Sauer, Carl O. *Sixteenth Century North America: The Land and the People as Seen by Europeans.* Berkeley and Los Angeles: University of California Press, 1971.

Shirley, John W., ed., *Thomas Harriot: Renaissance Scientist.* Oxford: Clarendon Press, 1974.

Stick, David. *Roanoke Island: The Beginnings of English America.* Chapel Hill and London: University of North Carolina Press, 1983.

Wright, Louis B. "Elizabethan Politics and Colonial Enterprise." *North Carolina Historical Review* 32(1955):254–70.

CHAPTER 3

Culpeper's Rebellion

Testing the Proprietors

Lindley S. Butler

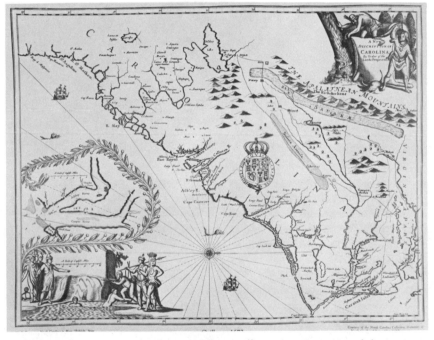

A New Description of Carolina, by John Ogilby, 1672 (Courtesy of the Division of Archives and History, Raleigh, N.C.)

By the mid-seventeenth century the Albemarle Sound country, northeastern North Carolina, was well known to Virginians. As early as 1622 John Pory, secretary of the colony of Virginia, had explored the region, reporting it to be "very fruitful and pleasant." Continuing explorations, a punitive expedition against the Roanoke valley Indians, and abundant promotional literature piqued the curiosity not only of the colonials but of Englishmen as well. By 1655 a fur trading operation, directed by Nathaniel Batts, was based at the junction of the Roanoke and Chowan rivers. Within the next few years, settlers from the southern Virginia counties began to filter through the swamps and down the river valleys north of the sound. The first generation of Carolinians chose the fertile necks between the rivers for their plantations, purchasing their land from the small, dwindling Indian tribes of the area—the Yeopim, the Pasquotank, the Meherrin, the Chowanoc, and the Perquimans.

When King Charles II conveyed the Carolina grant by a charter to the eight Lords Proprietors in 1663, the Albemarle region had been settled for at least five years by planters, who had on their own initiative traversed the Dismal Swamp and created a backwoods frontier settlement patterned on tidewater Virginia. It is not surprising that the Albemarle planters were reluctant to accept the governance of the Lords Proprietors, and the domination of the fledgling colony by the preproprietary planters would ultimately lead to contention, conflict, and revolt against their English overlords.

For more than twenty years the Lords Proprietors of Carolina reaped a bitter harvest of rebellion in Albemarle County, where governors were deposed, officials imprisoned, assemblies turned out, and courts overthrown. Many factors contributed to the general spirit of unrest in Albemarle County. The proprietors, who were principally involved in the development of the southern region of their colony, failed to establish an effective government. The weak government was embroiled in a continuing internal struggle for power between the preproprietary faction and the proprietary officials. Inconsistency characterized proprietary land policy, creating considerable uncertainty regarding land tenure. (Document 3.1) Geographic isolation contributed to self-sufficiency, individualism, and independence of thought and action. These characteristics led historian Wesley F. Craven to describe Albemarle County as "American," possessing "qualities better understood today than in that day."

Factional unrest began to emerge during the administration of Peter Carteret, who was chosen governor by the council in March 1670. The antiproprietary or popular faction was composed of the preproprietary settlers. The acknowledged leader of this faction was George Durant, who normally remained behind the scenes. Other planters in this faction, following Durant's lead, were John Jenkins, Valentine Bird, Richard Foster, John Willoughby, and John Harvey. These men owed no obligations to the proprietors. (Document 3.2) Indeed, they considered the proprietors as newcomers and meddlers. The proprietary or prerogative faction consisted of postcharter settlers, who were indebted to the proprietors for their land and political position. The leaders of the proprietary faction were Thomas Eastchurch, Speaker of the assembly, Thomas Miller, Timothy Biggs, and John Nixon.

Proprietary authority had been established within the county in the fall of 1664 with the appointment of William Drummond of Virginia as governor, and by the following summer the county had a representative assembly and courts. In January 1665, the proprietors promulgated a formal governance document, the "Concessions and Agreement," and it appears that in the following year, the Albemarle region came under the provisions of this constitution. The "Concessions and Agreement" allowed considerable self-government, establishing a unicameral assembly consisting of the governor, the council, and elected representatives.

By 1669, however, the Lords Proprietors had conceived a new plan of government, the "Fundamental Constitutions of Carolina," which provided for a complicated feudal state that was oriented toward protection of proprietary interests. The "Fundamental Constitutions" arrived in Albemarle in 1670. Although the local officials in good faith began incorporating aspects of the new system in the county, resentment arose over the restrictive provisions that superseded the more liberal "Concessions and Agreement."

Further discontent was fanned by drought, hurricanes, and generally unfavorable weather, which resulted in crop failures. Conditions were so severe in 1672 that the council considered it necessary for Governor Carteret to journey to England and petition the proprietors for assistance. Before his departure in May 1672, Carteret commissioned an influential council member, John Jenkins, to serve as deputy governor. Jenkins was authorized to serve until Carteret returned to the colony or until the proprietors commissioned a new governor.

Carteret's journey was in vain; by the time he arrived in England the proprietors were considering naming the imperious William Berkeley, governor of Virginia and a proprietor of Carolina, the sole proprietor of Albemarle County. The negotiations with Berkeley continued for several years, and while they were active, the proprietors were reluctant to make any suggestions concerning their northernmost settlement. Additional uncertainty was raised at this time by Virginia's attempt to lay claim to the Albemarle region.

The problems that arose from political conflict and a weak government were exacerbated by frontier isolation and tenuous economic growth. The Albemarle region was blocked from direct communication with England by the barrier islands now known as the Outer Banks. The shifting, sand-choked inlets limited access to shallow-draft coastal vessels sailing out of Boston, Salem, and other New England ports. (Document 3.3) Overland travel was difficult at best through the vast wilderness of the Dismal Swamp. Plantations in Albemarle County were small, producing chiefly tobacco as well as livestock and mixed grains. Albemarle tobacco, beef, and pork were transported to New England, Bermuda, Barbados, and other West Indian islands. The planters and their families tilled the fields with their indentured servants, Negro slaves, and Indian slaves. In the early years of the colony the agricultural exports were diversified—primarily grains and meat. By the 1670s tobacco dominated the economy, but overproduction drove the price down, causing the Albemarle planters to return in the next decade to their staples of grain, cattle, horses, and hogs. (Document 3.4)

Unfortunately, the coastal trade, so vital to the economic life of the colony, was increasingly hampered by the navigation acts passed by Parliament. Although the original intent of the acts was to eliminate the Dutch interlopers on British colonial trade, the acts favored England at the expense of the colonies. The Act of 1660 stated that certain enumerated articles, including tobacco, could be traded only to England. The New Englanders engaged in the intercolonial coastal trade thought that landing the tobacco in another English colony fulfilled the requirement of the law. Under the label of fish, traders would then illegally ship the tobacco to Ireland, Holland, Scotland, the Canary Islands, and France. (Document 3.5) Hoping to curb the illegal trade, Parliament passed the Plantation Duty Act of 1673, which placed a duty of one penny per pound on tobacco, to be paid at the port of purchase. Because of the sole dependence of the Albemarle settlers on the New England trade for the marketing of their tobacco crop, the Act of 1673 struck directly at the economy of the colony. The proprietors were greatly concerned about the illegal trade, and in their instructions to the governor in 1676, they ordered him to curb the New England traders who appeared to have a stranglehold on the economy of the colony. (Document 3.6)

The customs records of November 1677 show that the annual production of tobacco for Albemarle County was two thousand hogsheads. On the surface, the one penny per pound duty on tobacco does not appear to be high, but overproduction caused the price of tobacco in Virginia to plummet from 2s. 2 1/4 d. in the 1620s to one penny per pound by the 1630s, and the price never recovered its earlier levels. According to the accounts of Peter Carteret, the price of tobacco in Albemarle County for the period 1666–71 was sixteen shillings per hundred pounds, or two cents per pound. To reduce the gross from tobacco even further, Virginia (where most of the Albemarle trade was directed) levied an entry and clearing fee of two shillings per hogshead, and the average fee for shipping in 1675 was £7 per ton. By 1680 increased production of tobacco caused the price to go to 8s. 4d. per hundred pounds, or one penny per pound, and the price would remain low until the end of the century.

Governor Jenkins and the other precharter planters were not interested in having the Plantation Duty Act enforced, but Thomas Eastchurch and several members of the council were determined to follow the statutes. Eastchurch was opposed by the New England traders, who told the settlers that they would double their prices if the duty was collected. Upon hearing these plans, the local planters threatened some members of the council, and a crisis was averted only by appointing Valentine Bird, a member of the council and the antiproprietary faction, as collector of customs. Bird collected customs halfheartedly and inefficiently until the outbreak of the war with the Chowanoc Indians in 1676. Because the settlement was dependent on the New England traders for weapons, powder, and shot, the traders used the war as a pretext to escape the onerous duty. During the war period a band armed with weapons supplied by Zachariah Gillam, a New Englander, forced the remission of three farthings of the one penny duty to the traders.

In the summer of 1675 the proprietary faction began to ascend, but the antiproprietary faction received a welcome leader in John Culpeper, newly arrived from South Carolina, where he had been involved in political unrest. Culpeper and Jenkins conspired with other members of the antiproprietary faction to bring charges of treasonable and blasphemous words against proprietary leader Thomas Miller, and Miller, inclined to drink more than he should, gave them many opportunities. At the assembly in March 1676, Miller was presented with the charges and arrested by Governor Jenkins.

Realizing that the Palatinate Court was dominated by the proprietary faction and would return an acquittal, Governor Jenkins had Miller imprisoned until May and then sent him under guard to Jamestown to be tried before Governor Berkeley. Testimonies against Miller were signed by members of the antiproprietary faction. Miller was accused of critical statements about the king, of declaring the proprietors "fooles or sotts," and of comparing the elements of the sacrament of the Lord's Supper to "hogs wash putt in a piggs trough." Despite the damning accusations, Miller was acquitted by Berkeley and the Virginia council in June, and he promptly sailed for England to explain his actions to the proprietors.

Instead of weakening the proprietary faction, it appears that the arrest of Miller rallied them. The factional struggle was brought to a head by a case that Eastchurch lost in the county court and attempted to appeal to the Palatinate Court. Justice John Willoughby refused the appeal on the grounds that his court was the final authority. Soon afterward, Eastchurch had Willoughby summoned before the Palatinate Court, but he not only refused the summons but also thrashed the court officer. As a result of his rebellious actions, Willoughby was outlawed by the assembly and subsequently fled to Virginia.

A short time later, Thomas Cullen, a council member and a member of the antiproprietary faction, was outlawed by the assembly for trading with the Indians. At this point, events were going so well for Eastchurch that he decided to take control of the government. Governor Jenkins was deposed by the assembly in September 1675 and temporarily imprisoned. But Eastchurch had moved too soon. By the next March he was faced with a countercoup led by Durant and White, who raised a force that turned out the Palatinate Court, closed the assembly, and pursued Eastchurch into Virginia, where he boarded a ship for England. The antiproprietary faction was left in complete control, and Jenkins was returned as governor. (Document 3.7)

Eastchurch and Miller arrived in London and sought the aid of the proprietors in the early fall of 1676. Having heard little news from their settlement, the proprietors were inclined to believe Eastchurch, whom they characterized as a "Gent[n] of a good fame," who was related to the lord treasurer. (Document 3.8) With little difficulty Eastchurch secured a commission as governor, and his friend Miller received commissions as register (secretary) of the colony and collector of customs. Durant, the spokesman for the antiproprietary faction, soon arrived in London and presented his case to the proprietors but to no avail. Upon being told that Eastchurch had been appointed governor, Durant warned that if Eastchurch attempted to take office there would be a revolt.

In the summer of 1677, Eastchurch and Miller sailed for Carolina via the West Indies. Landing first at Antigua, they soon sailed to Nevis, where Eastchurch met an heiress, married her, and decided to remain in the islands for an extended honeymoon. Although he lacked the authority, Eastchurch commissioned Miller as president of the council and commander in chief.

Miller embarked from Bermuda on the shallop *Success*, which in July anchored off Currituck. He was not welcomed by the antiproprietary faction. Indeed, several days after his arrival, Miller was assaulted by Patrick White, who vowed that he would never allow the customs duties to be collected. Despite this volatile incident, Miller summoned the assembly, presented his commissions, and apparently satisfied the assembly as to his gubernatorial authority.

Miller took his obligations seriously and first settled the war with the Chowanoc Indians, who had continued sporadic raids on the colony. He then turned to the problem of the collection of customs. After removing Bird, Miller appointed Henry Hudson as deputy collector in Currituck and Timothy Biggs as deputy collector in Pasquotank. To increase the effectiveness of the customs law enforcement, Miller raised a militia force. In six months Miller's government collected 817 hogsheads of tobacco (327,068 pounds) and £1242 8s. 1d. from confiscation of illegal goods, including the seizure of the brig *Patience* for illegal trading. As his power increased, Miller arbitrarily began arresting antiproprietary men and charging excess fines. Although the opposition of the antiproprietary faction mounted, their resentment did not burst into rebellion until the return of Durant from London.

On 1 December 1677, the brig *Carolina* dropped anchor at Craw-ford's landing on the Pasquotank River with a cargo of trade goods and arms. This vessel was commanded by Gillam, and Durant was on board as mate. Miller boarded the vessel soon after its arrival and demanded from Gillam an accounting of tobacco shipped the previous year. Although Miller saw the ship's papers and the certificates of bond, he refused to accept this evidence, placing Gillam and his crew under arrest. Later that evening, upon hearing that Durant was aboard the *Carolina*, Miller rowed out to the vessel and arrested Durant at gunpoint. (Document 3.8)

When word of the arrests spread throughout the precinct, the aroused antiproprietary faction began to take action. Messengers announced a rendezvous, and on 3 December an armed party under Culpeper entered the house of Timothy Biggs and seized him with the county records that he possessed. Later in the day, Culpeper wrote the *Remonstrance*, a call to revolt for the entire county. (Document 3.9) The next day a group from Pasquotank precinct seized Miller and John Nixon, a member of the council. The leaders of the rebellion forwarded a letter to Richard Foster, the political leader of Currituck, instructing him to gather supporters, arrest Hudson, and bring him to trial at Durant's house. A few days later, Culpeper led a force into Chowan and seized the county marshal with his papers.

In Currituck, Foster had seized Hudson and summoned a meeting to elect burgesses to represent the precinct at the coming assembly. The crowd gathered in a surly mood and began raucously denouncing proprietary government. Foster, maintaining control of the mob, cautioned them against shouting rebellious words; but he insisted that they must stand for trade free from the king's duty. At this point the mob became so unruly that Hudson feared he might be murdered on the spot. Fortunately, cooler heads prevailed. It was then decided that Miller must be tried for his alleged crimes. After the mob rendered this decision, the meeting was adjourned, and preparations were made for the trip to the assembly at Durant's house.

In the meantime, the prisoners at Crawford's landing had been taken by boat to Durant's house. The next day a patrol searched Miller's property and found the box containing the county seal hidden in a tobacco hogshead. That afternoon amid the loud clamoring of the crowd, Miller was clapped into irons. Encouraged by an increasing flow of rum from Gillam's ship, the stocks and pillory were overturned by the mob and thrown into the river. Scouts were sent out to arrest, disarm, or exile all of those still opposing the rebellion. On 24/25 December Foster's party from Currituck arrived, and at the roll of a drum an assembly of eighteen members was elected with Thomas Cullen chosen as Speaker. From the assembly, a court was formed with Richard Foster elected chief justice.

Miller was dragged out in irons, and a grand jury was impaneled to indict him. Through ignorance the jury failed to return a true bill of indictment, and matters were not helped when it was found that the sheriff was "stark drunk." Miller feared for his life as the crowd muttered threats, but at that moment a proclamation condemning the rebels arrived from Governor Eastchurch, who had landed in Virginia a few days earlier. The assembly was dissolved after a guard of soldiers was sent to the border to prevent the entrance of the governor. Culpeper was elected collector of customs, and the customs receipts were divided, with some going to pay the soldiers. Miller was retained in irons, placed in a small log prison and allowed no communication with his friends. Durant, now the rebel attorney general, sailed for London to inform the proprietors of the momentous events that had taken place in their colony. (Document 3.10)

The antiproprietary faction was finally in complete control of the colony's government. It appears that John Jenkins, the former deputy governor, resumed that position, serving as the head of the rebel council. Governor Eastchurch, the only remaining threat to the rebels, died within five or six weeks of a fever. Everything went well for the rebels for the next seven weeks, but in February 1678, the wily Timothy Biggs escaped from prison and left for England to report the rebellion to the proprietors.

Upon arrival in London, Biggs made his presence known, bitterly denouncing the rebels before the proprietors. Because the crown was seeking justifications to recover the proprietary colonies, the proprietors decided to minimize the rebellion and satisfy the unrest as quickly and quietly as possible. To placate Biggs, the proprietors appointed him as comptroller of customs and surveyor general of the colony in September 1678. When the proprietor Seth Sothel was appointed governor, it was hoped that the rebellion would soon be settled. Unfortunately, the problem was not to be solved so easily; en route to Albemarle, Governor Sothel was captured by "Turkish" pirates and held for ransom in Algiers. As soon as the proprietors received the news of Sothel's kidnapping, they appointed John Harvey, who had the respect of both factions, as president of the council (acting governor).

To settle the controversy over the collector's position, the proprietors appointed Robert Holden as collector of customs. On the trip from England to Albemarle in June, Holden stopped in Boston and investigated the activities of the New England traders. While he was in Boston, Holden decided that Culpeper was not properly fulfilling his obligations as collector. Soon after his arrival in Albemarle, Holden evidently changed his opinion because by November he was serving on the council with the rebels. Holden was able to collect customs successfully and send returns to England.

To answer the charges of Biggs, Culpeper had been dispatched to London in the summer of 1678. After a hearing before the proprietors in November in which Culpeper admitted rebellious acts, he placed himself under a £500 bond with the stipulation that he would return the missing customs receipts within a year. This arrangement satisfied the proprietors, and they hoped that no further trouble would arise.

Miller, who had remained in prison since December 1677, had finally been charged by the rebels with treasonable and blasphemous words, the same offense for which he had been acquitted in 1675. During the August 1679 session he was brought before the Palatinate Court. The charges were restated, and he was released to the custody of the county marshal. Shortly thereafter, Miller escaped and sailed to England from Virginia.

Upon arrival in London, Miller presented a petition concerning the rebellion to the king, who issued a warrant for the arrest of Culpeper on 19 December. Culpeper was seized at Downes a week later on Gillam's ship *Carolina*, which was preparing to sail for Virginia. After several weeks of imprisonment, Culpeper requested that he be brought to trial. The crown ordered the proprietors to present a copy of their charter and a full report of the rebellion. Fully expecting the loss of their charter, the proprietors knew that Culpeper's conviction of treason would be an admission of failure on their part to keep order. They therefore decided to defend Culpeper to prevent such a conviction.

The investigation dragged on until 20 November 1680, when Culpeper was tried for high treason before the Court of King's Bench. Opening with the statement that there had been no legal government in Albemarle from the beginning, Lord Shaftesbury presented a masterful defense. If there had been no government, there could not have been a revolt. Shaftesbury further stated that Miller "*without any legall authority* gott possession of the government," committed many illegal and arbitrary acts, and drank to excess. Shaftesbury noted that since Governor Harvey and Collector Holden had taken office, they had been obeyed.

Two major elements in the defense were that Holden had returned customs receipts to the royal treasury and that the people of Albemarle had taxed themselves to repay the customs seized during the rebellion. (Document 3.11)

As a result of Shaftesbury's defense and the apparent settlement of the rebellion, an acquittal was secured for Culpeper. Thus ended the active rebellion but not the unrest. Although the antiproprietary faction remained in power, there were further conflicts with the proprietary faction, which was now led by Timothy Biggs. Another blow to the economic life of the colony was the Virginia statute of 1679, which prohibited the importation of Carolina tobacco. This statute tied the Albemarle colony even tighter to the New England trade. Surprisingly, the release of Governor Sothel in 1683 brought new trouble to the colony. Sothel, who had been appointed with such high hopes in 1678, eventually gained a reputation for being the worst governor that Albemarle ever had, and he was banished by the antiproprietary faction in 1689. With the appointment of Philip Ludwell that same year as governor of Carolina "north and east of Cape feare," Albemarle ceased to be a separate political unit and became a part of greater Carolina.

North Carolina historians have generally viewed the rebellion as an outgrowth of the internal factional struggle for power, with the specific crisis triggered by the potential effect of the tobacco duty of 1673. Unrest festered in the isolated frontier settlement, exacerbated by proprietary neglect, uncertain land policy, and rumors that the proprietors might convey the settlement to William Berkeley. Certainly the constitutional issue, used so well by Lord Shaftesbury in his defense of Culpeper, focused attention on the lack of government authority in the colony, and historian Mattie E. E. Parker in her study of the rebellion emphasized the importance of the constitutional crisis in the rebellion.

There may be a relationship between the Albemarle unrest and both Bacon's Rebellion in Virginia in 1676 and similar protest in Maryland. The Albemarle backwater was a likely refuge for Virginia rebels fleeing the wrath of Governor Berkeley, but there is no evidence linking the two uprisings. Although the Albemarle settlers were fighting Indians in 1676, the Chowanoc War remained on the periphery of events in Carolina, in clear contrast to Bacon's campaign against the Roanoke Valley Indians, which was at the heart of the Virginia rebellion. The Carolinians were surely aware of the uprising in Virginia and emboldened by it, but the swift and bloody vengeance exacted by Governor Berkeley was a vivid warning to proceed with caution.

The rebellion was not surprising, given the power struggle within the feeble proprietary government, for which the Lords Proprietors must bear full responsibility. The rebellion had indeed tested the proprietors, who for a variety of reasons were found wanting. The Albemarle planters had learned from the outset to rely on their own resources, and after many years of contention, the antiproprietary faction had won the right to govern the colony. The success of the government established by this faction was best described by the proprietors themselves, when in 1680 they admitted that all was "quyet" and that the customs fees were being "quyetly paid by the People."

Culpeper's Rebellion was the most important of the upheavals in Albemarle County, but there were four other incidents in the nearly three decades of the county's history when the governor was illegally deposed. Nor did rebellion die with the demise of the Albemarle colony. Shortly after Philip Ludwell took office there was an abortive effort by a Captain John Gibbs to overthrow the new governor. By 1691 Ludwell was appointed governor of Carolina with the seat of government in Charleston, and the northern region of the colony was administered by a deputy governor, a resident of the Albemarle area. This new arrangement coupled with the appointment of capable deputy governors brought a temporary calm to the region until the early eighteenth century.

In the eighteenth century, however, the proprietors were faced with renewed chaos during the Cary Rebellion, another internal power struggle between political/religious factions, which resulted in the permanent removal of the Quakers from participation in the government. Following closely on this rebellion was the devastating Tuscarora War. Despite the upheavals of the proprietary period the isolated colony prospered and new settlements appeared throughout the coastal plain.

When the crown purchased Carolina in 1729, the province was on the verge of significant economic and population expansion. Toward the end of the royal period the colony added to its reputation as a contentious and rebellious province with the War of the Regulation, the largest rebellion in America before the Revolution. The revolutionary patriots would have found common cause with the Albemarle planters in their protest over an oppressive tobacco duty and the arbitrary actions of the proprietary officials. Although small-scale and distinctly local in its consequences, Culpeper's Rebellion temporarily established a rebel government in the colony, but, more important, it began a tradition of provincial opposition to overseas rule.

DOCUMENT 3.1

Timothy Biggs to the Lords Proprietors, April 1678

I presume that y^r Lord^ps having beene out considerable summes of money for the well planting the south parts of your Province with hopes of a further Answere of your Expectacion then you may have hitherto had Possibly may be a Reason of unwillingnesse in your Lord^ps to Lance out no further But I humbly propose to your Lord^ps That notwithstanding you have not beene out as yet any thing upon that Country in ye Province called Albemarle yet ye Inhabitants have lived and gott Estates under y^r Lord^ps there by their owne Industry and brought it to the capacity of a hopefull Settlement and ere these had it had your Lord^ps smiles & assistance but a tenth part of what your Southern parts have had It would have beene a Flourishing Settlement But People having no assurance of their Lands (for that yet never any Patents have beene granted under yor Lord^ps to the Inhabitants) is matter of great discouragement for men of Estates to come amongst us because those already seated there have no assurance of their enjoyment.

William L. Saunders, ed., The Colonial Records of North Carolina, *10 vols. (Raleigh: State of North Carolina, 1886–90), 1:247.*

DOCUMENT 3.2

Representation to the Lords Proprietors of Carolina Concerning the Rebellion in That Country, 1679

That the Principalls and Heads of this Rebellion were not only prompted thereunto by ambition and envy or the private pekes and particular disgusts they had to those Gentlemen your Honors thought fit to entrust with the Government, but alsoe more especially those personall and particular crimes they knew themselves guilty of and accountable for whenever a Governor should come.

That this was a deliberate design of no sudden growth may be proved by their generall charge wherein all their former actions seem to have a naturall tendency to this their last and horrid end, At first their severall times disturbing the Courts, subverting the Government, dissolving Parliaments, Their industrious labor to be popular and continued making of factions and parties.

Their poysoning the peoples eares, unsetling and disquieting their minds, by diffusing and dropping abroad, by their Agents false and dangerous Reports tending much to the indignity of your Honors and reproach of your Government, and among divers others, that your Honors intended to raise the Quitrents to two pence and from two pence to six pence per acre. Now what they have done since is so notorious and obvious to every eye, as the imprisoning your Lordships' Deputies, putting the President who was likewise his Majesty's Collector into Irons, their Generall arming on the first appearance of Gilham's shipp in Pascotanke River, their seizing and carrying away the Records, Lastly their arrogating and assuming to themselves the supreme and sovereign power, by first dissolving then erecting Courts of Judicature, convening Parliaments without Writs, and as if they had the sovereign and absolute power they put out make New Officers not only in Courts and other publick services of the Country, but even where The King is more immediately concerned, turning out His Majesty's Collectors, putting in others, clearing and discharging Ships, but last of all their most horrid treasonable and tyrannicall actings in erecting a Court for tryall of life and death without the Lords Deputies or Commission of Oyer and Terminer or any other colour or pretence of Authority, either from His sacred Maj^{ty} or your Lordships, and particularly in the cases of Mr Thomas Miller and Mr Timothy Biggs.

But their speciall, particular and respective crimes are here annexed to their severall names here in the margin in the order following (vizt)

Capt Valentine Bird. He being appointed by the Country to be Collector of His Majesty's Duty of the penny per pound, for all Tobacco not exported for England, did without power from or the privity or consent of either my Lord High Treasurar or his Majesty's Commissioners of the Customs suffer the New England Traders to load and carry away the Tobacco of the Country without paying the said Duties, by which meanes they are now run in arreare to His Majesty one hundred and fifty thousand weight of Tobacco, and finding the hazard he had run in case another Collector should be sent he with above one hundred more, most whereof were Pastotankians, which after led the other Precincts into Rebellion there, with him subscribing a Paper against the payment of the said Duty, but after hearing by the report of Crawford that Mr Eastchurch was coming Governor and Mr Miller Collector, Bird and the rest of the subscribers were the first that took armes and opposed Miller at his first landing fearing they should be questioned for what they had done so, as soone as ever Gilham arrived they again take armes and by their Agents invite the other three Precincts to joyne with them, and till the generall elaps of the Country they were only in this defection and Bird was their Leader and drew the first sword, encouraged hereunto by Captain Zackery Gilham who supplied them with many fire armes and other weapons of War, came with some of his Seamen armed to Captain Crawford's house, where the President and two other of the Deputies were taken prisoners.

George Durant hath several times before not only contemned but opposed the authority established by your Honors, and in the head of a Rebell rout by force subverted the Government turning out and placing in whom he and they thought fit at pleasure, and openly threatning that, if ever Mr Thomas Eastchurch came in Governor, he would turn Rebell. And as if these were too small crimes, he hath viciated a Record of Court by adding, razing and other wayes altering the verdict of a jury, and as foreman giving it in contrary to what the whole Jury had returned upon oath, particularly in case of Mr Thomas Miller. And in fine hath all along when at home beene one of the most violent, active and the most outrageous of all the Conspirators and Insurrectors. . . .

Lieut: Col: John Jenkins being some time made Governor by the appointment of Cartwright was after for severall misdemeanours displaced and imprisoned; yet although never legaly discharged, raiseth a party of riotous persons in armes, and these with some others vote him Generalissime, neither he or they pretending to any other right or authority than what he derived from this Rebell Rout, these turne out the Palatines Court, dissolve the Assembly, place and displace whom he and they pleased by an arbitrary power and force. But yct although Jenkins had the title yet in fact Durant governed and used Jenkins but as his property, for of all the factious persons in the Country he was the most active and uncontrolable.

John Culpeper, a person that never is in his element but whilst fishing in troubled waters, he was forced to fly from Ashley River for his turbulent and factious carriage there. He both here and in New England with some of the discontented Traders plotted there and underhand here incouraged the hot headed people to this rash and ill-advised Rebellion. Culpeper being their Secretary or Register and one of their Caball or Grand Councill in matter of advise, this being the second disturbance he hath made here, besides what he hath done in Ashley River, New England and Virginia and therefore a man they much hearken to for his experience sake.

Saunders, Colonial Records, *ed.*, 1:256–59.

DOCUMENT 3.3

Thomas Miller vs. Robert Risco, 1673

By this publique Instrument of Protest, Bee it known & manifest to all whom it may concerne Whereas Robert Risco in the County of Albemarle in the province of Carolina master of the vessell called the good hope of the above said county by gods grace being intended or bound for ffoy [Fouey] in old England and in pursuance thereof & with an hearty Intention to performe the said voyage on the 20th day of March 1672 [1673] from Pascotancke River set saile & on the 22th of March aforesd was came before the New Inlet wch seemed to bee quite barred up for wee stood for the Middle thereof till wee came on ground. It pleased God the tide of fflood favouring of us wee gott her off againe & stood further to the Southward till shee came on ground the second time. Then wee carried out our Ancor and by the help of god gott her off againe then we stood almost to the Southside of the Inlet till wee found but ffive foote water and before wee were about, wee were on ground the third time But not soe fast but that wee got off with little trouble so being quite discouraged and quite out of hope of finding any channell that way wee stood quite over to the North Side where wee found Eight foote water but it showling for suddenly yt before could get the vessell about wee were fast on ground againe notwithstanding all our endeavors with Ancor & Cables and all the meanes wee could use shee cast thwart & Imediately there arose a violent storme or tempest of wind at Southwest or threabout which caused the Sea to breake sheer over her & shee beating soe violently that wee much feared shee would split in peeces. The time yt shee lay in this condition was from Nyne a Clocke in the morning till about five in the afternoone & the strength of the tide with the motion of the vessell wich the sea had wrought away ye sand afore and abaft and banked upon the lee side in the middle almost to the Bend which wee feared would have broke her backe But wee tryed the pump often but could not find her to complaine as yet But when it was almost night with great labour & paines & with the help of the flood wee got her off In which time wee received three or foure extraordinary knockes. But in the end wee being almost tyred and Desiring to take or rest wee went first to try the pump by wch wee found a great deale of water & that or vessell had received some harme by beating in which condition of leakines shee hath eversince continued for which cause the aforesd master did resolve to put into some port or place in New England. Wherefore knowe yee theerfore that the said Risko doth solemnly protest against the Showles

Tempest and Sea which wee met with coming out of the said Inlet against all Damages that wee have sustained.

Thomas Miller vs. Robert Risco, Newport, Rhode Island, 22 October 1673, pp. 11–13, North Carolina Archives, Raleigh.

DOCUMENT 3.4

Peter Carteret's Account, 1666–1673, 3 December 1674

Wee arived in Albemarle the 23^d of ffebr 1664/5 & went to Colleton Island acording to Instructions where I found a 20 foot dwelling howse a 10 foot hogg howse & apsell of wild hoggs butt Nothing towards a plantation soe that I was to make a plantation out of the wilderness wee cleered what ground we could on powells pointe & plant it with corne which produced litle by reason that wee were all Sick all the Sumer that wee could nott tend it & the Servants Soe weake the fall & Spring that they could doe little worke. . . .

1668 Wee cleered more grownd and repaired o^r fences planted both corne & tobacoe butt Such a great Drough happened for about 3 month y^t burnt up all the tob. and stented the corne that it produced litle ye 30th: July the raignes begone & continued untill the Later End of August soe y^t the great abundance of raignes did as much hurt as the drough had before we made 5 hod^s of tob & about 80 bars of of Oile—

1669 Wee repaired o^r fences planted both corne & tob: which was very hopfull the 2^d of August wee howsed a bout a hod of tob ye 18 ditto a violent haricane as bad as the former Only did nott last soe Long destroyed what tob was out broke & spoiled most of the corne this yeare wee have made 1 hod^e of tobackoe and aboutt 52 barrels of Oile/.

1670 Wee planted both Corne & tob: proportionable to the Number of Servants that I had left the 6th of August wee had a violent haricane that Lasted 24 howers broke downe timber trees blew downe howses destroyed both corne & tob: soe that it was Lick to bee a famine amongst us corne was sold in virginia for 3£ sterling a barell & with us at 250£ of tob: it blew downe to the ground the hogg howse & a howse on the South side of the Inlette wher was aboutt 30 barells broke & spoiled & caried away a small howse On the North P^t of the Inlette where was 4 tunes of corke redy trimed for to putt in On about ye beginninge of

Septemb^r we had an other storme but nott altogether soe violent as the former this yeare Very few whales came On Shoare wee made aboutt 38 bar's of Oile—. . . .

yor Lordshipps may plainly apperceive y^t my Industrie Labour & paines have Nott in the Least beene wanting And that it hath pleased God of his providence to Inflict Such a Generall calamitie upon the inhabitans of these countreys that for Severall yeares they have Nott Injoyed the fruitts of their Labours which causes them Generally to growne under the burtyn of poverty & many times famine.

William S. Powell, ed., Ye Countie of Albemarle in Carolina: A Collection of Documents, 1664–1675 *(Raleigh: State Department of Archives and History, 1958), pp. 62–64.*

DOCUMENT 3.5

Robert Holden to Commissioners of Customs, Boston, 10 June 1679

About 1/2 dozen traders of this place with their complices receive the greatest part of the production of tobacco in the County of Albemarle in the Province of Carolina annually & ℔ a person whom through their interest wth the people have factiously made one Mr Culpeper (a Gentleman I Know not) the Collector of his Ma$^{ty's}$ Customes, by which meanes they & he have played such notorious pranks with the specious pretences of doing justice and preserving the King's rights that a people and Customes Treasure were never more infatuated, cheated and exhausted by the current late received stamp in these parts of New England Christian policy.

And as the Tobacco trade current causeth their concourse thither & their wayes to leniate ye impost (which the other subjects of the King pay) resteth not there, for from thence brought hither, they have liberty without farther examination here to carry the same to Ireland, Holland, France, Spain or any other place under the notion of fish and such like goods by which the trade is so diverted from the true rules of Commerce that trafique in this Western world must be monopolized in this Commodity only to New England & the rest of His Majesty's people so trading must become Bostoniz'd or relinquish dealing if speciall care is not had thereto & a settlement of Customes here with the King's Officers.

Saunders, ed., Colonial Records, *1:244–45.*

DOCUMENT 3.6

Instructions of the Lords Proprietors to
Governor Thomas Eastchurch, November 1676

Item you are to doe all that in you lyes to deverte the trade of our People under you with those of New England and to bringe them with a more imediate Trade with England Itt beinge a certaine Beggery to our people of Albemarle if they shall buy goods at 2^d hand and soe much dearer then they may bee supply'd from England, and with all sell there To-bacco and other Commodities at a lower rate then they could doe in England. Besides the people of New England cannot be friends to the prosperity and Interest of our plantations which will certainly in tyme them one and render them inconsiderable.

Item in order to the Incourageinge a Trade with England and other places you are to send us an exact account of how many foot there is at Low water in your severall Inlets, what safety there is when a shipp is in and where she may doe best to unlade or take in Commodities for this has bine soe concealed and uncertainely reported here as if some persons amongst you had joyn'd with some of New England to engross that poore trade you have and Keepe you still under hatches.

Saunders, ed., Colonial Records, *1:232.*

DOCUMENT 3.7

Lords Proprietors to the Present Government and Assembly of Albemarle, 21 October 1676.

Wee have received your two Letters the one of the 17th November 1675 the other of the 28th March last per hands of Mr Thomas Miller; and doe in the first place assure you; that wee neither have nor ever will parte with the County of Albemarle to any person whatsoever But will alwayse maintaine our province of Carolina entire as itt is. The Reasons that induce us to this resolution are such that wee mayntaine and preserve you in the English Rights and Liberties and in the next place your scituation beinge contiguous to Virginia is of great importance to us for the well plantinge of the rest of our province which wee expected should have had longe since a better progress with you; and that the Rivers of Phampleco and Newse should have bin before this welplanted and a way and Intercource by Land should have bine discovered between you and our Plantation on Ashley River, and the neglect of these two has bine the Cause that heitherto wee have had noe more Reguard for you as lookinge upon you as a people that neither understood your own nor regarded our Interests. . . .

Wee doe alsoe further acquainte you that wee are very well pleased and sattisfied with your proceedure with Lieutenant Colonel Jenkins and your Order and settlement of the Councell and Government untill you heard further from us who observe to our great sattisfaction that in all your proceedings you maintaine the due Respect to us and regard to faire Justice among yourselves, But wee must blame you and utterly disallow and disapprove of your sending Mr Thomas Miller or any person whatsoever to be tried in Verginia or on of your owne Precincts which is a prejudice to the power and authority wee derive from his Majestie's Grant But however for what is past wee cannot reflect on you when wee consider the conjunction of time and the apprehensions you had of Sir Wm Berkeley's being sole Proprietor, and upon this occation wee thinke fitt to mind you that wee utterly dislike tryinge and condemninge any person either in Criminall or Civill causes without a Jury and that noe evidence clandestinely taken can bee of any validdity otherwise then to cause the Criminall person to be secured where the crime is of a great nature.

Saunders, ed., Colonial Records, *1:228–30.*

DOCUMENT 3.8

The Case Between Thomas Miller Collecto^r of His Maj^{ts} Customes & Capt. Zachariah Gilham Culpeper Durant Craford & Others . . . , 9 February 1680

The illness of ye harbours was the cause that this Northern p^{rt} of Carolina had no other vent for their Comodityes but either by Virginia where they paid dutyes to ye Governm^t or to New England who were the onely imediate Traders wth them; And ventur'd in, in small Vessells & had soe manadg'd their affayres that they brought their goods att very lowe rates, eate out & ruin'd ye place, defrauded ye King of his Customes & yet govern^d the people ag^t their owne Interest. to cure those evills the Prop^{rs} made choyce of one Mr Eastchurch to be their Govern^r a Gent^n of a good fame & related to the Lord Trea^r Clifford who had recommended him to ye Prop^{rs} formerly for that place & had ye promise of severall of us. In Summer 1677 we dispatched away the s^d Mr Eastchurch together with Mr Miller who was ye K^{gs} officer and made by us one of our Deputyes It happen'd soe y^t they went not directly for Virginia but took their passage in a ship bound for Nevis where Mr Eastchurch lighting upon a woman y^t was a considerable fortune took hold of the oppertunity marryed her and dispatched away Mr Miller for Carolina to settle affayres against his comeing who carryed with him ye Commission of ye Lds Prop^{rs} to their Deputyes and Comission from Mr Eastchurch himself that made Miller Presid^t of y^e Councill untill his arrival and gave him very full and ample powers. Miller arriveing in Carolina with these Comissions is quyetly received into y^e Governm^t & submitted to not onely as Govr but y^e K$^{g's}$ Collecto^r in y^e discharg of wch duty as Collecto^r he made a very considerable progress. But as Govern^r he did many extravagant things, making strange limitations for y^e choyce of y^e Parliam^t gitting pow^r in his hands of laying fynes, wch tis to be feared he neither did nor meant to use moderately sending out strange warrants to bring some of ye most considerable men of ye Country alive or dead before him, setting a sume of money upon their heads: these proceedings having startled and disaffected the people towards him there arrives Capt. Zachariah Gilham with a very pretty vessell of some force and together with him Durant and about the same time Culpeper they brought with them severall Armes wch were for Trade in ye Country and findeing that Miller had lost his reputation & interest amongst ye people stirr'd up a Comotion seized him and all the writings belonging to ye Prop^{rs} and all the Tobacco & writings belonging to ye Kings Customes, imploying ye K^{gs} Tobacco towards ye charge of maintaining & supporting their unlawful actions And wch aggravated the matter very much Durant had in England sometyme before this Voyage declared to some of ye Prop^{rs} that Eastchurch should not be Governo^r & threatened to revolt. Capt. Gilham was a fitt man for his turn having been turn'd out by some of ye Prop^{rs} of a considerable imploym^t in Hudson's Bay wherein he had very much abused them.

Culpeper was a very ill man having some tyme before fled from South Carolina where he was in danger of hang^g for laying the designe & indeavouring to sett the poore people to plunder the rich. These with Crafurd & some oth^r New England men had a designe (as we conceive) to gitt ye trade of this part of ye Country into their hands for some years att least And not onely defraud the King of all his Customes but buy the goods of ye Inhabitants att their owne rates for they gave not to them above halfe the vallue for their goods of wch the Virginians sold theirs for.

Not long after this imprisonment of Miller & that these generall men had formed themselves into w^t Mr Culpeper calls ye Govern^t of ye Country by their owne authority & according to their owne modell, Mr Eastchurch arrives in Virginia whose authority & Comission they had not ye least colour to dispute & yet they kept him out by force of armes soe that he was forced to apply to the then Govern^r of Virginia for aid and assistance from him to reduce them wch had been accordingly donne but y^t Eastchurch unfortunately dyes of a feavour Presently after this these Gentlemen that had usurped ye Govern^t & cast of and imprisoned our Deputyes that would not comply wth them sends over 2 Comiss^{rs} in their names to promise all obedience to ye Lds Propr^s but insisting very highly for right against Miller. The Prop^{rs} perswaded one of their owne Mem^{brs} Mr Southwell to goe over & be Gover^{nr} himselfe to whome they promised the utmost submission (he being a very sober discreet gentleman) & was allsoe authorized from ye Comiss^{rs} of ye Customes to take care of ye Kings concerns there which wee conceive he would have settled in very good order but that he was unfortunately taken by ye Turks in his passage thither, And upon whome the settlem^t of the place very much depends it being a very difficult matter to gitt a man of worth and trust to go thither. His redemption is every day expected and in ye meanewhile we have dispatched one Mr Holden with Comissions & Deputations for the Govern^r to those that we did imadgine would manage it with most moderation who sends us word that all is now quyett & peaceable.

Saunders, ed., Colonial Records, *1:286–88.*

DOCUMENT 3.9

The Remonstrance of the Inhabitants of Pasquotank, 3 December 1677

First the occasion of their secureinge the Records & imprisoning the Presid[t] is, that thereby the Countrey may have a free parlem[t] & that from them their aggreivances may be sent home to the Lords, w[ch] are breifely these; In the first place (omitting many hainous matters) hee denied a free election of an Assembly and hath positively cheated the Countrey of one hundred and thirty thousand pounds of Tobacco which hath raised the levie to two hundred and fifty pounds of Tob[o] ℔ head more then otherwaies it would have beene besides neer twenty thousand pounds of Tob[o] charge he hath brought upon us by his pipeing guard & now Capt. Gillam is come amongst us with three times the goods hee brought last yeare but had not beene two houers on shore, but for the slip of a word was arrested for one thousand pounds sterling & many affronts and indignities thrown upon him by y[e] Presid[t] himselfe, in so-much that had hee not beene earnestly perswaded by some hee had gone directly out of the Countrey and the same night (about midnight) hee went aboard with a brace of pistolls and presenting one of them cockt to M[r] Geo. Durants breast & wth his other hand arrested him as a Traytour and many other Injuries, mischiefes and grievances hee hath brought upon us, that thereby an inevitable ruein is comeing (unlesse prevented) which wee are now about to doe and hope & expect that you will joyne with us therein.

Saunders, ed., Colonial Records, *1:248–49.*

DOCUMENT 3.10

Affidavit of Henry Hudson, 31 January 1680

That in July 1677 M[r] Thomas Miller arived in Albemarle in Carolina wth sundry Commissions and Instructions relateing to his Majesty and the Lds Propriet[rs] affaires whereof one was to be Collect[r] of y[e] Customes their and after haveing by y[e] advice and assistance of y[e] then Counsell there reduced y[e] Indians and y[e] Governm[t] w[ch] y[e] yeare before and then alsoe lay in a tumultuous confusion, he setled his Majestyes affaires relateing to ye Customes . . . and soe for ye space of five months things went on in quiet and peaceable manner as to the Gener^ll (though some were factiously inclined untill X^ber following upon ye arivall of one Capt. Zach. Gillam of Lond^n that yeare the inhabitants then riseing up in Armes thier broke out a more violent resurrection then heretofore Even to an absolute subverting the whole authority derived both from ye King and ye Lds. Propriet^rs seazing and imprisoning ye said Miller and the Lds. Prop^rs Deputyes and all others in authority and office Yea and all such of the Inhabitants alsoe as would not joyne wth them they then writt a seditious letter to the Lower Pts. to one Mr Rich. Foster to give him an acco^t what they had donn above wth all requireing him to suṁons ye Inhabitants below to chuse Burgesses for a new Assembly (as they cald it) and to seaze this deponant prisson^r all wch was donn . . . notwithstanding this depon^t required assistance from them and gave caution thereof to ye s^d Foster and ye rest of ye Gang thier mett who instead of choseing Burgesses, they by a shout of one and all cryed out wee will have noe Lo^ds noe Landgraves noe Cassiques we renounce them all and fly to the King's protection soe downe went ye Lords Propriet^rs for about halfe an owre untill ye said Foster tould them that way would not doe, whereupon they cryed up ye Lo^ds againe and went to chusing thier Burgesses as they cald them wch Burgesses being thus chosen had instructions from ye Rable how they should p^rceed att thier assembly wch was, first absoelutely to insist upon a free traid to transport thier tobacco where they pleased and how they pleased without paying any duty to ye King; Upon wch some of them cryed out God dame ye Collecto^r and this Depon^t verily thought they would have murthered him: the next thing was that they should bring ye said Miller to a tryall for severall odious crymes they then contrived to tax him w^thall one espeacially for cheating the Country of 135,000 lbs of Tobacco wch was secured upon ye Kings acco^tt by ye said Miller wch as they said belonged to them and the wch if he had not done they nev^r would have troubled him about thier p^rtended imputation of treason or any thing else they had framed against him as Will: Crafford one of ye Cheefe Ringlead^rs often told this Depon^t while he was a prisson^r in his house then they were to seaze all his Maj^tys Customes into y^er hands: these Instructions being given the s^d Foster wth his Burgesses carryed this Dep^t a prisson^r along wth them to one George Durant's house wch was ye appointed place for y^er meeting and where ye afores^d Mr Miller and ye Lo^ds Deputyes and other Officers were prissoners and where they kept this deponant und^r a guard of thre files of soldiers takeing violently from this Depon^t all the Kings bonds acco^ts and consarnes whatsoever from him and after delivered them to Jo^n Culpeper thier Collect^r where ye afores^d Gillam was and countenancing them with his presence & furnishing them wth drink nor would he open store untill he see what would be done about ye Governm^t and was alsoe p^rsent when they created a P^rlement . . . in all about 18 of them this p^rlement seperated five of y^er Memb^rs vizt Jo^n Jenkins Willm Craford, James Blunt, Patrick White and Valantine Bird to joyne wth one Mr Richard Foster thier cheefe Judge to make a Court of, and then this Court impanelled a Grand Jury out of ye souldiers and confused Rable, the foreman whereof was one Mordecay Bowdon a New England Traider and one much indebted to ye King wch foreman consulting wth one Jo^n Culpeper (thier Collecto^r afores^d and cheefe scribe & counsellor) how he should bring in ye Inditem^t against ye sd Miller the s^d Culpeper told him he must Indosse Billa vera whereupon this Jury went out and quickly returned againe but ye s^d foreman instead of indossing Billa vera put downe Bill of Error whereupon the Court looking wishtly upon it as much amazed, the s^d Culpeper snatcht it from them and told them it was only a mistake in ye foreman, whereupon ye foreman p^rsently replyed he had donn as ye s^d Culpeper had bid him; but however w^thout a second goeing out or more adoe it was mended and soe passed for good the wch manner of p^rdeedings was not denyed but owned by Foster and others of ye Court when questioned by this Depon^t about it Upon this the Sheriffe was to Impanell a petty Jury upon ye s^d Miller ye foreman whereof was one Joseph Winslow another New England Traid^r and one much indebted to ye King for Custome wch was donn and would certainly then have proceeded to have taken away ye said Miller's life as this Depon^t had great cause to beleave (for besides the many irreverent speeches against all authority uttered by the rable) those that were upon this depon^ts guard and of ye said Miller's jury, this depon^t often heard them vowe and sweare that they would never depart thence untill they sawe ye said Miller dead or alive und^r ground but ye comeing in of ye Govern^rs Proclamation prevented it.

Saunders, ed., Colonial Records, *1:272–74.*

DOCUMENT 3.11

Answer of the Lords Proprietors of Carolina, 20 November 1680

Mr Thomas Miller *without any legall authority* gott possession of the government of the County of Albemarle in Carolina in the yeare 1677 and was for a tyme quyetly obeyed but doeing many illegall and arbitrary things and drinking often to excess and putting the people in generall by his threats and actions in great dread of their lives and estates and they as we suppose getting some knowledge that he had no legall authority tumultuously and disorderly imprison him and suddainly after Mr Biggs and Mr Nixon for adhering to Mr Miller and abetting him in some of his actions and revive an accusation against Mr Miller of treasonable words for which he had been formerly imprison'd *but never tryed* And appoynt Mr Culpeper to receive the Kings Customes dureing the imprisonment of Mr Miller and did many other tumultuous and irregular things.

Saunders, ed., Colonial Records, *1:326.*

SUGGESTED READINGS

Andrews, Charles M. *The Colonial Period of American History.* 4 vols. New Haven: Yale University Press, 1937.

Ashe, Samuel A. *History of North Carolina.* 2 vols. Greensboro: Charles L. VanNoppen, 1908.

Butler, Lindley S. "The Early Settlement of Carolina: Virginia's Southern Frontier." *Virginia Magazine of History and Biography* 79 (1971):20–28.

———. "The Governors of Albemarle County, 1663–1689." *North Carolina Historical Review* 46 (1969):281–99.

Craven, Wesley F. *The Southern Colonies in the Seventeenth Century, 1607–1689.* Baton Rouge: Louisiana State University Press, 1949.

Lefler, Hugh T., and Powell, William S. *Colonial North Carolina: A History.* New York: Charles Scribner's Sons, 1973.

Osgood, Herbert L. *The American Colonies in the Seventeenth Century.* 3 vols. New York: Columbia University Press, 1904.

Parker, Mattie Erma E. "Legal Aspects of Culpeper's Rebellion." *North Carolina Historical Review* 45 (1968):111–27.

———, ed. *North Carolina Higher-Court Records, 1670–1695.* Raleigh: Department of Archives and History, 1968.

Powell, William S., ed. *Ye Countie of Albemarle in Carolina*. Raleigh: Department of Archives and History, 1958.
Rankin, Hugh F. *Upheaval in Albemarle: The Story of Culpeper's Rebellion, 1675–1689*. Raleigh: Carolina Charter Tercentenary Commission, 1962.

CHAPTER 4

North Carolina in the First British Empire

Economy and Society in an Eighteenth-Century Colony

William S. Price, Jr.

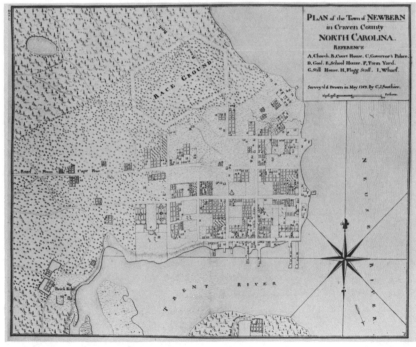

C. J. Sauthier's Map of New Bern, 1769 (Courtesy of the Division of Archives and History, Raleigh, N.C.)

The history of North Carolina as a distinct political unit within the British Empire may be said to have begun in 1689 with the designation by the Lords Proprietors of Philip Ludwell as governor of that part of Carolina lying north and east of Cape Fear. Although his commission designated Ludwell governor over virtually all of North Carolina's seaboard, as a practical matter the only viable white settlements at the time were clustered around Albemarle Sound. Reflecting the political instability characteristic of the early years of the colony, Ludwell was almost immediately opposed by another claimant for the governorship named John Gibbs. When Gibbs's efforts proved fruitless, the province entered a decade of much-needed political stability from 1691 to 1701. The county of Bath was formed south of Albemarle in 1696, and settlement around Pamlico Sound began increasing at a steady pace.

The first visible crack in this wall of stability appeared with passage by the colonial legislature of the Vestry Act in 1701 providing for organization and support for the Church of England. Even though the Lords Proprietors later disallowed the legislation, within the colony it had the effect of antagonizing a large proportion of the population who were dissenters, chiefly Quakers. These religious tensions in turn fueled the anxieties of established Albemarle settlers concerning the rapid growth of newer settlements in Bath County. Their orientation toward a Chesapeake-style plantation economy made leaders in Albemarle wary of the bold new men of Bath, who were making quick fortunes in a trade with Indians based on furs and skins. Heightening their anxiety was one of the more hateful aspects of membership in an empire: suffering the effects of a war essentially being waged in Europe. Queen Anne's War, known as the War of the Spanish Succession in Europe, began in 1702. Although North Carolina was not a battleground in the conflict, it was deeply affected by the scarcity of overseas transport resulting from the war. As shipping costs soared, Albemarle planters saw their tobacco economy falling into depression. Between 1702 and 1720, North Carolina underwent a politically spawned conflict (the Cary Rebellion), a decimating war (the Tuscarora War), and a provincial government so weak it cowered before pirates (the Blackbeard affair).

Similar patterns of political and economic tensions marked the subsequent decades of North Carolina's colonial years. The 1720s were characterized by uncertainty surrounding proprietary status (South Carolina had become a royal colony in 1719) and a land fraud controversy growing out of the survey of the boundary with Virginia; the 1730s, by the imposition of royal government and the explosive growth of a naval stores industry; the 1740s, by imperial conflicts and rapid population expansion in the western counties; the 1750s, by open hostility between white settlers and Indians in the western regions (culminating in the destruction of fifteen Cherokee towns in 1761) and the clearly disparate political representation favoring eastern counties over those in the west; the 1760s, by a growing anger over English control and a rancorous hostility between social classes in the colony; the 1770s, by the explosion that became the American Revolution and the attempt to define a new government. Although the tensions and conflicts that characterized these decades had their own specific causes and effects, each was also affected by North Carolina's uneasy status as a frontier outpost of a European "superpower." Likewise, one can enumerate sizable advantages from imperial status: the (usually unseen) protection of a dominant military power, a system of trade bounties particularly beneficial to North Carolina's naval stores industry, and a fundamental tradition of law and governmental process. Yet the perspective of history makes it clear that the "mother-child" relationship dictated by the colonial system was less beneficial to the child than to the parent.

Implicit in the imperial idea as it developed in seventeenth-century England was the concept of mercantilism. Mercantilists envisioned a self-sufficient empire in which colonies and mother country would be bound together by a variety of political and economic considerations hinging upon production of raw materials in the colonies and manufacture of finished goods in Britain. (Document 4.1) Through such legislative devices as the enumeration of certain products that could be shipped only to English ports and prohibitions against issuance of a plentiful supply of currency, the mother country sought to integrate the economy of her colonies with her own. As commerce grew in the eighteenth century, many colonists perceived this integration as subordination. With passage of the Molasses Act in 1733 designed to protect British West Indian planters from competition with their European counterparts, North American colonists began to comprehend the power that certain special interest groups could exercise in Parliament. It was becoming evident that pressure groups could wield sufficient influence in Parliament to effect passage of legislation beneficial to them alone rather than to the empire as a whole.

Imperial legislation was not always detrimental to the colonies. Parliament's passage of the Naval Stores Bounty Act in 1705 proved to be enormously beneficial to North Carolina. By providing a bounty of £4 per ton on exports of tar and pitch and £3 per ton for rosin and turpentine, England fostered the development of a major industry in the colony. Late in the 1760s North Carolina was producing 60 percent of the naval stores exported from the colonies.

So long as the colonies did not interfere with the course of trade or challenge the constitutional authority of Parliament, England permitted them wide latitude in administering their internal affairs through their own legislatures. With conclusion of the French and Indian War and the need to recoup the enormous costs of that conflict (which many Englishmen felt had been fought in defense of the colonies), the British government began to tighten its administrative control over the colonies. The upheaval generated by passage of the Stamp Act in 1765 opened a breach between England and the North American colonies that would not soon close. During that period many Americans began to see the empire less as an extension of the mother country than as a diverse domain of more or less equal parts. Conversely, certain British leaders began to view the colonies as self-concerned entities unappreciative of the protection and nurture offered by England. Out of such diverging perceptions the American Revolution sprang. (Document 4.2)

How does one measure the impact of imperial status on the economy and society of a given colony? Does one enumerate the various pieces of regulatory legislation growing out of a mercantilist system or the various pronouncements of the Board of Trade? Does one quote the available statistics on imports and exports? What about reviewing major legislation and executive orders within the colony itself? To be sure, such approaches are valid and important beyond question. Read solely on their own merits, though, they ignore some vital aspects of the economy and society of eighteenth-century North Carolina, for they fail to show to what a sizable degree certain basic rhythms of daily life went on regardless of who was governor of the colony, much less king of England. By the same token it is possible to read documents of the period which demonstrate that daily life could be profoundly touched by imperial and provincial policy.

Consequently, several documents are offered here that provide some sense of daily life in early North Carolina as well as describe certain aspects of imperial status. If such an approach fails to incorporate many of the undeniably important political, social, and economic themes of the day, it is hoped that that oversight will be partially compensated by providing a view of the frequent discomfort, hard work, and occasional triumph that characterized life in an outpost of empire.

Despite a wide variety of trading enterprises and increasing exports in the naval stores and lumber industries after 1730, North Carolina was a predominantly agrarian society. Several varieties of crops were grown, but throughout the colonial period the major farm exports remained tobacco and corn. Livestock, particularly hogs, were a major feature of the agricultural economy of the colony and often ranged about freely in the forests feeding on mast and wild plants. Pasturage abounded along the numerous streams of the province. (Document 4.3)

Throughout the eighteenth century many North Carolina settlers conducted trade with various Indian tribes for furs, usually deerskins. This trade was at its zenith in the years before the Tuscarora War began in 1711, but it remained an important factor in the commerce of the colony down to the American Revolution. (Document 4.4)

Until white settlement of the Lower Cape Fear region in the 1720s, North Carolina did not have a suitable deep-water port. The natural barrier created by a long, nearly unbroken chain of sand islands called the Outer Banks severely hampered the early commerce and settlement of the colony. Settlers around Albemarle Sound generally conducted their shipping through Virginia's Chesapeake ports, and farmers in the North Carolina backcountry, confronted with rivers and streams that flowed southeast, looked to Charleston for their shipping needs. Nevertheless, the colony grew steadily as the eighteenth century progressed, going from a population of about thirty-five thousand in 1730 to about seventy thousand in 1750 and increasing to nearly a quarter of a million in the 1770s. Thus between 1730 and 1750 the population doubled, and in the next two decades it more than tripled. This impressive demographic spurt resulted from large-scale immigration initially into the southeastern portions of the colony and then into the backcountry areas of the west. This backcountry settlement was largely overland from Pennsylvania through Virginia into North Carolina. Given such population growth the colony became increasingly more complex and diverse, both socially and economically.

If nature erected barriers to commerce through the Outer Banks, Britain erected man-made barriers through its various laws and proclamations severely limiting the flow of trade between the colonies and their neighbors as well as between them and Europe. Beginning with the Navigation Act of 1660, which enumerated certain articles of colonial growth and manufacture that could be shipped through England and its colonies, and continuing to an act of 1767 requiring that all previously nonenumerated goods bound for any part of Europe north of Cape Finisterre first be shipped through England, the British government consistently interfered with and frequently hampered the growth of colonial trade. Whatever one might argue about mercantilism, however, it is undeniable that North Carolina grew steadily and that the quality of life generally improved for the bulk of the white population during the colonial period.

Because of its early isolation from its northern and southern neighbors, North Carolina was frequently characterized as a bucolic society composed primarily of small landowners. Certainly, the colony never produced large numbers of planters equal in wealth to their counterparts in Virginia and South Carolina; but particularly after 1720, North Carolina's economy burgeoned to the extent that a number of sizable fortunes were made. The wealth of a merchant such as Samuel Cornell in New

Bern or a planter such as "King" Roger Moore on the Lower Cape Fear rivaled that of merchants and planters elsewhere in the South.

As the economy of North Carolina began expanding, perhaps the greatest single limiting factor was the lack of a sufficient labor supply. Indentured servitude, contract labor, and a steady flow of immigrants were insufficient to quench the thirst for economic expansion that parched the throats of many North Carolina entrepreneurs. As the eighteenth century progressed, the well of labor from which more and more planters began to draw was black. From an estimated population of fewer than five hundred Negroes in 1700 to the more than one hundred thousand slaves counted in the 1790 census, North Carolina's settlers came to rely heavily on chattel slavery for much of their labor force. Even for those whites who could afford few slaves or none at all, the racism that powered the engine of slavery was a dominant factor in society. At the lowest end of the economic and social scale, the slave served as an object for abuse and a symbol of dread (for the specter of widespread slave rebellion struck fear in many whites) as well as a source of labor. (Document 4.5)

Another constraint on the development of the economy was the difficulty of travel within the colony. Like the Outer Banks off the coast, the frontier wilderness of North Carolina made internal transportation arduous. Travelers and new settlers in the province frequently commented on the poor condition of the roads, but in fact few roads existed compared with later centuries. Consequently, given the abundance of streams and various waterways, much of the colony's traffic was waterborne. (Document 4.6)

If the average white settler in early North Carolina was an immigrant who had established himself on a small farm, he shared many experiences with other colonists in similar circumstances. He had entered North Carolina either overland or by water. In either case he had traveled a great distance, usually accompanied by his family. Many different factors accounted for settlement in North Carolina. The colony drew large blocs of religious dissenters including Christoph Von Graffenried's New Bern Palatines and the Moravians of Salem and ethnic groups such as the Highland Scots, but the primary attraction was for men drawn by the hope of owning their own land and of making some semblance of a fortune. (Document 4.7)

The first months of settlement were hard. Farmers had to plant their crops, build or acquire a home, and set up housekeeping. Virtually every newcomer went through a period of sickness shortly after arrival, ranging in degree from a general malaise to death. This period, referred to as "seasoning," resulted from Europeans, Africans, and native Americans coming together in one pool of contagion where each group passed its diseases to the other. Africans brought hookworm and dengue; Europeans, smallpox, typhus, and mumps. Indians were unusually susceptible to these maladies, and epidemics were an important factor in the devastation of the native American population in the eighteenth century.

Even after the "seasoning" period, sickness was a constant companion of life on a frontier. Infant mortality was very high; no statistics were kept, but extant eighteenth-century graveyards attest to the high death rate among the very young. A number of people in early North Carolina practiced medicine, but even when they had undergone training in Europe, their techniques sometimes impeded the natural healing process of the body. (Document 4.8)

A major facet in the overall health picture of the colony was the quality of the diet. Large quantities of meat were available: beef, poultry, and a variety of game offered a respite from the predominance of pork. Plentiful corn was the basis of most bread as well as being used in general cooking. Orchards and wild berries abounded, and such fruits were ultimately drunk as well as eaten. Carolinians' use of alcoholic beverages was sizable; in addition to making wine, cider, and brandy, colonists imported large quantities of rum and malt liquors. Despite the widespread availability of food, there was little knowledge of or attention to nutrition. As would be expected in a class-stratified society, the diet of the wealthy planter or merchant was a good deal more varied and wholesome than that of those at the lower end of the social ladder. (Documents 4.9 and 4.10)

The houses of typical white settlers were plainly furnished. Feather beds were prized commodities to be passed from one generation to another, as were table furnishings and other articles that modern families take for granted. A farmer with fifty or a hundred acres of land and a few head of cattle accumulated little movable wealth to pass on at his death. (Document 4.11)

Women, particularly those in frontier areas, often married at an early age. They bore and reared many children (one authority suggests that the average eighteenth-century family in North Carolina contained four children), conducted a variety of income-producing labors, and performed a staggering amount of domestic chores that might range from churning butter to making clothes. (Document 4.12)

Although there was a school in Pasquotank County as early as 1705, institutionalized education was rarely available to young North Carolinians. The chief educational instrument in the colony remained the family. Children were taught certain skills by their parents, and apprenticeships served to educate many. Even sons of the reasonably well-to-do often read law with a prominent local attorney rather than travel outside the province for more formal training. (Document 4.13)

Such schools as existed were generally associated with churches. Although the Anglican church had been established with tax support in acts of 1701 and 1703, it never flourished in North Carolina. Resentment over establishment and the absence of a resident bishop were but two factors retarding its growth. Missionaries sent to the colony by the Society for the Propagation of the Gospel were often less than ideal ministers. Dissenting sects proliferated; the first man known to preach in the colony (in 1672) was a Quaker. Lutherans, Presbyterians, Baptists, Methodists, and other sects existed, sometimes in the same community, throughout the province. Yet despite the variety of denominations and the appeal of certain sects, the fact is that most colonists had no religious affiliation. (Document 4.14)

The North Carolina colony in the eighteenth century was a child of England. It shared with the mother country a common language, political institutions, social systems, and other concepts and perceptions so fundamentally English that the American Revolution was in many ways a civil war. Yet there were undeniable differences between parent and child.

The existence of an awesome frontier, the presence of large red and black populations, and the general availability of land were but three factors that reminded settlers in North Carolina that they were not in Britain. When government leaders in England began to tighten administrative control over the colonies after 1763, many North Carolinians realized with their fellows in other provinces that, as members of an empire, they lacked control of their own political destinies. That realization led to increasing antagonism that in turn led to the explosion of 1775.

The catastrophe that was the American Revolution affected the life of every North Carolinian to some degree. Political events of enormous scale inevitably touch the lives of thousands. And yet, as some of the documents presented here show, many of the basic rhythms of daily life in North Carolina proceeded nearly oblivious to immediate questions of what the governor of the colony was doing or whether the king of France was angry with the king of England. The food people ate, the clothes they wore, and the state of their health were day-to-day concerns that seemed far removed from large-scale political matters.

The history of ordinary men and women has its own momentum. If some political leaders are motivated by grand schemes of conquest and empire, many workingmen are motivated by the hope of improving their lives and those of their families. Regardless of their status as members of the first British Empire, large numbers of eighteenth-century North Carolinians pursued that hope persistently and sometimes successfully. If the old concept of the New World as a land of freedom and opportunity has suffered from the realization that it brought slavery to many and ruin to others, it is nevertheless true that thousands of small-scale settlers in North Carolina realized the promise that had drawn them to America— they achieved a measure of control over their own destinies not available to their class brethren in Europe.

DOCUMENT 4.1

John Rutherfurd, *The Importance of the Colonies to Great Britain* (1761)

It is generally believed that one sixth, if not one fourth, of the white people in the colonies, for want of such encouragement, cannot with the produce of their lands purchase the manufactures of Britain; and for that reason have been obliged to manufacture for themselves, which by all means ought to be prevented, by putting it in their power with the produce of their lands to purchase British manufactures; it being most certain that in America, where lands are cheap and labour dear, that it must be against their inclinations and contrary to their interests to manufacture.

It becomes therefore the duty of the British legislature to be watchful that the colonies are not laid under the necessity of manufacturing, but are encouraged in raising and importing the beforementioned or any other valuable materials, which, when manufactured in Britain, may bring in foreign treasure.

This conduct towards our colonies would not only have the effect to increase the consumption of our manufactures, and render us independent of foreigners, but would make their dependence advantageous and mutually agreeable; WE SHOULD THEN BE SAID TO BE INDEPENDENT OF ALL NATIONS IN POINT OF TRADE, which it ought to be our study to carry to its highest point of advancement.

William Kenneth Boyd, ed., Some Eighteenth Century Tracts Concerning North Carolina *(Raleigh: Edwards and Broughton Company, 1927), p. 121.*

DOCUMENT 4.2

Maurice Moore, *The Justice and Policy of Taxing the American Colonies* (1765)

Nothing can be more consistent with the rights and liberties of a free people, than whenever the good of the community requires a part of the private property of individuals, that they should be allowed to give it in such manner and portions as their situation and circumstances can best afford; indeed they cannot be free without it: for if any sublunary power in being, can deprive them of part of their estate without their consent, the same power may take away the whole; and if it appears to them to be a measure of justice, proscribe 'em into the bargain.

The inhabitants of the Colonies upon the Continent (other than those acquired in the late war) have always thought, and I believe ever will think, all the constitutional rights and liberties enjoyed in Great-Britain, at the time they departed from it, their Birth-Right, and that they brought them over with them to America; among which, that of being taxed only by their own consent, is one of the most essential.

William S. Price, Jr., ed., Not a Conquered People: Two Carolinians View Parliamentary Taxation *(Raleigh: Division of Archives and History, 1975), p. 40.*

DOCUMENT 4.3

Report of Governor Arthur Dobbs to the Board of Trade (1755)

By my 128th Instruction I am commanded to lay before your Lordships the Wants & Defects of the Province, the chief Products, what new Improvements are made or may be made by trade, and which way his Majesty may contribute thereto.

What I have chiefly observed since I came here as to the wants & defects of this Province is first the want of a sufficient Number of Clergymen to instil good principals and Morality into the Inhabitants, & proper Schoolmasters to instruct their Youth, the want of which occasions an Indolence & want of Attention to their own good, which with the warmth of the climate & plenty they have of Cattle & fruit without Labour prevents their Industry, by which Means the Price of Labour is very high, and the Artificers and Labourers being scarce in comparison to the number of Planters, when they are employed they wont work half, scarce the third part of work in a Day of what they do in Europe, and their wages being from 2 Shillings to 3, 4 & 5 Shillings ⅌ diem this Currency, the Planters are not able to go on with Improvements in building or clearing their Lands, and unless they are very industrious to lay up as much as can purchase 2 or 3 Negros, they are no ways able to cultivate their Lands as Your Lordships expect and consequently the Clause of Cultivation must be lessened or relaxed, and only be kept as a Rod over them to prompt them to be industrious, and therefore young or new Planters could not venture to take up Lands, and those who are rich can't get hands to assist them to cultivate, until they can buy Slaves and teach them some handicraft Trades. . . .

Another Defect of the Province is the defenceless State of the sea Coast, and Want of a sufficient Depth of Water for large Ships to carry away Lumber in the Northern Part of this Colony, the River of Cape Fear being the only River capable of receiving Ships of considerable Burthen by having a Tide to carry them up a great way into the Country. . . .

The chief Products at Present in this Colony are Pitch, Tar, Turpentine, and other naval stores, Lumber of all kinds, Rice, Indian Corn, Pork, Beef, Hydes, Deer Skins & furs, Bees and Myrtle wax, Cotton, Indigo, which they are now enter'd upon wth great Spirit, as finding it from what has been tried to be equal to any in America, and all the back Lands, and other rich Lands near the sea Coast it thrives in to Admiration; The Climate is extremely proper for silk, Mulberry Trees from the seed become Trees in 3 or 4 years, Wines may be had higher up in the Country among the Hills near the Mountains, where there is a great Variety of native Grapes, which yield rich wines, which only want proper Vine Dressers to improve them Iron Mines also abound in the upper Countries and some of the upper Planters intend to erect Bloomeries or Forges. Hemp & Flax grow surprizeingly and flax seed has been exported by the way of Pensylvania from hence to Ireland, which has been found to exceed the best Pensylvania & New York Seed, but for want of a direct Trade to Ireland from hence being confined in our Exports, prevents the raising of Flax here, except for the Consumption of the Colony, which for want of having Returns to send to Britain and Ireland, all the back settlers are running into to serve themselves with their own Linnen; Besides these several Articles Tobacco wou'd thrive here and is of a better kind and yields more than in Virginia, but as that Article is rather over

stocked, and wou'd prejudice the Trade of that Colony we give no Encouragement here none except the Planters on the Virginia Line and
Roannock and Chowan being embarked in it as far as 2000 Hogsheads.

There are no Manufactures set up here but one or two Families who
make a few ill made coarse hats, and some of the Irish back Settlers
beginning to the Linnen.

I shall now beg Leave to lay before your Lordships the Difficultues we
ly under in this Province in Relation to our Trade, which is a great
Drawback upon our Improvements, and hope to make it appear to be
equally so to Britain.

The Prohibition of the Trade of Salt from all Parts of Europe except
Britain, to this & the southern Provinces on the Continent South of Cape
Henlopen or Delaware is a considerable Drawback upon our Trade the
English Salt is not found so good, as the French, Spanish or Portuguese in
curing our Pork & Beef being too mild and the Isle of May Salt Tatuga &
Turks Island Salt are too corrosive, eating away the Juices but the Bay
and Portugal Salt is a Medium between them and found here the only
proper Salt to cure Pork and Beef for the sugar Islands And therefore the
Enumeration and Limitation of this Trade obliges us to take that Salt at
great Disadvantage from New York and Pensylvania at double freight
and a further advanced Price to the Northern Importers, so that no more
salt is taken from England by the Restriction; But if the Trade was open'd
from hence to Portugal and Spain directly for salt & Wine which we can
have only from Madeira or the Azores Islands upon which Account the
Wines are risen to a great Price in England as well as here, we shou'd
open an immediate Trade with Portugal and Spain for their Wine and
Salt and shou'd carry to them all kinds of Lumber, Indian Corn, Bees
wax Ships, and Naval Stores, which they now take from foreigners and
have some Return in Bullion for to make Returns directly to Britain for
the choice Manufacture we must have from thence, when at present they
cost the planters here near 100 ℔ cent advance, having no Returns for
Britain. . . .

We are also greatly cramp'd in our trade to Ireland, having little or
nothing we can send from hence there except a little flax seed, for Lumber will not answer without an Assortment of other Produce from hence
so that Ships coming from Ireland must return empty; upon this Account
we are prevented from raising of flax, and what flax seed has been sent
as a Specimen to Ireland we have been obliged to ship from Pensylvania
or New York, to be carried from thence, which upon Tryal has been
found to answer better in Ireland than any Seed from the Baltick, or
Northern Colonies the Trade from Ireland being also limited to Lin-
nens and Provisions, which we don't want, and to Servants and Irish
Protestants who choose to come to reside in this Climate, the Ships for

want of Returns carry them all generally to Pensylvania from whence at a great Expence they come by Land in Waggons to the Province, but their Wealth being expended they are incapable of improving or cultivating the Lands they take up for sometime which is a great Loss to this Colony. The depriving therefore these Southern Colonies of sending most of the innumerated Commodities directly to Ireland being obliged to enter every Ship first in England and to land & reship their Goods, inhances the Price so much without Benefit to England that very little of the Produce from hence can be sold in Ireland and they are obliged to take all they want with ready Money from Norway to the Baltick.

William L. Saunders, ed., The Colonial Records of North Carolina, *10 vols. (Raleigh: State of North Carolina, 1886–90), 5:314–18.*

DOCUMENT 4.4

Christopher Gale to His Father, 5 August 1703

I cood wish Bro. Miles were w'th me Just now, for Tomorrow's light I sett out upon an Indian Voiage, in ord'r to followe a shallop's load off Indian goods, w'ch Voiage wood make him an expert Carolina Coaster, & Inure him soe far to ye Customes & language off ye Heathen, as to make him a well qualify'd Ind. Trader, by w'ch Imploym't . . . he may secure for himselfe a Comfortable being in ye world. Iff he comes, he shall not want Imploym't, butt I wood advice y'u to lett him marry before he comes away, provided he can marry a Fortune that wood encounter ye dangers off ye Atlantick Ocean, one penny in England is 3 w'th us, iff well laid out, & iff he cood butt bring w'th him 2 or 300 ll. w'th a wife, I cood putt him in ye way to live as happy as ye day is long.

Walter Clark, ed., The State Records of North Carolina, *16 vols. (Winston and Goldsboro: State of North Carolina, 1895–1907), 22:732.*

DOCUMENT 4.5

Governor William Tryon to His Uncle, 26 July 1765

The Calculation of the Inhabitants in this Province is one hundred and twenty Thousand White & Black, of which there is a great Majority of White People. The Negroes are very numerous I suppose five to one White Person in the Maritime Counties, but as you penetrate into the Country few Blacks are employed, merely for this Simple reason, that the poorer Settlers coming from the Northward Colonies sat themselves down in the back Counties where the land is the best but who have not more than a sufficiency to erect a Log House for their families and procure a few Tools to get a little Corn into the ground. This Poverty prevents their purchasing of Slaves, and before they can get into Sufficient affluence to buy Negroes their own Children are often grown to an age to work in the Field. . . . Numbers of families in the back Counties have Slaves some from three to ten, Whereas in the Counties on the Sea Coast Planters have from fifty to 250 Slaves. A Plantation with Seventy Slaves on it, is esteemed a good property. When a man marries his Daughters he never talks of the fortune in Money but 20 30 or 40 Slaves is her Portion and possibly [an] agreement to deliver at stated Periods, a Certain Number of Tarr or Turpentine Barrels, which serves towards exonerating the charges of the Wedding which are not grievous here.

William S. Powell, ed., "Tryon's 'Book' on North Carolina," North Carolina Historical Review *34 (1957):411.*

DOCUMENT 4.6

Moravian Travel Account, 1762

May 24. We passed the first rapid without trouble,—it does not amount to much,—and camped for the night on Mr. Smith's shore. Here the mosquitoes made us most welcome, in spite of our fires and the smoke. They were the worst we have seen, and the faces and arms of the Sisters and children were covered with bites. From Mr. Smith we bought a sheep and some chickens for our further trip.

May 25. We passed the so-called "Sugar Loaf," a white bluff on the bank which has something that shape. We also enjoyed the fresh water which here flows freely from the bluffs,—hitherto we have had very bad water, sometimes only that from the river, which has a distinct taste. This afternoon we safely passed a second and worse rapid. Not long after one of our boats stuck fast on a sunken log, of which there are millions in the river. We could not get loose until with a small canoe which happened to be near we put all the persons from the boat on shore. We camped here opposite Platen [Bladen] Court House, where court was in session.

Adelaide L. Fries, ed., Records of the Moravians in North Carolina, 11 vols. (1922–69; reprint, Raleigh: Department of Archives and History, 1968), 1:261.

DOCUMENT 4.7

Swiss Palatine Settlement Near New Bern, 1711

With a thousandfold greeting, I wish all true friends, neighbors, and acquaintances God's grace and blessing. I an my wife, two children, and my old father have, the Lord be praised, arrived safe and sound in Carolina, and live twenty English miles from New Bern. I hope to plant corn enough this year. The land is good, but the beginning is hard, the journey dangerous. My two children, Maria and Hansli died at Rotterdam in Holland and were buried in the common burial place.

This country is praised too lightly in Europe and condemned too much. I hope also in a few years to have cows and swine as much as I desire. Mr. Graffenried is our landgrave. Of vermin, snakes, and such like, there is not so much as they tell of in Europe. I have seen crocodiles by the water, but they soon fled. One should not trust to supporting himself with game, for there are no wild oxen or swine. Stags and deer, ducks and geese and turkeys are numerous.

I wish that I had my child with me, which I left with my father-in-law, together with forty-five pounds which I left behind me in the parish of Tofen. And if my father-in-law wishes to come to me I will give to him from my land. One can have as much swine and cattle as he wants without labor and expense. I am very sorry that Christian Balsiger took away his Uhli from me again at Bern.

Vincent H. Todd, ed., Christoph Von Graffenried's Account

of the Founding of New Bern *(Raleigh: North Carolina Historical Commission, 1920), pp. 312–13.*

DOCUMENT 4.8

Carolina "Countrey Disease" or Yaws, 1705

May the 30th: 1705

Taken in hand John Jenning Daughter Dorothey afflicted with malignous Sores and cachoetes ulcers in her right arme and Legg to the number of about thirty or fourthy, two in her arme to the bigness of 8 or 9 inches in Square, one in her legg about one foot Squarre the rest of less bigness; the said Dorothey having been afflicted maney years ago of the countrey disease with contractura in the tree great articles of her arme and her Knee, with an entire deperdition of use and motion of those parts; moreover attended with considerably athrophy, Cakexia and Jeteritia; unto whom I have in the name of God administred and applied both inward and outward Medicines, being Employed by her father; and Keept under my Cure the Said Dorothey Jenning with dayly dressing and attending, as much as it was possible, Sometimes twice a day with bathing fomenting, Phagedenicq waters, Compound ointments, Chymicall and Galenical remedies, Salves and ointments and powders until the 29th of August fallowing; in which time I brought the Said Dorothey's Arme to the last period of its cure; and I had performed with the Almighty blessing the cure of her, had not She by her unruliness, and unwillingness to follow my prescriptions, and to take inward Medicine, Stopt, and hindered the entire cure of her disease.

William S. Price, Jr., ed., North Carolina Higher-Court Records, 1702–1708 *(Raleigh: Division of Archives and History, 1974), p. 242.*

DOCUMENT 4.9

William Gordon to the Society of the Propagation of the Gospel, 13 May 1709

Here [Perquimans] and in Chowan the ways of living are much alike; both are equally destitute of good water, most of that being brackish and muddy; they feed generally upon salt pork, and sometimes upon beef, and their bread of Indian corn which they are forced for want of mills to beat; and in this they are so careless and uncleanly that there is but little difference between the corn in the horse's manger and the bread on their tables: so that with such provisions and such drinks (for they have no beer), in such a hot country, you may easily judge, sir, what a comfortable life a man must lead.

Saunders, ed., Colonial Records, *1:713–14.*

DOCUMENT 4.10

Town Ordinance, Wilmington, November 1763

Be it Ordained by the Mayor, Recorder, Aldermen and Freeholders of the Borrough of Wilmington convened in Common Council, and it is hereby Ordained by the Authority of the same, That all persons bringing any fresh Beef, Mutton, Veal, Pork, Fish, Butter, Cheese, Bacon, Poultry, and other provisions by land shall expose the same to sale under the Court house in Market Street. And that every person bringing any or either of the said Commodities or provisions by Water shall Expose the same to sale at the Publick Wharf in Market Street and at no other place within the said Borrough, and Custom or Usage to the Contrary notwithstanding.

Donald R. Lennon and Ida Brooks Kellam, eds., The Wilmington Town Book, *1743–1778 (Raleigh: Division of Archives and History, 1973), p. 150.*

DOCUMENT 4.11

Will of James Robertson, 17 January 1753

IN THE NAME OF GOD AMEN. I, James Robertson, of the County of Pasquotank in the Province of North Carolina, being of sound and perfect Memory, Do make this to be and Contain my last will and Testament, in manner and form following; this is to saw:

I Give and bequeath to my well beloved son, Mordecai, my manner plantation wheron I now live, containing fifty acres, More or less, to him and to his heirs for Ever.

I also give to my son Mordecai, one Ram and one Ewe, two Sows two Cows, and one beehive, to him and to his heirs forever.

I likewise give to my son, Malachi, two Sows, one Ewe and Ram, two beehives, and one Cow and Heiffer, to him and his heirs forever.

I Give to my Daughter, Euphan, one Feather bed and furniture, three pewter Basons, and one Dish, one Sow, and one Cow, to her and her heirs forever.

I give to my Daughter, Salley, three Basons, and one pewter dish, one Fethar Bed and Furniture, one Sow, and one Cow, to her and her heirs for ever. I also give to Each of my Daughters one Chest.

I also give all the rest of Moveable Estate to my Dear and Well beloved Wife, Sarah Robertson, and to her Disposal, whom I Nominate my Executrix, and my Trusty friend, Thomas Taylor, Executor to this my last will and Testament, hereby revoaking all other wills heretofore made,

Jams. Robertson (Seal)

Signd, Seald and Declared, this to be my last will and Testament. the 17th day of January, Annoq Dom. 1753, in the presents of:
SAMUEL OKELY, WILLIAM WOODLY, MARY TAYLOR

J. Bryan Grimes, ed., North Carolina Wills and Inventories *(Raleigh: Edwards and Broughton Co., 1912), pp. 375–76.*

DOCUMENT 4.12

John Brickell on Marriage and the Family, 1737

They marry generally very young, some at Thirteen or Fourteen; and she that continues unmarried, until Twenty, is reckoned a stale Maid, which is a very indifferent Character in that Country. These Marriages for want of an Orthodox Clergyman, is performed by the Governor, or the next Justice of the Peace: who reads the Matrimonial Ceremony, which is as binding there as if done by the best divine in Europe. . . .

The Women are the most Industrious in these Parts, and many of them by their good Housewifery make a great deal of Cloath of their own Cotton, Wool, and Flax, and some of them weave their own Cloath with which they decently Apparel their whole Family though large. Others are so Ingenious that they make up all the wearing Apparel both for Husband, Sons and Daughters.

John Brickell, The Natural History of North Carolina *(1737; reprint, Murfreesboro: Johnson Publishing Co., 1968), pp. 31–32.*

DOCUMENT 4.13

Apprentice Bond, 1720

Upon the Motion of Edwd. Outlaw by Thos. Henman to this Court that at the last Court held for Chowan Precinct Thos. Bond his Servant was taken from him by an Order of the said Court. It is Order'd by this Court that the Order of the said Precinct Court do Cease And that the said Thos. Bond dwell and Abide with the said Edward Outlaw, the said Edward Learning his said Apprentice to read and the art of a Shipwright.

William S. Price, Jr., ed., North Carolina Higher-Court Minutes, 1709–1723 *(Raleigh: Division of Archives and History, 1977), p. 216.*

DOCUMENT 4.14

C. E. Taylor to the Society for the Propagation of the Gospel, 20 August 1771

I have therefore settled myself for a while in St. George's Parish, Northampton County, void by the Resignation of Mr. Barnet one of the Society's Missionaries who I am informed has fled into Virginia being charged with Crimes too base to be mentioned. It is great pity but an American Episcopate were established if it tended to no other purpose than to take Cognizance of the Behavior of the Clergy some of whom (I am sorry to say) are the greatest Scandal to Religion we have. . . .

I have agreed with the vestry of the Parish 'till Easter; at which time (provided we unite in approbation) they are desirous of having me inducted. It is as wealthy a parish as any in the Province, but rather too large. I have four churches to attend, which in the course of every month lays me under the necessity of travelling very near 200 Miles, exclusive of my journeys to baptize and visit in Cases of Necessity I purpose (God willing) to administer the sacrament of the Lord's Supper next Sunday; which has not been administered but twice in this Parish in the Space of 7 Years. It is my Intention to order my affairs in such a Manner as to administer it 8 times in the Year, which will be twice at each Church in the Parish. I have communicated this plan to the Church wardens and several orderly People who seem very much rejoiced at it and are very desirous of receiving.

The People in general seem very fond of coming to Church and My Congregations are very much crowded. I have been in this Parish exactly a Month and have Baptized 66 White and 19 black Infants besides 18 Black Adults. I purpose to take a Journey Yearly thro' some Parishes, which are greatly in want of a Minister and but poor, who I understand have scarcely ever an opportunity of having their Children baptized yet preserve some Sparks of Religion among them. I should be very happy in my Parish were it not for some Sectarists who call themselves New Light Baptists, and harbour in the Skirts of my Parish and are very troublesome, but with the Blessing of God I hope to eradicate them by convincing them that the old Light is the only true one. I have talked with some of them, & find them in general a very ignorant set of People yet notwithstanding that they busy themselves with the most Mysterious Parts of Scripture, and believe they are absolutely bound to understand them.

Robert M. Calhoon, ed., Religion and the American Revolution in

North Carolina *(Raleigh: Division of Archives and History, 1976),*
pp. 3–5.

SUGGESTED READINGS

Crittenden, C. Christopher. *The Commerce of North Carolina, 1763–1789.*
New Haven: Yale University Press, 1936.
Crow, Jeffrey J. *The Black Experience in Revolutionary North Carolina.* Ra-
leigh: Division of Archives and History, 1977.
Ekirch, A. Roger. *"Poor Carolina": Politics and Society in Colonial North
Carolina, 1729–1776.* Chapel Hill: University of North Carolina Press, 1981.
Kay, Marvin L. Michael. "The Payment of Provincial and Local Taxes in North
Carolina, 1748–1771." *William and Mary Quarterly* 3d ser., 26 (1969):218–
40.
Lee, E. Lawrence. *The Lower Cape Fear in Colonial Days.* Chapel Hill: Univer-
sity of North Carolina Press, 1965.
Lefler, Hugh T., and Powell, William S. *Colonial North Carolina: A History.*
New York: Charles Scribner's Sons, 1973.
Main, Jackson T. *The Social Structure of Revolutionary America.* Princeton:
Princeton University Press, 1965.
Merrens, H. Roy. *Colonial North Carolina in the Eighteenth Century: A Study
in Historical Geography.* Chapel Hill: University of North Carolina Press,
1964.
Price, William S., Jr. "Men of Good Estates: Wealth among North Carolina's
Royal Councillors." *North Carolina Historical Review* 49 (1972):72–82.
Ramsey, Robert W. *Carolina Cradle: Settlement of the Northwest Carolina
Frontier, 1747–1762.* Chapel Hill: University of North Carolina Press, 1964.
Rights, Douglas L. *The American Indian in North Carolina.* Durham: Duke
University Press, 1947.
Watson, Alan D. *Society in Colonial North Carolina.* Raleigh: Division of Ar-
chives and History, 1975.

CHAPTER 5

The Regulation

Society in Upheaval

Alan D. Watson

Husband Tossing the "Taxes" on the Table before the Governor, from William
E. Fitch, Some Neglected History of North Carolina *(Courtesy of the Division*
of Archives and History, Raleigh, N.C.)

As one of the more momentous civil disturbances in the British North American colonies and one of the most divisive events in prerevolutionary North Carolina, the war of the Regulation deserves the attention of students who ponder the nature of society and government in early America. Arising from the demographic changes, social and economic tensions, and political turmoil of the mid-eighteenth century, the Regulation represented an outpouring of repressed frustration and thwarted ambition. The movement proceeded through various stages exemplified by political pressure at the local level, lawsuits, limited violence, petitions to provincial officials, and election campaigns before it concluded with the bloody struggle at Alamance.

Considering the magnitude of the war of the Regulation, it is not surprising that the movement has long been the subject of intense investigation and consequent dispute among historians. One of the more salient questions emerging from their scrutiny involves the essence of the protest. Was it a reaction to British tyranny, a class struggle, a sectional confrontation, or a matter of status anxiety? Indeed, did the movement relate to the imperial scene and the Revolution? In a broader context, how did it fit into the schema of North Carolina history? Were there precedents for such behavior? Can its influence be discerned after the realization of American independence? What was its impact beyond the borders of the colony? Was the Regulation solely a North Carolina phenomenon or did its influence extend to other provinces? These and other matters have interested historians for over a century and a half. Undoubtedly, they will continue to engender debate in the future.

As a formal agency of organized protest the Regulation may be dated from 1766 to 1771, but the origins of the movement long antedated those years. The tumult and weakness that had characterized North Carolina's government from its settlement in the seventeenth century somewhat abated after the crown purchased the colony in 1729. Still, the contentiousness of the first royal governor, George Burrington, the quitrent dissension, and the representation controversy from 1746 to 1754 promoted continued strife. Moreover, the settlement of the piedmont in the 1740s and 1750s proceeded at an incredibly rapid pace, leading to heightened tensions on the frontier. In addition to the roisterous nature of the colony and the peopling of the backcountry, the specific antecedents of the Regulation can be traced to the confusion created by the anomalous Granville tract, the efforts of speculators to engross western lands, the tribulations of the French and Indian War, and the attempt by imperial authorities to strengthen their control over the colonies.

Impeding settlement in the west were the Granville District and the speculative claims of Henry McCulloh and the Selwyn family. For many years the agents of the earl of Granville systematically extorted money from settlers by demanding excessive fees and other emoluments for their services. Protest in Edgecombe, Halifax, and Granville counties erupted in the form of the Enfield Riot of 1759. (Document 5.1) Discontent spread to the more westerly counties of Orange and Rowan in the 1760s, particularly after Granville closed his land office in 1763. Furthermore, the hostility toward the earl's officials was transmitted to public officers in general by 1765, when George Sims, a schoolmaster in Granville County, published his "Nutbush Address," which attacked with bitter invective the county sheriff, clerk, and various lawyers. (Docment 5.2)

Acquisition of land in the southwestern section of the province also proved difficult because the speculative efforts of McCulloh and Selwyn restricted entry. High prices, made particularly onerous by the demand for payment in scarce sterling rather than depreciated colonial currency, deterred prospective settlers. The matter reached a climax in 1765, when a group of armed, angry farmers attacked and badly beat members of a surveying team that was working on the lands of McCulloh and Selwyn. Occurring in the vicinity of Sugar Creek in Mecklenburg County, the so-called War of Sugar Creek elicited a royal proclamation from Governor William Tryon denouncing the action, though the rioters apparently escaped with impunity.

Turmoil over the Stamp Act intervened to divert attention from the western trouble, but the effective opposition of easterners to the obnoxious parliamentary statute may only have spurred westerners who sought redress for their grievances. In the first of the Regulator "advertisements" the Sons of Liberty were praised for their bold stand. Yet it was noted that those individuals who had redeemed the country from the tyranny of British oppression might easily lapse into corrupt and oppressive behavior if not held strictly accountable for their actions. Like colonials in general, the Regulators seemed obsessed with the concept of corruption, whether personal or governmental, that emanated from their pessimistic view of human nature.

Originating in the Sandy Creek Association of Orange County in 1766, the Regulator movement appeared immediately concerned with what was perceived to be an inequitable tax system, an extortionate fee structure, and an insensitive and corrupt local officialdom. These matters necessarily involved the accountability of public officers, most of whom were appointive rather than elective and many of whom exemplified the baneful influence of the courthouse ring. Although not seeking a twentieth-century democratization of their polity, the Regulators clearly intended to make government more responsive to its constituents, and by mobilizing a large number of the populace, whether politically or militarily, they contributed to an increased political awareness among the inhabitants of the backcountry. (Document 5.3)

Excessive taxation remained a principal complaint of the Regulators throughout the years of their protest, and their concern was genuine. The regressive nature of taxation in the colony intensified the burden. As much as 90 percent of the public revenues derived from poll taxes and import duties. Exacerbating the situation was the scarcity of circulating media. Specie was almost nonexistent in the backcountry, and the Currency Act of 1764 prohibited the use of paper as legal tender. Because the colony failed to manage its financial affairs properly, the existing paper depreciated so that it circulated well below its nominal exchange rate. Inefficiency and embezzlement on the part of public officials, especially sheriffs, were a further aggravation. Finally, the seat of government lay along the coast, and tax money often seemed expended for the benefit of easterners. Exemplary of such outlays was the funding of the extravagant "palace" in New Bern, perhaps the most impressive statehouse in the colonies but one which, according to a contemporary opinion, not one in twenty westerners would see. (Document 5.4)

From 1766 to 1768 the Regulators, who formally adopted that name in the latter year, attempted to achieve their goals by petition and negotiation. Herman Husband, the Quaker pamphleteer, Rednap Howell, William Butler, and James Hunter assumed leadership of the movement. Resentment eventually focused upon Edmund Fanning, a Yale graduate, personal friend of Governor William Tryon, assemblyman from Orange County, Superior Court judge, register of deeds, and militia colonel. After two years of peaceful protest and vain attempts to meet the public officers of Orange County, the Regulators declared in Advertisement Number 4 that unless forced they would pay no more taxes or public fees in excess of what the law allowed. Violence flared at Hillsborough in April 1768, when the sheriff of Orange County imposed distraint upon a Regulator's property for payment of taxes. Subsequently, Fanning assisted the sheriff in a daring raid that resulted in the capture of Husband and Butler.

In the meantime, resentment had spread to neighboring counties. A mob forced justices of the peace in Anson County to abandon court and offered support for the Regulators of Orange County. Johnston County justices and their supporters, however, successfully defended their court from Regulator assault. Still, some three hundred men in Rowan burned the county jail in Salisbury, and in Cumberland County rumors of civil conflict were current. Clearly the Regulation had become a widespread protest. (Document 5.5)

When Governor Tryon heard that several hundred Regulators were rendezvousing in Orange County, he decided to call upon the militia to protect the forthcoming session of the Superior Court at Hillsborough at which Husband and Butler were scheduled to stand trial. Although

Tryon's troops, exceeding a thousand, probably numbered less than those of the Regulators, variously estimated from eight to thirty-seven hundred, the appearance of the governor and the show of force sufficiently impressed the Regulators that they dispersed after receiving assurances of a fair hearing for their grievances. At the trial Husband was acquitted, but Butler and two other Regulators were fined and sentenced to prison. Tryon released the prisoners, suspended the fines, and issued a general pardon that excepted only the principal leaders of the movement. At the same court Fanning, who had been indicted for taking excessive fees, was adjudged guilty on six counts and fined the nominal sum of one penny and costs. The Regulators received some satisfaction, however, in that Fanning resigned his position as register of deeds for Orange County.

Although Tryon recognized the validity of many of the Regulators' complaints and worked to remedy improprieties in the financial and electoral systems, the imperial crisis involving the Townshend Acts and the Massachusetts Circular Letter diverted his attention. Neglected, the Regulators again resorted to violence to vent their anger. At the September 1770 session of the Hillsborough Superior Court they occupied the courtroom and proceeded to mete out their own brand of justice. After driving Associate Judge Richard Henderson from the bench, assaulting several lawyers, dragging William Hooper, future signer of the Declaration of Independence, through the streets, and brutally beating Fanning, the mob terrorized the town and held its own mock court. (Document 5.6)

At the next meeting of the provincial assembly, held in New Bern in December 1770, the legislators, a majority of whom were imbued with what James Iredell called "regulating Principles," passed several reform measures designed to placate the westerners. The statutes created four new counties in the piedmont, more strictly regulated attorneys' fees, established a more equitable system of fees for public officials, introduced a more palatable means for distraint and recovery of small debts, and provided for a more satisfactory militia organization. Rumors of an impending Regulator march on the capital, however, coupled with the general violence exhibited in the backcountry convinced many sympathetic assemblymen of the necessity of a far-reaching measure known as the Johnston Riot Act, which dealt harshly with rioters and allowed the governor to take necessary military measures to ensure the tranquillity of the colony.

Infuriated by the Riot Act, the Regulators continued to refuse to pay taxes, submit to distraint, or permit the operation of the courts. Tryon, having already accepted a commission as governor of New York, was equally adamant. He apparently determined to take advantage of the

Riot Act to bring about a military solution to the matter in order not to bequeath a rebellious province to his successor. With the approval of the council, Tryon gathered militia in preparation for another march to Hillsborough, ostensibly to protect the Superior Court but actually to crush lawlessness and opposition to the government. (Document 5.7)

Sending General Hugh Waddell ahead with the Cape Fear militia, the governor followed with contingents from several counties. Eventually Tryon's troops faced the numerically superior Regulators on the banks of Alamance Creek. When the Regulators attempted to open negotiations, Tryon rebuffed their efforts. A two-hour battle ensued in which the governor's well-equipped and well-led forces emerged victorious. To impress the Regulators with the totality of their defeat and to awe them with the power of the government, Tryon summarily executed one of the fifteen men taken prisoner. After a court-martial, twelve of the remaining prisoners were found guilty. Six were executed; the remainder received reprieves and subsequent pardons. In a series of proclamations, Tryon offered pardons to those Regulators who laid down their arms and swore allegiance to the government. Husband, Howell, Butler, and Hunter were excluded from the general amnesty. Within two months more than six thousand Regulators had signed oaths of allegiance and the Regulation as an organized movement had ended.

By the time that Josiah Martin, Tryon's successor, arrived in North Carolina calm had descended upon the province. After an investigation of Regulator grievances and a tour of the backcountry, Martin appeared convinced of the validity of the complaints. (Document 5.8) Although he attempted to rectify some of the injustices, Martin's general demeanor, the court crisis of 1773, and the increasing imperial tension embroiled the governor in controversy that negated most of his positive efforts to assist the westerners. In the meantime, many former Regulators escaped the confines of North Carolina by moving beyond the mountains to Kentucky, the Watauga and Holston settlements, and even the Mississippi country.

When the Whig historians of the nineteenth century began to investigate the history of North Carolina, they tended to see the Regulation as the opening salvo of the Revolution. In the words of John H. Wheeler, the Battle of Alamance represented "the first blood spilled in these United States, in resistance to exactions of English rulers, and oppression by the English government." The Whig view was conditioned by the relatively recent departure of the colonies from the British Empire, the continuing animosity between the United States and Great Britain, the need to produce a patriotic history for a young country, and the elitist background of the authors.

Upon the professionalization of history, greater availability of source materials, and the changing international political climate, the Whig approach was abandoned in the twentieth century by historians who saw the Regulation as a class struggle or a sectional contest, interpretations that had their origins in the pioneering work of John Spencer Bassett. Early in the century many scholars writing within the Progressive framework considered the Regulation as the essence of class contention in North Carolina and symbolic of the internal revolution that occurred throughout the colonies in conjunction with the attempt to secure independence from Britain. More recently, that view can be found in *Rebels and Democrats*, in which Elisha P. Douglass states that the events in North Carolina constituted the "most articulate, comprehensive, and violent" of all the colonial democratic protests "against aristocratic domination of government."

Adding greater sophistication and corroboration to the earlier impressionistic arguments, Marvin L. Michael Kay denies the Lockean conceptual framework of a liberal America and contends that the Regulation was a movement of "class-conscious agriculturalists" attempting to create a society that would protect their interests and those of productive, nonexploitative persons in society. This premodern, peasant mentality, apparent from investigations of early New England society, existed in part in North Carolina, though such feudal characteristics were in the process of being fused or integrated with incipient liberalism. On the whole, Regulator leadership may not have been poverty-stricken, but the movement showed a definite alignment of wealth versus poverty.

Vying with the class struggle approach has been the sectional argument, best represented among others by the work of Hugh T. Lefler and William S. Powell. Proponents of this interpretation see the Regulation as one of a series of clashes between the east and west. The provincial government was centered in the east, and there were obvious geographic, economic, religious, and ethnic differences between the regions; therefore, the conflict assumed the appearance of a sectional confrontation. Moreover, when viewed from a sectional perspective, the Regulation fits nicely in the continuum from Bacon's Rebellion and the Paxton Boys Riot to Shays' Rebellion and the Whiskey Rebellion, the last of which was led by Herman Husband, who had taken refuge in Pennsylvania and at the age of seventy protested the whiskey excise.

A variant critique of the Regulation, bearing some similarity to the class struggle thesis, is the status-anxiety approach posed by James P. Whittenburg, who sees the movement as one led by planters to ward off the increasing influence of merchants and lawyers in backcountry society. The migration to North Carolina in the 1740s and 1750s produced a large population wherein lawyers found a lucrative practice among the naturally litigious colonials. At the same time merchants discovered ample opportunity to conduct their trade at country crossroads and in the communities of Hillsborough and Salisbury. Often the familial, economic, and political connections of the lawyers and merchants enabled them quickly to supersede the agrarian elite of the backcountry.

Taking issue with Kay and Whittenburg is Roger Ekirch, who contends that the Regulators were fundamentally conservative in their principal values and goals. In fact, they were backwoods Whigs who found almost universal sympathy in the colonies beyond North Carolina. The Regulators were not democratic radicals. Instead, they protested a corrupt government dominated by eastern politicians, and their only crime was to demand greater political responsibility and responsiveness from the eastern officials.

Although the origin and impetus of the Regulation remain doubtful, the organized violence of the movement is undisputed. It was the most extensive and violent of numerous popular uprisings in the colonies. Drawing upon a long tradition of provincial insurgency and mob activity in Britain, these civil disturbances often served as extrainstitutional means of obtaining redress of grievances when normal channels of legitimate action were unavailable. Although mobs were appreciated for their extralegal check on power, such upheavals often threatened to run to excess. A strong deterrent to the acceptance of riotous behavior as well as truly republican, or democratic, government was the belief that democratic action tended to degenerate into anarchy. Nonetheless, the North Carolina assembly overreacted in 1771 when it passed the Johnston Riot Act. Many colonies enacted legislation similar to the English Riot Act of 1714, but only North Carolina was chastised by the crown for violating the fundamental liberties of Englishmen in its statute. (Document 5.9)

Bloodshed and death were minimal in most of the insurgent activities in the colonies. The established authority and law enforcement agencies generally proved so weak that excessive violence was obviated. The Regulation, however, was one of the few instances when the government was willing and able to muster effective opposition. Tryon, a man of military background, well remembered the Stamp Act affair and desired to leave the colony without another blemish on his record. Thus personal circumstance combined with the hysteria of the moment to demand action. The governor raised the militia for the second time in three years, and when the Regulators refused to submit, a substantial number of casualties resulted.

The violent nature of the Regulation was not its only nexus to the continental scene. It occurred contemporaneously with a civil disturbance of the same name in South Carolina, though the Regulators of the two Carolinas were not comparable in that those in the southern province were merely vigilantes seeking to establish law and order on the frontier. More important, newspapers along the coast gave lurid coverage to events in North Carolina, and a certain sympathy for the plight of the Regulators may have given impetus to the dissatisfaction in other colonies that impelled them toward revolution. At the same time the British may have seen the Regulation as symptomatic of the continuing liberal excesses in the provinces and indicative of the general drift toward independence that had to be checked.

Although the nineteenth-century interpretation of the Regulation as a prelude to the Revolution lacks credibility, matters in North Carolina were hardly divorced from the revolutionary situation. Only three years separated the Battle of Alamance from the incipient stages of revolution in North Carolina. The organization of backcountrymen into an association called the Regulation bore some similarity in design to the safety committees of 1774. The idea of conspiracy and the demand for more responsive government characterized both the Regulators of the 1760s and the revolutionaries of the 1770s. And, of course, the Regulation served as an object lesson to later revolutionaries in the use of armed resistance to authority and provided provincial leaders with valuable experience in dealing with a divided populace.

When considered against the backdrop of the revolutionary era, the Regulation reinforced a pattern of antiauthoritarian behavior that helped prepare many for the ultimate break with Great Britain. In the dispute over representation from 1746 to 1754, the brief interruption of the courts in 1760, the Stamp Act crisis, the Regulation, and the court crisis of 1773, the colonials either defied established government or necessarily resorted to their own devices when left without benefit of judicial protection. The colonials grew accustomed to fending for themselves. Liberties were more jealously guarded and the arrogation of power became more natural. The experience and behavior of the provincials in the three decades preceding the Revolution helped to produce an attitude that allowed many to accept the traumatic break with the mother country.

With the approach of the imperial conflict the backcountry assumed an increasing importance not only for its large population but also for its strategic position as a buffer between the east and the Indians. Governor Martin assumed that backcountry discontent would translate into loyalty to the crown. Whig leaders feared wholesale support in the west for Great Britain and ardently wooed former Regulators. Historians have divided in their opinion regarding Regulator affinities in the Revolution, in part because little evidence exists to substantiate loyalties. Largely for that reason recent scholarship suggests that the majority of former Regulators remained neutral, perhaps because the Whigs generally controlled the state during the war or perhaps because the westerners saw little future in a government dominated by an eastern elite, whether British or Whig.

The Regulation, in sum, manifested the continual efforts of aggrieved North Carolinians to challenge government authority. Considering their longstanding and manifold grievances, the Regulators were remarkably restrained in their protest. They used a variety of nonviolent tactics, including civil disobedience, before accepting the challenge of pitched battle. Though the Regulation cannot be dissociated from the Revolution, the Regulators were hardly revolutionaries. If they had triumphed at Alamance, it is inconceivable that they would have abandoned the empire or forsaken the province. Theirs was a struggle within the existing framework of government, a quest for reform, not wholesale change.

Although the Battle of Alamance destroyed the Regulator association, the ideas of the movement flourished. Instructions to delegates representing the western counties after 1773 in the assembly and provincial congresses reflected Regulator social and political attitudes. (Document 5.10) Although some of those sentiments materialized in the state constitution of 1776, they may have been even more effective in the western regions of Kentucky, Tennessee, and the Mississippi country to which North Carolinians migrated in substantial numbers. Of course, the state constitution and the reluctance of North Carolina to join the federal union reflected the distrust of centralized, aristocratic government. Long after the Revolution occurred and stable government appeared in the state and nation, the social unrest and sectionalism that had characterized the Regulation continued to shape the development of North Carolina.

DOCUMENT 5.1

Governor Dobbs and Riots, 1759

Answers of Arthur Dobbs Esqre Governor of North Carolina to certain resolutions made in a Committee of the Assembly of North Carolina to consider the distressed state of the Province. . . .

8th Resolution. That tho' the Governor was addressed by the Assembly in June last to take necessary measures to suppress the several Mobbs & insurrections which for many months in open violation of all law have with impunity assembled in great numbers in different Counties, erected sham Jurisdictions and restrained men of their liberty, broke open Goals [jails], released malefactors, dug up the dead from the Grave, and committed other Acts of Rapine and violence, no effectual steps have been taken to check the torrent of their licentious extravagancies. . . .

I must first observe that these Mobbs, Riots and Insurrections terrible as they are described were all confined to Lord Granville's northern district, and that all the outrages complained of were limited to the Counties of Granville & Edgecomb from which Halifax has been taken off since. . . .

But to lay open the cause and spring of that Mob I am under a necessity of hinting at part of the management of Lord Granville's Agents as well in England as in this Province. Mr. Child and Mr. Corbin were joint agents to His Lordship in this province when he was formerly Attorney General and acted in concert to make the most they could of the Fees and Perquisites in His Lordships Office for their own emolument at the expense of the people by which means they procured great sums to themselves but little for his Lordship.

William L. Saunders, ed., The Colonial Records of North Carolina, *10 vols. (Raleigh: State of North Carolina, 1886–90), 6:292–93.*

DOCUMENT 5.2

Extortion and Public Officials

An Address to the People of Granville County by George Sims June 6, 1765

Well, Gentlemen, it is not our mode, or form of Government, nor yet the body of our laws, that we are quarrelling with, but with the malpractices of the Officers of our County Court, and the abuses which we suffer by those empowered to manage our public affairs. . . . It is well known, that there is a law which provides that a lawyer shall take no more than 15/ for this fee in the County Court. Well Gentlemen, which of you have had your business done for 15/? Do not the Lawyers exact 30s for every cause, and 3, 4, or 5 pounds for every cause that is attended with the least difficulty? Yes: they do Gentlemen, and laugh at our stupidity and tame submission to these damned extravagancies. And besides the double fees, which they exact from you, do they not lengthen out your lawsuits, by artifices and delays, so long as they perceive you have any money to grease their fists with? And numberless other develish devices to rob you of your livings in a manner diametrically opposite to the policy of our State, and the intention of our Legislature. . . .

Need I mention one instance to set forth the misery which we groan under? Does not daily experience shew us the gaping jaws of ruin, open, and ready to devour us? Are not your lands executed your negroes, horses, cattle, hogs, corn, beds, and household furniture? Are not these things, I say, taken and sold for one tenth of their value? Not to satisfy the just debts which you have contracted; but to satisfy the cursed exorbitant demands of the Clerks, Lawyers and Sheriffs. . . . It is reasonable Gentlemen, that these Officers should be allowed such fees, as may give them a genteel maintenance, but then is it reasonable that they should rob the County to support themselves in such damned extravagancies, and laugh at us for being such simpletons as to suffer it? . . .

It is not a persons labour, nor yet his effects that will do, but if he has but one horse to plow with, one bed to lie on, or one cow to give a little milk for his children, they must all go to raise money which is not to be had. And lastly if his personal estate (sold at one tenth of its value) will not do, then his lands (which perhaps has cost him many years toil and labour) must go the same way to satisfy these cursed hungry caterpillars, that are eating and will eat out the bowels of our Commonwealth, if they be not pulled down from their nests in a very short time, and what need I say, Gentlemen, to urge the necessity there is for a reformation. If these things were absolutely according to law, it would be enough to make us turn rebels, and throw off all submission to such tyrannical laws. . . . But, as these practices are diametrically opposite to the law, it is our absolute duty, as well as our Interests, to put a stop to them, before they quite ruin our County. Or, Are [we] become the willing slaves of these lawless Officers, and hug our chains of bondage and remain contented under these accumulated calamities. . . ? Here I am this day with my life in my hand, to see my fellow subjects animated with a spirit of liberty and freedom, and to see them lay a foundation for the recovery thereof, and the clearing our County from arbitrary tyranny.

William K. Boyd, ed., Some Eighteenth-Century Tracts Concerning North Carolina *(Raleigh: Edwards and Broughton Company, 1927), pp. 186–92.*

DOCUMENT 5.3

Regulators' Advertisement No. 1, August 1766

Whereas that great good may come of this great designed Evil the Stamp Law while the sons of Liberty withstood the Lords in Parliament in behalf of true Liberty let not Officers under them carry on unjust Oppression in our own Province in order thereunto as there is many Evils of that nature complained of in this County of Orange in private amongst the Inhabitants therefore let us remove them (or if there is no cause) let us remove the Jealousies out of our minds.

Honest rulers in power will be glad to see us examine this matter freely there is certainly more honest men among us than rogues & yet rogues is harbored among us sometimes almost publickly, every honest man is willing to give part of his substance to support rulers and laws to save the other part from rogues and it is his duty as well as right to see and examine whether such rulers abuse such trust, otherwise that part so given may do more hurt than good, even if all were rogues in that case we could not subsist but would be obliged to frame laws to make ourselves honest and the same reasoning holds good against the notion of a Mason Club; this tho' it must be desired by all or the greatest number of men, yet when grievances of such public nature are not redressed the reason is everybody's business is no Bodys.

Saunders, ed., Colonial Records, *7:249–50.*

DOCUMENT 5.4

Poverty and Wealth

Petition of Citizens of Rowan and Orange Counties, October 4, 1768 To the Worshipful House of Representatives of North Carolina:

Your Poor Petitioners having been Continually Squez'd and oppressed by our Publick Officers both with Regard to their fees as also in the Laying on of Taxes as well as in Collecting together with Iniquitious Appropriations, and Wrong Applications of the same, & being Grieved thus to have our substance torn from us, and no ends nor Bounds were Like to be Set to such Illegal practices we applied to our public officers to give us some satisfaction on the several Heads which they Repeatedly denied, us. . . . We humbly supplicate your Worships to take under your serious Consideration, we labour under Extreem hardships about our Levies Money is very scarce hardly any to be had would we Purchase it at ten times its value & we exceeding Poor & lie at a great distance from Trade which renders it almost Impossible to gain sustenance by our utmost Endeavours, Gods Sake Gentlemen in an affairs of such Importance; on your Breath depends the Ruin or Prosperity of poor Families, and so to Gentlemen Rowling in affluence, a few shillings per man, may seem triffling yet to Poor People who must have their Bed and Bedclothes yea their Wives Petticoats taken and sold to Defray. . . . We Humbly begg of your Worships, to take it into your serious Considerations the sums to Erect a Publick Edifice it is a Pitiful Consideration to us poor Wretches to think where or how we shall Raise our Parts, of the sd. sums Designed for that Purpose; Good God Gentlemen what will become of us when these Demands come against us Paper Money we have none & gold or silver we can Purchase none of the Contingencies of Government Must be Paid, and which we are Willing to Pay, tho if we sell our Beds from under us and in this Time of Distress it is as much as we can support our selves under. . . . We Humbly Begg you would Consider the Laws as they now stand, Recovery of small Debts your own good sence will point out to you the hardships we Labour under by attending Courts of Justice at great Distances for small Triffles, or be forced to part with our small substance wrong. You can not but observe how Ruinous the Law as it now stands must be to the Poor but as an Honest good judge or Majestrate better even with a bad Cause than a Corapt one will do with the Best fram'd Laws on Earth we humble Begg you would be pleas'd to Use your Influence with our Worthy, Virtuous, Governor, to discontinue from time to Time such Officers as would be found to be ye Bane of Society and Put in the Common Wealth, at the same time to Encourage the Poor, and Despis'd to stand for them This would Cause Joy and Gladness to Spring from every Heart, this would cause Labour and Industry to prevail over Murmuring Discontent, this would Raise your poor Petitioners from an indigent Heartless to a flourishing Opulent and Hoping People otherwise Charge and disatisfaction and Melancholy must Prevail over such as Remain and Numbers, must Defect the Province and seek elsewhere an Asylum from Tyranny and Oppression.

Legislative Papers, North Carolina Archives, Raleigh.

DOCUMENT 5.5

Sheriffs and Taxes

Minutes of the Rowan County Court of Pleas and Quarter Sessions August 1769
Adam Allison Esqr Came into Open Court & Produced a Commission under the Seal of this province Signed by his Excelency William Tryon Esq Governor &c Appointing him the Said Adam Allison high Sheriff of said County.
The Said Adam Allison did at the Same Time Sign To this Court his Readiness and Earnest desire to Receipt of the said Officer of Sheriff for said County and Shew this Court that he was Willing To Take The Oaths Prescribed by Act of Assembly for a Sheriff and then in Open Court Sayth he Used his Utmost Endeavour to Procure Such Securities for his faithfull Execution of said Office According to Law but that his Frinds Absolutly Refused for This Reason (to wit) that they Doubted Not Either of his Integrity or honesty but the Confused State and Present Disturbances Together with the Scarcity of Circulating Money in this County[.] Each of his frinds Doubted it would be a Means Both to Involve him & them in to Intricate Lawsuits & Troubles.

Minutes of the Rowan County Court of Pleas and Quarter Sessions August 1770
This day Came into Open Court Andrew Allison Esquire late high Sheriff for the County of Rowan and Tendered a Settlement of his Collection of Taxes for the afd County for the Year 1768 and made Oath in Open Court that he had Collected Only Two hundred & Four Taxes for that Year and Offers for Reasons as follows That Owing to a Refractory disposition of a Sett of People calling themselves Regulators Refusing to pay any Taxes or other Publick money to a Sheriff or any Other Officer whatsoever by which means many Well disposed People neglects to discharge their Public dues as the Burden must Consequently fall very heavey on the well meaning Few & desires to be Recommended to his Excellency the Governor Councell & General Assembly for Such Redress as they in their Wisdom Shall Seem meet.

Minutes of the Rowan County Court of Pleas and Quarter Sessions, 1769, 1770, North Carolina Archives, Raleigh.

DOCUMENT 5.6

The Hillsborough Riot

Newbern, October 5, 1770

On Wednesday last a special messenger arrived in town from Granville county, to his Excellency the Governor, with the melancholy account of a violent insurrection, or rather rebellion, having broke out in Orange County, among a set of men who call themselves regulators, and who have for some years past given infinite disturbance to the civil government of this province, but now have sapped its whole foundation, brought its courts of Justice to their own controul, leaped the strong barrier of private property, and audaciously violated the laws of God and man.

These people have for a long time opposed paying all manner of taxes, have entertained the vilest opinion of the Gentlemen of the law, and often threatened them with their vengeance. Accordingly, as the Hon. Judge Henderson, and several other Gentlemen of the law, were returning from Salisbury circuit to Hillsborough, in order to hold the court there, they were waylaid by a number of them with their rifles; but happily, having notice of their hellish design, by taking a contrary rout they eluded their bloody plot. They still gave out their threats of meeting them at Hillsborough, and wrecking their vengeance on them there.

These menaces were treated with contempt, or rather the violent ravings of a factious and discontented mob, than any settled or fixed resolution of men of property to commit so daring an insult to the laws of the country; and accordingly the court was opened and proceeded to business. But on Monday, the second day of the court, the tragical scene began; a very large number of these people, headed by men of considerable property, appeared in Hillsborough, armed with clubs, whips, loaded at the ends with lead or iron (a stroke from which would level the strongest man) and many other offensive weapons, and at once beset the courthouse. The first object of their revenge was Mr. John Williams, a Gentleman of the law, whom they assaulted as he was entering the courthouse; him they cruelly abused, with many and violent blows with their loaded whips on the head and different parts of his body, until he, by great good fortune, made his escape, and took shelter in a neighboring store. They then entered the courthouse, and immediately fixed their attention on Colonel Fanning as the next object of their merciless cruelty. He expected his fate, and had retired to the Judge's seat, as the highest part of the courthouse from which he might make the greatest defence against these bloodthirsty and cruel savages; but, poor Gentlemen, vain were all his efforts, for after behaving with the most heroick courage he fell a sacrifice to numbers, and suffered a cruelty the richest language can but faintly paint. They seized him by the neck, dragged him down the steps, his head striking violently on every step, carried him to the door, and forcing him out, dragged him on the ground over stones and brickbats, struck him with their whips and clubs, kicked him, spit and spurned at him, and treated him with every possible mark of contempt and cruelty; until at length, by a violent effort of strength and activity, he rescued himself from their merciless claws, and took shelter in a house. The vultures pursued him there, and gave him a stroke that will probably destroy one of his eyes. In this piteous and grievously maimed condition, they left him for awhile, retreated to the courthouse, knocked down and very cruelly treated the deputy clerk of the Crown, ascended the bench, shook their whips over Judge Henderson, told him his turn was next, ordered him to pursue business, but in the manner they should prescribe, which was that no lawyers should enter the courthouse, no juries but what they should pick, and order new trials in cases where some of them had been cast for their malpractices. They then seized Mr. Hooper, a Gentleman of the law, dragged and paraded him through the streets, and treated him with every mark of contempt and insult. This closed the first day, but the second day presented a scene, if possible, more tragick. Immediately on their discovering that the Judge had made his escape from their fury, and refused to submit to the dictates of lawless and desperate men, they marched in a body to Colonel Fanning's house, and on a signal given by their ringleaders entered the house, destroyed every piece of furniture in it, ripped open his beds, broke and threw in the streets every piece of china and glass ware in the house, scattered all his papers and books in the wind, seized all his plate, cash, and proclamation money; entered his cellars, and after saturating and gorging their more than savage stomachs with his liquor, and lawless fury, they took his wearing clothes, stuck them on a pole, paraded them in triumph through the streets, and, to close the scene, pulled down and laid his house in ruins, Hunter and Butler, two of their chiefs, stripping in buff and beginning the heroick deed. They then went to a large handsome church bell that Colonel Fanning, at the expense of 60 or 70£, had made a present of to the church of Hillsborough, and split it to pieces, and were at the point of pulling down the church, but their leaders, thinking it would betray their religious principles, restrained them. Their revenge being not yet satisfied on this unhappy Gentleman, they again pursued him, cruelly beat him, and at length with dogs hunted him out of town, and with a cruelty more savage than bloodhounds stoned him as he fled. What heart but feels for the distresses of this unfortunate Gentleman! what hand that would not be uplifted in defense of such injured innocence.

When they had fully glutted their revenges on the lawyers, and particularly Colonel Fanning, to show their opinion of courts of justice they took from his chains a negro that had been executed some time, and placed him at the lawyer's bar, and filled the Judge's seat with human excrement, in derision and contempt of the characters that fill those respectable places. Would a Hottentot have been guilty of such a piece of brutality! or is there the most savage nation on earth whose manners are less cultivated!

A paragraph of a letter from a Gentleman, who was eye witness of the above dismal scene, says: "The merchants stores are broke and rifled, Mr. Cooke's house torn to pieces, and Mr. Edward's had not shared a better fate. The inhabitants have fled the town and the regulators live at their expense; they are in possession of their houses, and make the best use of the emergency to satiate their cursed passions, and appetites. Here my pen drops; I satiate with the painful recital."

· In short, all civil government in Orange County is relaxed, the courts of justice totally stopped, and every thing reduced to the power and controul of a set of men who call them selves regulators; but are in fact no other than a desperate and cruel banditi, actuated by principles that no laws can restrain, no honour or conscience bind.

Virginia Gazette *(Williamsburg)*, *25 October 1770.*

DOCUMENT 5.7

An Impetuous Governor

Samuel Johnston to Thomas Barker June 10, 1771

You will probably before this comes to hand see by the publick prints that the Govr: has had an Engagement with the Regulators in which they were routed. . . . We hear that since the engagement they have laid down their Arms and engaged to submit to Government The Govr. had eight field pieces which gave him greatly the advantage otherwise he & his party would have had nothing to boast of from this Action. Many think that the very heavy expense attending this extraordinary armament might have been saved to the province had not the Govr. been influenced by some who had received personal insults from these people and by the natural impatience & impetuosity of his own temper, as at the last Assembly an Act passed making Riots a Capital Offense and empowering the Courts to try the Delinquents in any other District than that wherein the offense was committed and after a Bill found and a proclamation for the Deft to appear within sixty days set up at the Court House of the County where he usually resided if at the end of that time he failed to appear he was deemed Guilty of the Offence and might be killed or destroyed with impunity. We are in Daily expectation of Mr. Martin our new Govr. and as we hear a very amiable Character of him are not uneasy at the approaching change most among us thinking Gov. Tryon however well calculated to discharge the duty of a Soldier, that his Talents are not so well adapted to the Station he is now in.

Hayes Collection, North Carolina Archives, Raleigh.

DOCUMENT 5.8

Josiah Martin's View of the Regulation

Governor Josiah Martin to Lord Hillsborough August 30, 1772

Since I had the honor of writing to your Lordship of my Intention to visit that part of this Province lying to the Westward of this Place I have made a Tour through the most broken difficult and rough Country I have ever seen as far as Salisbury. . . .

On my route My Lord I passed through the County of Guilford the residence of the principal Insurgents who had lately made their submissions to me. I received from them here the most pressing solicitations to be permitted to present themselves before me and . . . I consented that they should meet me at an appointed place; they came accordingly before me bearing in their countenance every mark of truest contrition and penitence. . . . After exhorting them to deserve his Majesty's Mercy to which they had now submitted themselves by future good conduct and informing them that I should soon apprize them of the measures to be taken in consequence of their surrender I dismissed them and I must own to your Lordship with sentiments of pity and compassion I never should have felt if I had not seen them and made myself acquainted with their barbarous ignorance that really surpassed all description.

My progress through this Country My Lord hath opened my eyes exceedingly with respect to the commotions and discontents that have lately prevailed in it. I now see most clearly that they have been provoked by insolence and cruel advantages taken of the peoples ignorance by mercenary tricking Attornies, Clerks and other little Officers who have practiced upon them every sort of rapine and extortion by which having brought upon themselves their just resentment they engaged Government in their defense by artful misrepresentations that the vengeance the wretched people in folly and madness aimed at their heads was directed against the constitution and by this stratagem they threw an odium upon the injured people that by degrees begat a prejudice which precluded a full discovery of their grievances thus My Lord as far as I am able to descern the resentment of Government was craftily worked up against the oppressed and the protection which the oppressors treacherously acquired where the injured and ignorant people expected to find it drove them to acts of desperation and confederated them in violences which as your Lordships knows induced bloodshed and I verily believe necessarily.

Saunders, ed., Colonial Records, *9:329–30.*

DOCUMENT 5.9

British Disapproval of the Riot Act

Additional Instruction to . . . Josiah Martin . . . , May 15, 1772

Whereas it hath been represented unto Us that a Law was passed in Our Province of North Carolina in 1771, intitled, "An Act for preventing Tumultuous and riotous Assemblies, for the more speedy and effectual punishment of the Rioters, and for restoring and preserving the public peace of this Province," enacting among other things, "That upon indictment found or presentment made against any person for any of the Crimes described in the Act the Judges or Justices of the Court, shall issue their Proclamation to be affixed or put up at the Court House and each Church and Chappel, of the county wherein such crime was committed, commanding such offender to surrender within 60 days and stand Tryal, on failure of which he shall be deemed guilty of the offense charged in the Indictment found or presentment made and it shall be lawful for any one to kill and destroy such Offender and his Lands and chattels shall be confiscated to the King for the use of Government," which said clause appears to Us to be irreconcilable with the principles of the constitution, full of danger in its operation and unfit for any part of the British Empire; But whereas it hath been also further represented unto Us, that the said Act, which also contains many useful and proper regulations for the preservation of the Public Peace of our said Province of late disturbed by Outrages and Insurrections of a very dangerous nature, is by its own limitations upon the point of expiring and that the total repeal of it might in the present state of Affairs, have very fatal consequences and revive that seditious spirit (not yet wholly subsided amongst some of the Inhabitants) which has been productive of so much tumult and confusion, We have therefore not thought fit to disallow the said Act, but it is nevertheless Our express Will and Pleasure, that in case it shall be found necessary to enact any new Law within our said Province of North Carolina for preventing tumults and riotous assemblies you do take especial care that the said laws be framed as near as may be agreeable to the Laws of this Kingdom and that you do not give assent thereto, unless the same shall appear to you to be entirely free from the Objections stated to the clause before recited.

Saunders, ed., Colonial Records, *8:515–16.*

DOCUMENT 5.10

Lingering Evidence of the Regulation

Instructions to the Delegates from Mecklenburg to the Provincial Congress at Halifax in November 1776.

2. That you shall endeavor to establish a free government under the authority of the people of the State of North Carolina and that the Government be a simple Democracy or as near it as possible.

3. That in fixing the fundamental principles of Government you shall oppose everything that leans to aristocracy or power in the hands of the rich and chief men exercised to the oppression of the poor.

4. That you shall endeavor that the form of Government shall set forth a bill of rights containing the rights of the people and of individuals which shall never be infringed in any future time by the law-making power or other derived powers in the State.

5. That you shall endeavour that the following maxims be substantially acknowledged in the Bills of Rights (viz.):

1st Political power is of two kinds, one principal and superior, the other derived and inferior.

2d. The principal supreme power is possessed by the people at large, the derived and inferior power by the servants which they employ.

3d. Whatever persons are delegated, chosen, employed and intrusted by the people are their servants and can possess only derived inferior power. . . .

6. That you shall endeavour that the Government shall be so formed that the derived inferior power shall be divided into three branches distinct from each other, viz.:

The power of making laws

The power of executing laws and

The power of Judging.

7. That the law making power shall have full and ample authority for the good of the people to provide legal remedies for all evils and abuses that may arise in the State, the executive power shall have authority to apply the legal remedies when the judging power shall have ascertained where and upon what individuals the remedies ought to be applied.

8. You shall endeavour that in the original Constitution of the Government now to be formed the authority of officers possessing any branch of derived power shall be restrained. . . .

12. That the law making power shall be lodged in the hands of one General Assembly composed of Representatives annually chosen by the people freely and equally in every part of the State. . . .

14. You shall endeavour that no officer of the regular troops or collector of public money shall be eligible as a member of General Assembly or if being elected he shall afterwards accept of such office or collectorship he shall thereby vacate his seat. And in general that no persons in arrears for public money shall have a seat in General Assembly. . . .

17. You shall endeavour that all Judges of the Court of Equity, Judges of the Court of Appeals and Writs of Error and all Judges of the Superior Courts shall be appointed by the General Assembly and hold their office during one year.

18. You shall endeavor that Trials by Jury shall be forever had and used in their utmost purity. . . .

And after the Constitution and form of Government shall be agreed upon and established and the General Assembly formed you shall endeavour that they may exercise the law making power on the following subjects of legislation (viz). . . .

3. You shall endeavour to obtain an appraisement law for the relief of the poor when their goods are sold by execution. . . .

5. You shall endeavour to diminish the fees of the Clerks in the Supe-

rior and Inferior Courts and make the Fee Bill more perspicuous and clear it of all ambiguities. . . .

13. You shall endeavour that so much of the *Habeas Corpus* Act and the Common and Statute law heretofore in force and use and favorable to the liberties of the people shall be continued in force in this State, excluding every idea of the kingly office and power.

14. That persons be chosen annually in every county to collect taxes.

15. That a General and equal land tax be laid throughout the State.

16. That people shall be taxed according to their estates.

17. That sheriff, clerk and register shall be chosen by the freeholders in every county, the register to continue in office during good behavior, the sheriff to be elected every year. The same person to be capable to be elected every year if all moneys due by virtue of his office shall be faithfully paid up.

18. That men shall be quieted in their titles and possessions and that provision shall be made to secure men from being disturbed by old and foreign claims against their landed possessions.

Saunders, ed., Colonial Records, *10:870a–870f.*

SUGGESTED READINGS

Adams, George R. "The Carolina Regulators: A Note on Changing Interpretations." *North Carolina Historical Review* 49 (1972):345–52.

Bassett, John S. "The Regulators of North Carolina (1765–1771)." American Historical Association, *Annual Report for the Year 1894*. Washington, D.C.: Government Printing Office, 1895.

Ekirch, A. Roger. "The North Carolina Regulators on Liberty and Corruption, 1766–1771." *Perspectives in American History* 11 (1977–78):199–256.

Haywood, Marshall DeLancey. *Governor William Tryon and His Administration in the Province of North Carolina.* Raleigh: E. M. Uzzell, 1903.

Henderson, Archibald. "Origin of the Regulation." *American Historical Review* 21 (1916):320–32.

Kay, Marvin L. Michael. "The North Carolina Regulation, 1766–1776: A Class Conflict." *The American Revolution: Explorations in the History of American Radicalism.* Edited by Alfred F. Young. Dekalb, Ill.: Northern Illinois University Press, 1976.

Lazenby, Mary Elinor. *Herman Husband: A Story of His Life.* Washington, D.C.: Old Neighborhood Press, 1940.

Powell, William S. *The War of the Regulation and the Battle of Alamance, May 16, 1771.* Raleigh: State Department of Archives and History, 1949.

Tilley, Nannie May. "Political Disturbances in Colonial Granville County." *North Carolina Historical Review* 18 (1941):339–59.
Wheeler, John H. *Historical Sketches of North Carolina.* 2 vols. in 1. Philadelphia: Lippincott, Grambo, and Co., 1851.
Whittenburg, James P. "Planters, Merchants, and Lawyers: Social Change and the Origins of the North Carolina Regulation." *William and Mary Quarterly* 3d ser., 34 (1977):215–38.

CHAPTER 6

Decision for Revolution

Don Higginbotham

Edenton Tea Party (Courtesy of the Division of Archives and History, Raleigh, N.C.)

At first glance, North Carolina did not appear to be a colony ripe for revolution in 1774. The merchants and planters of the Albemarle and Cape Fear sections, long the dominant figures in the colonial legislature, had earlier steered North Carolina into line with her sister colonies on the North Atlantic seaboard. North Carolinians had been willing to follow their traditional leaders in the years after 1763 in opposing a series of British acts designed to restructure the empire and impose parliamentary taxes on the king's American subjects. The settlers could be expected to oppose outside interference in their internal affairs and to balk at paying taxes to a distant body across the Atlantic. But whether a majority of North Carolinians would go so far as to take up arms in a fight that might well destroy the empire, to say nothing of deranging their own colony, was another matter.

By 1774 colonial unity in North Carolina had been tested in only the most superficial way. The colony lacked cultural and religious homogeneity, and it felt the instability and uncertainty of a veritable population explosion—from about 36,000 settlers in the 1730s to approximately 250,000 inhabitants four decades later. The support of these people, established folk as well as recent arrivals, would be questionable should North Carolina's political leaders join in a military confrontation with the mother country. In the northeastern counties and the backcountry there were enclaves of Quakers, longtime residents but pacifists in accordance with the principles of the Society of Friends. No more likely to take up arms were the Moravians, peace-loving Germans whose interior communities such as Bethabara and Salem hummed with the numerous endeavors of skilled craftsmen and farmers. Still another group, seemingly with little in common with the tidewater elite, was the Highland Scots. Living in farms and villages nestled in the upper valley of the Cape Fear River, most of them were recent arrivals in the early 1770s, although a sprinkling had come in the 1730s. Fiercely independent and dedicated to the preservation of their distinctive identity, they would be courted by both friend and foe of royal authority.

The vast majority of the newcomers, however, arrived from colonies to the north, usually winding their way down the Great Wagon Road, which ran southward from Lancaster, Pennsylvania, and ended at the Yadkin River in North Carolina. Along this route came the Moravians, other German strains, the numerous Scotch-Irish, and a sprinkling of other national stocks. They spread themsevles over the red-clay Piedmont, mostly on farms but also in fast-growing hamlets like Hillsborough, Salisbury, and Charlotte.

Many of these backcountry farmers in Orange, Granville, and Anson counties had recently raised the standard of rebellion in the war of the Regulation against the eastern-dominated assembly for its failure to deal with a variety of injustices. The Regulation was a complex episode. If the westerners had legitimate grievances, it is equally true that the North Carolina assembly was not unaware that some reforms were needed. Much of the difficulty stemmed from the colony's growth and expansion at a rate almost too rapid for the processes of government to digest.

Black and red Carolinians also added to the colony's peculiar mixture of peoples and cultures, and no revolt in the name of freedom was likely to produce any liberty for them. In fact, white Carolinians considered them potential allies of the crown; it was widely rumored that royal governors such as Lord Dunmore in Virginia and Josiah Martin in North Carolina would call all blacks to the royal standard. Eighty thousand strong in North Carolina, they could not be discounted. Red Carolinians, on the other hand, principally the more than fifteen thousand Cherokee living in some forty towns in the western Carolinas, eastern Tennessee, and northern Georgia, presented a distinct threat. The Cherokee held deep-seated grievances against their white neighbors who over the years had steadily encroached upon their lands. Not surprisingly, they looked to the British authorities for protection.

Until 1774, the non-English segments of North Carolina, located some distance from the seaboard, had not been directly involved in mounting demonstrations against Britain's new colonial policy. That policy had emanated from cabinet and Parliament following the Seven Years' War (or French and Indian War), which had concluded in 1763 with Britain triumphant over France and Spain. The North Carolina assembly had condemned parliamentary measures to raise revenues in America: the Sugar Act of 1764, the Stamp Act of 1765, and the Townshend Revenue Act of 1767. Even some colonists who would later be loyalists (or tories) in the Revolution believed these acts involved important constitutional issues. Never before had Parliament endeavored to extract pounds and pence from their pockets. They believed it to be a fundamental tenet of the British constitution that Englishmen—whether they lived in North Carolina or the mother country itself—could be taxed only by their own direct representatives; in the case of North Carolina, that would mean only by their colonial assembly. (Document 6.1) Carolinians participated in the boycotts of British goods that occurred up and down the Atlantic coastline. This strategy had led to Britain's retreat in every instance, although in repealing the Townshend taxes in 1770 Parliament had retained the obnoxious duty on tea as a symbol of its authority over America.

The crisis of 1774–75, however, posed the real threat of civil war and dismemberment of the empire. Parliament's endeavor in 1773 to assist the financially distressed East India Company in selling its dutied brew at a reduced price in the colonies was viewed by American leaders as a design to make them sacrifice their principles in exchange for a cheaper drink.

Violence in the form of the Boston Tea Party first erupted in Massachusetts on 16 December 1773, when local citizens emptied 340 chests of the leafy substance over the sides of three tea-laden vessels. Parliament retaliated with the Coercive Acts—Americans called them "Intolerable Acts"—which included closing the port of Boston and altering town and provincial government in Massachusetts. Throughout the colonies there were pledges of support for Boston and resolutions declaring the Coercive Acts illegal. Forty-seven North Carolina women from several counties met at the home of Elizabeth King in Edenton and affixed their signatures to an "Association," promising to uphold the patriot positon. (Document 6.2) This misnamed "Edenton Tea Party" was followed by a real tea party of sorts when Wilmington ladies "burnt their tea in solemn procession." Carolinians in Wilmington, Edenton, and New Bern raised quantities of food and clothing for the beleaguered Bostonians.

An added grievance was whether a new law should permit the provincial courts to attach property of defaulting debtors residing in England, a remedy most unpopular with British merchants and a controversy that resulted in wholesale judicial confusion in the colony after 1773 because Governor Martin and the authorities in London would accept no legislation providing for attachments. Doubtless the turmoil over the court law, which led to closing the regular judicial tribunals, helped generate anti-British sentiment in the interior, where parliamentary taxation and trade laws had been of less direct concern than in the coastal regions.

A more local issue that must have rankled the backcountry Scotch-Irish Presbyterians, especially in Mecklenburg County, was the Privy Council's disallowance of the Mecklenburgers' 1771 charter from the colonial assembly for an educational institution, Queen's Museum. The Privy Council said the act would "give great and permanent Advantages to a sect of Dissenters from the Established Church."

As the North Carolina whigs girded themselves for what seemed to be an oncoming storm, they contemplated how they could weld together their sprawling, heterogeneous colony, tidewater and piedmont, English and non-English. They assigned that task to an extralegal provincial congress. Such congresses were created in almost all the colonies because royal governors either refused to call duly constituted legislative assemblies or dismissed them.

The dominant figures in the old legislature—all tidewater aristocrats—continued to take the lead. They included John Harvey, Samuel Johnston, and Joseph Hewes of the Edenton-Albemarle region; Isaac Edwards and Richard Cogdell of New Bern; and Cornelius Harnett, William Hooper, John Ashe, and Robert Howe of the Wilmington–Lower Cape Fear country. But they also called upon such backcountry dignitaries as John Penn of Granville County, Dr. Thomas Burke of Orange County, and Thomas Polk of Mecklenburg County to mobilize patriot sentiment in their areas. (Document 6.3)

Acting independently of Governor Josiah Martin, these local stalwarts appealed to the counties to pick delegates to attend what became the first provincial congress. (Document 6.4) Sitting at New Bern on 25 August 1774, the delegates reaffirmed their constitutional rights, initiated trade boycotts of British goods, and elected representatives to an intercolonial gathering—the First Continental Congress—to be held at Philadelphia the following month.

But neither the resolutions nor the implied threats of the provincial congresses or the First Continental Congress brought about Parliament's repeal of the Coercive Acts or any promises from the ministry to give up taxing the colonies. Consequently, the North Carolina whigs, like those in other colonies, took further steps; they met again at New Bern, on 3 April 1775, as the second provincial congress. They repeated the positions of the earlier provincial gathering on the subjects of American rights and economic restrictions against Britain, reelected the same delegation to the forthcoming second meeting of the Continental Congress, and arranged for organizing still another provincial congress if necessary.

Then, on 3 May 1775, word arrived of the outbreak of fighting at Lexington and Concord on the nineteenth of the previous month. The strongest reactions came from Mecklenburg and Wilmington. One need not argue over whether the Mecklenburgers on 20 May permanently broke all ties with Britain in the "Mecklenburg Declaration of Independence," an alleged document which has not survived. The record shows that on 31 May the local citizens approved "Resolves" stating that all commissions from the king were "null and void" and that the people were to elect military officers "independent of the Crown of Great Britain." (Document 6.5)

As early as that same day, 31 May, the Wilmington patriot committee appealed to Samuel Johnston of Edenton for a third colonywide assemblage. The urgency of the situation did not escape Johnston, to whom the second provincial congress had entrusted the job of deciding when another congress should convene. Though a nephew of a former royal governor, Johnston, a forty-two-year-old planter-lawyer and veteran legislator, had warmly defended American rights over the preceding decade. He had encouraged his young brother-in-law, James Iredell, to write several essays in support of the colonists' constitutional position.

On 21 August, in response to Johnston's call, the congress began its deliberations at Hillsborough. There was no talk of independence or of severing all ties with Great Britain, but the provincial congress determined that only peace with honor was acceptable. As Boston-born, Harvard-educated William Hooper phrased it in an "Address" approved unanimously by the Hillsborough assembly, the Carolinians insisted on a return to the condition that they and the "other United Colonies" were in "before the year 1763."

Even if the "Address" was moderate in tone, it nevertheless might have been troublesome for the representatives to agree on the precise nature of that earlier relationship. Not a few of them had been positively influenced by the tracts of James Iredell, who pictured the true, legal connection between the colonies and Britain as resembling the present-day commonwealth of nations. In short, parliamentary overlordship did not extend beyond the shores of Britain, although the colonists had voluntarily accepted certain laws of England before and might do so again if they were just and beneficial to America as well as to the mother country.

But the provincial congress could not sit back and await Britain's response to such addresses and essays. It appointed a thirteen-man committee to employ "Argument and Persuasion" in encouraging the Moravians and former Regulators to join the whigs in defending the "Constitutional rights and privileges" of all Americans. The decision to hold this congress at Hillsborough, in the heart of Regulator country, helped gain the support of the former rebels by indicating to them the importance other North Carolinians attached to their region. Despite Johnston's earlier fear that the "old Regulators are all against us," the special delegation treated with the Regulator leaders and reported the resolution of several controversial matters. A second committee, appointed to meet with the Highland Scots, could not report its findings so quickly; it was to advise them to unite with the whigs "in defence of their rights."

Two matters of even greater moment caused the congress more difficulty—military readiness and a provisional government. As the congress wrestled to seek solutions, frustrations mounted and tempers flared. The normally cool, self-possessed Johnston confided testily to his brother-in-law Iredell that "we have more orators than men of business among us, which occasions great delays."

To serve as provincial troops, the congress authorized two regiments of five hundred men each, to be commanded by Colonels James Moore and Robert Howe, ranking militia officers and members of influential Cape Fear families. (The Cape Fear was the most vulnerable spot in the colony to a British invasion from the sea, just as it was exposed to the nearby Highland Scots should they decide to fight for the king.) In addition, North Carolina, like Massachusetts, was to have minutemen, a half-dozen battalions, to assemble on short notice in case of "Insurrections, Invasions or other Emergency." To finance these forces, the congress called for collecting back taxes and printing $125,000 in bills of credit.

At this point the colony needed a civil government to direct and coordinate all that the congress had set in motion. On 9 September, a committee composed of luminaries from all sections of the province brought forth a detailed plan, which the full assembly accepted as written. The new structure built upon and formalized the extralegal activities of local and district committees and the provincial congress. It clarified relationships, specifically defined authorities, and added as a capstone a body known as the provisional council, responsible only to the provincial congress to act in its name when the congress was not in session.

The Carolinians had fashioned, in the words of historian Allan Nevins, "the most elaborate provisional government on the continent." And they had not only made extensive military preparations but had attempted to bring together by cooperation and conciliation all the diverse elements that made up the white population of North Carolina in 1775. Only time would tell whether their efforts had been successful, whether they could respond effectively to a serious enemy threat in the months ahead.

Such a threat, not long in coming, was instigated by a man who resolutely opposed all they had done. He was thirty-seven-year-old Josiah Martin, a soldier by profession and chief executive of the colony since 1771. Honest and energetic, Martin was tough-minded, tactless, and little disposed to compromise when it came to upholding royal instructions. Despite his fuming and threatening, he had been unable to prevent the three provincial congresses from reducing his authority to a "shadow."

Even so, he remained convinced that most people were at heart loyalists, and were merely intimidated and lacked organization in the face of furious whig activity. From his watery asylum on H.M.S. *Cruizer*, anchored in the Cape Fear River, he bombarded his backcountry supporters along with General Thomas Gage in Boston and the London ministry with optimistic reports. Given arms for his followers, he claimed that he would smother the flames of rebellion in North and South Carolina. Indeed, he prophesied that the Highland Scots in the vicinity of Cross Creek on the Cape Fear River and the former Regulators would rise up almost to the last man and join him at his command. (Document 6.6) In London the ministry decided to do him one better by sending an expedition of regulars to the North Carolina coast to cooperate in the subjection of that colony and perhaps other provinces as well.

But Martin, frustrated and angry, scarcely cautious or reflective by nature, jumped the gun, mobilizing the loyalists too quickly, well before the British expedition could arrive unless it was blessed with near perfect sailing conditions, as scarcely ever happened in the eighteenth century. On 10 January 1776, he addressed a proclamation to all "His Majesty's subjects," ordering them to declare themselves and come forward, branding all who refused as "Rebels and Traitors." (Document 6.7) Simultaneously, he instructed influential loyalists in Bute, Surry, Cumberland, Chatham, Guilford, Orange, Anson, Mecklenburg, and Rowan counties to recruit units, seize supplies, and rendezvous their forces in time to reach the coast below Wilmington by 15 February.

On that date, however, the loyalist "army" had only recently assembled at Cross Creek, its designated place of departure, ninety miles from Wilmington. It included barely fourteen hundred men, no more than half of them armed, commanded by Brigadier General Donald MacDonald, an officer General Gage had sent south to aid Martin.

Where were the several thousand Highlanders and former Regulators that Martin had felt confident of raising? Aggressive action by local whig committees is a partial explanation; they intimidated the loyalists, and their county militia companies scattered and dispersed numerous small groups that set out for Cross Creek. It is also likely that Martin and his subordinates inflated crown support in the backcountry. Finally, credit belonged to the committees of the third provincial congress that sought to improve relations with the Highlanders and the old Regulators.

There was an even greater surge of preparations in the tidewater, for it was the region immediately threatened, by the loyalists from the interior and by Britain from the sea. Colonel Richard Caswell of the New Bern district mustered his minuteman battalion, and Colonel James Moore prepared his new regiment of provincial troops from Cape Fear to keep MacDonald's loyalist volunteers from reaching the coast and linking up with the British expeditionary force. In the first week of maneuvering, MacDonald proved to be an able opponent, darting here and there to avoid the patriot forces. But on the morning of 27 February, Caswell's militia in well-entrenched positions blocked MacDonald's passage over Moore's Creek Bridge. MacDonald's men charged across the bridge and into a hail of musketry and cannon fire. The result was a total disaster for MacDonald, who suffered heavy casualties; the majority of his survivors scattered and fled, most of them surrendering during the next few days to pursuing patriot parties. In all, four men out of the fourteen hundred who had earlier assembled at Cross Creek managed to join Martin, still aboard the *Cruizer*, the man with the grand, visionary design for restoring North Carolina to the royal fold. Nor was the governor pleased when the long-delayed British force, upon reaching the Cape

Fear, headed southward for what proved to be an ill-conceived attack on Charleston, South Carolina. (Document 6.8)

Men both individually (as in the case of Caswell and Moore) and collectively (as in the case of the third provincial congress) shape history. And the contribution of that congress was to create the machinery by which the loyalists were outmaneuvered for the minds of many people who might normally have gravitated to them, scattered and dispersed on their way to Cross Creek, and finally cornered and defeated on the field of battle.

Perhaps the most talked about single fact in North Carolina was not the actual victory, which was the first major clash between whigs and tories in the war (if not "the Lexington and Concord of the South") but rather the number of men who were mobilized on short notice. Samuel Johnston, among others, estimated that ninety-four hundred men were under arms. Many militia units that assembled were not put in motion because it was thought they would not be needed, at least until a formidable British army landed on the coast. The war was to demonstrate something that perceptive observers might have gleaned from the Moore's Creek campaign: that Britain was contending with a massive civilian rebellion, a countryside in arms, not primarily a professional American army.

Irregulars—militia, minutemen, and volunteers—were to prove best at the characteristic the North Carolina citizen-soldiers displayed early in 1776: combating disaffection at home. If Washington's army, somewhat fashioned along European lines, was necessary, so too were the irregulars, the home guard of the Revolution, to deal with the tories, the fifth column or internal subversives. (Document 6.9) And yet none of these implications of such colonial events registered with policy makers in London, nor, for that matter, with any shapers of opinion. The *Gentleman's Magazine*, for example, sneered that the Americans had "only reduced a body of their own people, supported by no one company of regular troops." Yet the *Annual Register*, possibly without recognizing the import of its own print, opined that loyalists might be less willing to rise after Moore's Creek and that the colony had called out nearly ten thousand armed whigs.

Finally, the patriots' éclat at Moore's Creek exerted a positive influence on the growing sentiment in the colony in favor of total separation from Britain. A colony that in 1774 scarcely appeared capable of achieving a measure of internal unity had seen its leaders put together an alliance of east and west that included a considerable admixture of former Regulators and Highlanders, the two elements that Josiah Martin had hoped to win over to the side of the crown. The pacifist groups, the Quakers and Moravians, had posed no obstacles, the latter having sold supplies to the whig military forces, albeit not always willingly. Despite rumors to the contrary, the slaves had not revolted against their whig masters, nor had the Indians as yet made serious warlike threats.

The confidence of North Carolinians now combined with a growing bitterness and disillusionment with the mother country, which had not only employed Governor Martin to make war on them, but which, at that very moment, was sending a fleet with soldiers to their coast. Furthermore, the North Carolina delegates to the Second Continental Congress—William Hooper, Joseph Hewes, and John Penn—had come around to the view that a final severance of the imperial cord could not be averted. The congressmen discovered that opinion in their province paralleled their own. Hewes, in sending Samuel Johnston a copy of Thomas Paine's strongly worded *Common Sense*, admitted he did so "not knowing how you might relish independence." But Hewes soon found out from Johnston, then at Halifax for the opening of the fourth provincial congress on 4 April, that independence seemed to be on almost all lips. Hooper, after traveling to Halifax, also assured Hewes that the colony's whigs now favored unfettered freedom for America. According to the future signer of the Declaration of Independence, it would be "Toryism" to consider reconciliation. If one entertained such thoughts, Hooper did not think it would be wise to voice them.

On 13 April, Samuel Johnston scrawled a terse but electrifying note to his brother-in-law James Iredell: "The House . . . last night agreed to impower their Delegates at Philadelphia to concur with the other Colonies in entering into foreign Alliances and declaring an independence on Great Britain. I cannot be more particular."

Johnston referred to the so-called Halifax Resolves, drafted by a special committee composed of Cornelius Harnett, Abner Nash, Allen Jones, Thomas Burke, Thomas Person (a former Regulator sympathizer), and John Kinchen—a nicely balanced group of three easterners and three westerners. Once again, the whig leadership had moved skillfully to unify the provincial congress. Indeed, the 148 delegates from thirty-four counties and eight towns voted without dissent on 12 April 1776 for the Halifax Resolves, a truly remarkable achievement. (Document 6.10)

The deed was done, and North Carolina was the first colony to permit its contingent in Congress to vote for independence.

DOCUMENT 6.1

James Iredell's *Address to the Inhabitants of Great Britain*, September 1774

As the king is supreme head of every legislature in the British dominions, his negative can prevent the actual injury to the whole of any positive law in any part of the empire.

I have hitherto considered the above rule upon the principles which generally support it in this controversy, though I am not ignorant that it has another basis, and that which I believe was the first suggestion of its political necessity; I mean, the great solecism of an *imperium in imperio* [recently stated by Sir William Blackstone].

The danger arising from this is, lest two independent legislatures should clash by different regulations about the same objects. Here neither can be executed, or distress and confusion must ensue. This is a real evil, certainly worth all the anxious care old authors have bestowed upon it. But what application does this make to the case of several distinct and independent legislatures, each engaged within a separate scale, and employed about different objects. The *imperium in imperio* argument is, therefore, not at all applicable to our case, though it has been so vainly and confidently relied on. The principal inconvenience attending our situation we readily admit; that it may not be always practicable to bring so many different legislatures to concur heartily in the prosecution and support of one common object. Judging of the future by the past, I do not think this would be found in practice so difficult as in speculation it may appear, but surely any remedy for the evil ought to be conducted on the basis of a general negotiaton, and not violently sought by an unjust usurpation of power.

To conclude: If our charters had not been so express as they are, if there had been some clerical defect, or any jesuitical craft in the penning of them, the confessed intention of the parties, and the original rights of mankind, should correct and alter them. We would not be cheated out of our liberties by a few artful syllables. Our ancestors looked for freedom in this country, and thought they possessed it. They fondly flattered themselves that they had transmitted this blessing to their posterity, and they no doubt hoped that their posterity would not be base enough to resign it. God forbid we should disappoint this reasonable expectation. We desire to stand upon manly ground; not upon scholastic and trifling refinement. Such a power as you long continued to exercise, for your and our mutual benefit (though our particular interests were often made subservient to yours), we will cheerfully and readily submit to. Without critically inquiring whether you may not, constitutionally, be possessed of this power, as properly resulting from the relation between us, we are ready to offer our obedience to it as a proof of our regard and attachment, and our desire to cement a lasting union with you. This alone will put millions in your power. A power of taxing, and harassing us with cruel, oppressive, and inconvenient laws, we will not give you; because it is a novel claim, and can never be exercised but to our destruction; any instance to the contrary, however, we think would only form exceptions to a general system of weakness and injustice. We cannot divest ourselves of every vestige of freedom to please you, nor even to remove some inconveniences with which the situation we contend for is certainly accompanied. But we are ready, at any time, to enter into a fair negotiation, by which means to concert a plan of cementing the general interest of the empire upon a broad basis, at once securing a proper union of counsel, and authority, and the individual freedom of each member of the empire, so far as is consistent with the general welfare. But this object must not be secured by any partial and contracted plan of ruining whole societies to make the business of government go on more smoothly. This your plan, which you are now proceeding to enforce with fire and sword. Which of the two is the most equitable, let Heaven and the world judge.

Don Higginbotham, ed., The Papers of James Iredell, 2 vols. (Raleigh: Department of Cultural Resources, 1976), 1:266–67.

DOCUMENT 6.2

Association Signed by Ladies of Edenton, North Carolina, 25 October 1774

The Provincial Deputies of North Carolina, having resolved *not* to drink any more *tea*, nor wear any more British cloth, etc. many ladies of this Province have determined to give a memorable proof of their patriotism, and have accordingly entered into the following honourable and spirited association. I send it to you to shew your fair countrywomen, how zealously and faithfully, American ladies follow the laudable example of their husbands, and what opposition your matchless Ministers may expect to receive from a people thus firmly united against them.

As we cannot be indifferent on any occasion that appears nearly to affect the peace and happiness of our country, and as it has been thought necessary, for the public good, to enter into several particular resolves by a meeting of members deputed from the whole Province, it is a duty which we owe, not only to our near and dear connections, who have concurred in them, but to ourselves, who are essentially interested in their welfare, to do everything as far as lies in our power, to testify our sincere adherence to the same; and we do therefore accordingly subscribe this paper, as witness of our fixed intention and solemn determination to do so.

"Extract of a letter from North Carolina, Oct. 27," Morning Chronicle and London Advertiser, *16 January 1775.*

DOCUMENT 6.3

William Hooper to James Iredell, 26 April 1774

With you I anticipate the important share which the colonies must soon have in regulating the political balance. *They are striding fast to independence, and ere long will build an empire upon the ruin of Great Britain;* will adopt its constitution purged of its impurities, and from an experience of its defects will guard against those evils which have wasted its vigor and brought it to an untimely end. From the fate of Rome, Britain may trace the cause of its present degeneracy, and its impending destruction. Similar causes will ever produce similar effects. The extent of the British dominion is become too unwieldy for her to sustain. Commerce hath generated a profusion of wealth, and luxury and corruption, the natural attendants of it. Those to whom are entrusted the conduct of the state are too much absorbed in debauchery to attend to the rights of the constitution, or too enervated to dare to support them.

Higginbotham, ed., Iredell Papers, *1:231.*

DOCUMENT 6.4

Samuel Johnston to William Hooper, 5 April 1774

Colonel Harvey and myself lodged last night with Colonel Buncombe, and as we sat up very late the conversation turned on Continental and provincial affairs. Colonel Harvey said during the night, that Mr. Biggleston told him, that the Governor did not intend to convene another Assembly until he saw some chance of a better one than the last; and that he told the Secretary that then the people would convene one themselves. He was in a very violent mood, and declared he was for assembling a convention independent of the Governor, and urged upon us to co-operate with him. He says he will lead the way, and will issue handbills under his own name and that the committee of correspondence ought to go to work at once. As for my part, I do not know what better can be done. Without Courts to sustain the property and to exercise the talents of the Country, and the people alarmed and dissatisfied, we must do something to save ourselves.

William L. Saunders, ed., The Colonial Records of North Carolina, *10 vols. (Raleigh: State of North Carolina 1886–90), 9:968.*

DOCUMENT 6.5

The Mecklenburg Resolves, 31 May 1775

CHARLOTTE TOWN,
MECKLENBURG COUNTY

This day the Committee of this county met and passed the following resolves:

Whereas by an address presented to his majesty by both Houses of Parliament in February last, the American colonies are declared to be in a state of actual rebellion, we conceive that all laws and commissions confirmed by or derived from the authority of the King and Parliament are annulled and vacated and the former civil constitution of these colonies for the present wholly suspended. To provide in some degree for the exigencies of this county, in the present alarming period, we deem it proper and necessary to pass the following resolves, viz:

1. That all commissions civil and military heretofore granted by the Crown to be exercised in these colonies are null and void and the constitution of each particular colony wholly suspended.

2. That the Provincial Congress of each Province under the direction of the great Continental Congress is invested with all legislative and executive powers within their respective Provinces and that no other legislative or executive power does or can exist at this time in any of these colonies.

3. As all former laws are now suspended in this Province and the Congress has not yet provided others we judge it necessary for the better preservation of good order, to form certain rules and regulations for the internal government of this county until laws shall be provided for us by the Congress.

4. That the inhabitants of this county do meet on a certain day appointed by the committee and having formed themselves into nine companies ... eight in the county and one in the town of Charlotte do choose a Colonel and other military officers who shall hold and exercise their several powers by virtue of this choice and independent of the Crown of Great Britain and former constitution of this Province.

5. That for the better preservation of the peace and administration of justice each of these companies do choose from their own body two discreet freeholders who shall be empowered ... to decide and determine all matters of controversy arising within said company under the sum of twenty shillings and jointly and together all controversies under the sum of forty shillings that so as their decisions may admit of appeal to the convention of the selectmen of the county and also that any one of these shall have power to examine and commit to confinement persons accused of petit larceny.

6. That those two select men thus chosen do jointly and together choose from the body of their particular body two persons properly qualified to act as constables who may assist them in the execution of their office.

7. That upon the complaint of any persons to either of these selectmen he do issue his warrant directed to the constable commanding him to bring the aggressor before him or them to answer said complaint.

8. That these eighteen selectmen thus appointed do meet every third Thursday in January, April, July and October, at the Court House in Charlotte, to hear and determine all matters of controversy for sums exceeding forty shillings, also appeals, and in cases of felony to commit the person or persons convicted thereof to close confinement until the Provincial Congress shall provide and establish laws and modes of proceeding in all such cases.

9. That these eighteen selectmen thus convened do choose a clerk to

record the transactions of said convention and that said clerk upon the application of any person or persons aggrieved do issue his warrant to one of the constables . . . directing said constable to summon and warn said offender to appear before the convention at their next sitting to answer the aforesaid complaint. . . .

16. That whatever person hereafter shall receive a commission from the Crown or attempt to exercise any such commission heretofore received shall be deemed an enemy to his country and upon information being made to the captain of the company in which he resides, the said company shall cause him to be apprehended and conveyed before the two selectmen of the said company, who upon proof of the fact, shall commit him the said offender to safe custody until the next sitting of the committee, who shall deal with him as prudence may direct.

17. That any person refusing to yield obedience to the above resolves shall be considered equally criminal and liable to the same punishment as the offenders above last mentioned.

18. That these resolves be in full force and virtue until instructions from the Provincial Congress . . . shall provide otherwise or the legislative body of Great Britain resign its unjust and arbitrary pretensions with respect to America.

19. That the eight Militia companies in this county do provide themselves with proper arms and accoutrements and hold themselves in readiness to execute the commands and directions of the General Congress of this Province and of this Committee.

20. That the committee appoint Colonel Thomas Polk and Dr. Joseph Kennedy to purchase three hundred pounds of powder, six hundred pounds of lead and one thousand flints for the use of the militia of this county and deposit the same in such place as the committee hereafter may direct.

Signed by order of the Committee,
Eph. Brevard,
Clerk of the Committee.

Saunders, ed., Colonial Records, *9:1282–85.*

DOCUMENT 6.6

Governor Martin Assures Lord Dartmouth the Scots and Former Regulators Will Support Britain, 12 November 1775

I have the satisfaction, I think on good information, to assure your Lordship that the Scotch Highlanders here are generally and almost without exception staunch to Government, and on the same authority I am persuaded to believe that loyal subjects yet abound and infinitely outnumber the seditious throughout all the very populous Western Counties of the Province. I am also told for a certainty that their indignation against the late Congress held at Hillsboro ran so high that they would have broke it up if they had been provided but with a small quantity of ammunition.

Saunders, ed., Colonial Records, *10:325.*

DOCUMENT 6.7

A Proclamation by Governor Martin

Whereas a most daring, horrid and unnatural Rebellion has been exerted in the Province against His Majesty's Government, by the base and insidious artifice of certain traitorous, wicked and designing men, and the same is now openly avowed and declared, and actually threatens the sole subversion of the laws and Constitution of the said Province, and the liberties and privileges of His Majesty's subjects, inhabitants thereof, I have thought fit to issue this Proclamation, hereby to signify to all His Majesty's liege subjects within this Province, that I find it necessary, for the safety and preservation of the rights, civil and religious, and for the maintenance of His Majesty's Government against the said desperate, unnatural Rebellion, to erect His Majesty's Royal standard and to collect and unite the force of His Majesty's people under the same, for the purpose of resisting and subduing, with the assistance of the Almighty, the said impious and unnatural Rebellion, and to restore the just rights of His Majesty's Crown and Government, and the liberties of his people; and I do hereby exhort, require and command in the King's name, all His Majesty's faithful subjects, on their duty and allegiance, forthwith to repair to the Royal standard, hereby promising and assuring every aid, encouragement, and support to all such as shall come to vindicate and support the violated laws and Constitution of their country; at the same time pronouncing all such Rebels as will not join the Royal Banner Rebels and Traitors; their lives and properties to be forfeited. All such as will join shall be forgiven any past offences, even admitting they had taken up arms, not doubting that every man who knows the value of freedom and the blessings of a British subject, will join his heart and hand to restore to his country that most glorious, free and happy Constitution and form of Government, which the most desperate and abandoned Traitors only can wish to disturb or alter; or, in times of danger, like the present, forbear to hazard everything that is dear to support it.

Given under my hand and seal-at-arms, on board His Majesty's Sloop *Scorpion*, in Cape Fear River, this 10th day of January 1776, and in the sixteenth year of his Majesty's reign.

JOSIAH MARTIN.

God save the King.

Saunders, ed., Colonial Records, *10:396–97.*

DOCUMENT 6.8

Colonel Moore's Report to the Provisional Council on the Battle of Moore's Creek Bridge, 2 March 1776

Just when I was prepared to march I received an express from Colonel Caswell, informing that the Tories had raised a flat which had been sunk in Black River, about five miles above him, and by erecting a bridge, had passed it with their whole army.

I then determined, as the last expedient, to proceed immediately in boats down the Northwest River to Dollison's Landing, about sixty miles from them; and to take possession of Moore's Creek Bridge, about ten miles from them, at the same time acquainting Colonel Caswell of my intentions, and recommending him to retreat to Moore's Creek Bridge, if possible; but if not, to follow on their rear.

The next day, by four o'clock, we arrived at Dollison's Landing; but as we could not possibly march that night, for want of horses for the artillery, I dispatched an express to Moore's Creek Bridge, to learn the situation of affairs there, and was informed that Colonel Lillington, who had the day before taken his stand at the bridge, was that afternoon reinforced by Colonel Caswell, and that they had raised a small breastwork and destroyed a part of the bridge.

The next morning (the 27th) at break of day an alarm gun was fired; immediately after which, scarcely allowing our people a moment to prepare, the Tory army, with Captain Macleod at their head, made their attack on Colonel Caswell and Colonel Lillington, and, finding, a small entrenchment next the bridge on our side empty, concluded that our people had abandoned their post, and in the most furious manner advanced within thirty paces of our breastwork and artillery, where they met a very proper reception. Captain Macleod and Captain Campbell fell within a few paces of the breastwork, the former of whom received upwards of twenty balls through his body; and in a very few minutes their whole army was put to flight and most shamefully abandoned their general, who was next day taken prisoner.

The loss of the enemy in this action, from the best accounts we have been able to learn, is about thirty killed and wounded; but as numbers of them must have fallen into the creek, besides many more that were carried off, I suppose their loss may be estimated at about fifty. We had only two wounded, one of which died this day.

Thus, sir, I have the pleasure to inform you, has most happily terminated a very dangerous insurrection and will, I trust, put an effectual check to Toryism in this country.

Henry S. Commager and Richard B. Morris, eds., The Spirit of Seventy-Six: The Story of the American Revolution as Told by Participants *(New York: Harper & Row, 1975), p. 115.*

DOCUMENT 6.9

The Militia Forces the Issue for Revolution

Three months ago, a very small number had not any thing to apprehend; a few troops landing and a general amnesty published would have secured them all at home. For I do not suppose them of such a martial spirit as voluntarily to have joined either's standard. At present the martial law stands thus: An officer or committeeman enters a plantation with his posse. The Alternative is proposed, Agree to join us, and your persons and properties are safe; you have a shilling sterling a day; your duty is no more than once a month appearing under Arms at Wilmington, which will prove only a merry-making, where you will have as much grog as you can drink. But if you refuse, we are directly to cut up your corn, shoot your pigs, burn your houses, seize your Negroes and perhaps tar and feather yourself. Not to chuse the first requires more courage than they are possessed of, and I believe this method has seldom failed with the lower sort. No sooner do they appear under arms with the implacable cruelty of the king of Great Britain, who has resolved to murder and destroy man, wife and child, and that he has sworn before God and his parliament that he will not spare one of them; and this those deluded people believe more firmly than their creed, and who is it that is bold enough to venture to undeceive them. The King's proclamation they never saw; but are told it was ordering the tories to murder the whigs, and promising every Negro that would murder his Master and family that he should have his Master's plantation. This last Artifice they may pay for, as the Negroes have got it amongst them and believe it to be true. Tis ten to one they may try the experiment and in that case friends and foes will be all one.

Janet Schaw, Journal of a Lady of Quality . . ., *ed. Evangeline W. Andrews and Charles M. Andrews (New Haven: Yale University Press, 1923), pp. 198–99.*

DOCUMENT 6.10

The Halifax Resolves, 12 April 1776

It appears to your committee, that pursuant to the plan concerted by the British Ministry for subjugating America, the King and Parliament of Great Britain have usurped a power over the persons and properties of the people unlimited and uncontrouled; and disregarding their humble petitions for peace, liberty and safety, have made divers legislative acts, denouncing war, famine, and every species of calamity, against the Continent in general. The British fleets and armies have been, and still are daily employed in destroying the people, and committing the most horrid devastations on the country. That governors in different Colonies have declared protection to slaves, who should imbrue their hands in the blood of their masters. That ships belonging to America are declared prizes of war, and many of them have been violently seized and confiscated. In consequence of all which multitudes of people have been destroyed, or from easy circumstances reduced to the most lamentable distress.

And whereas the moderation hitherto manifested by the United Colonies and their sincere desire to be reconciled to the mother country on constitutional principles, have procured no mitigation of the aforesaid wrongs and usurpations, and no hopes remain of obtaining redress by those means alone which have been hitherto tried, your committee are of opinion that the House should enter into the following resolve, to wit:

Resolved, That the delegates for this Colony in the Continental Congress be impowered to concur with the delegates of the other Colonies in declaring Independency, and forming foreign alliances, reserving to this Colony the sole and exclusive right of forming a Constitution and laws for this Colony, and of appointing delegates from time to time (under the direction of a general representation thereof), to meet the delegates of the other Colonies for such purposes as shall be hereafter pointed out.

Saunders, ed., Colonial Records, *10:512.*

SUGGESTED READINGS

Alden, John R. *The South in the Revolution, 1763–1789.* Baton Rouge: Louisiana State University Press, 1957.

Butler, Lindley S. *North Carolina and the Coming of the Revolution, 1763–1776.* Raleigh: North Carolina Department of Cultural Resources, 1977.

Douglass, Elisha P. *Rebels and Democrats.* Chapel Hill: University of North Carolina Press, 1955.

Ganyard, Robert L. *The Emergence of North Carolina's Revolutionary State Government.* Raleigh: North Carolina Department of Cultural Resources, 1978.

Higginbotham, Don. "James Iredell's Efforts to Preserve the First British Empire." *North Carolina Historical Review* 49 (1972):127–45.

———, ed. *The Papers of James Iredell.* 2 vols. to date. Raleigh: North Carolina Department of Cultural Resources, 1976.

Hoyt, William H. *The Mecklenburg Declaration of Independence.* New York: G. P. Putnam, 1907.

Morgan, David T., and Schmidt, William J. "From Economic Sanctions to Political Separation: The North Carolina Delegation to the Continental Congress, 1774–1776." *North Carolina Historical Review* 52 (1975):215–34.

Price, William S., ed. *Not a Conquered People: Two Carolinians View Parliamentary Taxation.* Raleigh: North Carolina Department of Cultural Resources, 1975.

Rankin, H. F. "The Moore's Creek Bridge Campaign." *North Carolina Historical Review* 30 (1953):23–60.

Sellers, Charles G. "Making of a Revolution: The North Carolina Whigs, 1765–1775." In J. Carlyle Sitterson, ed., *Studies in Southern History*, pp. 23–46. James Sprunt Studies in History and Political Science, vol. 29. Chapel Hill: University of North Carolina Press, 1957.

Taylor, H. Braughon. "The Foreign Attachment Law and the Coming of the Revolution in North Carolina." *North Carolina Historical Review* 52 (1975):20–36.

CHAPTER 7

Joining the Federal Union

J. Edwin Hendricks

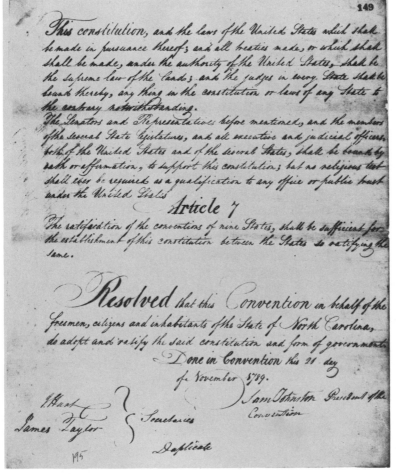

North Carolina's Ratification Document of the United States Constitution,
21 November 1789 (Courtesy of the Division of Archives and History,
Raleigh, N.C.)

The role of North Carolina in the creation of the federal union has been misunderstood and misinterpreted. Much research and writing about the participation of the state in the nation-making process has produced general agreement on the basic facts but an interpretive consensus has not emerged. Much of the problem stems from a simplistic view of North Carolina's relationship to the adoption of the federal Constitution. Either the state is lumped with Rhode Island as opposing the Constitution in any form, or emphasis is placed on North Carolina's refusal ("rejection" is a frequently used though erroneous term) to ratify the Constitution in its first ratification convention in 1788. It is also erroneously implied that North Carolina, like Rhode Island, ratified only as a result of threats by the new government to exclude the nonratifying states from the proposed tariff union. A closer examination of North Carolina's role in shaping the union reveals a different story, especially when seen in the broader perspective of the colonial and revolutionary periods. Concern for individual rights and the power of the state government were the major factors that shaped North Carolina's role in the formation of the federal union. This story, long known to scholars and serious students of North Carolina history, deserves a wider audience.

In the Halifax Resolves of 12 April 1776, North Carolina took the first state action toward independence and also implicitly approved steps toward forming a more stable union among the newly independent states. The Continental Congress, in response, appointed a committee to formulate a plan of action at the same time that it appointed a committee to draft the Declaration of Independence. While Congress was debating the precise form of the Articles of Confederation and Perpetual Union, North Carolina's delegation was changed to include Cornelius Harnett, John Penn, and Thomas Burke.

All these men were protective of the rights of individual states, but Thomas Burke seemed particularly obsessed with the issue of state sovereignty. He was almost solely responsible for the inclusion of the second article: "Each state retains its sovereignty, freedom and independence, and every Power, Jurisdiction and right, which is not by this confederation expressly delegated to the United States, in Congress assembled."

In debate through the fall of 1777 Penn and Harnett joined with other delegates to limit the power of the proposed Confederation government over the states, reserving power over taxation, commerce, tariffs, and western land claims to the states. Although some wished to create a stronger national government, most of the delegates appear to have agreed with the North Carolinians that the power of the new government should be limited. The resulting federal union was much like the state government created by the new North Carolina constitution of 1776. Weak enough to entice even the most recalcitrant states into a national union, the Confederaton government proved strong enough to conduct the revolutionary war and survive until a stronger national government could be forged.

In the debate over the nature of the Confederation, Burke, Harnett, and Penn reflected the differing views of their North Carolina constituency. Despite the inclusion of Article 2 and its protection of state sovereignty, Burke referred to the efforts at union as a "chymerical Project." He proposed a bicameral form of government that was defeated. Penn, slow to make his position known, finally supported the union, but then joined with the Virginia delegates in an unsuccessful attempt to have representation in Congress be based on population. Harnett was concerned that the apportionment of tax levies among the states be based only on land under "Patent or Deed," the system he thought best for North Carolina. He and Penn united in opposing any move to give the central government control over ungranted western lands. Continued differences in the delegation and in the state are reflected in Harnett's report of 13 November to Burke (who had returned home), "The child Congress has been big with these two years past is at least brought forth. I fear it [the Confederation] will by several Legislatures be thought a little Deformed; you will think it a Monster." Harnett, however, thought it was the best government that could be formed, considering the number of states and their different interests.

Harnett was fearful that the opposition of Burke and others would keep the North Carolina legislature from ratifying the Confederation. Burke did lead the opposition to ratification in the General Assembly in November and December 1777 and produced a negative committee report, which the assembly approved. Harnett, from Philadelphia, continued his correspondence with state leaders urging that the Articles of Confederation be adopted. His and other efforts succeeded when on 24 April 1778, the General Assembly ratified the Articles without reservations. In other states problems over ratification had arisen, and suggestions or demands for modifications would delay unanimous ratification for months. The Continental Congress, however, proceeded almost as though the Articles were in effect; and North Carolina and the other states for the most part made similar assumptions.

Although progress was evident in many areas, numerous problems remained as the revolutionary war continued. Many difficulties stemmed from the need to create a new government and from inefficiencies and inequities in the system that was created. The committees of safety, which served North Carolina until a constitution could be written, were frequently inexperienced and arbitrary in their actions. The new state constitution of 1776 provided for an almost powerless governor, and although it gave the appearance of democracy it proved not to be so in practice. Free, white, Protestant landowners dominated the government; and the county representation system gave entirely too much power to the east. The legislature was the seat of most government power, especially in that it chose both executive and judicial officials. An important feature was a Declaration of Rights with guarantees of individual liberties taken from the new constitutions of Maryland, Virginia, and other sources including the English Bill of Rights. (Document 7.1) Conservatives and radicals clashed in preparing the new constitution, many of whom would take the same positions in the debates over the national Constitution more than a decade later. The final document that framed the new state government was a compromise, with the conservatives holding the upper hand but not too firmly. Perhaps the constitution's most significant flaw was the absence of a procedure for amendment.

The end of the fighting of the revolutionary war did not end the difficulties of the revolutionary government. Inhabitants of all states were troubled about the exchange of prisoners, evacuation of American territory, collection of debts owed to Englishmen, conflicting claims over confiscated loyalist property, and the failure to regain trading rights with English markets. Most of these concerns affected North Carolinians, but the one that brought the state into conflict with the peace treaty and the wishes of the Confederation government (including some of the state's own delegation) was the issue of loyalist property. The state confiscation acts of 1777 and 1779 had provided that loyalist property could be seized by the state and sold to support the Revolution. With the end of hostilities a more humane approach prevailed, and many tories were covered by the "Act of Pardon and Oblivion" of 1783. But the state continued to sell confiscated property until the case of *Bayard* v. *Singleton* (1786–87) in which the state supreme court declared the confiscation acts unconstitutional because they were in conflict with the state constitution of 1776. Whether this action had any influence on George Mason and John Marshall, who are generally credited with establishing the doctrine of judicial review on the national level, is unknown.

One reason for the delay in ratifying the Articles of Confederation was the issue of the western lands claimed by some of the states. North Carolina's claims to the lands beyond the mountains were based on the charter of 1663, and by the time of the Revolution settlers were already moving into the territory that became the state of Tennessee. Several colonies that did not have claims stretching to the Mississippi or beyond wanted all claims to be surrendered before the Confederation became a reality. Maryland withheld its ratification until 1781 largely over this issue.

Opinion in North Carolina over the proper disposition of these lands varied greatly. Its delegates to the Congress at first opposed ceding the lands to the national government on the grounds that the state could make better use of them. As other states made whole or partial cessions of their lands, the North Carolina delegation began to press for similar action so as not to appear niggardly and provincial. Some state leaders thought the lands should be used to pay state debts or be credited to the state's account with the Confederation government if the territory were placed in the public domain. Others favored cession because of the lawless character of the inhabitants and the difficulties of governing and protecting the area. Westerners generally favored cession but with exceptions. In this complex situation and with potentially great sums involved, it is not surprising that some individuals sought to use the lands to their own advantage, with profits going to themselves rather than to the state or the national government.

In the Cession Act of 1784 the General Assembly offered to cede the lands to the national government provided certain conditions were met. In Congress, Hugh Williamson decided that the gesture had not been carefully considered, and he aided William R. Davie and others in getting the offer quickly rescinded. John Tipton and John Sevier fought over goals and personalities but finally united in an effort to get Congress to recognize the state of Franklin with Sevier as its governor. Having withdrawn its cession offer, North Carolina made efforts to conciliate the western factions and joined with Virginia in preventing congressional recognition of Franklin. Like the earlier Transylvania (Kentucky) statehood movement, the Franklin movement seemed ill-timed and poorly conceived. From 1785 to 1789 all the Tennessee counties were represented in the North Carolina Assembly even though political strife continued in places. In 1789, after finally ratifying the Constitution, North Carolina ceded its western lands to the United States, perhaps as a gesture of its willingness to cooperate with the new government. In 1790 the area was made a part of the Territory South of the Ohio, and in 1796 Tennessee became the sixteenth state.

Finance provided another area of tension between North Carolina and the Confederation government. North Carolina was a poor state, and its government was not well established financially. It had difficulty meeting its own financial needs and found the assessments from the Confederation government very difficult to meet. Rather than burden its citizens with an unbearable tax load, which they would not accept, the state resorted to fiat financing, issuing unbacked paper currency, which the inhabitants did accept. Although the currency rapidly depreciated, it met the immediate needs of the state. Such depreciation was in truth a subtle method of taxation paid by those who used the currency in its depreciated form. The fiat financiers were willing to suffer the ill effects of their policies: inflation, declining trade, and recurrent shortages of both specie and currency because they saw no other alternative for North Carolina's nonindustrial economy.

Having chosen a different approach from most of the other states (although one similar to the central Confederation government), the fiat financiers opposed abandoning that path for the hard money proposals to strengthen the Confederation. Although they supported trade duties to create a uniform tariff system that would help North Carolina, they opposed any other form of congressional taxation. North Carolinians had borne their burdens in order to pay their militia and continental forces; they did not want to assist other states in meeting their unpaid obligations. From these fiat financiers came much of North Carolina's antifederalism and opposition to the Constitution when it was proposed to mend the weaknesses of the Confederation.

Weaknesses in the Confederation government were evident from the beginning. Although it was perhaps the strongest government that could have been formed at the time, and although it had accomplished military, economic, and political miracles in successfully fighting the Revolution and staving off bankruptcy and anarchy, changes clearly were needed. Several amendments were proposed, and North Carolina supported most of them. In 1781, for instance, the General Assembly voted to give Congress the right to levy a duty on foreign goods being imported, but the proposal failed to get the required unanimous approval of the states needed to amend the Articles. After the revolutionary war was concluded, support for the Confederation declined even further. Most states, North Carolina included, failed to deliver the full amounts of taxes levied by Congress. Delegations from the states were weak and underpaid. They frequently arrived late to Congress and sometimes not at all. North Carolina seems to have performed on about the same level as most other states during these critical years of the Confederation.

In September 1786, in response to a call from the Virginia Assembly, delegates from the commercial states gathered at Annapolis to consider the trade of the United States. North Carolina appointed five delegates to the convention, but only Hugh Williamson went, and he arrived just after the delegates had adjourned. From this ill-fated effort, however, came a call for another convention to meet in Philadelphia the second Monday in May 1787, to consider strengthening the national government.

The General Assembly met in Fayetteville in November 1786 and in a joint election by both houses chose Governor Richard Caswell, Alexander Martin, Richard Dobbs Spaight, William R. Davie, and Willie Jones as delegates to Philadelphia. When Jones refused to serve and Governor Caswell decided not to go, the governor, as authorized by the assembly, appointed Hugh Williamson and William Blount to join the delegation.

North Carolina's delegates to the Constitutional Convention were generally capable, relatively young like their colleagues, and men of position and property. All but Martin were from the eastern part of the state and earlier had served in Congress. Blount and Martin participated little in the convention and were not highly regarded by their fellow delegates. Davie and Spaight made modest contributions to the debates and to the finished form of government. Williamson was by far the most involved and the most influential of the North Carolina delegates. He was usually the spokesman for the delegation, made more than seventy speeches, and served on five committees. In the tedious process of forming a new government for the nation, Williamson's participation meant that North Carolina had a part in shaping the finished product. He and the other delegates generally supported the large state position but voted for the compromises that permitted representation by population in the House of Representatives. They unsuccessfully opposed the final form of the executive branch but successfully protected the interests of their state in the three-fifths and slave trade compromises. Essentially, Williamson and the delegation favored giving much more power to the central government than existed under the Confederation, but not so much as to endanger the rights of North Carolina.

In September 1787, the Constitution was completed and ready for signing. Blount, Williamson, and Spaight signed for North Carolina, although they all had some reservations about the nature of the proposed government. Martin and Davie had already returned home; Davie would be one of the leading supporters of ratification. Martin did not take an active part in the procedure. In North Carolina as well as in several other states the struggle for ratification proved difficult, reviving old political animosities between conservatives and radicals as well as between geographical sections.

Even before the Constitution had been completed, a propaganda campaign had begun to rally support for or against the proposed system of government. The conservatives pointed to the disordered and distracted condition of the country and to the need for a stronger central government. Calling themselves Federalists, these men relied on the writings of James Iredell and others to point out the advantages of the Constitution and to demonstrate that the government it proposed would not endanger the liberties of the people or the powers of the states. They also distributed copies of the *Federalist Papers* and other material supporting the Constitution. Generally, the Federalists were from among the upper classes, from the larger towns of the eastern part of the state, and from areas whose economic and cultural interests crossed state lines.

The Antifederalists, as the opponents of the Constitution came to be called, were generally less well-to-do, from the backcountry and the less populated portions of the state, and from areas whose interests were mostly within the boundaries of the state. Some of their most able spokesmen, including Willie Jones, Thomas Person, Timothy Bloodworth, and Lemuel Burkitt, were men of property and position who felt that the new central government would infringe on the rights of individuals and reduce the authority of the state.

The choice of delegates for the legislature that convened in November 1787 and for the convention it authorized to meet in Hillsborough in July 1788 gave rise to bitter campaigning and heated debates. Old and new animosities surfaced as Federalists and Antifederalists fought to gain support. Violence, attacks on character, and even bodily injury accompanied the debates in many areas. (Document 7.2)

Opponents of the Constitution were predominant in both the legislature and the Hillsborough convention. The Federalists were a powerful political bloc, however, and succeeded in getting an item-by-item deliberation of the Constitution, while a secretary of their choosing recorded the debates. By the time the convention met, ten states had already ratified the Constitution, and New York became the eleventh while the convention was in session. Although it was evident that opponents of the Constitution outnumbered its supporters, the Antifederalist leaders recognized that the Confederation was at an end and that a new government was being formed. Willie Jones at this point took a suggestion that Thomas Jefferson had earlier made to James Madison—that some states refuse to ratify until a Bill of Rights and other limitations were appended to the Constitution. Several states had already accompanied their ratification with suggested amendments, but the North Carolina Antifederalists apparently did not feel that merely proposing amendments was a sufficiently strong statement of their position. They were willing to remain outside the new union to assure that their voice would be heard. After much parliamentary maneuvering, the convention determined neither to ratify nor reject the Constitution and proposed amendments that would make it more acceptable to North Carolina. (Document 7.3) The amendments included a declaration of rights virtually identical to the amendments proposed by Virginia upon its ratification and a series of other proposals that would protect the rights of individuals and the states.

After refusing to ratify the Constitution, the members of the Hillsborough convention took action to assure the rest of the nation that they did not want to separate themselves from the newly formed union. Federalists and Antifederalists resolved that whenever Congress should levy a tariff on goods imported into the United States, North Carolina should levy the same tariff and turn the proceeds over to Congress. They also recommended that the General Assembly take measures to redeem the paper currency that was troubling the economy. The decision of the convention neither to ratify nor reject the proposed Declaration of Rights and other amendments and the resolutions on the tariff and paper money were ordered sent to Congress and to the other twelve states. The convention delegates seemed very concerned that although North Carolina would not participate in the formation of the new union, all should know that she was holding back because of concern about the nature of the new government. (Document 7.4)

As soon as the convention was over, the Federalists indicated that they had not abandoned the struggle. Iredell and Davie led the way with the publication and distribution of the debates of the Hillsborough convention. Newspapers and pamphlets were circulated in attempts to persuade the people of North Carolina that they would be better off within the new union. There was an increasing awareness in the backcountry that a stronger central government meant a more stable currency and economy and more protection against the Indians, the Spanish, and the British. Shortly after the adjournment of the Hillsborough convention in August 1788, news had arrived of New York's ratification, and this action solidified the views of many. In elections for the North Carolina Assembly shortly thereafter, many Antifederalist leaders were elected. The call for a new convention was approved, but Willie Jones succeeded in delaying it until November 1789, when the new government would already be functioning. When the new government went into effect in the spring, the choice of George Washington as president inspired confidence and further undercut the Antifederalists.

Hugh Williamson had remained in the Confederation Congress as long as that body existed and then served as North Carolina's unofficial representative to the new government. In New York, he directed his actions toward assuring that North Carolina was not isolated from the other states or linked with Rhode Island in opposition to the Constitution. On 17 September 1788 he had published in the *New York Daily Advertiser* an "Apology" for North Carolina signed "A Republican" in which he presented the state's position in as favorable a light as possible. (Document 7.5) Williamson was appointed as a commissioner to settle the issue of which North Carolina claims would be counted against the state's obligations to the national government. Governor Samuel Johnston of North Carolina, a strong Federalist, directed Williamson to remain in the national capital and worked within the state to encourage the calling of a second convention.

Williamson's prime tasks were to assure that North Carolina was not excluded from any tariff union the United States might form and to press for revisions that would make the Constitution acceptable to his state. At first, Williamson had encountered a belligerent attitude in Congress and even was forced to withdraw from the chamber while votes were being taken. His representation of North Carolina's position must have been successful, however, because soon her interests were being considered and she was being enticed rather than bludgeoned into the new union. (Document 7.6) Admission of products grown and manufactured in North Carolina into the United States free of duty and the entrance of North Carolina vessels into United States ports free of tonnage duties until January 1790 made it clear to North Carolinians that they were being encouraged to join the new nation. At the same time, the threat of eventual exclusion was becoming evident to Federalists and Antifederalists alike.

Williamson also worked to make it clear that North Carolinians were concerned about the absence of a Bill of Rights in the new Constitution and that the other amendments proposed by the Hillsborough convention needed attention as well. Pressure from New York, Virginia, and other states that had already ratified as well as from North Carolina and Rhode Island led Madison to announce that he would consolidate the proposals and recommend them to Congress. The House of Representatives accepted seventeen of his proposals, and Congress submitted twelve to the states for ratification. Williamson, Governor Johnston, and the other North Carolina Federalists were delighted because this action countered Antifederalist claims that promises of a Bill of Rights would be forgotten once the Constitution had been ratified.

By now it was generally accepted that North Carolina would ratify when the delegates gathered for a second convention at Fayetteville on 16 November 1789. Willie Jones, who had led the opposition at Hillsborough, refused to serve. Other Antifederalists changed their votes, and even though some sought to delay action until the Bill of Rights actually became a part of the Constitution, North Carolina ratified on 21 November 1789.

The state government and the central government moved quickly to make North Carolina a full partner with the other states. The legislature chose senators, provided for the election of representatives, and ratified the Bill of Rights amendments. Lands west of the mountains were once more ceded to the United States, and this time the cession was accepted by Congress. President Washington welcomed the state into the Union, and Congress quickly incorporated it into the tariff and tonnage union and into the federal judiciary system. The leading Federalist, James Iredell, was named to the United States Supreme Court. By the time of Washington's tour through the state in 1791, North Carolina was thoroughly a part of the federal union.

North Carolina's ready acceptance of the responsibilities of participation in the new government belied its reluctance in approving the Constitution. Federalist leaders hoped that approval of the tariff, participation in the federal judiciary system, cession of western lands, and other such actions would lead to a favorable settlement of the state's accounts with the national government, a process Hugh Williamson had been coordinating while a member of the Confederation Congress and which he would continue while serving in the House of Representatives. Williamson and his fellow negotiator, Abishai Thomas, succeeded in getting principles of equity established and many of North Carolina's debts that had been paid with the fiat currency counted as a part of the state's claims against the central government. Nevertheless, largely because of poor recordkeeping in the state and unfavorable interpretations of many of North Carolina's claims, when the accounts were tallied it was ruled that North Carolina owed the United States slightly more than $500,000. The immediate costs of joining the federal union proved high for the state, which had been willing to remain outside in order to imprint state and individual rights more firmly into the fabric of the new order.

The role of North Carolina in the formation of the federal union was shaped by a concern for the rights of the state and the individual, a concern that was tempered by an enlightened self-interest that recognized a need for a national government strong enough to function. The interplay of these concerns would lead to an alternating predominance of Federalist and Jeffersonian Republicans during the state's first decade within the new union. Jeffersonianism, with a focus on state and individual rights, would triumph in North Carolina as it did in the remainder of the nation after 1800 and was even more firmly established in North Carolina because of its agrarian economy and a general withdrawal from national affairs. In part because of the state's role in shaping the federal union, state and individual rights (at least for the controlling white male population) were protected within the United States. Not until changing times and circumstances again threatened these principles would North Carolina strive to bring its influence to bear on the nature of the federal union.

DOCUMENT 7.1

North Carolina Declaration of Rights, 1776

A Declaration of Rights made by the Representatives of the Freemen of the State of North Carolina.

I. That all Political Power is vested in, and derived from the People Only.

II. That the People of this State ought to have the sole and exclusive Right of regulating the Internal Government and Police thereof.

III. That no man or Set of men, are intitled to exclusive or separate Emoluments or Privileges from the Community, but in Consideration of Public Services.

IV. That the legislative, executive and supreme judicial Powers of Government, ought to be forever separate and distinct from each other.

V. That all Powers of suspending Laws, or the Execution of Laws, by any Authority, without Consent of the Representatives of the People, is injurious to their Rights and ought not to be exercised.

VI. That Elections of members, to serve as Representatives in General Assembly ought to be free.

VII. That in all Criminal Prosecutions every man has a Right to be informed of the accusation against him, and to confront the Accusers and Witnesses with other Testimony, and shall not be compelled to give Evidence against himself.

VIII. That no Freeman shall be put to answer any Criminal Charge but by Indictment, Presentment or Impeachment.

IX. That no Freeman shall be convicted of any crime, but by the unanimous verdict of a Jury of good and lawful men, in open Court, as heretofore used.

X. That excessive Bail should not be required, nor excessive Fines imposed, nor cruel or unusual Punishments inflicted.

XI. That General Warrants, whereby any Officer or Messenger may be commanded to search suspected Places, without Evidences of the Fact committed, or to seize any Person or Persons not named, whose Offence is not particularly described and supported by Evidence, are dangerous to Liberty, and ought not to be granted.

XII. That no Freeman ought to be taken, imprisoned, or disseized of his Freehold, Liberties, or Privileges, or outlawed or exiled, or in any manner destroyed or deprived of his Life, Liberty, or Property, but by the Law of the Land.

XIII. That every Freeman restrained of his Liberty is intitled to a Remedy to inquire into the Lawfulness thereof, and to remove the same if unlawful, and that such Remedy ought not to be denied or delayed.

xiv. That in all Controversies at Law respecting property the ancient Mode of Trial by Jury is one of the best Securities of the Rights of the People, and ought to remain sacred and Inviolable.

xv. That the Freedom of the Press is one of the great Bulwarks of Liberty, and therefore ought never to be restrained.

xvi. That the People of this State ought not to be taxed, or made subject to the Payment of any Impost or Duty, without the consent of themselves, or their Representatives in General Assembly, freely given.

xvii. That the People have a Right to bear Arms for the Defence of the State, and as Standing Armies in Time of Peace are dangerous to Liberty, they ought not to be kept up, and that the military should be kept under strict Subordination to, and governed by the Civil Power.

xviii. That the People have a Right to assemble together, to consult for their common Good, to instruct their Representatives, and to apply to the Legislature for Redress of Grievances.

xix. That all men have a natural and unalienable right to worship Almighty God, according to the dictates of their own consciences.

xx. That for redress of grievances, and for amending and strengthening the laws, elections ought to be often held.

xxi. That a frequent recurrence to fundamental principles is absolutely necessary to preserve the blessings of liberty.

xxii. That no hereditary emoluments, privileges, or honours, ought to be granted or conferred in this State.

xxiii. That perpetuities and monopolies are contrary to the genius of a free State, and ought not to be allowed.

xxiv. That retrospective laws punishing acts committed before the existence of such laws, and by them only declared criminal, are oppressive, unjust and incompatible with liberty, wherefore no *ex post facto* law ought to be made.

xxv. The property of the soil in a free government being one of the essential rights of the collective body of the people, it is necessary, in order to avoid future disputes that the limits of the State should be ascertained with precision.

William L. Saunders, ed., The Colonial Records of North Carolina, *10 vols. (Raleigh: State of North Carolina, 1886–90), 10:1003–5.*

DOCUMENT 7.2

Kinston Election Riot, 1788

NEWBERN, April 16

Agreeable to the resolve of the General Assembly, the freemen of the county of Dobbs met at the Court House in Kinston, on the last Friday and Saturday in March, in order to elect persons to represent them in Convention at Hillsborough, on the third Monday in July next; accordingly Richard Caswell, James Glasgow, John Herritage, Bryan Whitfield and Ben Sheppard Esqrs. were candidates supposed to be in favor of the Federal Constitution; Jacob Johnston, Morris Westbrook, Isaac Groom, Abraham Baker, and Absalom Price, were supposed to be the opposers of the Federal Constitution;—The whole number of voters were three hundred and seventy-two; at sunset on Saturday the Poll was closed and the sheriff proceeded to call out the tickets; two hundred and eighty two tickets were called out, the hindmost in number on the Poll of the Antifederalists had one hundred and fifty-five votes, the foremost in number of the Federalists had only one hundred and twenty one, and the tickets coming out fast in favor of the Antifederalists, the other party seemed fully convinced they should lose their election and appeared to be much exasperated at the same, especially Col. *B. Sheppard*, who with sundry others cast out many aspersions and very degrading and abusive language to the other candidates, which was not returned by any of the candidates, or any person on their part with so much as one provoking word. At length Col. A. Sheppard went upon the bench where the sheriffs, inspectors, and clerks were attending their business, and swore he would beat one of the inspectors who had been peacably and diligently attending to his business, and having a number of clubs ready prepared, the persons holding the candles were suddenly knocked or pulled down and all the candles in the Court House were instantly put out; many blows with clubs were heard to pass (but it being dark they did the most damage to the Federalists). The Antifederal candidates being unapprized of such a violent assault, and expecting better treatment, from men who would wish to wear the character of gentlemen, were in no posture of defense, and finding their lives in danger, thought it most advisable to retire privately in the dark, but one of them (to wit) Isaac Groom was overtaken in the street, by a party of their men consisting of twelve or fifteen—with clubs, who fell on him and much abused him, in so much that he was driven to the necessity of mounting his horse and riding for his life; the sheriff also related that in the time of the riot on the Court

House he received a blow by a club and that the ticket box was violently taken away.

North Carolina Gazette *(Newbern), 16 April 1788.*

DOCUMENT 7.3

Declaration of Rights Laid before Congress by the Hillsborough Convention, 1788

Resolved, That a declaration of rights, asserting and securing from encroachment the great principles of civil and religious liberty, and the unalienable rights of the people, together with amendments to the most ambiguous and exceptionable parts of the said Constitution of government, ought to be laid before Congress, and the convention of the states that shall or may be called for the purpose of amending the said Constitution, for their consideration, previous to the ratification of the Constitution aforesaid on the part of the State of North Carolina.

DECLARATION OF RIGHTS

1. That there are certain natural rights, of which men, when they form a social compact, cannot deprive or divest their posterity, among which are the enjoyment of life and liberty, with the means of acquiring, possessing, and protecting property, and pursuing and obtaining happiness and safety.

2. That all power is naturally vested in, and consequently derived from, the people; that magistrates, therefore, are their trustees and agents, and at all times amenable to them.

3. That government ought to be instituted for the common benefit, protection, and security, of the people; and that the doctrine of nonresistance against arbitrary power and oppression is absurd, slavish, and destructive to the good and happiness of mankind.

4. That no man or set of men are entitled to exclusive or separate public emoluments or privileges from the community, but in consideration of public services, which not being descendible, neither ought the offices of magistrate, legislator, or judge, or any other public office, to be hereditary.

5. That the legislative, executive, and judiciary powers of government should be separate and distinct, and that the members of the two first may be restrained from oppression by feeling and participating in the public burdens; they should, at fixed periods, be reduced to a private station, return into the mass of the people, and the vacancies be supplied by certain and regular elections, in which all or any part of the former members to be eligible or ineligible, as the rules of the constitution of government and the laws shall direct.

6. That elections of representatives in the legislature ought to be free and frequent, and all men having sufficient evidence of permanent common interest with, and attachment to, the community, ought to have the right of suffrage; and no aid, charge, tax, or fee, can be set, rated, or levied, upon the people without their own consent, or that of their representatives so elected; nor can they be bound by any law to which they have not in like manner assented for the public good.

7. That all power of suspending laws, or the execution of laws, by any authority, without the consent of the representatives of the people in the legislature, is injurious to their rights, and ought not to be exercised.

8. That, in all capital and criminal prosecutions, a man hath a right to demand the cause and nature of his accusation, to be confronted with the accusers and witnesses, to call for evidence, and be allowed counsel in his favor, and a fair and speedy trial by an impartial jury of his vicinage, without whose unanimous consent he cannot be found guilty, (except in the government of the land and naval forces;) nor can he be compelled to give evidence against himself.

9. That no freeman ought to be taken, imprisoned, or disseized of his freehold, liberties, privileges, or franchise, or outlawed or exiled, or in any manner destroyed, or deprived of his life, liberty, or property, but by the law of the land.

10. That every freeman, restrained of his liberty, is entitled to a remedy to inquire into the lawfulness thereof, and to remove the same if unlawful; and that such remedy ought not to be denied or delayed.

11. That, in controversies respecting property, and in suits between man and man, the ancient trial by jury is one of the greatest securities to the rights of the people, and ought to remain sacred and inviolable.

12. That every freeman ought to find a certain remedy, by recourse to the laws, for all injuries and wrongs he may receive in his person, property, or character; he ought to obtain right and justice freely without sale, completely and without denial, promptly and without delay; and that all establishments or regulations contravening these rights are oppressive and unjust.

13. That excessive bail ought not to be required, nor excessive fines imposed, nor cruel and unusual punishments inflicted.

14. That every freeman has a right to be secure from all unreasonable searches and seizures of his person, his papers and property; all warrants, therefore, to search suspected places, or to apprehend any suspected person, without specially naming or describing the place or person, are dangerous, and ought not to be granted.

15. That the people have a right peaceably to assemble together, to consult for the common good, or to instruct their representatives; and that every freeman has a right to petition or apply to the legislature for redress of grievances.

16. That the people have a right to freedom of speech, and of writing and publishing their sentiments; that freedom of the press is one of the greatest bulwarks of liberty, and ought not to be violated.

17. That the people have a right to keep and bear arms; that a well-regulated militia, composed of the body of the people, trained to arms, is the proper, natural, and safe defence of a free state; that standing armies, in time of peace, are dangerous to liberty, and therefore ought to be avoided, as far as the circumstances and protection of the community will admit; and that, in all cases, the military should be under strict subordination to, and governed by, the civil power.

18. That no soldier, in time of peace, ought to be quartered in any house without the consent of the owner, and in time of war, in such manner only as the laws direct.

19. That any person religiously scrupulous of bearing arms ought to be exempted, upon payment of an equivalent to employ another to bear arms in his stead.

20. That religion, or the duty that we owe to our Creator, and the manner of discharging it, can be directed only by reason and conviction, not by force or violence; and therefore all men have an equal, natural, and unalienable right to the free exercise of religion, according to the dictates of conscience; and that no particular religious sect or society ought to be favored or established by law in preference to others.

Jonathan Elliot, Debates in the Several State Conventions on the Adoption of the Federal Constitution, *5 vols. (Philadelphia: J. B. Lippincott & Co., 1859), 4:242–47.*

DOCUMENT 7.4

An Antifederalist View of the Hillsborough Convention

Thomas Person to General John Lamb

Goshen 6th, August 1788

Sir

Your favor of the 19th May last, was only Received the 23rd of July & then open, the third day after our Convention had assembled, whose conclusions on the extraordinary Change of Government proposed for our Acceptance I transmit to you with pleasure, firmly persuaded that our proceedings which were temperate and calm as well as the result of our Political Contest in the cause of Republican Liberty, will be highly pleasing to you & your friends in your state & thro the Union.

It is my decided opinion (& no man is better acquainted with the public mind) that nine tenths of the people of this State are opposed to the adoption of the New System, without very considerable Amendments & I might without incurring any great hazard to err, assure you that very Considerable numbers conceive an idea of a General Government on this extension impracticable & dangerous. But this is a subject on which I feel myself more disposed to concur with better judges than to Dogmatically decide & only state it as a doctrine gaining ground in this part of the World.

Our Convention met at Hillsborough on the day appointed & on the 22nd resolved itself into a committee of the whole house & continued thro discussion from day to day (Sundays excepted) until the 1st Inst on which we called the decisive question when there appeared, for non-concurrence 184 & 83 for adopting—but recommending numbered amendments which were repugnant to their Eloquence & reasoning in debate, a circumstance something surprising, but proves nevertheless that even its advocates think the plan radically bad, by these exertions to render it virtually better.

However I can assure you if the total rejection had been proposed, even in terms of Reprobation, the motion would have succeeded, but we conceived it more decent & moderate to refer it in the mode you will see prefixed to our bill of Rights & Amendments, in confidence that the Union & Prosperity of America may yet be preserved by temperance & wisdom, in defiance of perception & some arts which I suspect tho I cannot enumerate or trace them. There is so little Security left now for obtaining Amendments, especially if your state is adoptive, that it may probably be wise in these states, or the minorities in them, to oppose all representation until Amendments are obtained or to send into the new

Congress only such men of unequivocal characters as will oppose every operation of the system until it is rendered consistent with the preservation of our Liberties too precious to be sacrified to authority, name, ambition, or design. Your proposition for opening a correspondence I embrace with great cheerfulness. It meets with my cordial approbation as well as my Friends. Urged only by motives for the prosperity of the Union and I have only to lament that such measures were not persued earlier, as they would in my opinion have prevented or abated the mischief which the public cause has already received, I take the freedom to request, that you may forward the proceedings of your Convention & anything else you may think conducive to the public weal. Our Assembly will meet the 1st Monday in Nov. next at Fayetteville when we would easily as well as cheerfully receive anything which you might think interesting to the good people of this State. I have the Honor to be with profound respect to you Sir & thro you to the Federal Republican Committee

YR   .   .   .

Thomas Person

Stuart Wright, Historical Sketch of Person County *(Danville, Va.: Womack Press, 1974), pp. 48–49.*

DOCUMENT 7.5

Williamson's "Apology" for North Carolina

From the *New York Daily Advertiser* of September 17 [1788]

The State of North Carolina by not adopting the new constitution is lately become the subject of much criticism and censure. In this instance, having done what is supposed to be wrong, it is hardly admitted that ever she did any thing that was right. We are told that during the war her exertions were trifling—that she had never contributed to the national expence—and that she now refuses to confederate, from a desire to promote the fraudulent tender of paper money. Charges against the unpopular are usually listened to with avidity, but happily none of these charges are well founded, however current they are in circulation. During the whole of the late war, whenever the neighbouring states were invaded, North Carolina was sure to lend them assistance. We have seen in the course of one campaign, six or seven thousand men of the North

Carolina militia in one of the neighbouring states, or on the march to its relief; and she now counts three or four thousand of her citizens who fell a sacrifice in Georgia or South Carolina, to their zeal for the safety of the union. We say nothing of her continental line, nor of those who fell within the state while the enemy pervaded every part of it. Is it probable that such armies were supported without money? Surely not.— But North Carolina has uniformly paid and supported her own militia, though they were in the continental service, and she has furnished provisions to a considerable part of the continental troops in the southern armies. Who have paid for the vast stores that have been consumed by such bodies of armed men? In other states commissioners have been appointed to settle the claims of individuals against the United States, and certificates for many a million have been issued by those commissioners; but no such officers have had occasion to settle accounts in North Carolina, because the state has taken upon itself all the debts that were due to her citizens by the union, except a small balance that was due to her continental line. These debts have amounted to several million. Some part is already paid—there is a large balance remaining. From the public accounts it would *appear*, that in the years 1782 and 1783, North Carolina paid nothing toward the specie requisitions, while South Carolina had paid her quota, but this is a difference only in *appearance*—for the state last mentioned has a specie credit for all supplies furnished the army from the beginning of 1782, while North Carolina that furnished large supplies, stands without any credit, because she has not brought up her accounts. For several years North Carolina has been oppressed by discharging the debts she had assumed to her continental line, and some others of her citizens—but she has lately begun to make effectual payments into the national treasury. On the last year she paid near 30,000 dollars in specie, and we are told she has another large payment ready to be made. It is true that paper money has been issued in that state, and it was made a legal tender, but it is also true, that the general sense of the people is not in favour of fraudulent payments—on the contrary, it is common for juries, in actions of debts, to consider the depreciation and assess damages accordingly. Has the virtue of their citizens done the same thing in other states where bad money is a legal tender? But North Carolina has not adopted the new constitution, and therefore it is alleged that she is antifederal, and an enemy to good government. This is the last charge, and like the rest, it is worse founded than people are apt to believe. It is now generally agreed that the new constitution will admit of some amendments—they have been pointed out. It will also admit of several explanations or alterations, by which it may be rendered, not a better system, but a safer one against the machinations of wicked men. Some of those explanations will doubtless be

made by the general concurrence of the states, because they obviate powers which no man can advocate:—But North Carolina has proposed one
amendment, marked No. 7, which others of the states may not be disposed to make, and yet experience has taught her, as well as Virginia,
that such amendment is extremely proper. The state wishes to see the
alterations made which she pointed out, and for this very reason she
wishes to see the new government commence. If eight states only had
confederated when the Convention of North Carolina sat, perhaps they
ought to have made the ninth, but ten states had confederated, consequently the general system was secure.

The pause that North Carolina has made can occasion no delay in the
necessary measures, and no state, except herself can be injured by it. We
are told, indeed, that she ought to have adopted the new system, that she
so might have assisted in making the proposed amendments; but she
replies that, if other states are seriously disposed to make reasonable and
profitable alterations, they can do it in a short time without her assistance; but if they are dissembling—if they are about to drop the spirit of
accommodation, and to hold by majorities what they have gained by
consent, she is safest where she stands.

State Gazette of North Carolina *(Edenton)*, *6 October 1788*.

DOCUMENT 7.6

Exchange of Addresses between the Independent State of North Carolina and the Newly Elected President of the United States

EDENTON, July 9, [1789]

The following ADDRESS of the Governor and Council of this State, has
lately been presented to General *Washington*, President of the United
States; to which he has been pleased to return the ANSWER thereto sub-
joined.

To his *Excellency* George Washington, *Esquire, President of the United
States*, SIR,

AMIDST the congratulations which surround you from all quarters,
We, the Governor and Council of the state of North Carolina, beg leave
to offer ours, with equal sincerity and fervency with any which can be
presented to you. Though this state be not yet a member of the union

under the new form of government, we look forward with the pleasing hope of its shortly becoming such; and in the mean time consider ourselves bound in a common interest and affection with the other states, waiting only for the happy event of such alterations being proposed as will remove the apprehensions of many of the good citizens of this state, for those liberties for which they have fought and suffered in common with others. This happy event, we doubt not, will be accelerated by your Excellency's appointment to the first office in the union since we are well assured the same greatness of mind, which in all scenes has so eminently characterized your Excellency, will induce you to advise every measure calculated to compose party divisions, and to abate any animosity that may be excited by a mere difference in opinion. Your Excellency will consider (however others may forget) how extremely difficult it is to unite all the people of a great country in one common sentiment upon almost any political subject, much less upon a new form of government materially different from one they have been accustomed to, and will therefore rather be disposed to rejoice that so much has been effected, than regret that more could not all at once be accomplished. We sincerely believe that America is the only country in the world where such a deliberate change of government could take place under any circumstances whatever.

We hope your Excellency will pardon the liberty we take in writing so particularly on this subject; but this state, however it may differ in any political opinions with the other states, cordially joins with them in sentiments of the utmost gratitude and veneration for those distinguished talents and that illustrious virtue, which we feel a pride in saying we believe, under God, have been the principal means of preserving the liberty and procuring the independence of your country. We cannot help considering you, Sir, in some measure, as the father of it, and hope to experience the good effects of that confidence you so justly have acquired, in an abatement of the party spirit which so much endangers a union on which the safety and happiness of America can alone be founded. May that union, at a short distance of time, be as perfect and more safe than ever! And in the mean while, may the state of North Carolina be considered, as it truly deserves to be, attached with equal warmth with any state in the union, to the true interest, prosperity, and glory of America, differing only in some particulars in opinion as to the means of promoting them!   SAMUEL JOHNSTON
                                          By order and on behalf of the Council
                                          JAMES IREDELL, President
                                          By order,
                                          Wm. JOHNSTON DAWSON
                                          Clerk Council

May 10, 1789

To the GOVERNOR and COUNCIL of the state of North Carolina
Gentlemen,
    It is scarcely possible for an address to have given me greater pleasure
than that which I have just received from you: because I consider it not
only demonstrative of your approbation of my conduct in accepting the
first office in the union, but also indicative of the good dispositions of
the citizens of your state towards their sister states, and of the probability
of their speedily acceding to the new general government.
    In justification of the opinion which you are pleased to express of
my readiness "to advise every measure calculated to compose party divisions, and to abate any animosity that may be excited by mere difference
of opinion," I take the liberty of referring you to the sentiments communicated by me to the two Houses of Congress. On this occasion, I am
likewise happy in being able to add the strongest assurances, that I entertain a well grounded expectation that nothing will be wanting on the
part of the different branches of the general government to render the
union perfect, and more safe than ever it has been. A difference of opinion on political points is not to be imputed to freemen as a fault; since it
is to be presumed that they are all actuated by an equally laudable and
sacred regard for the liberties of their country. If the mind is so formed in
different persons as to consider the same object to be somewhat different
in its nature and consequences, as it happens to be placed in different
points of view, and if the eldest, the ablest, and the most virtuous statesmen have often differed in judgment as to the best forms of government—we ought, indeed, rather to rejoice that so much has been effected, than to regret that more could not all at once be accomplished.
    Gratified by the favorable sentiments which are evidenced in your ad-
dress to me, and impressed with an idea that the citizens of your state
are sincerely attached to the interest, the prosperity, and the glory of
America, I most earnestly implore the divine benediction and guidance in
the councils which are shortly to be taken by their Delegates on a subject
of the most momentous consequence, I mean the political relation which
is to subsist hereafter, between the state of North Carolina, and the states
now in union under the new general government.
                            G. WASHINGTON
New-York, June 19, 1789.

State Gazette of North Carolina *(Edenton), 9 July 1789.*

SUGGESTED READINGS

Elliot, Jonathan. *Debates in the Several State Conventions on the Adoption of the Federal Constitution.* 5 vols. Philadelphia: J. B. Lippincott & Co., 1859.

Ferguson, E. James. *The Power of the Purse: A History of American Public Finance, 1776–1790.* Chapel Hill: University of North Carolina Press, 1961.

Gilpatrick, D. H. "Contemporary Opinion of Hugh Williamson." *North Carolina Historical Review* 17 (1940):26–36.

Lefler, Hugh T., ed. *A Plea for Federal Union: North Carolina, 1788.* Charlottesville: Tracy W. McGregor Library, University of Virginia, 1947.

Morgan, David T., and Schmidt, William J. *North Carolinians in the Continental Congress.* Winston-Salem: John F. Blair, 1976.

Morrill, James R. *The Practice and Politics of Fiat Finance: North Carolina in the Confederation, 1783–1789.* Chapel Hill: University of North Carolina Press, 1969.

Morris, Francis G., and Morris, Phyllis M. "Economic Conditions in North Carolina about 1780, Parts I–II." *North Carolina Historical Review* 16 (1939):107–33, 296–327.

Newsome, Albert Ray. "North Carolina's Ratification of the Federal Constitution." *North Carolina Historical Review* 17 (1940):287–301.

Pool, William C. "An Economic Interpretation of the Ratification of the Federal Constitution in North Carolina." *North Carolina Historical Review* 27 (1950):119–41, 289–313, 437–61.

Trenholme, Louise Irby. *Ratification of the Federal Constitution in North Carolina.* New York: Columbia University Press, 1932.

Zornow, William F. "North Carolina Tariff Practices, 1775–1789." *North Carolina Historical Review* 32 (1955):151–64.

CHAPTER 8

An Agrarian and Evangelical Culture
Robert M. Calhoon

Old East Building, the University of North Carolina at Chapel Hill, drawing by John Pettigrew, 1797 (Courtesy of the Division of Archives and History, Raleigh, N.C.)

North Carolina in the early nineteenth century appeared to its most articulate critics—as it has to its most influential twentieth-century historians—to be the "Rip Van Winkle state," a lethargic, pastoral, culturally blighted society. Certainly the political hegemony of conservative eastern planters, the torpid quality of life in towns and cities, the undeveloped transportation facilities, the lack of educational opportunities, the migration to the West of two hundred thousand of the state's most energetic people, and, overshadowing all else, slavery and racism profoundly inhibited social change and economic growth. The impact of these conditions on human behavior and upon the thoughts, aspirations, and desires of individuals, however, remains a little-explored frontier of historical understanding for students of the North Carolina past.

Contemporaries were certain that there was a connection between the social environment and the public character of their society. The Reverend Henry Pattillo saw pious, orderly family life as a way of creating an environment conducive to public and private virtue. (Document 8.1) Joseph Caldwell, president of the University of North Carolina, bemoaned the failure of county justices to locate county seats where they would encourage social virtue. Such towns, he recommended, should be established on convenient, healthful, and pleasant sites so that people visiting from the surrounding countryside would return home with their various business in courts and stores finished and their public spirit gratified by the "scene of general activity and prosperity." In actuality, Caldwell lamented, county seats were the scenes of "wildness and rudeness, intemperance, ferocity, gaming, licentiousness, and malacious litigation." Caldwell's jeremiad is intriguing in that it depicts a society that was anything but stagnant or moribund. Even Caldwell's moralistic and idealistic terms—"rude, intemperate, licentious"—described a society teeming with human activity—sensuous, gratifying, complex, authentic, and worthy of dispassionate analysis. Other ministers were concerned about these cultural perils. (Document 8.2) What Caldwell was talking about in these remarks was the culture of his own society. *Culture* connotes much more than public taste and artistic expression; it is the unifying spirit of a society, the inhibitions placed on its members, the constraints people most readily and widely accept, the communal impulses and sense of a shared tradition that coercively or voluntarily bind groups and individuals into a social fabric. Culture, in short, expresses accepted standards of behavior.

The early years of the University of North Carolina, chartered in 1789, were torn with controversy over the nature of a good society and the values the state and its university ought to inculcate among the people. In 1795, two early trustees and builders of the nation's first state university, William R. Davie and Reverend Samuel E. McCorkle, proposed rival curricula and differed sharply on the nature of education. McCorkle stressed the classics and a strict student regimen of piety, prayer, and religious instruction, whereas Davie placed the classics on an equal footing with the sciences, history, and moral philosophy and responded tartly to clerical criticisms that the university was "a very dissipated and debauched place" that "nothing . . . goes well that these *men of God* have not had some hand in." McCorkle proposed not only a curriculum but a full-scale system of governance and discipline for the university. Adopted by the trustees in February 1795, these rules specified a reading knowledge of Latin and mastery of Greek grammar for admission and required an additional year of Latin and two of Greek for graduation. Although McCorkle included mathematics, science, history, and moral philosophy, these subjects remained subordinate to the classics and to religious instruction in the life of the school. Another father recommended a similar program of moral self-improvement for his daughter. (Document 8.3) Mandatory morning prayer, divine service on the Sabbath, and Sunday evening examinations on the general principles of religion and morality; prohibitions on gambling, drinking, association with "evil company"; and a rigid schedule of recitation, lecture, and study, leaving only the hour following breakfast for amusement all promoted the values of discipline, subordination, and reverence.

Though he probably voted to adopt McCorkle's rules, Davie soon concluded that they were gravely deficient, and in December 1795 he persuaded the trustees to adopt a broader and more flexible course of study. He added French to the foreign languages taught at the university, made foreign language study optional at the request of a student's parents, and created a degree in science with no foreign language requirement for admission or graduation. Mastery of the English language, he emphasized, was the primary objective, and the other languages were but auxiliaries. Although McCorkle soon thereafter left Chapel Hill, Davie's ambitious plans never went into effect and the presidency of Joseph Caldwell (1804–35) confirmed the classical and Presbyterian character of the institution.

The clash between Davie and McCorkle involved more than opposing egos or differences over curriculum; the two men represented different understandings of republicanism—the social and political creed spawned by the American Revolution, which rejected any hereditary claim to office or eminence and held that the exercise of power ought to be regulated by representative bodies acting in the public interest. Davie was a typical "young man of the Revolution"—he was twenty-one years old and a graduate of Princeton when independence was declared and was thrust by the war into a series of important military and civilian offices; in the 1780s he emerged as a political leader, lawyer, and planter, and he was an important delegate to the Constitutional Convention and an advocate of ratification. In Davie's view, the country desperately needed political and social leaders steeped in Enlightenment philosophy, eloquent and persuasive in the use of language, and imbued with lofty, nationalist ambitions. The first "professorship" in his plan for the university was to teach "moral and political philosophy and history" through the study of constitutionalism, national law, Enlightenment, legal and social theory (Paley, Montesquieu, Vattel), and the skeptical and critical historical writing of Hume and Priestley. McCorkle, also a Princeton graduate, saw the training of leaders for society as a moral enterprise and the destiny of the nation a spiritual mission. Reason, scientific curiosity, and the utilitarian value of knowledge were meaningful for McCorkle because they enhanced man's understanding of the Creator.

The two had very different assumptions about the relationship of a university to society. Since the people are the source of law in a free government, Davie expected them to receive an education that would enable them to formulate the law within the existing constitutional framework. Davie believed that his curriculum would produce "useful and respectable members of society." McCorkle, on the other hand, wanted to instill into students a sense of awe and exhilaration at being part of a chosen people. All history, McCorkle declared, proved that the United States was a specially favored nation—singled out by God for blessings and responsibilities as no other people had been since the Old Testament Israelites. Because churches that shared this sense of God's will were the most influential and effective institutions in the state and because articulate laymen and clergy—especially Presbyterians—were among the most assertive and confident of North Carolina's social and political leaders, McCorkle believed that the university should become a repository of and a rallying point for Protestant idealism.

The dispute was emblematic of the great transformation in American culture that began with the Revolution and was completed by the age of Jackson. Davie epitomized the old order of the Revolution in which America's destiny was to preserve and enhance traditions of liberty and virtue inherited from Britain, from the Reformation, and from classical antiquity. McCorkle represented the conviction that this heritage was the gift of God, which was available to Americans only as they humbled themselves before the throne of grace. By conversion and Christian sanctification Americans would become new men and women—free, capable, and assertive.

These visions did not wash unimpeded across the social landscape of North Carolina during the two generations following independence. They swirled around powerful political and social realities, foremost among them the rise of a new class of commercial farmers and professional men who owned slaves, were ambitious to modernize agriculture, finance, and transportation, and reached for opportunities in places beyond their own localities. Although historians have only begun to explore the values and cultural influence of these people in detail, two early studies (one by Bennett H. Wall on the Pettigrew family and the other by Edward W. Phifer on slavery in Burke County) provide a framework for examination of agrarian culture and social development.

Between 1779 and his death in 1807, the Reverend Charles Pettigrew of Edenton, an Episcopalian clergyman, purchased land and developed two plantations in Tyrrell and Washington counties. Over the next three decades his son, Ebenezer, made the Pettigrew plantations among the most efficient and productive in the state. The senior Pettigrew purchased land with money belonging to his first wife, Mary Blount. With the aid of several parishioners who were land speculators, he bought and drained swampland and planted corn and rice. He devised an elaborate system of ditches and floodgates, and the reclaimed land proved to be enormously fertile. As his landholdings increased, lumber became a principal product of the estate. His chief difficulty was lack of access to market. He shipped corn and rice by flatboat to Edenton but was at the mercy of merchants and shippers, who charged exorbitant rates to transport crops to Baltimore and New York. The cornerstone of their work as planters was the Pettigrews' diligent supervision of their slaves. Reverend Pettigrew used white overseers sparingly. The slaves at his Lake Phelps plantation, he discovered with relief, usually worked better by themselves with a little direction than they did under the direction of overseers. On the Pettigrew plantations a little direction was, in fact, an elaborate system of rewards and penalties. His slaves had their own garden plots, earned credit at the plantation store, and were encouraged to hunt for game during the winter. Ebenezer's son, William S. Pettigrew (born in 1818), who became an active Episcopal priest and in the 1850s spent long periods away from the plantation, relied entirely on black overseers with whom he corresponded regularly and whose work he checked closely on his return to the plantation. At the heart of the family creed was an understanding of slavery as a mixture of loyalties, obligations, and deep moral antagonism. (Document 8.4) Charles Pettigrew regretted the necessary conjunction of slavery and tyranny, the requisite exercise of authority to produce an obedient and useful slave.

Slavery in Burke County in the foothills of the Appalachians was as integral an element in the social order as it was on the Pettigrew plantations. In 1790, 7 percent of the county's population was slave, and by 1830 the figure had risen to 14 percent. Though slaves did not make up a critical portion of the labor force, the institution was an important economic stimulus. Burke County had no planter class, but the 38 percent of landowners who owned slaves invariably also owned the best agricultural land—alluvial valleys in the rolling foothills of the county. Most of these landowners were professional men—preachers, merchants, bankers, teachers, lawyers—for whom land- and slaveowning and agriculture were speculative ventures that accelerated their upward social mobility. The market value of slaves rose sharply in the region throughout the antebellum period, and though slaveowners tried to avoid splitting families, the settlement of estates frequently necessitated doing so. As in the lowcountry, slavery in western North Carolina buttressed the position of the newly emergent elite of enterprising landowners.

In an uncertain and risky world, men desperately needed a visible moral code that defined them to others and gave them a sense of identity. Looking back on raising his children in Haywood County in the early nineteenth century, Bazil Edminston, a western North Carolina landowner and member of a powerful family, attempted to set appropriate examples of industry, truth, honesty, justice, and civility for his children. Concluding that he had succeeded in his task, Edminston declared that "every test now has to stand on its own bottom." For better or worse, his children's lives were a compound of those values and their own volition.

Between 1827 and 1829, William S. Pettigrew's teacher prescribed handwriting exercises using moral maxims. How seriously Pettigrew regarded the content of these lessons is hard to judge, although his handwriting certainly improved steadily during this period. Considering his subsequent reputation for integrity and ability as a planter and Episcopal priest, these lessons at least indicate the dutiful and watchful milieu in which he was raised. Forty-three—nearly all—of the maxims in his copybooks dealt with questions of character, motivation, and discipline. Of these, the largest number simply prescribe behavior modification: "Diligence is industry and constant application in work," "Love the society of your parents and receive good advice," and "Love your studies."

These injunctions to self-control, to mastery of one's own social space, to wariness about the moral pitfalls of the world, and yet to regard the world as morally ordered and comprehensible express well the ethos of the planter and well-to-do farmer. One North Carolina political leader who exemplified those virtues was Senator Nathaniel Macon (1757–1837), a rigid agrarian who, in contrast to commercial farmers like the Pettigrews and upwardly mobile townsfolk like the slaveowners in Burke County, deeply distrusted the role of money, influence, commercialism, and economic development in politics. Macon believed that a rural, democratic society—supported unfortunately but necessarily by slavery—was the purest and freest state of human existence. In his popular contemporary biography of Macon, published in 1840, Edward R. Cotton emphasized that happiness and success depended on the individual's maintaining a delicate balance between desire and duty and that the life of the planter was peculiarly suited to the proper blend of self-assertion and self-control.

In an agrarian culture, members of aggressive and articulate local elites therefore occupied strategic positions from which to advocate and exemplify social and personal values; in doing so, they drew on several common pools of experience and understanding—republicanism, economic improvement, local folkways, and slave management. They made a new culture from materials at hand; though they were an elite, or perhaps more precisely a cluster of local elites, and had limited sympathy for the plight of the poorest and most exploited of their contemporaries, these arbiters of culture espoused views widely emulated throughout the middle ranks of the social order. (Document 8.5)

In contrast, a major source of ideas and influences on behavior was the religious movement of evangelical Protestantism, which arose from the lowest ranks of society and penetrated upward. Evangelicalism in the South arose, first, from the migration during the last half of the eighteenth century into the piedmont of thousands of children of the first Great Awakening and, second, from a growing sense of psychological dislocation and spiritual crisis among people in isolated rural areas throughout the region, which burst the bounds of conventional worship in the Great Revival of 1800–1803. The Reverend Shubal Stearnes in 1755 led a band of fifteen Separate Baptists from Connecticut to a new home in Sandy Creek in present-day Randolph County. A follower of Isaac Backus, the New England leader who made the Separate Baptists a major religious force in that region during the generation following the first Great Awakening, Stearnes provided preaching and a personality that filled a vacuum of leadership and culture, and in three years the membership of the Sandy Creek Church grew from 16 to 606. By 1772, his followers had established forty-two Separate Baptist congregations in the southern backcountry. One of Stearnes's many converts, who had come out of curiosity to hear the famous preacher, reported that Stearnes's penetrating gaze was inescapable and that his preaching produced such mental anxiety that the listener fell to the ground. Another man, who came to mock and disrupt a creekside baptismal service, found that Stearnes's enchanting voice and his penetrating gaze induced "trembling" and then "dread and anxiety," which did not abate until he had professed his faith in Christ.

It was this sense of the barrenness of their own lives and the galvanizing personal embodiment of the Spirit by preachers and lay people, whose lives had been made whole and vibrant by evangelical conversion, that was at the core of southern religious life in the late eighteenth and early nineteenth centuries. Methodist circuit riders fanned out systematically over the region after 1784 and brought evangelical worship to isolated settlements on a regular basis. Presbyterians adopted revivalism as a means of recruiting new members and fusing congregations together with a new sense of rapturous joy. Baptists, who first brought revivalism to North Carolina, made their highly autonomous congregations into joyful, supportive communities.

Southern evangelicalism was, therefore, an intense form of social bonding. With its Christocentric theology and heightened sense of human awareness, evangelicalism taught converts that they had direct access to the throne of grace, to the ear of the Savior. An offshoot group of Methodists in Virginia and North Carolina, led by the Reverend James O'Kelly and calling themselves "O'Kellians" or "Republican Methodists," made this posture the basis of their belief and policy. They insisted that their denominational organization had no power whatsoever over individual clergy and laity. O'Kelly not only insisted on radical Christian freedom for himself and his followers; he denounced the institution of slavery in one of the most uncompromising abolitionist tracts ever written in the South. (Document 8.6) In this regard O'Kelly was no more radical than his former colleagues among southern Methodist circuit riders who tirelessly and courageously barred unrepentant slaveowners from the communion table for a quarter century after the founding of the American Methodist church in 1784. Not until 1819 did the Methodists succumb to lay pressure in the South and cease to make slaveowning a barrier to church membership.

Evangelicalism emerged in the late eighteenth century as a revolt by plain folk against the haughty, "careless," hedonistic style of aristocratic gentlemen. It was, writes Donald G. Mathews in *Religion in the Old South*, "a volatile social movement providing a value system to raise converts in their own esteem, give them confidence in themselves and their comrades, and create the moral courage to reject as authoritative for themselves the life-style and values of traditional elites." An excellent illustration of how "volatile" this process could become is the revival that swept North Carolina in 1801, when thousands of people—young and old, men and women, slaves and whites of all economic conditions—joined in spontaneous conversion experiences. Although the record is obscure on the racial composition of these ceremonies, Scott Strickland has discovered strong circumstantial evidence that these services placed "blacks and whites, standing side by side, shaking hands, breaking into tears over one another's religious experiences, singing together, walking hand in hand to baptism, relating spontaneously as equals in the Christian communities." Both Strickland and Thomas C. Parramore have emphasized the intensity of wild rumors of imminent black insurrection that swept this region of North Carolina only a year later. The breaching of established racial barriers in the revival heightened tensions between blacks and whites in a complex way. Certainly the revivals gave the slaves unprecedented opportunities to gather and converse excitedly in public. And the religious message of liberation proclaimed by the revivals bore striking resemblance to black testimony during the 1802 scare that slaves wanted "the breath of liberty as free for us as for themselves."

Evangelical belief and practice permeated North Carolina society by the 1820s. Churches, even more than the court system or political parties, became critical institutions bringing people together, establishing norms of conduct, providing arenas for leadership and outlets for feeling. By insisting on abasement and humility, evangelical theology showed people that their anxieties and distresses were internal and personal and that the struggle to come to terms with one's own nature and character would be won through the intervention of Christian grace. (Document 8.7) Its very momentum and relevance meant that evangelicalism would absorb and partake of elements of the society it sought to transform. The early antislavery witness of James O'Kelly and the Methodist itinerants and the biracial character of the Great Revival gave way to accommodation with slavery. The failure of the revivals to usher in a new era of goodness and harmony paved the way for bitter quarrels in the 1820s and 1830s over the structure and function of evangelical churches. Revivals became routine matters. As southern evangelicals grew more conscious of their sectional loyalties, the sense of mission that in the eighteenth century had inspired all Protestants was vitiated. Agrarianism and evangelicalism were, therefore, not unchanging, immutable forces; but during the formative period in the making of North Carolina and southern society, from the Revolution to the Civil War, these traditions gave coherence and form to a culture undergoing rapid and far-reaching changes.

DOCUMENT 8.1

The Farmer as a Republican Father

To Heads of Families
My Friends and Brethren,
    I consider the station in which Providence has placed you, as one of the most important in life. I consider you as either a husband, a father, a master; or as all these in one; and he who acts these several parts well, *hath purchased to himself a good degree*, and one of the most useful members of civil society. A family is a little community within itself; of which smaller bodies, states and kingdoms are composed. Out of your families are to arise the future citizens of these States. *Cast back your eyes to the American revolution.* Never forget the wonders God hath wrought for your country. The acknowledged *independence of America*, is an event that engages the eager attention of all *Christendom*. . . .
    But my dear friends, though I earnestly wish you that moderate competency, unincumbered with riches, which has been the aim of the wise and virtuous in all ages; yet I am still more felicitous respecting your happiness as candidates for eternity, than as citizens of *America*. You are the inhabitants of the happiest country under heaven, could you refuse the temptation of riches; and avoid debts and foreign frippery—but are you securing a *better country, that is an heavenly?* Come, my beloved countrymen; a friend of yours is come to enquire after your spiritual health, and religious prosperity; and you must allow him to be as particular as the prophet of old. . . .
    1. *Is it well with thyself?* Thou hast a dwelling in this land of liberty; but hast thou secured a residence in *the house not made with hands?* Thou ownest a farm within these states, but art thou not like the sons of *Reuben and Gad*, so captivated with the balsam groves of *Gilead*, the pools of *Hesbbon*, and the rich pastures of *Basban*, that thou hast no lot in the promised land beyond the flood? . . . *To be a man of the world*, can no more qualify us for the heavenly state, than spending our youth at the plough could qualify us to teach law, physic or divinity. Until you can prove, then, That to pay your public and private debts, is *rendering to God the glory due unto his name*—That to cultivate your field is to *work out your own salvation*—That to fill your barns with plenty, is to *lay up treasure in heaven*—That to love your country, family, friends and neighbours, is *to love the Lord with all your heart* . . . you must never believe that the man of the world is the man of God. . . .
    2. *Is it well with thy wife?* She is the woman of thy choice whom thou

hast singled out from all the daughters of thy people. She preferred thee
to all others; forsook her natural relations for thy sake; put herself under
thy care and protection; and entered with thee the nearest and dearest
relation upon earth. She is the painful mother and careful nurse of thy
children. Is it thy constant endeavour to promote her happiness? . . . My
sister; my daughter; how is it with thee? . . .

3. *Is it well with your children?* If you are living without God in the
world, what becomes of them? If worldly pursuits and conversation be
all they see and hear about their father's house, they will naturally conclude, that they were made for no other purpose but to laugh and play
while they are children; and to make crops and clothes when they are
men and women. . . .

4. *Is it well with your servants?* I must flatter myself, that my country
increase in humanity. The slaves you own, generally grew up with yourselves, or have been raised with your children. You feel, then, a kind of
brotherly or paternal affection for them. They have so often fed from
your hand; played at your door, and shown such a willingness to please
and oblige you, that you consider them as your *humble friends,* and
perhaps the best you have. . . . *Wait, I say, upon the Lord, and he shall
give thee the desires of thine heart. And though it tarry long, yet wait for
it.* Thou you sow in tears and disappointment, you may yet reap in joyful
harvest: and you and your household meet at last with joy unspeakable
before your judge and Saviour; and you be able to say, *Here, Lord, I am,
and the family thou gavest me.* Amen.

Henry Pattillo, The Plain Planter's Family Assistant . . . *(Wilmington:
James Adams, 1787), pp. 7, 10–15, 18–25, 27–28.*

DOCUMENT 8.2

Agrarian Life and Moral Discipline

My Dear Sons,—Life is precarious, and it is not likely that I shall remain
long with you. . . . My sons, I feel myself greatly interested in the turn
you may take. Could I stay but long enough to guard you from the rocks
and shoals which are so numerous, and so dangerous to youth, as just
launching out into the troubled ocean of this life; and more especially,
could I be so happy, as with success to direct your feet into the paths of

virtue, religion and happiness, with a rational hope that you would persevere therein, the bed of earth would be rendered comparatively soft, easy and comfortable. . . .

Never . . . be too self-confident, but rather jealous over your own heart; for such is the imperfection of human nature, that men are often deceived in themselves, while exposed to the eye of the world, in a very different light from that in which they are accustomed to view themselves.

Let me then entreat you to let simple honesty, and undisguised truth characterize your transactions, both civil and social, and particularly in your matters of trade and traffic. Honesty is, and will ever be found, the best policy.

There is nothing more disgraceful to a man, than a disposition to deviate from the simplicity of truth, either by misrepresentation, prevarications, or a passion for idle story-telling, whereby some men who might otherwise have been respectable, have rendered themselves very ridiculous, and even contemptible. In respect to these things, I wish you never to be off your guard.

The world is envious and ill-natured. I have found it so, particularly since I became possessed of property. To possess more than some others, is a crime sufficient to make the naturally envious and splenetic one's enemies. From a general notion that wealth gives power and influence, those who may be below you in this respect, will always view you with a jealous eye, and be ever ready to misconstrue your best actions. When you see this observation verified, let it not excite your resentment, but endeavour to overcome *this evil with good*; at the same time maintain your firmness, in the exercise of religion, and those noble and manly virtues which I have mentioned. I have more than once seen such a conduct make an enemy ashamed of himself, and in some instances even convert him into a friend. . . .

The character of a christian and a gentleman are very consistent. The latter is highly improved by the softening and meliorating influence of the former. I wish you, my sons, to unite them, that you may be in favour with both God and man.

To this end cultivate the softer tempers, in the exercise of resolution and firmness. Beware of giving up the reins to passion; unbridled passion will grow daily more and more turbulent, and at last spurn all restraint from the rules of decency and good breeding. This renders a man a truly pitiable object. To manage *negroes* without the exercise of too much passion, is next to an impossibility, after our strongest endeavours to the contrary; I have found it so. I would therefore put you on your guard, lest their provocations should on some occasions transport you beyond the limits of decency and christian morality.

Let this consideration plead in their favour, and at all times mitigate your resentments. They are slaves for life. They are not stimulated to care and industry as white people are, who labor for themselves. They do not feel themselves *interested* in what they do, for arbitrary masters and mistresses; and their education is not such as can be expected to inspire them with sentiments of honor and gratitude. We may justly expect rather that an oppressive sense of their condition would naturally have a tendency to blunt all the finer feelings of nature, and render them callous to the ideas of honor and even honesty.

Rev. Charles Pettigrew, Last Advice of the Reverend Charles Pettigrew to His Sons *(N.p., 1797), pp. 3, 5–6, 9–10.*

DOCUMENT 8.3

Moral Self-Improvement as Preparation for Life

Pittsborough—February 10th 1824
My Dearest Child—
    My promised letter to you should have been written long ago, if I had not been so constantly engaged as to be unable to take the time. . . .
    You tell your Mother that you are reading European History. That is very proper and I offer you my thanks and my congratulations for so useful and so agreeable an appropriation of your time. Our lives are only happy in proportion as they [are] employed in acquiring knowledge and practicing virtues. But let me add, that occasional reading of a single volume or a defective treatise upon one subject and then of another is of very little value. System and Diligence are essential to the acquisition of correct or extensive knowledge and that alone is of value. When you read therefore, read, in retirement, well selected books and devote all your thoughts to them; endeavour to impress important events upon your memory and to apply the moral consideration arising out of them, by reflection, to your own heart and improvement. But I would have you remember one Book above all the rest. The Book of Life,—which I trust you read daily and devoutly. The Bible is the fountain of Truth and the revealed will of God to man: In every line it contains wholesome instruction, reproof or comfort and is worthy of being studied and known of all men. But it is the surest school for those who desire to cultivate good feelings towards God and man, to learn our true nature and destiny and

to live in meekness and humility. There are [to be found] all proper tempers and dispositions for a fine woman and nothing would give me more pain than to see you indifferent to them. I never knew a woman that professed Infidelity or was careless about Religion who duly felt the weight of any duty or was useful in any of the relations of life or was kind in her disposition or was happy. If my opinion be entitled to any influence with you, you will not neglect your religious duties: Remember your prayers and your Bible and fail not daily to seek for instruction in the former and to acknowledge your dependence in the latter—as you have been accustomed to observe in your excellent Mother. . . .

Write often to your Mama and brother and sisters—You will shew your affectionate remembrance of them by doing so, besides affording the means of improvement to yourself and the children. I need not say, that I shall expect letters myself. Offer my kind regards to all our relations; and receive, my Child, the assurances of the tender affections of your Father and Friend.

Thomas Ruffin.

Thomas Ruffin to Catherine Ruffin, 10 February 1824, J. G. de Roulhac Hamilton, ed., The Papers of Thomas Ruffin, *4 vols. (Raleigh: North Carolina Historical Commission, 1918–20), 1:289–91.*

DOCUMENT 8.4

Slavery and Moral Virtue

A wise Legislature will always consider the character, condition, and feeling, of those to be legislated for. In a government and people like ours, this is indispensable. The question now under debate [admission of Missouri as a slave state] demands this consideration. To a part of the United States, and that part which supports the amendment, it cannot be important, except as it is made so by the circumstances of the times. In all questions like the present in the United States, the strong may yield without disgrace even in their own opinion; the weak, cannot; hence, the propriety of not attempting to impose this new condition on the people of Missouri. . . . The Senate was intended by the long time for which its members are elected, to check every improper direction of the public mind. It is its duty to do so; and never was there a more proper occasion than the present. The character of the present excitement is such, that no man can foresee what consequences may grow out of it.

But why depart from the good old way, which has kept us in quiet, peace, and harmony—every one living under his own vine and fig tree, and none to make him afraid? Why leave the road of experience, which has satisfied all, and made all happy, to take this new way, of which we have no experience? The way leads to universal emancipation, of which we have no experience. . . .

It is a fact, that the people who move from the non-slaveholding to the slaveholding states, when they become slaveholders by purchase or marriage, expect more labor from them than those do who are brought up among them. . . . The old ones are better taken care of than any poor in the world, and treated with decent respect by all their white acquaintances. I sincerely wish that he, and the gentleman from Pennsylvania . . . would go home with me, or some other Southern member, and witness the meeting between the slaves and the owner, and see the glad faces and the hearty shaking of hands. . . .

The owner can make more free in conversation with his slave, and be more easy in his company, than the rich man, where there is no slave, with the white hireling who drives his carriage. He has no expectation that the slave will, for that free and easy conversation, expect to call him fellow-citizen or act improperly.

Speech to the Senate by Nathaniel Macon, 20 January 1820, Annals of the Congress of the United States . . . Sixteenth Congress, First Session (Washington, D.C.: Gales and Seaton, 1855), pp. 222, 225–26.

DOCUMENT 8.5

Self-Consciousness and Spirituality as Preparation for Life

The Church at Powell's Point has had an addition of 102 members in the last 12 months, and others have had considerable additions. . . . We are encouraged this year to address you on the nature, fruits and evidences of christian experience. And we need not state to you that both conversation and writing, have often been rendered vague, for want of fixing properly the sense of the terms used to express the subject discoursed on. We have reason to fear that some, when talking of christian experience, use the term in so indistinct a manner as to render it scarcely intelligible, while others affix to it such ideas as render it undeserving of the name. . . .

Experience, in its general acceptation, conveys the idea of knowledge obtained by experiment. Christian experience is that religious knowledge which is acquired by any exercise, employment, or suffering either of body or mind. Knowledge consisting in a train of tho'ts formed entirely by the efforts of reason, is called speculation: So far as this is confirmed by experiment or practical proof, it is experience. The design of religion is not only to furnish the understandings of men with a regular system of truth, but also to effect the heart, and to quiet the mind; hence, the objects which it exhibits cannot fail to be grand and important. The great author of our existence has revealed to us, so much of his works of creation, of providence, and grace, together with the original, present, and future state of man, that nothing but the most wilful inattention can prevent us from discovering the necessity, the nature, the author, the means, and the end of salvation. . . .

Are we elevated or depressed, let us be careful to know the reason, and if we can assign no reason, such enquiry may lead us to correct our levity or to dissipate our melancholy. In a dreary moment, we may be led to adapt the language of the Psalmist, and say, "*Why art thou cast down O my soul! and why art thou disquieted within me? Hope thou in God, for I shall yet praise him for the help of his countenance.*" To know the origin of the various affections of the mind, and to carefully mark the dangers to which we are incident thereby, is truly desirable, because we thereby are enabled to form a proper idea of our character, and so become acquainted with what ought to be the pursuit of all, viz, a knowledge of ourselves. . . .

Therefore use your experience to put on your guard in an hour of temptation, to guide you in time of difficulty, and to fortify your minds under the pressure of affliction: like David, recollect the time and the place when, and where the Lord blessed you, that you may repose a cheerful confidence in him for the future.

Rev. Jeremiah Ethridge, "Circular Letter," Minutes of the North Carolina Chowan Baptist Association . . . (Petersburg, Va.: Pescud, 1823), pp. 6–7, 9, 10.

DOCUMENT 8.6

Slavery and Sin

A slave is looked upon as the property of the master, who is his own legislator (as touching the slave) to curse, abuse, drive rigorously, sell, change, give, etc., yea, beat without restrictions; mark, brand, and castrate him and even when life itself is taken away, it is but very little regarded. Perhaps there may be a small stir if one is murdered, but it is nothing but a sham-inquisition! His wife and children (if slaves) are all saleable property; so that slave cannot say that even his life is his own. They see their wives and children in suffering circumstances, but have no way to relieve them! They see their bleeding backs but dare not say, "Why is this abuse?" They are torn from each other to satisfy debts, and to be parted among the favored legatees. This is tolerated by the sons of liberty, who risked their lives to deliver themselves from political bondage. The stain of the blood may, perhaps, still be found! The tears of the fathers, mothers, and widows have not yet ceased flowing. Yet the worst of slavery is tolerated with all its train of inhuman consequences!

And what still serves to augment my pain, my beloved Methodist brethren approve of it. But not all. Where shall I turn mine eye from seeing of evil, or mine ears from hearing of blood! The sorrows of my heart are enlarged by hearing, and mine eyes affecteth my soul, in beholding the sorrowful scenes that have lately fallen within my province. . . .

We now proceed to inquire whether the motives which introduced slavery, were from the lust of the flesh or the divine impulses of the Holy Ghost. The spirit of God works tender-heartedness, bowers of mercy and love, with the fruits thereof. Love is the fulfilling of the law: it is the very basis of the Christian Religion, taught by the eternal Son of God. Our Lord gives it as his commandment, that we should *love one another.* This is the charity that *seeketh not her own, but is kind. Bear ye one another's burdens, and so fulfill the law of Christ.*

We are an enlightened people, and therefore God requireth us to do justice and to love mercy. Micah 6. The works of the flesh are manifest in this grand abomination, from the rise thereof to this present period. Ask your consciences, why you keep slaves? Cannot I answer in behalf of thy bribed conscience: "for the sake of ease, honor and self-interest." *The flesh lusteth to envy.* Be ye well assured that slavery is a work of the flesh, assisted by the devil; a mystery of iniquity, that works like witchcraft to darken your understanding, and harden your hearts against conviction. And will ye live after the flesh and die? Or, through the Spirit mortify the deeds of the body and live? Beyond contradiction, great is the mystery of this grand abomination. And we must declare slavery to be robbery, spoil, yea, cruelty, and opposition. . . . Can anyone have the assurance to suppose that in order to give us carnal pleasure in indulging our idleness, feeding our pride and lust, like fed horses . . . that God would ruin and butcher so many thousands of our inoffensive fellow creatures? . . .

Let us ransack the sweet bowels of Christ for arguments. Let us venture nearer to God than we ever did. . . . Let us persuade the Lord to conquer our people by the power of religion, and not to give them up to the curse of judicial blindness. Let us never distrust the Almighty. Lay all your shoulders to the mountains of slavery. I believe I am leaning now on the main pillars on which it stands. If God would give me my power, I would bow till my heart broke, so it would be to the destruction of this bloody oppression.

Rev. James O'Kelly, Essay on Negro Slavery *(Philadelphia: Richard Hall, 1789), pp. 7–8, 10, 12, 33–34.*

DOCUMENT 8.7

Life and Death in Evangelical Consciousness

I, Aaron Spivey, was born in the County of Birtie and in the State of N. Carolina July 28th, 1763 and my Father's name was Moses Spivey and my mother's Jemima. . . . One thing I wish to state with gratitude that from my cradle until this time my moralls were strickly attended to by my parents—but with much regreat I must confess I soon took a different course in my conduct and as continued for some time heaping up sin upon sin and tho' frequently promising my own convicted conscience that I would amend my life if not before whenever I got married falsely supposing if I had of morral character it would be injurious to my Honour, as religion was generally dispised in that day by men of Character as they call them—but so it was by the Almighty's good Providence that on the 28th of Dec. 1786 I intermarried with Eliza Grimes the Daughter of Samuel Grimes of the County and State aforesaid, with whom I enjoyed mutual Happiness untill the Lord was pleased to take her to himself which melancolly day hapned on the 10th of July 1796 aged 25 years 1 months and 8 days leaving me as tokens of her conjugal affections two only sons (viz.) Moses and Samuel having enjoyed in a great degree as much happiness as I promised in this state and being left with a large family I soon found the necessity and disposition to reinstate my self in my former situation again which took place on the 5th of January 1797 with Polly Moss. . . . My former promise I was to reform for the better after a few days elapsed. My mind was exercised on Various subjects and instead of entering on the important subject of a reformation (having acquired in my new state of life a small Family) my mind began to solicit wealth in order to accomidate my Family this rationally appeared my Duty and I in a measure being in the circumstance of the Prodigal Son thought I would put off the Work a little longer untill a more convenient Season that is untill I had gotten our Domesti[c]al affairs in such a train these would be no obstruction in the way. Coming to this conclusion I vested tolerable contented but now and then had some emotions of mind for nearly six months when the bell of mortallity began to be inlarged in the neighbourhood and death had and was about removing sum of my neighbours and near Conections out of time and while one of them (an old comrade too) lay on his death bed I was sent for to visit him on whom I attended alternately untill his Death, finding while I was there to human probability he must leave this World to go to Eternity—this discovering induced me to consider the consequence as soon as this thought took place on my mind it was attended with such gloomeness and horrour. . . . O! What a confused mind tongue cannot express here I found all my human exertions would profit me nothing in point of Justification and I was ignorant of a redeemer as my religious as well as other Education was best scanty. When I would attempt to read the word of God I found myself so dearly condemned which added to my grief I declined for several days reading any in it and tried to reconcile my mind against the worst of miserys being well pursuaded it would be just in God to eternally frown on me but O! How painfull was the thought but still I was induced from some secret impulse to still plead for mercy. At length as I was riding the road in the evening I think the first Wednesday in July being under uncommon prayer pleading with God to show me how it was possible for my Soul to be saved. Jesus Christ then for the first time was revealed to me a sufficient Saviour. The next inquiry was is he my Saviour? My own heart with a Dread replied no, tho I confess with joy I had some gleam of hope from a discovery I had of the blessed Redeemer as the Saviour of Sinners. . . . Night sleep departed from my eyes and I think I can truly say with the prophet my Couch was witness to my tears. Near 12 O'Clock at night my Soul was so overwhelmed with grief I was induced to try to pray (notwithstanding I was often afraid when I was attempting to pray I was agravating my wo) but I proceeded (as I had been shown that the blessed Jesus was the Saviour of Sinners) now my prayers was that I might discover him to be my Sav[i]our after fervently beseching the fountain of Wisdom to reveal him into me not only as a Sufficient but a willing Sav[i]our to save such a unworthy wrech as I was, in this adress I found some inducement to wait with more patience I also was directed to the word of God under this impression I took a little repose being much discomposed for the want of it accordingly in the morning I took courage to search the Book of God praying in the mean while that I might be rightly directed I opened at the XI Chapter of St. Mathew's Gospell and when I read the last verse of that Chapter particularly the Words "Come unto me, all ye that labour and are heavy laden, and I will give you rest" were repeated in my mind several times from hence I began to pay greater attention to the meaning of them and they were explained thus to me that I Jesus Christ is the inviter the object invited are those who are labouring under a weight of their own guilt and condemnation and they who comes must through themselves wholy on his will and mercy and be willing to suffer all things for his Sake which I was induced to do and the Words sumed inactly sutable to my care and believing my self to be the invited.

Rev. Aaron Spivey, "A Succinct Account," Cashie Baptist Church Record Book, 1791–1832, Baptist Collection, Wake Forest University Library, Winston-Salem, N.C.

SUGGESTED READINGS

Boles, John B. *The Great Revival, 1787–1805: The Origins of the Southern Evangelical Mind*. Lexington: University of Kentucky Press, 1972.

Calhoon, Robert M. "A Troubled Culture: North Carolina in the New Nation, 1790–1834." In Jeffrey J. Crow and Larry E. Tise, eds., *Writing North Carolina History*, pp. 76–110. Chapel Hill: University of North Carolina Press, 1974.

_____. *Religion and the American Revolution in North Carolina*. Raleigh: North Carolina Department of Cultural Resources, 1976.

Franklin, John Hope. *The Free Negro in North Carolina, 1790–1860*. Chapel Hill: University of North Carolina Press, 1943.

Geertz, Clifford. *The Interpretation of Cultures: Selected Essays*. New York: Basic Books, 1973.

Gutman, Herbert G. *The Black Family in Slavery and Freedom, 1750–1925*. New York: Pantheon Books, 1976.

Johnson, Guion Griffis. *Ante-bellum North Carolina: A Social History*. Chapel Hill: University of North Carolina Press, 1937.

Mathews, Donald G. *Religion in the Old South*. Chicago: University of Chicago Press, 1977.

Parramore, Thomas C. "Conspiracy and Revivalism in 1802: A Direful Symbiosis." *Negro History Bulletin* 43 (1980):28–30.

Phifer, Edward W. "Slavery in Microcosm: Burke County, North Carolina." *Journal of Southern History* 28 (1962):137–60.

Robinson, Blackwell P. *William R. Davie*. Chapel Hill: University of North Carolina Press, 1957.

Strickland, Scott. "The Great Revival and Insurrectionary Fears in North Carolina: An Examination of Antebellum Southern Society and Slave Revolt Panics." In Robert C. McMath and Orville V. Burton, eds., *Class, Conflict, and Consensus: Antebellum Southern Community Studies*, pp. 57–95. Westport: Greenwood Press, 1982.

Wall, Bennett H. "The Founding of the Pettigrew Plantation." *North Carolina Historical Review* 27 (1950):395–418.

Wyatt-Brown, Bertram. "The Ideal Typology and Antebellum Southern History: A Testing of a New Hypothesis." *Societas* 5 (1975):1–29.

———. *Southern Honor: Ethics and Behavior in the Old South*. New York: Oxford University Press, 1982.

CHAPTER 9

Confronting the Issue of Slavery

Larry E. Tise

NEGROES
FOR SALE.

I will sell by Public Auction, on Tuesday of next Court, being the **29**th of November, *Eight Valuable Family Servants*, consisting of one Negro Man, a first-rate field hand, one No. 1 Boy, **17** years of age, a trusty house servant, one excellent Cook, one House-Maid, and one Seamstress. The balance are under **12** years of age. They are sold for no fault, but in consequence of my going to reside North. Also a quantity of Household and Kitchen Furniture, Stable Lot, &c. Terms accommodating, and made known on day of sale.

Jacob August.
P. J. TURNBULL, *Auctioneer.*
Warrenton, October **28**, **1859**.

Printed at the *News* office, Warrenton, North Carolina

Handbill for Slave Sale, Warrenton, N.C., 1859 (Courtesy of the Division of Archives and History, Raleigh, N.C.)

Slavery in North Carolina was both one of the most complex issues ever faced by the people of the state and a harsh reality that affected the lives and aspirations of nearly everyone—enslaved and enslavers, Indians and free blacks, and the thousands of persons who never owned slaves or lived in slaveholding regions of the state. Nevertheless, the North Carolina experience with slavery was fundamentally different from that of other southern colonies and states, not in the ways it affected the enslaved or the enslavers but in its effect on the society and on North Carolinians' perceptions of their state, America, and the world. Except that it was a system that considered men as chattel, slavery in North Carolina cannot be seen as a mere extension of the institution elsewhere in the South.

The differences were both qualitative and quantitative. Although slavery was introduced into North Carolina almost from the time of earliest settlement by Virginians who came to the Albemarle region, before the Civil War no industry or way of life that required a substantial and concentrated work force developed in the state. Partly as the result of natural and geographic features, North Carolina never produced a farming economy comparable to the plantation systems of either lowcountry South Carolina or tidewater Virginia, with the possible exception of the Lower Cape Fear. As a consequence, although North Carolina eventually acquired a substantial slave population, individual slaveholdings were always small compared to those in other southern states and were widely dispersed except for a few areas in the westernmost extremities.

The North Carolina experience was different also in that, unlike other southern states, it was settled in a haphazard manner by a variety of people whose national traditions did not include experience with slavery and who, if not entirely inimical to the institution, were at least convinced that they had no need for slave labor. The vast numbers of Quakers and other dissenting religious groups, Germans of all persuasions, and Scotch-Irish who peopled the piedmont and mountain areas of North Carolina during the second half of the eighteenth century eventually owned small coteries of slaves but never became fully convinced that their lives and livelihoods depended upon the institution.

A third factor, and perhaps the most important, was that North Carolinians' contact with slaves and the institution of slavery and their experiences with the implications of slavery's existence among them were almost always secondhand or dependent upon circumstances elsewhere in America. Because the colony and state never developed a viable seaport and inland transportation system connecting the backcountry with the coast, most imported goods, including slaves, arrived largely through the ports of Norfolk or Charleston. The same could be said of the laws, customs, and practices regarding the operation of the institution of slavery. North Carolina was perpetually a generation or more behind adjacent areas in creating the legal, economic, and cultural framework that made slavery an immovable fixture in those societies.

A final and crucial factor in the North Carolina experience derived from the third. Because both slavery and the customs for operating the institution were imported from surrounding areas, North Carolinians, from the earliest days until the conclusion of the Civil War, were constantly forced to react to events occurring outside their boundaries. Ranging from pressures to purchase slaves recently imported from Guinea and to establish laws that would restrict movement of slaves and free Negroes into and out of the state to demands to join other southern states in stamping out the influences of abolitionism and to unite in a southern Confederacy to defend the institution in war, North Carolinians faced a series of choices concerning slavery that they preferred to avoid. Because their views concerning slavery were never united, they rarely participated fully and happily in shaping their own destiny as a people but were continual victims of decisions made and initiatives taken first in England, later in Philadelphia and Washington, and finally in Charleston, Richmond, and Montgomery, Alabama.

The fact that North Carolinians never really decided as a people how to deal with the institution of slavery also produced paradoxical circumstances and experiences that characterized the history of slavery in the state. A vast network of manumission societies emerged and continued their witness against slavery until well after such activity had been banned elsewhere in the South. Avowed abolitionists operated openly for years without opposition. Despite the enactment of harsh and restrictive laws, slaves pursued business, industry, and in at least one instance the arts with the open support of the elected leaders of the state. For a generation, debate on the virtues and evils of slaveholding was intense, but North Carolina did not produce a single recognized spokesman for the defense of slavery. In fact, many continued until the onset of the Civil War to denounce slavery as a curse on the land and to dream of its removal.

Despite the many anomalies that distinguished North Carolina's experience with slavery, to all outward appearances and in the broad outlines of its history slavery looked little different there than in surrounding areas. Although a few Negro slaves had been brought to North Carolina in connection with the ill-fated Spanish settlement of Lucas Vasquez de Ayllon in 1526 and again by Sir Francis Drake to the first English settlement on Roanoke Island in 1586, the first permanent slaveholdings did not appear until 1663, when at least four settlers in the Albemarle region spilling over from Virginia are known to have possessed slaves. The inducements to bring slaves increased dramatically with the issuance of the

Carolina Charter and the establishment of provisions by the Lords Proprietors of Carolina to grant any person immigrating to the newly established colony a specified amount of land per slave. (Document 9.1)

Although it was a common practice in North Carolina as elsewhere to enslave the captives from numerous skirmishes and wars with the colony's native Indian population, the bulk of North Carolina's slave population derived from the importation of blacks either directly from Africa or from the West Indies through Virginia or South Carolina. And although there were a few free blacks in the Albemarle region as early as 1701, slavery in North Carolina quickly developed as a racial institution that involved virtually only blacks and characterized the condition of nearly all blacks in the colony. Enslaved blacks almost always outnumbered free blacks by twenty to one. On the other hand, North Carolina's white population outnumbered its black population throughout most of the colonial period six to one. By the time of the first decennial census in 1790, the ratio of the state's white to black population was roughly three to one; by the eve of the Civil War it was two to one. In 1860 North Carolina's population consisted of 629,942 whites, 331,059 slaves, and 30,463 free blacks, the last number having increased from 5,041 or 1.27 percent of the population in 1790 to 3.07 percent of the population in 1860.

Although North Carolina clearly originated as a slaveholding colony, the General Assembly did not enact a firm and comprehensive slave code until 1741, long after similar laws had been established in Virginia and South Carolina. (Document 9.2) On the surface the North Carolina code paralleled the restrictive systems of laws that grew up in other slaveholding colonies, but in implementation and interpretation, it apparently provided both protection and rights to slaves and free Negroes not available in other areas. The code was amended at nearly every sitting of the General Assembly and of the state's courts, either in reaction to external events or to protect further the rights of slaves and slaveholders. The most notable revision followed the publication of David Walker's *Appeal* in 1829 (Document 9.3) and in 1831, when the General Assembly moved quickly to eliminate many rights formerly belonging to free blacks and to establish new mechanisms to control all blacks, whether slave or free.

Despite North Carolinians' disparate views about slavery, there is little reason to believe that the life of the individual slave in North Carolina was any better than in other slaveholding regions of the Western world. (Document 9.4) Although few extensive plantations existed in North Carolina outside of the extreme northeast and southeast making use of large numbers of slaves in stereotypical dehumanizing work systems, it is not difficult to document the evils of the institution in the state's history. Blacks were brought unwillingly into North Carolina ports, sometimes directly from Africa, and introduced to unrelenting toil in the swamps and forests of eastern North Carolina. Many were brutalized by masters with the whip, with the branding iron, and with other forms of inhumane treatment. Without any thought of judicial retribution, some were killed for attempting to escape their bondage or when suspected of involvement in fomenting insurrection. Family life among slaves was frequently not respected, and masters and courts sold off black relatives in the lively intra- and interstate slave trades that particularly characterized the early nineteenth century. (Document 9.5) And even though free blacks enjoyed a separate legal status throughout the antebellum period, many, though not all as witnessed by John Chavis and Moses Horton, continued to be treated in the manner of their enslaved brethren. (Document 9.6)

Nor was North Carolina immune to the madness that surrounded periodic rumored slave insurrections. Any society that attempts to fetter a portion of its population seems subject to fears of internal conspiracy and to brooding about the security of the enslaving populace. These fears, combined with the fact that those held in bondage were of a different, misunderstood, and constantly degraded race made North Carolina just as subject to scares of slave revolt as any other slaveholding region. Although there was never an insurrection of the magnitude of those of Gabriel Prosser in 1800 and Nat Turner in 1831 in Virginia and of Denmark Vesey in South Carolina in 1822, massive and intensive scares were frequent and were handled as blindly, brutally, and unthinkingly as any real insurrection elsewhere in America. (Document 9.7)

Against the realities of slavery that made the North Carolina experience similar were the conditions, events, and people that ensured a different outlook upon the institution from that of their fellow southerners. Of the seven southern "plantation" states, North Carolina in 1860 had fewer slaves than any except Louisiana and the smallest ratio of blacks to whites. In 1850 only 27 percent of North Carolina families owned slaves whereas in Virginia the figure was 33 percent, in South Carolina, 48 percent, and in Georgia, 70 percent. In 1860, 72 percent of North Carolina families owned no slaves at all and of those who did 67 percent owned fewer than ten. Throughout the antebellum era, despite the wide dispersion of slaveholding throughout the state, only sixteen counties—all in the coastal region—ever had a greater number of slaves than whites.

Because a majority of North Carolinians never had any personal stake in slavery, they could question the value of the institution. During the latter part of the eighteenth century North Carolina's large and formerly politically powerful Quaker population witnessed against slavery through letters and tracts, petitions to the General Assembly, and the manumission of their own slaves. Although other religious groups, notably the Methodists and Baptists, occasionally denounced the institution as a moral evil, none equaled the persistence and tenacity of the Quakers. By the end of the eighteenth century the Quakers had largely rid themselves of slaves and were working to get other North Carolinians to follow their example. Encouraged by the rising tide of interest in either manumitting slaves or colonizing them in Africa, a number of Quakers in 1816 formed the North Carolina Manumission Society near Greensboro and organized at least forty-one male and perhaps as many female branches throughout central North Carolina. (Document 9.8)

The work of the Manumission Society and all other efforts to rid the state of slavery reached a hiatus beginning in 1829 with the publication of the *Appeal* by David Walker, a former North Carolina free black who had relocated to Boston, the Nat Turner rebellion in 1831, and the appearance of radical abolitionism through the North in 1835. (Document 9.3) This six-year period proved to be the turning point in North Carolina's experience with slavery. Until that time, the attitude of North Carolinians was singular, questioning, and frequently openly hostile. After 1835, however, public statements about the institution increasingly assumed the rhetoric and values expressed by other southerners. And although North Carolinians constantly berated the harangues and actions of fire-eating slaveocrats throughout the South, their fortunes became more deeply intertwined with those of other southerners, particularly those who viewed slavery as the cornerstone of a distinctive regional culture.

It is notable, however, that both direct and indirect questioning of slavery continued in North Carolina throughout the antebellum period. Although the Manumission Society held its last formal meeting in 1834, those Quakers who led the society continued their witness against the institution through the Society of Friends and through occasional tracts. In the late 1840s and again on the eve of the Civil War Quakers and many others in the central region of the state openly supported Methodist clergymen who came to North Carolina to organize a host of local antislavery societies under the banner of Wesleyan Methodism—and were successful. Although the abolitionists were ultimately arrested and forcibly sent out of the state, that they were able to work unmolested for as long as three years without public censure was remarkable given the climate of the South in the thirty years preceding the Civil War. (Document 9.9)

It is also notable that during the antebellum period North Carolina did not produce a single articulate proponent of slavery. Although a few native sons moved elsewhere and were vocal defenders of slavery, North

Carolinians remained virtually silent on the merits of slavery while other southerners and many transplanted northerners poured forth weighty tomes on its positive moral, economic, and social values. Indeed, it appears that almost the only articulate defenses of slavery that appeared in the presses of North Carolina were written by northern transplants (clergymen George Washington Freeman, Moses Ashley Curtis, and George Patterson of Massachusetts, Elisha Mitchell of Connecticut, and Thomas Meredith of Pennsylvania), who were as concerned with the inflammatory influences of abolitionism as with the merits of slavery.

The attitude of North Carolinians toward slavery was sufficiently ambivalent that they frequently found their views disconsonant with those expressed elsewhere in America. For example, when Calvin H. Wiley, founder of the state's common school system, wrote *A Sober View of the Slavery Question* in 1849, he began by postulating that "Negro slavery is assumed to be a curse; a curse to the slave and to the master," and proceeded to recommend the gradual abolition of the institution by dispersing the slave population throughout the American continent so that ultimately each state or territory could bear an equitable portion of blacks. (Document 9.10) Even more discordant with the prevalent debate was perhaps the most renowned statement on the subject of slavery written by a North Carolinian, Hinton Rowan Helper's *Impending Crisis of the South* (1857). (Document 9.11) Although the book was thoroughly rejected by the political and social leadership of the state as subversive, Helper daringly expressed the views of many North Carolinians when he argued that slavery was a curse on the South that had hampered the region's overall economic development and that the economic burden for sustaining slavery fell squarely on the backs of the modest nonslaveholding southern farmers who constituted the vast majority of the state's population. (Document 9.12)

Citizens of North Carolina hardly knew what direction to take in the steady march toward war that faced them in the late 1850s. Their expressions of disgust with southern fire-eaters throughout the prewar years and even on the eve of the war suggested that North Carolinians had little desire to fight to perpetuate slavery. Indeed, on the only occasion when they had an opportunity to vote on secession, in 1861, they voted not to convene a convention to consider the subject. Considering the strength of unionist sentiment in the state and the continuing doubts on the subject of slavery, it is perhaps not surprising that North Carolina was the last of the southern states to secede from the Union on 20 May 1861.

Despite thirty years of living amid the slavery debate, it was remarkable that even in the crisis of the Union North Carolinians still had no clear position on the matter and more or less drifted into the war. As on earlier occasions their actions were in large measure dependent upon the positions taken by South Carolina and Virginia. Although they eventually became among the most dedicated of Confederates and contributed heavily to the southern war cause, it is perhaps fair to say that as a people North Carolinians were reluctant rebels. Had it been clear that the imminent war was primarily designed to perpetuate slavery, North Carolinians probably would have had no part of it. They could understand and relate to those who saw the southern Confederacy as a means to protect their homes and their political prerogatives, but as a people they had not yet truly confronted the issue of slavery. Had they been forced to face that issue squarely and independent of other factors, their long-term ambivalence would clearly have prevented them from joining in a slaveholders' war.

DOCUMENT 9.1

Concessions and Agreement, 1665

Item, We do hereby grant unto all persons who have already adventured to Carolina, or shall transport themselves or Servants before the first day of January which shall be in the year of our Lord one thousand Six hundred Sixty five, these following proportions. . . . : whoever shall send Servants at that time shall have for every able man Servant he or she so sends, Armed and provided as aforesaid, and arriving there, the like quantity of one hundred and fifty acres; And for every weaker Servant or Slave, male or female, exceeding the age Fourteen years, which any one shall send or Carry, Arriving there, Seventy five acres of land.

Mattie Erma Edwards Parker, ed., North Carolina Charters and Constitutions, 1578–1698 *(Raleigh: Carolina Charter Tercentenary Commission, 1963), pp. 122–23.*

DOCUMENT 9.2

"An Act Concerning Servants and Slaves": The Slave Code of 1741

1. *Be it enacted by his excellency* GABRIEL JOHNSTON, *Esquire, Governor, by and with the advice and consent of his majesty's council, and the General Assembly of this province, and it is hereby enacted by the authority of the same* . . . That if any person or persons whatsoever, shall, directly or indirectly, at any time . . . tempt or persuade any negro or negroes, or other slave or slaves, to leave his, her, or their master or mistress' service, out of an intent and design to carry or convey away him, her or them out of this government, or shall harbour or conceal him, her or them, for that intent or purpose, and be thereof convicted . . . such person or persons shall, by the next two justices of the peace, be committed to gaol . . . and being thereof lawfully convicted, shall, by the said court, be adjudged to pay, to the master or mistress, for each negro or other slave so enticed or persuaded . . . the sum of twenty-five pounds, proclamation money, or the value thereof. . . .

30. That when any runaway servants or slave shall be brought before any justice of the peace within this government, such justice shall, by his warrant, commit the said runaway to the next constable, and therein also order him to give the said runaway so many lashes as the said justice shall think fit, not exceeding the number of thirty-nine, well laid on, on the bare back of such runaway; and then to be conveyed from constable to constable, until the said runaway shall be carried home, or to the public goal. . . .

35. That no slave shall go armed with gun, sword, club or other weapon, or shall keep any such weapon, or shall hunt or range with a gun in the woods, upon any pretence whatsoever . . . and if any slave shall be found offending herein, it shall and may be lawful for any person or persons to seize and take, to his own use, such gun, sword, or other weapon, and to apprehend and deliver such slave to the next constable, who is enjoined and required, without further order or warrant, to give such slave twenty lashes on his or her bare back, and to send him or her home. . . .

38. That no slave shall go from off the plantation or seat of land where such slave shall be appointed to live, without a certificate of leave, in writing, for so doing, from his or her master or overseer. . . .

39. That no slave shall be permitted, on any pretence whatsoever, to raise any horses, cattle or hogs. . . .

41. That where any such negro, mulatto, or Indian, bond or free, shall

... be found to have given a false testimony, every and such offender shall, without further trial, be ordered by the said court, to have one ear nailed to the pillory, and there stand for a space of one hour, and the said ear to be cut off, and thereafter the other ear nailed in like manner, and cut off, at the expiration of one other hour; and moreover, to order every such offender thirty-nine lashes, well laid on, on his or her bare back, at the common whipping-post. . . .

44. That if in the dispersing any unlawful assemblies of rebel slaves or conspirators, or seizing the arms and ammunition of such . . . or in apprehending runaways, or in correction by order of the county court, any slave shall happen to be killed or destroyed, the court of the county where such slave shall be killed . . . shall put a valuation, in proclamation money, upon such slave so killed, and certify such valuation to the next session of assembly; that the said assembly may make suitable allowance thereupon, to the master or owner of such slave.

Henry Potter, comp., Laws of the State of North-Carolina, 2 vols. (Raleigh: J. Gales, 1821), 1:152, 159, 162–63, 164, 165, 166, 167.

DOCUMENT 9.3

David Walker: Appeal to the Coloured Citizens of the World, 1829

I am fully aware, in making this appeal to my much afflicted and suffering brethren, that I shall not only be assailed by those whose greatest earthly desires are, to keep us in abject ignorance and wretchedness, and who are of the firm conviction that Heaven has designed us and our children to be slaves and *beasts of burden* to them and their children. I say, I do not only expect to be held up to the public as an ignorant, impudent and restless disturber of the public peace, by such avaricious creatures, as well as a mover of insubordination—and perhaps put in prison or to death, for giving a superficial exposition of our miseries, and exposing tyrants. But I am persuaded, that many of my brethren, particularly those who are ignorantly in league with slave-holders or tyrants, who acquire their daily bread by the blood and sweat of their more ignorant brethren. . . . Yea, the jealous ones among us will perhaps use more abject subtlety, by affirming that this work is not worth perusing, that we are well situated, and there is no use in trying to better our condition, for we cannot. I will ask one question here.—Can our condition be any worse?—Can it be more mean and abject? If there are any changes, will they not be for the better, though they may appear to be for the worse at first? Can they get us any lower? Where can they get us? They are afraid to treat us worse, for they know well, the day they do it they are gone. But against all accusations which may or can be preferred against me, I appeal to Heaven for my motive in writing—who knows that my object is, if possible, to awaken in the breasts of my afflicted, degraded and slumbering brethren, a spirit of inquiry and investigation respecting our miseries and wretchedness in this *Republican Land of Liberty*!!!!!!

David Walker, Appeal in Four Articles: Together with a Preamble to the Coloured Citizens of the World *(1829; reprint, New York: Hill and Wang, 1965), p. 2.*

DOCUMENT 9.4

John Brickell: "The Present State of North Carolina," 1737

The NEGROES are sold on the Coast of *Guinea*, to the Merchants trading to those Parts, are brought from thence to *Carolina, Virginia,* and other Provinces in the hands of the *English,* are daily increasing in this Country, and generally afford a good Price. . . . There are great Numbers of them born here, which prove more industrious, honest, and better Slaves than any brought from *Guinea;* this is particularly owing to their Education amongst the *Christians,* which very much polishes and refines them from their barbarous and stubborn Natures that they are most commonly endued with. I have frequently seen them whipt to that degree, that large pieces of their Skin have been hanging down their Backs; yet I never observed one of them to shed a Tear, which plainly shows them to be a People of very harsh and stubborn Dispositions.

There are several Laws made against them in this Province to keep them in Subjection, and particularly one, *viz,* That if a *Negroe* cut or wound his Master or a Christian with any unlawful Weapon, such as a *Sword, Scymiter,* or even a *Knife,* and there is Blood-shed, if it is known amongst the Planters, they immediately meet and order him to be hanged, which is always performed by another *Negroe*, and generally the Planters bring most of their *Negroes* with them to behold their fellow *Negroe* suffer, to deter them from the like vile Practice. . . .

Notwithstanding the many severe Laws in force against them, yet they sometimes rise and Rebel against their Masters and Planters, and do a great deal of mischief, being both treacherous and cruel in their Natures so that mild Laws would be of no use against them when any favourable Opportunity offered of executing their barbarities upon the *Christians*, as hath been too well experienced in *Virginia*, and other Places, where they have rebelled and destroyed many Families.

When they have been guilty of these barbarous and disobedient Proceedings, they generally fly to the Woods, but as soon as the *Indians* have Notice from the *Christians* of their being there, they disperse them; killing some, others flying for Mercy to the Christians (whom they have injured) rather than fall into the others Hands, who have a natural aversion to the *Blacks*, and put them to death with the most exquisite Tortures they can invent, whenever they catch them.

When any of these *Negroes* are put to death by the Laws of the Country, the Planters suffer little or nothing by it, for the Province is obliged to pay the full value they judge them worth to the Owner; this is the common Custom or Law in this Province to prevent the Planters being ruined by the loss of their Slaves, whom they have purchased at so dear a rate. . . .

There are some *Christians* so charitable as to have the Negroes born in the Country, baptized and instructed in the *Christian Faith* in their Infancy, which gives them an abhorance of the Temper and Practice of those who are brought from *Guinea*. This Freedom does not in the least exempt them from their Master's Servitude. . . . The Planters call these *Negroes* thus Baptized, by any whimsical Name their Fancy suggests, as *Jupiter, Mars, Venus, Diana, Strawberry, Violet, Drunkard, Readdy Money, Piper, Fiddler, &c.*

Their *Marriages* are generally performed amongst themselves, there being very little ceremony used upon that Head; for the man makes the Woman a Present, such as a *Brass Ring* or some other Toy, which if she accepts of, becomes his Wife. . . . It frequently happens, when these Women have no children by the first Husband, after being a Year or two cohabiting together, the Planters oblige them to take a second, third, fourth, fifth, or more Husbands or Bedfellows: a fruitful Woman amongst them being very much valued by the Planters. . . .

There are several *Blacks* born here that can Read and Write, others that are bred to Trades, and prove good Artists in many of them. Others are bred to no Trades, but are very industrious and laborious in improving their Plantations, planting abundance of *Corn, Rice* and *Tobacco*, and making vast Quantities of *Turpentine, Tar,* and *Pitch,* being better able to undergo fatigues in the extremity of the hot Weather than any *Europeans.*

The *Children* of both Sexes wear little or no Cloaths, except in the *Winter,* and many of the young Men and Women work stark naked in the Plantations in the hot Season, except a piece of Cloath (out of decency) to cover their Nakedness; upon which Account they are not very expensive to their Planters for their Cloathing. The Planters at their Death used to make some of their favourite *Negroes* free, but there is now an established Law . . . that if they do not quit the Province in about Eleven Days after their Freedom, whoever takes them they become his Property. . . . The Planters seeing the Inconveniencies that might attend these kind of Priviledges to the Negroes, have this and all other Laws against them continually put in practice, to prevent all Opportunities they might lay hold of to make themselves formidable.

John Brickell, The Natural History of North Carolina *(Dublin: For the Author, 1737), pp. 272–76.*

DOCUMENT 9.5

Johann David Schoepf: Another Slave Auction at Wilmington, 1783

The day after our arrival at Wilmington we attended a public auction held in front of the Court-house . . . negroes were let for 12 months to the highest bidder, by public cry. . . . A whole family, man, wife, and 3 children were hired out at 70 Pd. a year; and others singly, at 25, 30, 35 Pd., according to age, strength, capability, and usefulness. . . . The keep of a negro here does not come to a great figure, since the daily ration is but a quart of maize, and rarely a little meat or salted fish. Only those negroes kept for house-service are better cared for. Well-disposed masters clothe their negroes once a year, and give them a suit of coarse woollen cloth, two rough shirts, and a pair of shoes. But they who have the largest droves keep them the worse, let them run naked mostly or in rags, and accustom them as much as possible to hunger, but exact of them steady work. Whoever hires a negro, gives on the spot a bond for the amount, to be paid at the end of the term, even should the hired negro fall sick or run off in the meantime. The hirer must also pay the negro's head-tax, feed him and clothe him. Hence a negro is capital, but out at a very high interest, but because of elopement and death very unstable.

Other negroes were sold and at divers prices, from 120 to 160 and 180 Pd., and thus at 4–5 to 6 times the average annual hire. Their value is determined by age, health, and capacity. A cooper, indispensable in pitch and tar making, cost his purchaser 250 P., and his 15-year old boy, bred to the same work, fetched 150 Pd. The father was put up first; his anxiety lest his son fall to another purchaser and be separated from him was more painful than his fear of getting into the hands of a hard master. "Who buys me,["] he was continually calling out, "must buy my son too," and it happened as he desired, for his purchaser, if not from motives of humanity and pity, was for his own advantage obliged so to do. . . .

One cannot without pity and sympathy see these poor creatures exposed on a raised platform, to be carefully examined and felt by buyers. . . . If the negresses are put up, scandalous and indecent questions and jests are permitted. The auctioneer is at pains to enlarge upon the strength, beauty, health, capacity, faithfulness, and sobriety of his wares, so as to obtain prices so much the higher. On the other hand the negroes auctioned zealously contradict everything good that is said about them; complain of their age, longstanding misery or sickness, and declare that purchasers will be selling themselves in buying them, that they are worth no such high bids: because they know well that the dearer their cost, the more work will be required of them.

Johann David Schoepf, Travels in the Confederation, *1783–1784, trans. Alfred J. Morrison (Philadelphia: William J. Campbell, 1911), pp. 147–49.*

DOCUMENT 9.6

John Chavis: Advertisement for White and Black Students at Raleigh, 1808

John Chavis takes this method of informing his Employers, and the Citizens of Raleigh in general, that the present Quarter of his School will end the 15th of September, and the next will commence on the 19th. He will,

at the same time, open an EVENING SCHOOL for the purpose of instructing Children of Colour, as he intends, for the accommodation of some of
his Employers, to exclude all Children of Colour from his Day School.

The Evening School will commence at an hour by Sun. When the white
children leave the House, those of colour will take their places, and
continue until ten o'clock.

The terms of teaching the white children will be as usual, two and a
half dollars per quarter; those of colour, one dollar and three quarters. In
both cases, the whole of the money to be paid in advance to Mr. Benjamin S. King. Those who produce Certificates from him of their having
paid the money, will be admitted.

Those who think proper to put their Children under his care, may rely
upon the strictest attention being paid, not only to their Education but to
their Morals which he deems an *important* part of Education.

Raleigh Register, *25 August 1808.*

•

George Moses Horton: Slave Poet's Plea for Assistance, 1853

Sept. 11, 1853
Chapel Hill, N.C.

To Mr. Greeley
Sir,

From the information of the president of the University of North
Carolina, to wit, the honorable D. L. Swain, who is willing to aid me
himself, I learn that you are a gentleman of philanthropic feeling. I therefore thought it essential to apply to your beneficent hand for some assistance to remove the burden of hard servitude. Notwithstanding, sire,
there are many in my native section of country who wish to bring me
out, and there are others far too penurious which renders it somewhat
dubious with regard to my extrication. It is evident that you have heard
of me by the fame of my work in poetry, much of which I am now too
closely confined to carry out and which I feel a warm interest to do; and
sir by favoring me with the bounty of 175 dollars, I will endeavor to
reward your generosity with my productions as soon as possible. I am
the only publick or recognized poet of colour in my native state or perhaps in the union born in slavery but yet craving that scope and expression whereby my literary labour of the night may be circulated throughout the whole world. Then I forbid that my productions should ever fall
to the ground but rather soar as an eagle above the towering mountains
and thus return as a triumphing spirit to the bosom of its God who gave

it birth though now confined in these loathsome fetters. Please assist the cowering vasal to arise and live a glad denizen the remnant of his days and one of active utility.

> Yours respect.
> George M. Horton
> Of Colour

George Moses Horton to Horace Greeley, 11 September 1853, David Lowry Swain Papers, Southern Historical Collection, University of North Carolina, Chapel Hill.

DOCUMENT 9.7

Moses Ashley Curtis: Diary of an Insurrection Scare, New Hanover County, September 1831

Sept 9th. Horrible! A set of runaway negroes have murdered about 50 persons in Southampton County Va. & left their carcasses headless & abused as a prey to the buzzards. . . . The outrages being in the vicinity of this state created much excitement here, particularly among [the] women & roused people to adopt measures [of] precaution among ourselves. . . .

Sept 10th. News to day of an intended insurrection in Wilmington & vicinity. This is a fine charge for our women after the previous priming [of] news [from] Virginia. It appears that a Baptist camp meeting was to be holden about the first of Oct. at which the blacks from several counties were to assemble & commence their work. . . .

Sept 12. Bless me! now the explosion has taken place indeed & the women (some of them he women) are in a desperate taking. . . . Fear & despair, what confusion! The women were all flying or fled with their trinkets & mattresses to the garrison. . . . When I reached the garrison there were 120 women packed in a small dwelling half dead with fear. One was stretched out on a mattress in the hysterics, a number fainted, & one was jabbering nonsense in a fit of derangement. A few men too I noticed with tremulous voices, & solemn visages, pacing back & forth in fearful anxiety. . . .

Sept 13. Morn. We did not wake this morning & find our throats cut, & in this house had as quiet sleep as ever. . . .

Evening—At 5 o'clock the inhabitants met to form a corps of defense. I enrolled my own name, took a musket & ammunition & came home, with a requisition to meet them at 7 o'clock. . . .

Sept 21st. Four of the insurgents have been condemned in W[ilmington] & have received the reward [of] acknowledged guilt. One was deeply affected at his situation. . . . Their heads are sticking on poles in different parts of the town. Four more are to be shot today or tomorrow. . . .

Sept. 23. Four men to be hung in Onslow County this day. There are daily arrests in W[ilmington] & it seems probable that as many blacks will be executed for this intended insurrection in N. C. as were destroyed for their violence in Va.

Moses Ashley Curtis, Personal Diary, 1830–36, Moses Ashley Curtis Papers, Southern Historical Collection.

•

North Carolina General Assembly: "A Bill to Prevent All Persons from Teaching Slaves to Read or Write, the Use of Figures Excepted," 1830

Whereas the teaching of slaves to read and write has a tendency to excite dissatisfaction in their minds and to produce insurrection and rebellion to the manifest injury of the citizens of this state: Therefore

Be it enacted by the General Assembly of the State of North Carolina, and it is hereby enacted by the authority of the same, that any free person who shall hereafter teach or attempt to teach any slave within this State to read or write, the use of figures excepted, Shall be liable to indictment in any court of record in the State having jurisdiction thereof, and upon conviction shall at the discretion of the court if a white man or woman be fined not less than one hundred dollars nor more than two hundred dollars or imprisoned and if a free person of colour shall be whipped at the discretion of the court not exceeding thirty nine lashes nor less than twenty lashes.

Be it further enacted that if any slave shall hereafter teach or attempt to teach any other slave to read or write the use of figures excepted, he or she may be carried before any justice of the peace and on conviction thereof shall be sentenced to receive thirty nine lashes on his or her bare back.

Legislative Papers, 1830–31 Session of the General Assembly, North Carolina Archives, Raleigh.

DOCUMENT 9.8

Preamble to The Constitution of the Manumission and Colonization Society of North Carolina, 1819

The Committee appointed by the above mentioned Society at their General Association, to revise and amend their constitution, & take into consideration the condition of the oppressed Africans, are of the opinion that at this eventful era, when the attention of Europe & America are arrested by the Sufferings of Africa, or of the African race,—that it behoves us as a Nation, to consider whether we are acting consistent with the liberal ideas of freedom, we have long held forth to the world. Without entering into a critical disquisition of the matter we are free to observe, that we adhere to the Declaration made by our country Men in the year (1776) Viz, "that all men are created equal, that they are endowed by their creator with certain Unalienable rights, that among these are life liberty & the pursuit of happiness,"—That the command of the great father of Mankind is, that we do unto others as we would be done by,— and that the human race however varied in color are Justly entituled to Freedom, & that it is the duty of Nations as well as Individuals, enjoying the blessings of freedom to remove this dishonor of the Christian character from among them,—But more especially in this United States where the principles of freedom are so highly professed—The toleration of Slavery must be more degrading in proportion to our profession of being more enlightened,—from an Impression of the truth of these principles, from an earnest wish to bear our testimony against Involuntary Slavery, to spread it abroad as far as the Sphere of our influence may extend, & to afford our friendly assistance to those who may be engaged in the same laudable pursuit, and in the hope of Support from the supreme being, who takes as an offering to himself, those benevolent acts we perform to our fellow Creatures.

H. M. Wagstaff, ed., Minutes of the North Carolina Manumission

Society, 1816–1834 *(Chapel Hill: University of North Carolina Press, 1934), p. 39.*

DOCUMENT 9.9

George C. Mendenhall: In Defense of Adam Crooks and Jesse McBride, Abolitionist Emissaries from the North, 1850

In discharge of my duty as an Attorney, I appear to see that these men have a full, fair trial. Nor do I arise to try and please those around me or to make half a plea. . . . It has been charged upon them that they have come into our midst unasked for. . . . They are here as regular ministers of the Gospel; . . . they were sent for by your own citizens; . . . one has been here three years, and the other not quite so long. They preach against intemperance . . . and against war. The Quakers, from which I sprung protest, and have for a hundred years, against *slavery.*

For doing nothing more, these men must be dragged up before this court as fellons, and compared with Nat Turner. . . .

Is it in testimony that these men have at any time interfered with slaves? . . . These men have a right to use means to gain proselytes; and believing, as they do, that slavery is sinful, they'll have a right to convince masters and freemen that it is wrong. . . . I'll show . . . that other ministers have brought and circulated things as bad as this little pamphlet ["Ten Commandments"] and that every intelligent Methodist minister keeps and circulates books equally as strong against slavery. Presbyterians and Quakers do the same. . . .

Here, by permission of the court Mr. M. read and commented on extracts from the writings and sayings of the following distinguished statesmen and divines, viz., Patrick Henry and Thomas Jefferson. . . . The narrative of the doings of the North Carolina Yearly Meeting of Friends on the subject of Slavery within its limits . . . Petition of the Presbyterians to their General Assembly—printed in Washington and circulated everywhere . . . Governor Swain, of North Carolina, scorching; . . . Address of Hon. Wm. Gaston, before the students at Chapel Hill, N.C.—clear masterly, and pithy—circulated everywhere, admired by everybody. Fourth edition, printed at Raleigh, capital of North Carolina.

Now, gentlemen of the jury, I have not read these things to convince

212 · *The North Carolina Experience*

you that slavery is wrong, but to show you that if the "Ten Command-ments" is incendiary, then these are equally so, and to show you that the defendants have done nothing more than other ministers. . . . I venture the assertion, that if this pamphlet had been given out by a Methodist Episcopal preacher, there would not have been one word said about it. . . .

Mr. M. after reading from his notes fifteen reasons why the defendants should be acquitted . . . concluded his last manly defense of three hours and a half, which was delivered in a clear dignified, and masterly man-ner; and, notwithstanding its length, was heard by all with the most profound interest and breathless attention.

Transcript of the trial of Adam Crooks and Jesse McBride for the distribution of incendiary literature in Salem, 7 October 1850, in Elizabeth Willets Crooks, The Life of Rev. A. Crooks *(Syracuse, N.Y.: D. S. Kinney, Wesleyan Methodist Publishing House, 1875), pp. 45–65.*

DOCUMENT 9.10

Calvin H. Wiley: A Sober View of the Slavery Question, 1850

We have a common country, a common hope, and a common destiny; let us, therefore, calmly and frankly reason together before we condemn each other and invoke to our councils that first born of hell, the Demon of fraternal strife. . . .

Negro slavery is assumed to be a curse; a curse to the slave and to the master. . . . Has slavery proved a curse to the negro? While there is nothing more ennobling in its tendencies than well regulated liberty, the inevitable effect of slavery is to debase; and the end of all human progress is the emancipation of our race from every species of debasing vassalage. . . .

If slavery is to be abolished, directly or indirectly, immediately or gradually, it must be the voluntary act of those that own slaves; they must be allowed to manage their own burdens, and to discover and re-pent them of their own sins. . . .

How is slavery to be abolished? Is it to be immediate? Of course it cannot be; in the present state of the world it is unreasonable, nay, it is utterly absurd to ask men to make such vast sacrifices on the score of humanity. . . . The humble writer can see but one solution. Startling as his proposition may at first seem, the writer believes, that of those who anxiously and honestly examine this subject many will [sic] agree with him, that the only hope for the slave and for the master is, *in an extension of the area of slavery*. . . .

The extension of the area of slavery will not increase the number of slaves; for, as all know, there can be no new importation of this class of persons into the United States. The extension of the area would diminish the proportion of slaves in any given place; and hence the following conclusions seem irresistable, the first being obviously true, and the others plainly susceptible of proof:

First. The extension of the area of slavery will diminish the proportion of slaves in any given place.

Second. Those States where the proportion of slaves is the smallest, are the most likely to become free.

Third. The extension of the area of slavery must therefore hasten the period of the slaves' emancipation.

Does any rational man doubt the truth of any one of these proposition[s]?

Calvin H. Wiley, A Sober View of the Slavery Question: By a Citizen of the South *(N.p., 1850), pp. 1–2, 4–5.*

DOCUMENT 9.11

Hinton Rowan Helper: Impending Crisis of the South, 1857

In our opinion, an opinion which has been formed from data obtained by assiduous researches, and comparisons, from laborious investigation, logical reasoning, and earnest reflection, the causes which have impeded the progress and prosperity of the South, which have dwindled our commerce, and other similar pursuits, into the most contemptible insignificance; sunk a large majority of our people in galling poverty and ignorance, rendered a small minority conceited and tyrannical, and driven the rest away from their homes; entailed upon us a humiliating dependence on the Free States; disgraced us in the recesses of our own souls, and brought us under reproach in the eyes of all civilized and enlightened nations—may all be traced to one common source, and there find solution in the most hateful and horrible word, that was ever incorporated into the vocabulary of human economy—Slavery!

Reared amidst the institution of slavery, believing it to be wrong in both principle and in practice, and having seen and felt its evil influences upon individuals, communities and states, we deem it a duty, no less a privilege, to enter our protest against it, and to use our most strenuous efforts to overturn and abolish it! Then we are an abolitionist? Yes! not merely a freesoiler, but an abolitionist, in the fullest sense of the term. We are not only in favor of keeping slavery out of the territories, but, carrying our opposition to the institution a step further, we here unhesitatingly declare ourself in favor of its immediate and unconditional abolition, in every state of this confederacy, where it now exists! Patriotism makes us a freesoiler; state pride makes us an emancipationist; and a profound sense of duty to the South makes us an abolitionist; a reasonable degree of fellow feeling for the negro, makes us a colonizationist. . . . We love the whole country, the great family of states and territories, one and inseparable, and would have the word Liberty engraved as an appropriate and truthful motto on the escutcheon of every member of the confederacy.

Hinton Rowan Helper, The Impending Crisis of the South: How to Meet It *(New York: A. B. Burdick, 1857), pp. 25–26.*

DOCUMENT 9.12

Frederick Law Olmsted: A Backcountry View of Slavery, 1854

I stopped last night [west of Asheville] at the pleasantest house I have yet seen in the mountain; a framed house, painted white, with a log kitchen attached. The owner was a man of superior standing. I judged from the public documents and law books on his table, that he had either been in the Legislature of the State, or that he was a justice of the peace. There were also a good many other books and newspapers, chiefly of a religious character. He used, however, some singularly uncouth phrases common here. He had a store, and carried on farming and stock raising. After a conversation about his agriculture, I remarked that there were but few slaves in this part of the country. He wished that there were fewer. They were not profitable property here, I presumed. They were not, he said, except to raise for sale; but there were a good many people here who would not have them if they were profitable, and yet who were abundantly able to buy them. They were horrid things, he thought; he would not take one to keep it if it should be given to him. 'T would be a great deal better for the country, he believed, if there was not a slave in it. He supposed it would not be right to take them away from those who had acquired property in them, without any remuneration, but wished they could all be sent out of the country—sent to Liberia. That was what ought to be done with them. . . .

"Do most of the people here in the mountains think as you do about slavery?" [Olmsted asked].

"Well, there's some thinks one way and some another, but there's hardly any one here that don't think slavery's a curse to our country, or who wouldn't be glad to get rid of it."

Frederick Law Olmsted, A Journey in the Back Country *(New York: Mason Brothers, 1863), pp. 262–64.*

SUGGESTED READINGS

Bassett, John Spencer. *Slavery and Servitude in the Colony of North Carolina.* Baltimore: Johns Hopkins Press, 1896.
———. *Slavery in the State of North Carolina.* Baltimore: Johns Hopkins Press, 1899.
Berlin, Ira. *Slaves without Masters: The Free Negro in the Antebellum South.* New York: Pantheon Books, 1974.
The Black Presence in North Carolina. Raleigh: North Carolina Museum of History, 1978.
Blassingame, John E., ed. *Slave Testimony: Two Centuries of Letters, Speeches, Interviews, and Autobiographies.* Baton Rouge: Louisiana State University Press, 1977.
Crow, Jeffrey J. *The Black Experience in Revolutionary North Carolina.* Raleigh: Division of Archives and History, 1977.
Degler, Carl N. *The Other South: Southern Dissenters in the Nineteenth Century.* New York: Harper & Row, 1974.
Franklin, John Hope. *The Free Negro in North Carolina, 1790–1860.* Chapel Hill: University of North Carolina Press, 1943.
Genovese, Eugene D. *Roll, Jordan, Roll: The World the Slaves Made.* New York: Pantheon Books, 1974.
Gutman, Herbert G. *The Black Family in Slavery and Freedom, 1750–1925.* New York: Pantheon Books, 1976.

Johnson, Guion Griffis. *Ante-bellum North Carolina: A Social History*. Chapel Hill: University of North Carolina Press, 1937.

Jordan, Winthrop D. *White over Black: American Attitudes toward the Negro, 1550–1812*. Chapel Hill: University of North Carolina Press, 1968.

Morgan, Edmund S. *American Slavery, American Freedom: The Ordeal of Colonial Virginia*. New York: W. W. Norton, 1975.

Wood, Peter H. *Black Majority: Negroes in Colonial South Carolina from 1670 through the Stono Rebellion*. New York: Alfred A. Knopf, 1974.

CHAPTER 10

"Old Rip" and a New Era

Harry L. Watson

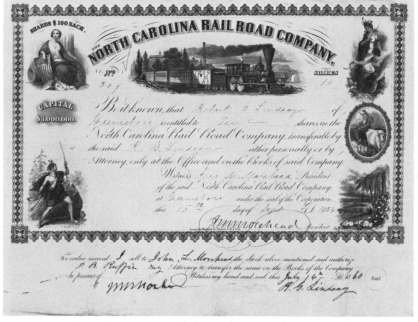

Stock Certificate for the North Carolina Railroad Company, 1854 (Courtesy of the Division of Archives and History, Raleigh, N.C.)

At the beginning of the nineteenth century, most of the free inhabitants of North Carolina lived on self-sufficient farms. With the labor of parents and children, each family produced the cornmeal, pork, flax, wool, and leather that were necessary for its own food and clothing. Cooperative neighbors and relatives aided each other with tasks that were too onerous for one family, but they did not expect wages for their help. To pay their taxes and to buy items they could not make, the yeoman farmers produced a few articles for sale, but they were not deeply enmeshed in the intricacies of the market economy. They could not afford to be, because transportation costs were too high to justify reliance on commercial agriculture.

In places where nature had made traveling less difficult, some North Carolinians practiced a different kind of agriculture and experienced a different way of life. Farmers who did not face high costs for transportation could raise crops for sale in addition to growing their own food. They used slaves to do the extra work because few free men would work for wages in a country where land was cheap and the frontier beckoned. The staples grown by these commercial farmers varied from region to region, but the basic pattern remained the same. The slaveowner organized his bondsmen into large gangs or efficient work teams and operated one or more plantations to produce one or two major crops for sale. After the harvest the planter sold his surplus to a merchant, who sold it to a commodity dealer in New York or Liverpool. Then the planter made a payment on the debt he had contracted to buy his land and slaves, and he purchased imported manufactured goods to provide him with the comforts of a gentleman. Some plantations were self-sufficient in food and fodder, but self-sufficiency was not the planter's basic goal. Instead, he hoped to make a large cash income in the international market economy. Small slaveholders who could not duplicate this pattern tried to approximate it as best they could. Slaveownership and commercial agriculture were therefore almost synonymous in the antebellum period.

Only a small number of North Carolina families participated in this market-based economic system. Because shipping costs consumed most of the profits, few farmers would take the risks to go into debt, buy slaves, and produce large crops for the market. Some planters near the rivers, an even smaller number of merchants and artisans in the towns, and a handful of lawyers and other professionals were almost the only North Carolinians who depended on trade for a living.

In spite of their small numbers, these commercially oriented men and their families were the most powerful members of society. The planter class and the merchants, lawyers, and professionals associated with them had more wealth, more education, and more connections with the outside world than did the small family farmers. They dominated the legislature, the courts, the executive offices, and the delegations to Congress. Even in backcountry counties where slavery was rare, the man who had acquired a few more "hands" than his neighbors enjoyed extra prestige and political influence. The power of planters was not overtly oppressive to the other free whites, and it depended on their ongoing consent, but the dominance of the slaveholders pervaded the state. No group seriously challenged their power before the end of slavery.

During this period of minimal growth and change, outsiders began to refer to North Carolina as the "Rip Van Winkle" state. The label was not entirely fair, for the state was sleeping only in the sense that its society was relatively static. Compared to some farming regions in the world at that time, it was not an extremely primitive society, but it was unlikely to change very much without deliberate initiative.

Some North Carolinians thought the state needed change very badly, and they pointed to the census statistics to show why. The population continued to increase, but every decade the rate of growth sank, finally reaching a low of 2 percent in the 1830s. Families were very large, and much land was thinly settled, but the population did not grow fast because many children who reached adulthood chose to move to other states where ambitious farmers faced fewer obstacles than in North Carolina. Between 1790 and 1830, North Carolina's population declined from third to fifth place among the states.

The emigration movement deepened the state's economic stagnation. Real estate values declined as the few land buyers picked and chose among the crowd of land sellers. Slaves left the state as masters sold or transported the bondsmen whom they could not keep busy on their own plantations. Alert legislators worried over these conditions, for they remembered that taxes on land and slaves were the principal supports of state government. Legislators were landowners, too, and they suffered personally from the state's lack of growth. They also knew that if North Carolina's population leveled off while that of other states kept growing, the state would lose seats in Congress, votes in the electoral college, consideration in patronage appointments, and political influence on questions of national policy. By the 1830s, some leaders had even decided that emigration was destroying family life and loosening the citizen's attachment to the interests of the state.

The advocates of reform were mostly planters or professional men who were closely tied to the market economy. They hoped to change society by improving transportation facilities and thereby expanding the system of commercial agriculture. If shipping costs for planters and farmers could be reduced, critics argued, they could produce more for the market and enjoy larger incomes without having to move to other states. Population would grow faster, land values would rise again, and

Rip Van Winkle would wake up to a safer and steadier future. In effect, the reformers wished to transform North Carolina by replacing self-sufficiency with regional economic specialization and by supplanting the exchange of goods with money in a market economy. There is no evidence, however, that the reformers wished the plantation system to give way to a more developed system of industrial capitalism that would have resembled the business economy of the northern states.

Many articulate North Carolinians called for these new policies in the first half of the nineteenth century. Perhaps the most forceful and persuasive advocate of change was the famous Orange County lawyer and planter Archibald DeBow Murphey. While serving in the state senate between 1815 and 1819, Murphey prepared a series of reports calling for a system of canals, roads, and reopened coastal inlets to be constructed at state expense. The network of internal improvements would link North Carolina's major rivers, open up the west to inland navigation, and concentrate commerce in one or more eastern ports. (Document 10.1)

In the following decade the potential of rail transportation became manifest to some of the state's leaders. President Joseph Caldwell of the University of North Carolina updated Murphey's ideas by calling for a state-supported railroad, and in the 1830s Governor David Lowry Swain and other political leaders began to make solid accomplishments on the basis of Murphey's and Caldwell's suggestions. A depression hit the state in 1837 and prevented further progress for a decade, but when the North Carolina Railroad was chartered in 1849, the state began a second phase of railroad construction that did not end until secession. (Document 10.2)

While the railroads began stretching across North Carolina, the state made other political decisions that affected its economic future. A commercial society needed banks to provide credit and a flexible paper money supply. The state accordingly invested large sums in bank stock, not only because the investments were very profitable but also to ensure that business interests would not suffer. (Document 10.3) The government also attempted to create more valuable farm acreage by draining swamplands in the east. This effort was not very productive, but an attempt to promote industrialization was more successful. Businessmen pointed out that cotton culture would be more profitable if the fiber were turned into yarn before it left the state. The government agreed and supplied the infant mills with loans from the Literary Fund when private banks refused to accept the risk. In the 1850s, the state supplemented its subsidies of railroads and navigation companies with generous subscriptions to plank road companies. Ultimately, these investments were vindicated. The population growth rate recovered, agriculture revived, small cotton mills opened, and the railroad companies paid reasonable dividends before the end of the 1850s. Nevertheless, federal census takers discovered in 1860 that North Carolina still had the nation's highest illiteracy rate among native white adults, just as it had in 1840. They also found that North Carolina workers received the lowest or next to lowest wages in the nation in the six occupations for which they collected data. The rewards of progress were slender and unevenly distributed.

The need for internal improvements seems so obvious to twentieth-century citizens that it has been hard to understand the position of the opponents of state aid for that purpose. The policy of state-sponsored economic development was controversial, but it was not simply a struggle between eastern planters and western yeomen. Many eastern planters wanted internal improvements, and if the representatives of the west did not speak for actual planters, they spoke for farmers who wanted to become planters. Nor was the debate over internal improvements purely a political quarrel between the Whig and Democratic parties. At the time the second American party system originated, most friends of internal improvements became Whigs and most opponents remained Democrats. Before the party system ended, however, many Democrats were as committed to the policy as were the Whigs.

Finally, it is not enough to say that eastern conservatives fought internal improvements because they were parsimonious. Some easterners did resent the cost of these projects, but they feared the consequences of change more than they begrudged the price. Internal improvements might enrich the state, but as Congressman Willis Alston of Halifax County reminded his constituents on 4 July 1824, riches bred luxury, luxury corrupted morals, and immorality threatened the foundations of republicanism. "A system devised in heaven," he warned, "would fail to command the respect of a licentious and abandoned people. *The tables of Sinai could not control the Jews—so* must the provisions of our constitution lose their influence over *us*, when we reject our simplicity of manners and our regard for virtue." Alston conflated the moral order and the political and economic systems and suggested that any change in one could lead to the downfall of the others. A letter writer to the *Tarboro Free Press* in 1832 articulated a similar complaint more specifically. The correspondent, who signed himself "Another Friend to Edgecombe," opposed the projected Central Railroad because it would throw wagoners out of work. They would be forced to return to farming or "resort to some dishonest means for a livelihood. . . . If the former, it would . . . reduce the prices of our own produce. If the latter, it would be still worse." The association of crime and economic change was apparently very strong. (Document 10.4)

Nathaniel Macon, the uncle of Willis Alston, was a United States senator from Warren County and one of the most important opponents of internal improvements. He spoke for many conservatives when he opposed federal aid to transportation because he thought he saw the fatal consequences of broad constitutional interpretation. If Congress could build roads and canals, Macon thought that it could free slaves. The same objection did not apply to improvements undertaken by the state, but Macon viewed state banks and other corporations as gaming shops and get-rich-quick schemes that would undermine the morals of the country. Fundamentally, Macon doubted the ability of men to improve the world by their own efforts. He even regarded most moral reform organizations as tainted with the spirit of abolitionism. "We have abolition-colonizing bible and peace societies," he observed to his protégé, Bartlett Yancey.

The common theme of all these objections to reform was the conviction that economic change would unsettle society, release individuals from a sense of restraint, lead them to ask dangerous questions about the value of established institutions, and tempt them into selfish, dishonest, or immoral practices. The conservatives sometimes hinted that economic development would erode the popular commitment to slavery, but more commonly they warned against a more general threat to moral and social stability. They did not distinguish between private morals and loyalty to the existing social and political order. The tendency to pursue private interests or convictions in a departure from the status quo might lead one man to change his job or start a new business, but it might inspire another man to sell his vote, steal a watch, kite a bill, or free the slaves. It was therefore better to change nothing than to jeopardize everything. (Document 10.5)

The conservatives' concern over personal virtue was an extension of their desire for social stability. This concern was not unique. The friends of internal improvements were just as worried about popular morality and the safety of slavery as their opponents were. After all, the advocates of modernization were planters, too, and they had an equal stake in social tranquillity. They differed from their opponents in thinking that the alternatives to reform were worse than inaction. Murphey's first report pointed to the decline of agriculture and complained that "this perversion of things is gradually undermining our morality." A similar criticism appeared in the writings of other friends of internal improvements.

Many state leaders came to realize, moreover, that North Carolina's problems were shared by the entire upper South. Virginia, for example, had ample natural facilities for water transportation, but she suffered from population losses, backwardness, and illiteracy just as did North Carolina. Stagnation also appeared in the South Carolina economy and affected that state's experience in the nullification crisis. Thoughtful politicians throughout the region began to ask how safe southern institutions would be in the Union when the South lacked fundamental economic strength. As early as 1838, one North Carolina congressman had a grim answer. In a letter to Governor Edward B. Dudley, Edward Stanly wrote,

> I have always felt, and still feel the most anxious desire to see our Legislature show some State pride, to encourage internal improvements, both by railroads and canals. We can never rival in prosperity our sister states, until this is done—It will increase our resources and advance our prosperity as well as strengthen the bonds of our Union in peace, and it will make us more respected and independent, if in the manifold changes, to which all things are liable in this world, we should cease to form a part of the Union—a thing not to be thought of, unless abolition forces [it] upon us.

Most state politicians were not expecting secession in 1838 but by the 1850s many were becoming sensitive to the problems to which Stanly alluded. (Document 10.6) Even when legislators did not express doubts about the future of the Union, a consensus grew that modern technology, an improved balance of trade, and a prosperous and stable population were essential to the public welfare and even to the public safety. The antebellum South built its railroads with a much larger proportion of public funds than other sections, a practice that reflected the political determination of its leaders to strengthen the economic infrastructure even if the necessary ventures were unattractive as private investments.

The commercialization of agriculture, the rise of towns, the development of factories, and the other changes advocated by the friends of internal improvements were potentially disruptive. Many historians and social scientists have observed that community disorder, the rise of crime, the deterioration of common values, and challenge to established authority sometimes accompany rapid economic development. In this sense, the conservatives' fears were legitimate. The progressive planters' confidence that they could regulate the pace and direction of social change was an important aspect of their decision to support internal improvements. The common school system was the instrument through which they expected to maintain social control.

The relationship between education, personal morality, and social stability is a persistent theme in the literature of the common school movement. It was no accident that Archibald Murphey was the first major advocate of public instruction as well as the first great proponent of internal improvements. Schools were essential to Murphey's plan. He pointed out in his first report on education that "a republic is bottomed upon the virtue of her citizens," but he observed that "thousands of unfortunate children are growing up in perfect ignorance of their moral and religious duties." He reiterated many times that the state must impose discipline on these unruly children and place them in schools where "the precepts of morality and religion should be inculcated, and habits of subordination and obedience be formed." (Document 10.7)

Like Murphey, Joseph Caldwell was a learned pamphleteer for education and internal improvements. In his 1832 pamphlet *Letters on Education*, Caldwell insisted that in a modern school, "the government of the passions becomes habitual. . . . It is made as distinctly an object to repress selfishness, impatience and insolence, as it is to communicate the knowledge of the rule of three or practice in arithmetic." Likewise, the 1838 report of the Committee on Education and the Literary Fund, which led to the establishment of common schools, addressed itself to "the Virtuous, the Intelligent, and the wealthy." The committee asked, "Can you employ more wisely a small sum from your abundance, than in diffusing intelligence amongst the ignorant, who have so important an influence over your property, thereby reclaiming the vicious . . . and . . . cementing and strengthening their attachment to their country and its institutions?" The supporters of education and internal improvements thus resembled the conservatives very closely in the way they connected private morals and public order. The major difference between the two groups was that the reformers saw more danger from inaction than from regulated change. The state did not establish common schools out of an abstract love of learning or democracy but from a sense of possible social crisis that grew out of specific economic and political developments.

The early advocates of public education related undisciplined personal behavior to vague predictions of social chaos. In the 1850s, a direct connection appeared between the need for common schools, the need for economic development, and the need to protect the institution of slavery. Calvin H. Wiley, who became state superintendent of common schools in 1853, wrote *The North Carolina Reader* as a school textbook because he thought existing textbooks encouraged the emigration movement by disparaging North Carolina and because some textbooks criticized slavery and favored abolitionism. By contrast, *The North Carolina Reader* inculcated in almost every lesson love of stability, admiration of economic progress, and loyalty to the state. (Document 10.8)

Going a step further, Wiley's annual reports during the secession crisis related the common schools to the fundamental interests of the South. Wiley reminded legislators that they must protect the interests of non-slaveholders just as they must continue to be good masters to their slaves, for nothing but the practice of benevolent paternalism justified the rulers' power over both races. Wiley also stressed that "*sufficient means for the religious and mental education of the masses . . . are most essential to the peace, security, and prosperity of the States where Afri-*

can slavery exists." If there were no common schools, he argued, poor whites would sink to the level of free blacks and slaves and "become a source of demoralization to the African element, a reflection on the progress of the whites, and a source of constant danger to the peace and order of the Commonwealth." Wiley's arguments succeeded, and most schools stayed open through the war. (Document 10.8)

The dedication of the North Carolina Railroad in 1856 was the culmination of the campaign for internal improvements and a decisive event in the development of contemporary North Carolina. The railroad fulfilled Archibald Murphey's dream and joined western North Carolina to the sea. Because of superior rail connections, the villages along its tracks became the populous industrial cities of the modern piedmont crescent. The speech John W. Ellis delivered at the dedication of the railroad summarized the ideas of the modernizers and announced the beginning of a new era in the state's history. Ellis stressed the physical marvels of the new technology, the wisdom and responsibility of the state and its leading men, and the prosperity and social unity the railroad would bring. He spoke of the great changes that the railroad caused, but in his eyes, the railroad fulfilled and enhanced the traditions of the older society. (Document 10.9)

Most historians of North Carolina have accepted the claims of the reformers that by 1860, the state had rejected the backwardness of the past and had started to construct a new order. They suggest that internal improvements, common schools, and the growing belief that positive government should serve the public welfare were making North Carolina more like the rest of the United States. They imply that economic improvements would have continued unabated in the direction of modern industrial capitalism had not the Civil War intervened. These conclusions are supported by the work of recent econometric historians, whose findings indicate that the antebellum southern economy was prosperous and growing rapidly by 1860.

Other scholars interpret these facts differently. They point out that the prosperity of the 1850s depended on a temporary surge in cotton prices, which rose and later fell because of developments in the English textile industry. In their opinion, the boom did not reflect increased strength in the southern economy but showed instead the South's dependence on the industrial countries that purchased its staples. These historians suggest that the modern technology that affected North Carolina and the rest of the South tended to streamline the plantation system but did not prepare the region for continued economic development. Even if the war had not intervened, they argue, the improved plantation economy would have lingered in a state of agrarian dependency.

It may be beside the point to speculate on what might have happened if the Civil War had not erupted. Whatever success the slave South enjoyed was a political threat and a moral affront to northern society, based as it was on the principles of civil freedom for all citizens and economic freedom for workers and employers alike. The reverse was also true; northern success and expansion implied a threat and a rebuke to slave-based society. Whatever the abstract economic potentialities, these historians argue, it was humanly impossible for such radically different systems to prosper and endure in the same nation, so the Civil War was truly an irrepressible conflict.

This debate among historians has not yet ended, but the economic history of antebellum North Carolina tends to support the second view. North Carolina leaders did encourage a measure of industrialization, but mostly they sought to replace subsistence farming with an expanded system of slavery and commercial agriculture. By 1861, they had made significant strides in this direction. When the moment of crisis finally came, they suppressed their lingering misgivings, joined the Confederate States of America, and devoted themselves to the ultimate political fulfillment of plantation ideals. It was therefore fitting that John W. Ellis, the governor who led North Carolina through secession, was also the man who dedicated the North Carolina Railroad.

DOCUMENT 10.1

Archibald D. Murphey: To Provide for the Inland Navigation of the State, 1815

The time has come when it behooves the legislature of North-Carolina to provide efficiently for the improvement of the inland navigation of the state. To delay this provision, is to postpone that national wealth, respectability and importance which follow only in the train of great internal improvements. With an extent of territory sufficient to maintain more than ten millions of inhabitants, under a system which would develope the possible resources of our agriculture, we can only boast of a population something less than six hundred thousand; and it is but too obvious that this population, under the present state of things, already approaches its maximum. Within twenty-five years past, more than two hundred thousand of our inhabitants have removed to the waters of the Ohio, Tennessee and Mobile; and it is mortifying to witness the fact, that thousands of our wealthy and respectable citizens are annually moving to the west in quest of that wealth which a rich soil and a commodious navigation never fail to create in a free state; and that thousands of our poorer citizens follow them, being literally driven away by the prospect of poverty. In this state of things our agriculture is at a stand; and abandoning all idea of getting rich, by the cultivation of the soil, men are seeking the way to wealth through all the devious paths of speculation. In this way individual prosperity contributes but little to the national wealth; and what is still more lamentable, habits of speculation are succeeding to habits of steady industry; and our citizens are learning to prefer the fortuitous gains of the first, to the slow yet regular gains of the second. This perversion of things is gradually undermining our morality, and converting the character which we bore of being industrious, enterprising farmers and thriving mechanics, into that of shopkeepers and speculators. This rage of speculation has given a fictitious value to houses and lots in the several towns of the state, but has not advanced the price of lands in the country; and whilst the people, whom we have sent to work the soil of other states and territories, have raised the price of their lands from two to four fold, the price of ours has remained stationary. What is the cause of this strange condition of things? Is the soil of this state too poor to reward the labors of the husbandman with its products? Have we no navigable streams by which those products can be taken to market? We have as good a soil as any of the southern Atlantic states can boast of—fine rivers intersect our state in different directions, furnishing superior means and facilities for an extensive internal commerce, to those enjoyed by any of our neighboring states; but hitherto we have not availed ourselves of the means which Providence has thrown in our way—We have suffered year after year to pass by without seizing opportunities to improve our condition; and whilst we admit that internal improvements are essential to our prosperity, we seem to act upon a contrary principle, and to expect that national prosperity will come without national labor. It is surely worse than folly to expect the rewards of industry without its toils, or national prosperity without exertion; and we ought always to bear in mind, that it is the duty of the government to aid the enterprise of its citizens, and to afford to them facilities of disposing, to advantage, of the products of their industry.

Archibald D. Murphey, "Report of the Committee on Inland Navigation," North Carolina Senate Journal, 6 December 1815.

DOCUMENT 10.2

J. Seawell: The Present Languishing Condition of North Carolina, 1833

Upon comparing the present languishing condition of the agricultural resources of North Carolina with the improved and prosperous condition of even the most inconsiderable member of the Union, the picture portrays the contrast, characteristic of a community worn down by the hand of adversity, in colours too strong to be concealed. That in North Carolina, it is apparent the reward of labor has ceased to be a stimulus to industry and enterprise; that agriculture has ceased to yield to the land owner a compensation equivalent to the expense attending the transportation of his surplus produce to market. The consequent result of this state of things is, that real estate throughout the country has so depreciated in the hands of farmers, as to be considered not to possess a fixed value estimated upon its products. Hence our citizens are daily abandoning the places of their birth for situations in other States less healthy, and often not superior in fertility of soil; but which, by the improvement of those States, rendered so by the fostering aid of Legislative patronage, the facilities to wealth and the means of acquiring the necessaries of life, the profits of labor hold out stronger inducements to agricultural pursuits than is to be found in North Carolina. Nor does the evil stop here. The tide of emigration, which never ebbs, not only carries with it a great portion of the enterprise and prime of our youth, but much of the productive and most valuable description of the State's wealth. These are facts of "ominous import," which should admonish us to guard against the fatal issue with which they are pregnant. Can it be our interest so to shape our policy as to render our State the mere nursery for the Western and Southwestern States? Surely not. We not only thereby lessen the political influence of the State in the councils of the General Government, but we evidently weaken the ties of patriotism of our citizens to the land of their nativity.

The social relations of family connections evidently constitute the most lasting cement of the political permanency of any country. Indeed, what else is it but the social ties of family connections, when rendered happy and prosperous by their own industry, that stamps a value upon society? Or will it be contended that the present scattered condition of the family connections of North Carolina has a tendency to increase either the happiness or the devotion of its inhabitants to the interest of the State? Go into any neighborhood, and inquire of the seniors or heads of families, "how many children they have raised, and in what State do they reside?" and in nine cases out of ten, the answer will be, "I have raised some six or eight children; but the major portion of them have migrated to some other State;" and adds the parent, "I am anxious to sell my lands, to enable me to follow them." Thus, it will appear that the lands of nine-tenths of the farmers of the State are actually in market; and what does it arise from? Evidently from the fact, that the distance to, and expense of sending the staple products of the soil to market, so far lessen the profits upon agricultural labor, that the farmer has no inducements to effort. Therefore, it is that all our farmers are land sellers, and no land buyers.

The cause of these evils is apparent; but no less so, than is the remedy. Throw open the agricultural interest of our State to the action of trade or commerce; open its wide spread avenues, by constructing railroads from the interior of our fertile back country to markets within the State, at least, so far as nature in the distribution of her favors has rendered them feasible; connect by railroads the rivers of the State at given points, whereby the produce of their fruitful valleys may be sent to an export market. This done, and it will reflect to the State all the substantial benefits to be derived from an export depot—such at least as will locate a capital within its influence, equal to the amount of exports.

J. Seawell, "Report of the Committee on Internal Improvements," Legislative Documents, *1833, in Charles L. Coon, ed.,* The Beginnings of Public Education in North Carolina: A Documentary History, *1790– 1840, 2 vols. (Raleigh: North Carolina Historical Commission, 1908), 2:632–38.*

DOCUMENT 10.3

The Joint Select Committee on Currency and Banks

That, in the opinion of the committee, the present condition of the currency of the State loudly calls for the prompt action of the legislature. It may almost be said that the State, at this time, is destitute of a circulating medium: it has scarcely any of its own, and of that which our people are compelled to employ, there is a deficiency in quantity and quality.

This state of things is altogether owing to the circumstances of the existing Banks now winding up their business, collecting their debts, and withdrawing their notes from circulation. The stockholders in these institutions consider this necessary, since after December next, they are restricted by law from doing any new business.

Nothing ever more powerfully disturbs the business of a community, and affects its prosperity, than a rapid and continued reduction of the general currency. It brings embarrassments on the people, destroys confidence in credit, checks trade, and invariably depresses the prices of labor and property. We have seen, if, at any time, in other States, a reduction of 10 or 15 per cent takes place in the amount of the currency, it is followed by bankruptcies and distress. Can it be a matter of wonder, then, that there should be a stagnation of business in North Carolina, that industry should be paralized, and the energies of our people depressed, when we consider what a great reduction our currency has undergone during the past few years? The wonder is, how our people have sustained themselves as well as they have, under this severe operation. . . .

The official returns of the Banks in this State, will show the progress of this diminution. The amount of their notes in circulation was, in 1825, $3,052,687; in 1830, $1,216,060.

No returns of the present year have been received, of later dates than June and July. From these, however, it appears that the reduction is still going on, and, as the Banks wind up, must continue to go on. Probably, at this time, the whole amount of notes in circulation falls short of one million of dollars; while the debt due to these Banks, alone, is considerably more than two millions. . . .

Owing to this state of things, at no former period in our history has the condition of North Carolina presented so depressed an aspect. We know that there are other causes; but we believe this to be one of the main ones. Besides the evils already alluded to, we may mention, as another consequence, the tide of emigration which is now setting to the South and West from our borders. Many of our most intelligent, wealthy and enterprising citizens have already gone, or are preparing to go; all who go, take from us wealth, capital and enterprise, and, what is worse, prepare the way for others to follow; thus unsettling our population, and turning their minds from improvements at home, to the advantages of the new States. The committee believe that a restoration of a sound circulating medium, commensurate with the wants of the community, will contribute much towards reviving trade, awakening the enterprise of our citizens, and, as a necessary consequence, lead on the public mind to ameliorations in our moral and physical condition. Under these views of the subject, we unite in the opinion, that this Legislature ought not to adjourn without the establishment of a Bank or Banks, of some character or other.

Report of the Joint Select Committee on Currency & Banks, *signed Chs. Fisher, Chairman (Raleigh: Lawrence & Lemay, 1833)*.

DOCUMENT 10.4

Speculators, Bank Officers, Shopkeepers, and Livers upon Their Wits

Senator Robert Strange, March 6, 1838

If no check is put to the present progress of events, no one will attain to wealth and honor, who does not receive them at the hands of the bank aristocracy. . . . And yet the paper system is applauded to the skies, as the wing upon which England has soared to her present prosperous height. Sir, England has thriven in spite of her paper system, and not by reason of it; and the same answer applies to the panegyrics which has been poured forth upon the wonders attributed to the banks in this country. They have, it is said, caused the wilderness to blossom, built up towns in the desert, opened our lands, constructed our railroads, and caused the steam-moved palaces to float upon our waters. If this were so, they would indeed deserve our gratitude and praise; but I have thought, and still think, that we owe all these things to the enterprise and industry of our citizens, and the abundant resources with which it has pleased Heaven to bless our country. Through them all these wonders have been accomplished, and the banks supported besides. . . .

And this brings me to the consideration of another evil of the paper system, and that is, its tendency to call men off from the most productive employments to those which are less so, or not so at all; drawing them off from the cultivation of the soil to become speculators, bank officers, shopkeepers, and livers upon their wits. All values are created by the spontaneous production of the earth, by human labor, by animal procreation, or by some or all of these united. The spontaneous production of the earth is, of course, the most profitable to him who can avail himself of it of any other; and the production of the earth, combined with human labor, furnishes at last the basis of all wealth. Human labor may, after the production of the earth is completed, put into more advantageous forms, and in more advantageous places, what has been produced; but to the earth we must go back for the origin of all wealth. Wealth to a nation is happiness; that is to say, the more aggregate wealth a nation possesses, provided it be sufficiently distributed, the more people does it place in possession of the means of procuring the essentials of happiness. The larger portion of a nation's population engaged in the production of values, and the more advantageously engaged, the better for that nation. Labor applied to bringing into action the productive powers of the earth, is, as a general rule, the most advantageous mode of producing values. Every thing, therefore, which has a tendency to divert any considerable portion of a nation from agricultural pursuits, by turning them to specu- lation, professions, merchandise, or even to manufactures, where that nation possesses a suitable field for agricultural pursuits, has, as a gen- eral rule, the effect of diminishing the wealth of that nation. But I can pursue this topic no further. I conclude that Congress has not the right, and if it had, it would not be expedient for it to undertake the creation and regulation of a common paper medium through banks. . . .

Sir, I have little hope that the paper system will be soon arrested. . . . Its swiftly moving car may roll on; but let it not drag after it every thing dear to the earthly hopes of man. Let the inflated balloon ascend if it will; but let it not, in its ascent, wrench from their foundations the insti- tutions of our country. While they remain within their sacred enclosure, the seeds of public virtue will sprout and vegetate. Planted on their firm battlements, the flag of freedom will yet soar aloft, and attract the admir- ing gaze of nations. Protected by their time-honored walls, the tree of liberty will spread forth its branches, inviting all who choose to come and repose beneath its shade. But if the parasite vine of the paper system is allowed to twine about it, it will wither and decay. If it is suffered to insinuate itself among the crevices of our institutions, it will gradually force out the cement which holds them together.

Speech of Mr. Strange of N.C. on the Independent Treasury Bill in the Senate, 6 March 1838, Congressional Globe, 25th Cong., 2d sess., Appendix, 145–54.

DOCUMENT 10.5

Your Dratted Plank Road: Jacup Jones to the *Fayetteville Observer*, 1855

SPUNK.—We received the annexed letter by this morning's mail. We have not the pleasure of an acquaintance with Mr. Jones, but as his letter bears the post mark of "Snow Camp, N.C., 11th mo. 2d," we presume he is a genuine character.

Mr. Jones threatens to subscribe for a newspaper; and we really think he needs one,—but not *our'n*, for neither our spelling nor our politics conform to his, which we faithfully copy below:—

ALEMANCE COUNTY NC
Snow Camp P.O. Oct 18 1825 [sic]

Messurs Edytors,—i sene in your paypor sum time back a peice consernin a muster somwhare away doun the country whar they as you say made a picter of old general Harison on a pine tree and shot at hit and cut it about mity bad. Now I tel you jist what it Is I dont bleve people would do sich, now I tel you If we had a muster up her and old general harison wast thar he would see fits cause every one of uss up her is real old dimecrats, and democrats to the core now iff any off your Droted whigs wus to show his face in thes parts he woud git his due if he went to medlin a long with our musterin sertun. Now I have bin to fayett and Ive ben to raley and Ive seen all your big works and I have never seen any of you whigs that I kerd a sent for never seed one that I axed a bit of ods. Now I reckon ther is jist as gud democrat papers as yourn is a whig and I mean to subscribe for won but It wont be yourn case you is always makin fun of the democrats and hard shel Baptusts. case the have sertain ways for themselves and case they bleve in the lord and do jist rite and case you hi floun whigs gits licked every onse and a while your awai a maikin things on us to try and injur our Karecktors. I tel you, you whigs is jist past goin case we democrats are hemin you inn on both sides we are a goin to quit to fayett and send our flower to Norfolk and you will not get to cheet uss any more sartain nor have me up any moor about not whantin to pay toll on your Dratted plank Road you see we democrats up her aint a gon to be runover no longer

Yours & C soforth
JACUP JONES

N B you can do jist as you like about puttin this in your paypor as I dont Kere who knous my principles   JA. JONES
E. J. HALE & SUN.

Fayetteville Observer, *5 November 1855.*

DOCUMENT 10.6

William W. Holden: We Must Live Independent of Northern Products, 1854

It is becoming more and more apparent every day, that the feeling in the non-slaveholding against the slaveholding States is stronger now than it ever was before. This feeling has been aroused and is gathering in volume and power simply because it was proposed in the Senate of the United States, by Senator Douglas, in introducing the Nebraska and Kansas bill, that the people of the slaveholding states should be permitted to enjoy equal rights in the common territories with those of the non-slaveholding States! So reasonable, so fair, so just a request, and yet such bitter and unrelenting opposition! . . .

The true course of the Southern people is to unite as one man, to sustain those of both parties, whether here or in the free States, who are standing by their rights; and to put forever from their fellowship and confidence the Whigs of the non-slaveholding States. The question is one of existence, and cannot be postponed. The South must also look more and more to the development of her resources, and to building up sea-ports and markets within her own limits. To this end, systems of internal improvement should be pushed forward, and agriculture, mining, manu-factures, and the arts generally promoted and encouraged. We must learn to live, as far as possible, independent of Northern fabrics, Northern commercial advantages, and Northern products. The North so wills it—there is no other safe course for us as a people. As we grow weaker in the free States and in Congress we must grow stronger at home. As we de-cline there we must increase here, else when "the evil day" comes it will find us divided and defenseless before our enemies.

North Carolina Standard, *24 May 1854.*

DOCUMENT 10.7

Archibald D. Murphey: A Judicious System of Public Education, 1816

A republic is bottomed upon the virtue of her citizens; and that virtue consists in the faithful discharge of moral and social duties and in obedience to the laws. But it is knowledge only, that lights up the path of duty, unfolds the reasons of obedience, and points out to man the purposes of his existence. In a government, therefore, which rests upon the public virtue, no efforts should be spared to diffuse public instruction; and the government which makes those efforts, finds a pillar of support in the heart of every citizen. It is true, that knowledge and virtue do not always go hand in hand; that shining talents are sometimes united with a corrupt heart; but such cases only form exceptions to a general rule. In all ages and in all countries, the great body of the people have been found to be virtuous in the degree in which they have been enlightened. . . .

To effect this benevolent purpose, a judicious system of public education must be established. Few subjects present more serious difficulties; none is of more vital importance. To frame a system which shall suit the condition of our country and the genius of its government; which shall develope the faculties of the mind and improve the good dispositions of the heart; which shall embrace in its views the rich and the poor, the dull and the sprightly; is a work of great magnitude and requires details to give it efficacy, which the little time allowed to your committee will not permit them to attempt. They will, however, give their general views upon the subject, and recommend to the legislature to appoint men to fill up their outlines in detail and make report to the next general assembly. . . .

This general system must include a graduation of schools, regularly supporting each other, from the one in which the first rudiments of education are taught, to that in which the highest branches of the sciences are cultivated. It is to the first schools in this graduation, that your committee beg leave to draw the attention of the legislature at this time, because in them will be taught the learning indispensable to all, Reading, Writing, and Arithmetic. These Schools must be scattered over every section of the state, for in them education must be commenced, and in them it will terminate as to more than one half of the community. . . . It is important, therefore, that in these Schools the precepts of morality and religion should be inculcated, and habits of subordination and obedience be formed. One of the greatest blessings which the state can confer upon her children, is to instill into their minds at an early period moral and religious truths—Depraved must be the heart, that does not feel their influence throughout life. It is a subject of deep regret, that at this time in North Carolina, the early education of youth is left in a great measure to chance. Thousands of unfortunate children are growing up in perfect ignorance of their moral and religious duties: Their parents, equally unfortunate, know not how to instruct them, and have not the opportunity or ability of placing them under the care of those who could give them instruction. The state, in the warmth of her affection and solicitude for their welfare, must take charge of those children, and place them in schools where their minds can be enlightened and their hearts can be trained to virtue.

Archibald D. Murphey, Report on Education Made to the General Assembly of North Carolina at Its Session of 1816 *(Raleigh: Tho. Henderson, Ja., 1817), in William H. Hoyt, ed.,* The Papers of Archibald D. Murphey, 2 vols. *(Raleigh: North Carolina Historical Commission, 1914), 2:51–54.*

DOCUMENT 10.8

Calvin H. Wiley: The North Carolina Reader, 1851

LESSON XXXIII.
SUCH is our beloved North-Carolina!

Does it not seem to you a goodly land to live in, and a proper place to rest after the toils of life? Is it not a desirable place to run your own career, and to leave your children in? Within its borders is found every variety of climate that can be desired: on its soil grows every kind of grain and plant and fruit found within the borders of the United States, and under its soil abounds, every useful, and every rare and beautiful mineral. It is a land of corn and wine; it is a land of gold and gems; it is a land of flocks and herds, of orchards and meadows.

It is a land, too, of good morals and steady habits; a land of virtue and honour and honesty.

It is a land of domestic affections; a land where filial reverence, parental tenderness, and conjugal love and fidelity are flowers of perpetual bloom.

It is a land of historic renown—a land consecrated by memories as enduring as time, and as glorious as the stars of heaven. It is the land of our ancestors, just and free in their day, and hopeful in their death; and their honoured ashes mingle with its soil, and their patriotic spirits hover through its air.

It is the land of our nativity; a land endeared by the recollections and the associations and the sweet dreams of the days of our innocence.

It is a land between extremes; it knows not the rigours of a Northern winter, and it is free from the tornadoes and earthquakes of the South. Equally exempt it is from the gloomy fanaticism and chilling selfishness of the north, and from the bloody scenes and blazing passions of the South.

It is a land whose advances, though slow, are sure; a land whose natural resources, though rugged, are exhaustless; and whose moral and political foundations are laid upon a rock. And when the genius of desolation shall sit and howl on the deserted sites of Mammon, and among the falling splendours of the Pacific—when ambition and vanity and avarice and fanaticism have done their work in other places, and set their seal of blood and gloom and rottenness and ruin and terror upon them, the sun, as he walks the heavens in his diurnal round, will still look down on one spot of beauty and happiness, where the glory of his beams is rivalled by the light of humanity and love. That land will be our own North-Carolina; and from the hearts of its free men and virtuous women will still ascend a sweet savour, grateful to Heaven, and calling down its continual blessings!

Calvin H. Wiley, The North Carolina Reader (Philadelphia: Lippincott, Grambo, & Co., 1851), pp. 23–24, 51–52, 77–78, 89–90.

DOCUMENT 10.9

John W. Ellis: The North Carolina Railroad: Wonderful Achievement of a Wonderful Age, 1856

Here we are to day, far among the hills of North Carolina, more than two hundred miles from the ocean, and eight hundred feet above its level, to celebrate an event, which brings that ocean to our very doors. . . . Wonderful achievement of a wonderful age! And full in view, Stands the Agent by which all this has been accomplished. The rail-way is here, and the locomotive; in all its length, and breadth, and full proportions. Look upon it! those of you who have seen it in other places, and welcome its coming hither. Look upon it! those of you who now See it for the first time; and feed your growing curiosity, without stint and without blush; for it will ever challenge, the curiosity of the most learned and most wise. In it, the fictions of other days are realized, in all the fullness of truth. . . .

Let us pause! My fellow citizens, in the midst of our congratulations, to acknowledge a debt of gratitude, which we owe the authors of this noble enterprise. Those patriotic and public Spirited citizens, who have contributed their energies and their means to its advancement, will receive their well merited reward, in the lasting thanks of a grateful community. It will be remembered too, that the liberal aid of North Carolina has been extended to it from the beginning. North Carolina has done this; our own native, beloved, North Carolina. . . . Let us this day, thank her for the generosity displayed in this County. Let these assembled thousands, of her native Sons, in the midst of their rejoicings, with hearts filled with gladness and with hope, raise that name in honor upon their united voices, and speak out the true Sentiments of the bosom: "The old North State forever."

But, fellow citizens, it is not this mere structure of earthenwork, nor the long trail of iron rail, nor yet the admirable mechanism, by the mysterious workings of which, these astonishing results are attained, that awakens the deep and universal interest manifested by this assembly. Wonderful as all these are, our toil and our treasure, were expended to little purpose, did they accomplish nothing more. No gentlemen! this is no idle pageant. We are here to celebrate a triumph over material nature, whence will flow blessings to our latest posterity. Hence forth, the hand of labor will be stimulated, for the laborer will be sure of his reward. Blessed by Providence with a kind and fruitful Soil, we will be led by the prospect of remuneration, to introduce all the useful improvements of agriculture and the farm. The whole community will be quickened to a lively industry; for industry will now have its fascinations.—the most powerful of human incentives; the assurance of a competency; of independence; of wealth. Every where, upon every hill and in every valley, our fields will in due Season, teem with the "golden harvests." Convenient and comely homes will be established for our people; for homes here, will now have all their natural attractions. Yes, gentlemen! henceforth, we are to have homes here in Western North Carolina; homes that will check that Spirit of emigration, which has already Scattered so many members of dissevered families through the wide spread dominions of this Republic; homes where we may live contentedly and in peace, loving and fearing God, Surrounded by all who are dear to us in life. Cities and towns, the necessary appendages of a prosperous country, will Spring up amongst us, under the stimulant of an active and buisy commerce. Our moral condition too, will receive its due Share of this general improvement. Possessed of the means, all conditions of men will be enabled to enjoy the blessings of education and a moral culture. Everywhere over the land, will arise the temples of the living God, whose mercies have been visited so bountifully upon us, where will ascend, Sabbath after Sabbath, praises to his holy name. This is no mere creation of the imagination. It will all follow, most certainly and Surely, as it has followed elsewhere, a fair and just remuneration of labor; which we not have guarrantied to us. . . .

In this manner, it has been considered, and well considered too, that the railway tends to equalize the conditions of men. Indeed, it may be regarded as the boldest agrarian of the age; yet, it pulls down no man's fortunes; it does its work in a manner more grateful to the philanthropist, and more acceptable to God; by elevating the poorer and more humble. It tolerates no inferior dependent class of men; but dispels social inequality and Social despotism, that necessary hand maid of political tyranny. It is a fact to be noted, that the railway enterprises of the present day, are doing more than any other Single agent to Spread the liberal principles of free government throughout the world. In what country then, Should they be more fostered, than in this Republic of ours? by whom more cherished, than republicans like us. . . ?

I would fellow citizens, that all the people of North Carolina could witness the Spectacle presented here this day. Could they look, as we do, upon these thousands of happy faces beaming with gladness and joy; could they See the rich man and the poor, all ages and all conditions of people, rejoicing together over a common blessing; could they behold the Schackles that have been thrown off from a pent up and imprisoned community; there would arise from their generous bosoms but one voice,—a strong, unbroke aye, for a rail way beyond the mountains to our utmost State limits. There would be no discordant Sounds of East and West, Whig and Democrat, to mar the harmony of that voice; but North Carolina would be united, as she was upon another memorable occasion, and a great public good, would prove the fruit of that union.

Noble J. Tolbert, ed., The Papers of John Willis Ellis, *2 vols. (Raleigh: State Department of Archives and History, 1964), 1:142–47.*

SUGGESTED READINGS

Brown, C. K. *A State Movement in Railroad Development*. Chapel Hill: University of North Carolina Press, 1928.
Cathey, C. O. *Agricultural Developments in North Carolina, 1783–1860*. Chapel Hill: University of North Carolina Press, 1956.
Engerman, Stanley L. "A Reconsideration of Southern Economic Growth, 1770–1860." *Agricultural History* 49 (1975):343–61.
Hinshaw, Clifford Reginald, Jr. "North Carolina Canals before 1860." *North Carolina Historical Review* 25 (1948):1–57.
Jeffrey, Thomas E. "Internal Improvements and Political Parties in Antebellum North Carolina, 1836–1860." *North Carolina Historical Review* 55 (1978):111–56.
Johnson, Guion Griffis. *Ante-Bellum North Carolina: A Social History*. Chapel Hill: University of North Carolina Press, 1937.
Morgan, J. Allen. "State Aid to Internal Improvement in North Carolina: The Pre-Railroad Era." *North Carolina Booklet* 10 (1911):122–54.
Noble, M.C.S. *A History of the Public Schools of North Carolina*. Chapel Hill: University of North Carolina Press, 1930.
Standard, Diffie W., and Griffin, Richard W. "The Cotton Textile Industry in Ante-Bellum North Carolina." *North Carolina Historical Review* 34 (1957):15–35, 131–64.
Starling, Robert B. "The Plank Road Movement in North Carolina." *North Carolina Historical Review* 16 (1939):1–22, 147–73.
Ward, James A. "A New Look at Antebellum Southern Railroad Development." *Journal of Southern History* 39 (1973):409–20.
Watson, Harry L. "Squire Oldway and His Friends: Opposition to Internal Improvements in Antebellum North Carolina." *North Carolina Historical Review* 54 (1977):105–19.

CHAPTER II

Reemergence of the Two-Party System
Max R. Williams

Whig Political Banner (Courtesy of the Division of Archives and History, Raleigh, N.C.)

Although there were political factions in colonial and revolutionary America, the Founding Fathers did not anticipate the formation of political parties. Nevertheless, by the mid-1790s vigorous, well-organized parties were active in advancing policies, putting forth candidates for office, and mobilizing followers in pursuit of electoral victories. Federalists and Jeffersonian Republicans vied for control of the state and national governments. This first American two-party system entered a period of arrested development in 1800, and by 1816 the Jeffersonians were so firmly entrenched that an Era of Good Feelings in national politics ensued. By 1820, however, the first party system was nearly defunct. The Federalists offered no presidential candidate after 1816, and only in Massachusetts could they expect to compete on a statewide basis. Even that New England bastion of Federalism became Republican in 1823.

The early political history of North Carolina followed the national pattern. After 1800, Federalist fortunes declined as the Republican party dominated the legislature, the governorship, and most of the congressional seats. Although badly outnumbered, the Federalists showed remarkable staying power, contesting the Republicans in several areas of the state until 1816. Subsequent political campaigns in North Carolina were determined by personalities, although the Republican party doctrine and leadership retained some identity.

The presidential campaign of 1824 marked the end of Republican unity in North Carolina. Dissident politicos and voters, resentful of the caucus candidate William H. Crawford of Georgia, flocked to support Andrew Jackson, who ran on a "People's Ticket." Except for the plantation east, Jackson showed surprising strength in all sections of the state. His majority was 4,794 votes in a total poll of 36,036. Denied the presidency in 1824 by what most North Carolinians believed to be a "corrupt bargain" between John Quincy Adams and Henry Clay, Andrew Jackson was the state's clear choice in 1828. "Old Hickory" defeated Adams in all but nine counties. His 1832 victory was even more impressive; he received 84.5 percent of the vote and carried sixty-three of sixty-four counties. These figures, however, are misleading: despite his overwhelming victories at the polls, Jackson faced potentially strong opposition in the Old North State.

Ironically, Andrew Jackson's actions contributed to the rise of the second party system. His war on the Second Bank of the United States seemed intemperate and vindictive; it raised the specter of executive tyranny. As demonstrated in the election of 1832, most North Carolinians would have sustained Jackson had he stopped with vetoing the bank recharter bill—an 1832 measure designed by his opponents to embarrass him before the electorate. Instead, alleging that the bank was a "hydra of corruption," President Jackson determined to withdraw government deposits from the bank and to place them in carefully selected state banks. In September 1833, three years before the bank's charter expired, Jackson accomplished his purpose. To do so, he had to dismiss arbitrarily two recalcitrant treasury secretaries. In his unreasoning hostility to the bank, Jackson had blundered politically. The premature removal of government deposits became a rallying cry for anti-Jackson men everywhere.

North Carolina became a veritable political battleground and divided fairly evenly into pro- and antiadministration forces. Seven of thirteen congressmen, for example, supported a return of deposits. Senator Bedford Brown was staunchly loyal to Jackson, but Senator Willie P. Mangum joined the opposition. Both men were important leaders within their parties. (Document 11.1) An amalgam of states' righters and nationalists, strict and loose constructionists, nullifiers and unionists were linked in an uneasy alliance to form an organized opposition that was increasingly called "Whig." Unable to agree on national policies, the Whigs denounced executive despotism at the hands of a "violent and intemperate chief," citing as evidence the Bank War, especially the removal of deposits. In North Carolina the national wing of the party would eventually gain hegemony; meanwhile, the Whigs there adopted a broad anti-Jackson and anti-Van Buren posture. Jackson's friends and supporters rushed to his defense, taking the name "Democratic." By the end of 1834 the second party system was a reality.

The era of the second party system was unique in American political experience. From 1840 through 1852, the dominant political parties were truly national in scope for the only extended period in American history. Both Whigs and Democrats succeeded in subordinating local and regional biases to the quest for power and preferment. In every state and region either party might have emerged victorious in a given election. But this competitive party system was artificially contrived. Sectional feelings, particularly regarding slavery, were barely submerged in the public consciousness. Eventually the slavery issue would disrupt both parties (the Whig in 1854 and the Democratic in 1860), and regional politics would become paramount. The demise of national parties boded ill for the Union.

North Carolina political developments paralleled the general pattern in nearly every respect except for the Whig revival in 1859. The late 1830s were devoted to perfecting party organization and devising techniques necessary to win elections. Although the Whigs were initially more vigorous and imaginative in this effort, by 1840 both parties were formidable institutions.

Political parties are electoral machines, which nominate and promote the elections of candidates to public office. Throughout the second party system, they maintained individual identities, distinctive names, and complex organizational structures from the national to state levels. Selecting candidates, campaigning for office, and vote-gathering were activities that took precedence over party platforms. From 1836 to 1848 both Whigs and Democrats emphasized national issues because of difficulty in harmonizing diverse factions within the state parties. After 1848 more attention was given to state issues; the most pressing national question—slavery extension—was too divisive. In short, it is apparent that political parties in this period were more interested in winning elections than in espousing consistent political philosophies.

The activities of political parties are largely determined by the environments within which they function. North Carolina, in comparison to Virginia and South Carolina, was a relatively primitive state socially, economically, and culturally. Geographically it was a large state in which transportation was particularly difficult. With few exceptions the river highways were inadequate, so that citizens west of the coastal plain were more likely to have commercial contacts with South Carolinians or Virginians than with their eastern counterparts. As a consequence, in essentially rural North Carolina, localism was a political creed. Opposition to any extension of government authority, especially if additional taxes were involved, was likely to be vigorous.

By 1840 the components of party machinery common to both North Carolina Democrats and Whigs were in evidence. The legislative caucus—a remnant from the first party system—was one effective device by which party leaders determined policy, selected candidates for office, and imposed discipline among legislators. In secret sessions decisions were made which all participants were obligated to support. As popular democracy became a reality, however, it was necessary to broaden the scope of party leadership and rank-and-file involvement. To this end, the convention at the county, congressional district, and state levels became a standard fixture in party organization. With delegates from every county eligible, both parties held their first statewide conventions in the 1840 campaign. Thereafter, biennial state conventions, usually held four or five months before an election, were conducted to adopt party platforms, to nominate gubernatorial candidates, and to impress those assembled with the comparative virtue and excellence of their party. Between state conventions it became customary to give responsibility for party affairs to a central committee, which varied in size from fewer than ten to as many as forty. Geography and poor transportation dictated that nearly all members came from Wake or the immediately surrounding counties. In most instances a quorum was possible if all Raleigh members attended. In addition to planning and announcing the next state convention, the central committee promoted party candidates, directed political campaigns, and distributed partisan literature in the form of addresses, speeches, tracts, and pamphlets. Another crucial function of the central committee was to ensure the existence and circulation of party newspapers.

Although most party leaders and candidates were either lawyers, businessmen, or prominent agriculturalists, political journalists played vital roles in both parties because newspapers were the principal means of mobilizing public support for a particular candidate, cause, or party. Initially there were substantially more Whig than Democratic papers in North Carolina. The most prominent Whig party organ was the *Raleigh Register*; but several regional newspapers including the *Fayetteville Observer*, the *Greensborough Patriot*, and the *Hillsborough Recorder* were excellently edited and enjoyed influence far exceeding what their modest circulation might suggest.

But if Whig journalists were more numerous, the Democrats had William Woods Holden, longtime editor of the *North Carolina Standard* (Raleigh) and the most effective political editor the state has yet produced. A native of Orange County, Holden was apprenticed to Dennis Heartt, editor of the *Hillsborough Recorder*, who taught him the newsman's craft and inspired him to embrace Whig principles. In 1843, having been frustrated in efforts to acquire a Whig newspaper, the ambitious young Holden accepted the editorship of the Democratic *Standard*. Long thereafter castigated for his apostasy, he became a political partisan par excellence. Many a Whig candidate lamented Holden's vitriolic wit (Document 11.2), and many a turn in the Democratic party's policy and practice originated with him. He fervently called Democrats to action and drove them and himself without stint. Although his political peregrinations confounded his opponents, Holden's course was predicated on the assumption that North Carolina and her people would prosper under Democratic administrations.

Aside from the obvious functions of nominating candidates and winning elections, political parties were intended to provide a means whereby concerted actions might be taken on the pressing issues of the day. North Carolina Whigs and Democrats faced a multiplicity of local, state, and national issues. Because both parties were composed of supporters from all vocations, geographic sections, and social classes, it was difficult for the membership to agree on controversial subjects. The high degree to which party regularity prevailed, despite temporary defections resulting from local issues or interests, was a striking characteristic of the second party system.

One insight into party development may be found in the attitude taken toward the use of political power within the state. Despite their criticism of "executive tyranny," from the mid-1830s to about 1850 Whigs advocated positive government action to effect change. In particular, they favored a progressive state program of internal improvements, public education, and humanitarian measures on behalf of debtors, criminals, the physically impaired, and the insane. During the same period Democrats generally preferred an essentially negative government. By the late 1840s, the Whigs, who had held the governorship since 1836, became more cautious in the use of power. The Democrats, prompted largely by Holden, shed their negative philosophy and espoused an activist state government. Ironically, in the 1850s the Democrats completed much of the progressive program initiated by the Whigs in the 1840s. A consideration of three key issues—internal improvements, constitutional reform, and southern rights—will reveal the fluctuations that were peculiar to the second party system in North Carolina.

Geographic realities had long determined that North Carolina would be fragmented into sections and that the relative isolation of many of her people would characterize the society. There were no great rivers linking the various sections of the state. Commerce west of the fall line was difficult at best; westerners frequently had more contacts with neighboring states than with eastern North Carolina. Before the 1830s little could be done to remedy nature's deficiencies. Plank roads, canals, and steamboats held little long-term promise in a state with such a varied topography. All was changed, however, by the application of steam power to overland transportation. Railroads held untold promise for North Carolina; but the cost of building, equipping, and maintaining a railroad system seemed prohibitively high in a state whose capital was heavily invested in agriculture and slaves. State support was badly needed. By adopting a program of positive government action, including encouragement for railroads, the nascent Whig party gained an initial advantage in the second party system. Citizens in all sections who favored government aid for internal improvements were likely to find Whiggery appealing. The dilemma confronting North Carolina Whigs was to promote state development without raising taxes or borrowing extensively.

In 1837 North Carolina received $1,433,756.39 from the federal government under provisions of the Distribution of the Surplus Act of 1836. This windfall, produced largely by the sale of the public domain, provoked a telling debate over how the money was to be used. (Documents 11.3 and 11.4) Committed to a negative government philosophy, Democrats favored banking the distribution money, liquidating the modest state debt, reducing taxes, or some combination of those alternatives. Whigs, on the other hand, saw distribution as the answer to pressing state needs. The Whigs, who controlled the legislature in 1837, overwhelmingly enacted measures to stimulate banking and commerce; to promote internal improvements; and, because investments in bank stock and railroad securities totaling $1,100,000 were assigned to the Literary Fund, to establish a public school system. Given their preference for progressive government policies, which were usually expensive, it was understandable that North Carolina Whigs would oppose all attempts to lower the price of western lands or to permit preemption by land-hungry settlers. From 1836 to 1850 distribution was a cornerstone of Whig philosophy in state and national elections.

Railroad construction received a great impetus from Whig governors and legislators. Assured of the possibility of state assistance, private entrepreneurs formed companies, obtained state charters of incorporation, sold stock, and began building railroads in eastern North Carolina. The Wilmington and Raleigh Company (whose name was changed in 1854 to the Wilmington and Weldon) was financed largely by Wilmington capitalists, who, despairing of adequate support from Raleigh investors, built their line to Weldon, a small town on the Roanoke River, which afforded access to Richmond and Petersburg railroads. Piqued by this development, Raleigh investors built a railroad from their city to Gaston, also a small town on the Roanoke with connecting lines into southern Virginia. Both ventures—boldly undertaken with private capital—required substantial state assistance before completion.

Despite the drain on the public treasury caused by these early railroads, the people of North Carolina demanded that more be built. Plans were discussed for roads in all sections to join east and west and to link up with South Carolina and other Virginia towns. Finally, in late 1848, believing that political exigencies and state conditions required a more progressive outlook, William W. Holden abruptly shifted editorial ground. He urged Democrats to abandon their past opposition and boldly asserted that railroads were a boon to the state, even if public financing was necessary. (Document 11.5) Most Democrats responded slowly to Holden's clarion call. In 1849, however, it was the tie-breaking vote of Democratic House Speaker Calvin Graves that saved the bill creating the North Carolina Railroad Company. Chartered with a capitalization of $3 million ($2 million of which were to be subscribed by the state), the North Carolina Railroad stretched from Goldsboro through Raleigh to Charlotte. In January 1856, the 223-mile railroad began operations, stimulating agriculture and commerce by opening the west and piedmont to distant markets. In the 1850s state support for internal improvements—especially railroads—was one subject upon which Democrats and Whigs could agree.

Harmony among partisan North Carolina politicians was a rarity, but constitutional revision was an issue upon which both parties followed the dictates of the ballot box. Although the impetus for the constitutional changes effected in 1835 predated the second party system, the nascent Whig party was the principal beneficiary of these reforms. For several years, the Whigs, who also espoused a philosophy of positive government, enjoyed a reputation as the more progressive of the two parties. This fact provided an important, if partial, explanation of Whig electoral successes in the late 1830s and 1840s.

The potency of constitutional issues as vehicles of political success was not lost on the North Carolina Democrats. In 1848 Democratic gubernatorial candidate David S. Reid, a native of Rockingham County, suggested to the party leadership that he emphasize a single issue—free suffrage. Thousands of balloters who were qualified except for the want of a fifty-acre freehold were prevented under provisions of the 1776 constitution from voting for state senators. Reid proposed to correct this inequity. In a debate with the Whig candidate, Raleigh attorney Charles Manly, in early May, Reid explained the need for constitutional revision and coined the phrase "free suffrage" before calling upon Manly to respond. An astonished Manly pled unpreparedness on that occasion. The next day, 11 May 1848, having had no opportunity to consult other Whig leaders, he staked out a position. After complaining that the issue had been unsportingly sprung on him, Manly claimed that this reform had no support among the electorate and concluded that the Founding Fathers had wisely established the Senate as protector of the landed interest. In a reversal of roles, Manly's foursquare opposition to equal suffrage placed the Whigs in a conservative position while allowing the Democrats to present themselves as advocates of a constitutional amendment that appealed to the masses.

Initially Whig editors supported their candidate in opposition to abolition of the fifty-acre freehold. Later, when the issue became increasingly popular with the people, they sought to ignore it. Privately many prominent Whigs believed that their man had blundered, noting that the end of this modest property qualification would make little difference. It is still difficult to assess the impact of free suffrage on the outcome of the 1848 gubernatorial election. Manly narrowly defeated Reid by a majority of 854 in a total poll of 84,218, which compared very unfavorably with the majority of 7,859 by which William A. Graham, his Whig predecessor, had carried the state in 1846. Clearly, the Democrats were on the move.

Two years later, at the prompting of Holden, the reluctant Reid agreed to run again. (Document 11.6) In 1850 free suffrage was again the cornerstone of his campaign, along with a Holden proposal that state judges be popularly elected. A beleaguered Governor Charles Manly, once more in the field, recognized that his prospects were fading before Reid's promises of political equality. Finally, in the west, Manly tacitly embraced free suffrage and linked that constitutional reform to a change in the basis of commons representation from federal (five blacks were counted as three whites) to free white. Although popular in the west, this linkage was anathema to the east, where the slave population was greatest. Free suffrage presaged no important changes, but abandonment of the federal principle threatened a fundamental shift in power from east to west. Proponents of slavery saw this measure as a threat to the peculiar institution in North Carolina. Manly's proposal probably lost as many votes as it gained. In any event, David S. Reid was elected governor by a majority of 3,345 in a vote of 88,019, though the removal of the fifty-acre freehold requirement was not accomplished until an amendment was submitted to and ratified by the people in 1857. The white basis for allotting representation was not seriously considered before the Civil War; nonetheless, even lip service to such an idea allowed the Whigs to reclaim something of their former reputation as advocates of progressive constitutional revision.

In the late 1850s the Whigs also supported ad valorem taxation, proposing to amend the constitution so that slaves would be taxed as property rather than as polls. Although the chief proponent of the ad valorem principle was Wake County Democrat Moses A. Bledsoe, the official Democratic posture was to oppose it. In the gubernatorial campaign of 1860, John Pool, candidate of a resurgent Whiggery, championed the ad valorem principle to the discomfort of incumbent Democrat John W. Ellis, who was seeking a second term. Governor Ellis denounced ad valorem taxation, warning that even a family's chickens, furniture, and cooking utensils would be taxed if Pool and the Whigs prevailed. Thereafter the 1860 gubernatorial canvass was known as the "pots and pans campaign." Ellis won, but the Democratic majority fell from sixteen to six thousand votes.

The Whig gains were more remarkable because they had not offered a candidate since 1854 and had only recently reorganized in the wake of the national party's demise. It seemed that the Whig party, at least in North Carolina, might recover sufficiently to give the Democrats an equal contest in the future. But North Carolina politics were irrevocably altered by the election of Abraham Lincoln, the attack on Fort Sumter, and secession. On 20 May 1861 North Carolina left the Union to join the Confederacy. (Document 11.7) Neither Whigs nor Democrats gained political advantage from secession. Although the vestiges of old political alignments were discernible until 1864, southern rights, long a potent issue in state politics, had at last rendered the second party system obsolete.

Although North Carolina was predominantly a state of small farms and only about 30 percent of white families owned slaves at any one time, slavery—the socioeconomic basis of southern life—lay at the heart of the southern rights question. Any real or imagined threat to the peculiar institution was likely to cause a furor. North Carolinians reacted with alarm to the abolitionist literature that began to appear in the South around 1830. (Document 11.8) Slavery was firmly entrenched as a social and economic necessity when the second party system materialized, and both the Democratic and Whig parties were committed to its perpetuation. Both were equally determined that the constitutional rights of the minority South should be vigorously defended against northern encroachments. But neither party was monolithic; and, of course, there were differences within and between the parties as to what these rights were and how they could best be maintained.

By the 1850s most North Carolinians believed that they enjoyed the right to own slaves without restriction, to have fugitive slaves returned, and to establish slavery in United States territories. As more northerners became abolitionists or free soilers (determined that western territories must be free) and southerners sought more effective means of upholding their rights, the key issue ultimately became the nature of the Union. Was the Union merely a creature of the sovereign states from which any state might easily withdraw, as John C. Calhoun had claimed, or was it indissoluble and inviolable, as Abraham Lincoln and others believed? Opinions on this question changed with circumstances. Each North Carolina political party contained conservative, moderate, and ultra secessionists and unionists. In general, Democrats were more likely to be ardent secessionists and Whigs to be devoted to the Union, but within limits both shifted ground in conjunction with national party policy changes. For example, in 1837 North Carolina Whigs favored the annexation of Texas; by 1844, because of Henry Clay's negative position on the acquisition of western territories, they opposed it.

The national Whig party disintegrated over the issue of slavery in the middle 1850s, allowing most northern Whigs to join the emergent Republican party but leaving southerners with few options. North Carolina Whigs chose among several alternatives: becoming Democrats; joining the American or Know-Nothing party; remaining Whig, which promised little except political impotence; or abandoning politics altogether. (Document 11.9) Fortune favored the Democrats. Gradually within the state and nation the Democratic party became the haven for slaveholders and their sympathizers. Even so, the national Democratic party could not long avoid the divisive slavery–southern rights predicament. In 1860, the party split along sectional lines over whether the territories were to be slave or free. Including the Republican nominee, Abraham Lincoln, there were three sectional candidates in the field. Only the Constitutional Union party, hastily contrived by old-line Whigs, had national appeal, and its aborted efforts were too little and too late. Although Lincoln received only 40 percent of the popular vote, he won an overwhelming victory in the electoral college. Without the restraint of national political parties, sectionalism triumphed. It would appear that the demise of the second party system contributed to the death knell of the Union.

The second party system provided the milieu in which two evenly matched political factions contended for advantage, a circumstance without parallel in North Carolina history. The Democratic and Whig parties were formed during the second Jackson administration. At that time, the Democrats supported the president's policies, and the Whigs railed against executive tyranny and called for a national bank and the distribution of government treasury surpluses. National issues were paramount in the election process and in political rhetoric until the late 1840s, when state issues were given more prominence. Both political parties were a conglomeration of men from all sections, vocations, and strata of society. In general, it would appear that the Whigs had their greatest appeal among large slaveholders, professional men—especially lawyers—townsmen, and those whose interests lay in internal improvements. The Democrats always enjoyed great strength in areas where plantation agriculture was predominant. Once formed, political alliances were altered reluctantly.

North Carolina Whigs and Democrats were vigorous in their pursuit of election victories. Initially the Whigs were better organized and led; they had a broader appeal because of their support of constitutional reforms in 1835 and their positive government philosophy. By the late 1840s, however, the Whigs had become cautious and complacent, while under the prodding of Holden and the *Standard*, the Democrats had abandoned their negative concepts of government, to their political advantage. Between 1836 (when the governor was first popularly elected) and 1854 (when the national Whig party collapsed), the Whigs elected governors seven times, the Democrats three. The Democrats carried the state in presidential contests in 1836 and 1852, the Whigs in 1840, 1844, and 1848. In the same eighteen-year period, forty-eight Whigs and forty-four Democrats were elected to seats in the national House of Representatives. The contests for state legislative hegemony were especially competitive. On joint ballot the Democrats had a one-vote majority in the legislature of 1836 and working margins in 1842, 1850, and 1854. The Whigs had majorities in the legislatures that convened in 1838, 1840, 1844, 1846, and 1852. In 1848 there was a tie in both houses. Because United States senators were elected by the state legislature, the Whigs enjoyed an advantage in possessing senatorships. Two Whigs and one Democrat were appointed to cabinet posts; and, in 1852, William A. Graham was the Whig vice-presidential nominee.

Questions naturally remain about the precipitous decline of the apparently vigorous Whig party after 1852. Some historians have accepted Holden's contention that free suffrage was the issue upon which party fortunes turned. Others suggest that the defection of the influential western congressman Thomas L. Clingman was decisive. An examination of gubernatorial election returns suggests, however, that neither Reid's free suffrage campaign in 1848 nor Clingman's 1852 support of Franklin Pierce and 1854 political conversion were as important as previously believed. Beginning in 1842, except for 1846 when the disorganized Democrats faced a popular incumbent, the trend was toward smaller Whig majorities. Clingman failed to deliver his district to the Democrats until after the demise of the Whig party.

The Whig decline may be attributed to several factors—disgruntlement with the party managers of the central clique, failure to accomplish substantial internal improvement projects in the piedmont and west, loss of initiative as older leaders became more conservative without relinquishing power, and vacillation on democratic constitutional reforms. But perhaps the crucial factor was the revitalization of the state Democratic party at about the same time the vocal northern wing of the Whig party, in a prelude to party disintegration, adopted free soilism. Apparently, like the Federalists before them, the Whigs required national party affiliations. When these ties were broken, the second party system had little chance of survival, despite Whig optimism over the 1860 state election. North Carolina has been predominantly a one-party state ever since.

DOCUMENT 11.1

Willie P. Mangum's Dilemma

The present state of parties, and the great results that may be achieved by the efforts of this Winter, & knowing that those efforts on the part of the *Kitchen* are prodigious, lead to this communication.—You will pardon me for addressing you with the purpose I have in this matter.—I know that your position makes it matter of great delicacy to touch general politics.—Nor would I, if I could have you to violate in the slightest degree the decorums of your station—& yet I feel that the country is entitled to the influence of your great popularity & weight of Character in the pending struggle.—The next six or eight months will probably settle the question of the next Presidency—& with that question every thing else is fixed—For it is obvious, that the whole policy of the Country to a very great extent is controuled by that result. The Campaign this Winter on the part of Mr. Van Buren's friends will be exceedingly active—All the resources of that bad influence *around & under & over* the throne will be actively employed. . . .

All opposition here to bad influences, is attributed to *enmity to the hero*, to National republicanism & to nullification.—In these bad times, no man can be honest without being denounced with the sins of hatred of Jackson, nullification &c &c—

The popularity of Jackson on the one hand & the unpopularity of nullification on the other, give the party in power great advantages in the South—& they rely upon them for success—. . . .

As the U.S. Bank will not apply this session & probably not to this Congress, for a recharter, I regret that the Bank question has been thrown before the Legislature—The naked question of recharter is much weaker, I presume, than the *Deposite* question—The battle should be fought on the *latter*.—The removal deeply involves the question of *good faith*, as well as all the considerations of policy, & upon the question of faith, I think N.C. will be found strong, if sufficiently enlightened.—I predicate this upon the belief, that we are less corrupted than are the most of our neighbours.—My opinion is, that North Carolina disagrees with the Adm^n. in reference to the *public domain*—Clay's Bill upon its great principles, I speak not in reference to all its details, I think falls in with the views of the State generally—

I have twice voted against the measure, upon the ground that until the Tariff was adjusted, I would not *without instruction* entertain any question, that by abstracting from the public revenue, would to that extent be a sort of make-weight in aid of the continuance of the Tariff—No vote of mine has been given on the *merits*—Might not the Legislature, in the event of a movement, such as I anticipate, move that question advantageously?— . . .

Though on the one hand far short of So. Ca. nullification yet on the other equally adverse to the antagonist principle of Consolidation.—I foresee that in No. Ca. *The Independents*, as I presume to call myself, or the absolute *submissionists*, (I mean submission to the bad influences here) will wage the war.—There are fearful odds on the side of the submissionists—all the holders, & hopers for office, will be with them, & besides the power of Gen. Jackson's name will be so used, as to be a tower of strength with the multitude.— . . .

My course is taken—I shall give a cordial support, where I can to the admn: But I shall also give what aid I can to the exposure of abuses.—It is on this latter point where there is most sensibility.—I clearly see now, as I have clearly foreseen for several months, that my course would subject me to the most unsparing vituperation of the Collar press here & in No Carolina.—

The only check to as absolute power, as that in Russia is found in the Senate.—The policy of men in power is to destroy that body in public opinion.—Every other branch of the Gov^t. is unquestionably & almost unqualifiedly subservient to the will & passions of One Man—or to speak more truly, to the will & passions of a Cabal that gives a decided direction to the Executive.—

Senator Willie P. Mangum to Governor David L. Swain, 22 December 1833, confidential, in Henry T. Shanks, ed., The Papers of Willie P. Mangum, *5 vols. (Raleigh: North Carolina Department of Archives and History, 1950–56), 2:51–55.*

DOCUMENT 11.2

William W. Holden Comments on the "Reluctant" 1844 Gubernatorial Candidacy of William A. Graham

When and where did the delicate lawyer-like hands of William A. Graham become accustomed to the handles of the plough? Will nobody enlighten us? The truth is, the idea is perfectly ridiculous. This reluctant "breaking away" from "agricultural pursuits" was put in for no other purpose than that of conveying to the minds of the farmers of the State the impression that he is a practical farmer. . . . We believe Mr. Graham does live in the center of a 10-acre patch. The extensive farm is bounded on the south by the waters of the Enoe—on the north by the Oxford road—on the east by a magnificent branch at least two feet wide—and on the west by the ancient village of Hillsboro, and over all look proudly down the Ocanechee Mountains. We shall therefore call him the Ocanechee Farmer, a pretty title and romantic. And now imagine him out at work. Of course his coat is off, his sleeves rolled up, and his whole soul set against being broken off from his "agricultural pursuits." He ploughs along; and ever as he gets to the turning row he kicks the mud from the ploughshare with his elegant slipper, and swears, with all the sternness of a man bent on making corn that he will farm it. Anon he denounces the late Federal Convention for "breaking in" upon his "agricultural pursuits," casts a last melancholy look at his beloved grubbing hoe; and then in a spirit of beautiful desperation, rushes to his office, seizes his pen, and signs the letter of acceptance. The deed is done. Henceforth his corn will grow; but oh! agony! he will not see it.

North Carolina Standard, *3 January 1844.*

DOCUMENT 11.3

Distribution: A Whig View

But notwithstanding the duty prescribed in this case is so obvious and palpable, there are yet some who appear inclined to disregard it, and to make disposition of the public lands favorable alone to the new states, and violatory of all the deeds of cession.—It is . . . then high time for the people of the old states to look seriously to this matter, and repel with indignation all attempts to deprive them of their rights; of their equal and just share of the proceeds of the public lands.

The revenue from this source last year amounted to about five millions of dollars, which if divided among the states would give to North Carolina nearly three hundred thousand dollars. This distributive share would probably increase every year as the sales increased and the settlements extended. With this sum annually flowing into our treasury, rail roads and canals might be constructed in every direction through the state. A new impulse would be given to the industry, enterprise and commerce of the country; and the whole land, in a short time, might be made to blossom as the rose. After accomplishing these great objects, a system of schools might be established, so as to give every poor man in every neighbourhood, opportunities of education free from all expense or taxation of any kind whatever. These are bright and cheering prospects, it is true, but not more so than can be fully realized, if the Representatives of the people are true to the trust reposed in them, and will do what is right, regardless of all extraneous or improper influence: For let it be remembered that a portion of the money arising from the public lands belongs to us; it is our property, and we should claim it as a matter of justice. Shall we not then avail ourselves of it? shall we not take it, and apply it to our own use and benefit, instead of permitting others to riot upon it at our expense? Surely we ought. Enlightened patriotism, wise policy, and inflexible justice, all demand that we should take and use what belongs to us.

The great obstacle to internal improvements in our state, is the want of money; and the objection to borrowing it, is the difficulty of paying the interest. But according to the plan here suggested these impediments can be easily overcome. In the first place, if the state choses to do so, she can go on and construct three hundred thousand dollars worth of internal improvements every year without taxation, which in a few years, would amount to a great deal. But if she should prefer to progress faster than this, she might borrow between five and ten millions of dollars, which would be amply sufficient for all our purposes, and pay the interest annually without taxation. After the works shall have been completed, and become a source of profit to the state as they soon would do, the three hundred thousand dollars, from sales of the public lands, still flowing into our treasury, would be disengaged from the payment of the first loan, and could be applied to the making of new loans for the accomplishment of other desirable objects. Thus, without one cent of burden, or tax of any kind upon the people, all these advantages may be enjoyed—who can be so unwise as to reject them? I hope no one and I trust, fellow citizens, you will look to it, and see that your interest is faithfully maintained.

Congressman Lewis Williams, "To the Citizens of the Thirteenth Congressional District of North Carolina" (broadside), 1835, pp. 7–8.

DOCUMENT 11.4

Distribution: A Democratic View

Voters of Rockingham County   January 23, 1837
    Of all other subjects you perhaps feel most anxious to hear the result of the deliberations of the Legislature in regard to the Surplus Revenue alloted to the State under the deposit act of Congress. . . .
    We take the act of Congress on this subject to be what it is, and can view the sum of One Million nine hundred and eleven thousand Six hundred and Seventy Six dollars and fifty three cents which the State received under this act, in no other light than a *deposit* and not a *gift,* and that the State pledges herself to refund it to the General Government when called for, upon the terms stipulated in the act. Perfectly aware that the past Legislature was looked to with considerable Solicitude to give an impulse to some general system of Internal Improvement, but with our

views of this Subject, had objects presented themselves in which our Constituents could have been *immediately* interested, we Should have doubted much the propriety of investing the Surplus Revenue so as to put it beyond the reach of the State if called on for it, much less could we think of voting for a system so extravagant in its nature, but, extravagant as it is, it gives nothing to those we represent. Yes, the Surplus Revenue of which so much has been said and so many promises made, is disposed of before it is received, and altho' you do not directly participate in its benefits, if it is demanded by the General Government you will *partici-pate* directly in its repayment. It was said that the money must be returned to the *people*, but where is it? The answer is, you are bound for your part in it and still get *none*. The distribution of the Surplus Revenue is a hoax! it is a gross imposition on the people and the events of every day more fully demonstrates the fact! We are indeed sorry that more money was Collected from the people than was necessary for the expenditures of an economical Government. But we were told that a Surplus had unavoidably accrued in the Treasury and that it must be returned to the people and none were then to be found to contend that this as a principle was not unjust and dangerous in its tendency, but it is a lamentable fact that there are some now who propose it as a general system. Reduce the taxes you pay on your necessaries of life to the wants of the General Government and you have no Surplus in your Treasury, but have it in your *pockets* subject to your own disposal: it is hoped that the number is few who will ask a boon from the National Treasury when it is perfectly obvious that for every dollar we get we must previously pay one and a half; this is well calculated to make the Treasury rich and the people poor, it is not believed that there are many who for *party devotion* will nurse a doctrine so inemical to the Constitution and dangerous to the Country. We have little hesitation in saying that time will confirm the correctness of the views we have so often repeated to you on this subject. It is hoped that it is not understood that we are opposed to Internal Improvement for such is not the fact, for we are devoted to it when conducted upon principles of equity with an eye to all the great interests of the State, but can not consent to a system of *Log rolling*, more particularly with the *funds* of the General Government.

David S. Reid and Philip J. Irion, To the Voters of Rockingham County, 23 January 1837, David S. Reid Papers, North Carolina Archives, Raleigh.

DOCUMENT 11.5

Holden Advocates Internal Improvements

We have no hesitation in expressing the belief, that a very large majority of the people of the State, of both parties, confidently expect that the present legislature will devise some general system of Internal Improvements; and that unless their expectations are responded to, those members who may come up here, two years hence, to take charge of the public interests, will find the State five hundred thousand dollars worse off than it is now. This is strong language, but in all sincerity we believe it to be true; and we should be false to our convictions, and wanting in that candor and frankness which ought to characterize the conductor of a public press, if we failed to give expression to it. Our young men are leaving us, by fifties and by hundreds, to seek their fortunes and to win distinction in other and distant lands; our Commerce languishes, and our Farmers and Planters, as a general rule, scarcely realize enough to keep their estates together; and with the exception of a few localities, favored by nature, and fortunate in the enterprise and energies of their inhabitants, the whole State labors under a weight and encounters disadvantages, which nothing but a bold, a general, and a vigorous system of Internal Improvements can remove. Here, then, is work for *North Carolinians* to do, and to which, we make no doubt, they are fully equal. Let the voice of party, as to this question, at least, be silent; and let us all resolve, happen what may, that some plan shall be fixed upon and the work begun.

North Carolina Standard, *13 December 1848.*

DOCUMENT 11.6

Holden Comments on Politics, 1850

I have read and re-read your confidential letter, but cannot, for my life, percive [*sic*] that your reasons for declining are conclusive. . . . You are the strongest man with *the masses* ever presented to the people, and the leaders *dare not* oppose you, or even appear indifferent. I know it.

Just look, if you please, at the condition of things. Both the Mountain Banner and the Asheville News, Whig papers, are *pledged against* Manly, and for "State Reforms." Also, the Whigs of Buncombe, who have just had a Meeting. I shall publish a Communication next week headed "Who shall be the Nominees?" and pressing your name, from a well informed Rutherford Democrat, who assures me that you will beat Manly in Rutherford 500 votes. John Gray Bynum is running for the Senate in that County *against* Manly; and in Halifax and Granville the Whigs are disorganized, and cannot get candidates. Besides, Clay has just attacked Taylor in the strongest terms, and Whigs in this State *must* decide between the two. Several Whig papers have already denounced Taylor; and next week the Raleigh Star will denounce Stanly, the North State Whig, and the Raleigh Times, in the fiercest terms. These things, all together, may not indeed give you any *Whig* votes, but they *must* produce lukewarmness in the Whig ranks ... which cannot fail to diminish Manly's vote. For the last two months I have carefully kept back from the Standard all evidences of Manly's unpopularity, in the hope that he would again be the candidate; there is now no doubt that he will be; and I have all these evidences filed away, to be used as soon as he is nominated.

So far as the Central Road is concerned, you have taken, in your letter to me, *the right ground, and the very ground which I have all along told our friends you would take.* Allow me to assure you that though Raleigh is for the Road, *you* are the first choice of every Democrat here. . . . Your election, under the circumstances, could not injure the Rail Road Democrats, who have nothing more to ask in the way of appropriations, while it would give confidence to the anti-Rail Road Democrats, because they could trust you on the subject. . . . I can speak for them; and besides, being for the Road, I have a right to require them, by every favorable consideration, to sustain you. They will do it, almost, if not quite, unanimously. Again: If you will run, you are obliged to get the same vote, at least, you got last year west of Raleigh, and I think you will increase it. *Eight or ten Counties in the centre might have elected you before, by polling their full strength.* With you in the field, I shall call on these counties by name, point to the vote, and *prove* to them what they can do; and I will address every leading man in them in relation to his duty . . . and they will be *bound* to do their duty towards you.

It is not necessary that you should stump the State at all. You have done it once. You are universally known as Manly's former competitor, *and as the author of Equal Suffrage.* All you will have to say, will be, that you and the Governor have already stumped the State once, and that, while you are willing to do it again, so far as the time will allow, *you await the movements of "His Excellency."* This will throw the blame on him of leaving his duties here.

In regard to the Nashville Convention, that is a dead question. *I knew, four weeks ago, that you were opposed to it;* or rather that you thought it inexpedient now; but what of that? We are all for secession at the proper time; and in going for it I but yielded to the will of the majority, and did not dream of proscribing anyone. . . . All you will have to do, in this regard, if you accept, is to endorse the Resolutions of the Convention. In regard to Clay's Compromise and Taylor's plan, you need not advocate either; but you might say, if compelled to choose, that you would take Clay's plan. In your letter of acceptance, you enforce Equal Suffrage—go for Judges, etc. by the People, and in regard to "State Reform" generally, called for by the Buncombe Whigs, you might say you were for "State Reforms," and would, if elected, cheerfully co-operate with the Assembly in bringing it about. *Manly could not say that, without condemning his own party,* which has had the State government fourteen years. . . .

I write the universal opinion of our friends here when I say you are, by far, the strongest man, and that your election is certain. I have not conversed with a single Democrat who speaks otherwise; and *Whigs* have told me you would certainly beat Manly. So far as I am concerned, I am for you against the world; and if you will consent to run, I will omit neither expense, nor labor, nor pains, so far as they will go, to ensure your success. I will publish the Standard twice a week from the Convention until the election, and labor for you, *with an assurance of triumph,* day and night.

William W. Holden to David S. Reid, 1 June 1850, David S. Reid Papers, North Carolina Archives, Raleigh.

DOCUMENT 11.7

Secession

Heard today that on the 20th, it being the anniversary of the Signature of the Mecklenburg Dec of Independance, the Convention of NC signed the ordinance of Secession. The scene is said to have beggared description. So soon as the Ordinance had been signed & the Speaker had announced that North Carolina "abjured her allegiance to the U S" & solemnly "assumed her own Sovereignty," Ramseur's Battery stationed outside fired a Salute of a hundred Guns! This seemed a signal for men, women & children to flock to the State House. The men shook hands, the women rushed into each other's arms, every body congratulated everybody else. Persons who had not spoken for years exchanged the most cordial & fraternal greeting. When quiet was restored after a brief interval, the President put the Question as to whether North Carolina should join the Southern Confederacy, which was carried by acclaim first, then by individual vote without one dissentient! So now we are under Mr. Davis rule! "Hurrah for Jeff Davis!"

Beth Gilbert Crabtree and James W. Patton, eds., "Journal of a Secesh Lady": The Diary of Catherine Ann Devereux Edmonston, 1860–1866 (Raleigh: Department of Cultural Resources, 1979), 22 May 1861, p. 63.

DOCUMENT 11.8

Denunciation of Abolitionists, 1837

For two years past the country has been much agitated by these misguided and deluded fanatics. They have been endeavoring to enlist the people of the North in a crusade against the domestic institutions of the South, the certain consequence of which would be a dissolution of the Union, which we should all regard as a great political evil. The South never ought, and never will submit to the least interference from any quarter with her own domestic and internal concerns. If slavery be an evil, it is one which the South alone has the right to consider and relieve. The abolitionists, however, are regardless of consequences, and have pressed this delicate and dangerous question upon the consideration of Congress. They commence with the abolition of slavery in the District of Columbia, as being most plausible; but this is only an entering wedge to further operations. Swarms of petitions praying for the abolition of slavery in the District of Columbia, were addressed to us at the commencement of the last Congress. Their reception was objected to; and upon this abstract right to petition, the most angry speeches were made on both sides of the question, well calculated to produce the most unhappy excitement in all quarters of the Union. All other business stood still, while the subject of slavery was agitated day after day for nearly two months. This agitation was the very thing the abolitionists desired.

Congressman Abraham Rencher, "To the People of the Tenth Congressional District of North Carolina" (broadside), 1837, p. 7.

DOCUMENT 11.9

A Whig Becomes a Democrat

Your kind favor had just come to hand when a multitude of business interests engaged my attention, which have prevented my answering until now.

I have bestowed much anxious reflection upon the political condition of our country and I am distressed with apprehensions for her future safety. I see no prospect for the termination of the war on slavery. The occasion in which the Republican party had its origin will probably pass away—but the result of the contest on the subject of the "legislative restriction" on the progress of slavery has been, I fear, to abolitionize the mind of the free states, and what was a mere contest in regard to a constitutional question—has become a contest in regard to slavery itself. That a party is organizing with this characteristic cannot be doubted. It must in conformity to all laws, progress, in power and activity and sooner or later will push all the South before it. This evil may be parried and delayed, but cannot be defeated. The frightful consequence is ever before me so that really I take no interest whatever in politics or political parties. Every other question has lost its interest to my mind, before the great and manifest danger of the South & the Union. The Northern Whig party have unquestionably betrayed its Southern supporters. The American Party is impotent save for division and destruction. The democracy have as yet a powerful national organization, which is held together by the "cohesive power" of ambition of sympathy and of interest. What it can do in this crisis I know not. It will be conquered I fear . . . by the combination of opposing elements. Should it be so, our worst apprehensions will be realized. For look at the matter as we may, the Democratic party is the only one affording any formidable resistance to the Black Republicans. The duty of Southern men in the crisis hopeless as it is, is to hold themselves in readiness by as little division of sentiments among themselves as possible upon secondary and collateral subjects. I hope these views are not too gloomy, and may never be realized. And I trust that the kind Providence which has ever taken care of our economy will protect it still.

James W. Osborne to Edward J. Hale, 10 July 1857, Edward J. Hale Papers, North Carolina Archives, Raleigh.

SUGGESTED READINGS

Craven, Avery O. *The Growth of Southern Nationalism, 1848–1861.* Baton Rouge: Louisiana State University Press, 1953.

Folk, Edgar E., and Shaw, Bynum. *W. W. Holden: A Political Biography.* Winston-Salem, N.C.: John S. Blair, 1982.

Hamilton, J. G. de Roulhac. *Party Politics in North Carolina.* Durham: Seeman Press, 1916.

Hoffman, William S. *Andrew Jackson and North Carolina Politics.* Chapel Hill: University of North Carolina Press, 1958.

Jeffrey, Thomas E. "Internal Improvements and Political Parties in Antebellum North Carolina, 1836–1860." *North Carolina Historical Review* 55 (1978):111–56.

_____. "National Issues, Local Interests, and the Transformation of Antebellum North Carolina Politics." *Journal of Southern History* 50 (1984):43–74.

_____. " 'Thunder from the Mountains': Thomas Lanier Clingman and the End of Whig Supremacy in North Carolina." *North Carolina Historical Review* 56 (1979):366–95.

Jones, Houston G. "Bedford Brown: State Rights Unionist." *North Carolina Historical Review* 32 (1955):321–45.

Kruman, Marc W. *Parties and Politics in North Carolina, 1836–1865.* Baton Rouge: Louisiana State University Press, 1983.

McCormick, Richard P. *The Second American Party System.* Chapel Hill: University of North Carolina Press, 1966.

Norton, Clarence Clifford. *The Democratic Party in Ante-Bellum North Carolina, 1835–1861.* Chapel Hill: University of North Carolina Press, 1930.

Pegg, Herbert Dale. *The Whig Party in North Carolina.* Chapel Hill: Colonial Press, 1968.

Sitterson, Joseph Carlyle. *The Secession Movement in North Carolina.* Chapel Hill: University of North Carolina Press, 1939.

Sydnor, Charles S. *The Development of Southern Sectionalism, 1819–1848.* Baton Rouge: Louisiana State University Press, 1948.

Watson, Harry L. *Jacksonian Politics and Community Conflict: The Emergence of the Second Party System in Cumberland County, North Carolina.* Baton Rouge: Louisiana State University Press, 1981.

Williams, Max R. "The Foundations of the Whig Party in North Carolina: A Synthesis and a Modest Proposal." *North Carolina Historical Review* 47 (1970):115–29.

CHAPTER 12

Unwilling Hercules

North Carolina in the Confederacy

Paul D. Escott

1. Blockade runners were loaded with cotton here   4. Cape Fear River
2. Porter's Flagship   5. Town Hall
3. Custom House

View of Wilmington's Front Street, 1865, With Released Prisoners Marching to Their Transports, from Harper's Weekly, *27 February 1865 (Courtesy of the Division of Archives and History, Raleigh, N.C.)*

The Civil War took a heavy toll in death and destruction in a state that only recently had begun to awaken from lethargy and backwardness. But in addition to the costs of war, North Carolina suffered the travail of constant conflict and dissatisfaction within the framework of the Confederate government. Citizens of the Old North State complained bitterly of government oppression in the form of taxes, impressment, conscription, and suspension of the writ of habeas corpus. Their governor challenged the constitutionality of the draft and Confederate shipping regulations. The people generally felt that their defense and their interests were ignored by the central government. Internally, class tensions and open disaffection with the southern cause reached such proportions that North Carolinians sometimes fought each other and gave much support to a powerful, if ultimately unsuccessful, peace movement. Truly, North Carolina presented, in aggravated form, all the internal problems of the South's new nation.

Why did so many discontents and difficulties concentrate in one state? Two factors hold the key to North Carolina's experience in the Confederacy: psychology and circumstance. During the war circumstances conspired to weigh down a people whose psychological commitment to southern independence was already weak. Material suffering intensified spiritual suffering and gave people a doubly heavy burden to carry. Together the psychological condition of North Carolinians and the exceptionally heavy demands that were placed on them ensured an unhappy sojourn as part of the Confederate States of America.

To understand the psychology of North Carolinians one must start with the secession movement. The people of North Carolina were singularly unenthusiastic about the prospect of leaving the Union and joining a new southern government. Despite the influence of an actively pro-secession governor, John W. Ellis, they refused even to hold a convention and showed their intention of sending a large majority of unionist delegates to the convention, had it been approved. Judge Thomas Ruffin and others represented North Carolina in a peace conference called by Virginia, which presented to Congress seven proposals to amend the Constitution in order to obtain sectional harmony. President-elect Lincoln and Republican congressmen declined, however, to support these proposals, and the likelihood of conflict grew.

After Lincoln decided to resupply Fort Sumter in Charleston Harbor, Confederate troops bombarded the fort on 12 April 1861. The war had begun, and Lincoln promptly called for troops from loyal states to suppress the "insurrection." "You can get no troops from North Carolina," Governor Ellis told the United States secretary of war, and he was right. The outbreak of fighting had turned North Carolinians into Confederates. "We are all one now," said former Unionist John A. Gilmer to

George Howard. As Zebulon B. Vance later wrote, "I preferred to shed Northern rather than Southern blood. If we had to slay, I had rather slay strangers than my own kindred and neighbors." On 20 May 1861, North Carolina seceded from the Union and joined the Confederacy. Nevertheless, the decision had come with a reluctance that was significant. (Document 12.1)

The war immediately occasioned many problems for North Carolina. Federal troops occupied coastal portions of the state as early as August 1861 and steadily expanded their control thereafter, menacing eastern counties throughout the rest of the war. The Union's naval blockade quickly produced shortages of many luxury items and such essentials as salt. Volunteering and conscription carried off the greatest part of the labor force in many areas and contributed to the widespread poverty in the Confederacy, which was severely aggravated by inflation and speculation or extortion. (Document 12.2) To maintain its existence, the Richmond administration relentlessly increased its demands for men, money, and supplies to wage the war.

North Carolina's geographical location contributed to its difficulties. Throughout the conflict most of the state remained inside Confederate lines. As the Confederacy lost more and more territory on its periphery, it had to draw more and more heavily on the resources of its core. Thus North Carolina was compelled to furnish a lion's share of the resources that stoked the furnaces of the war machine. Nearly one-fourth of all the conscripts in the southern armies, 21,348 men, came from North Carolina. In a state whose normal military population (white males aged eighteen to forty-five) was estimated at 116,000, approximately 120,000 served in the Confederate army and 40,000 died. Although the state had only about one-ninth of the Confederacy's white population, it furnished one-sixth of its fighting men. In nonhuman resources the story was the same, for the huge Confederate bureaucracy focused its attentions on the areas that it could control and made heavy demands on the state's citizens.

It is not surprising that North Carolinians resisted. Most of them had not wanted the war in the first place; once in the Confederacy, they found it, on the whole, to be a tragic experience. (Document 12.3) Thus although North Carolina made exceptional sacrifices for the cause, the historian discovers the complementary fact that North Carolina made exceptional protests. Probably no state raised more obstacles to the execution of policies of the central government.

The conscription law aroused anger not only because it caused hardship but also because it favored the rich. (Document 12.4) As a result, at least 23,000 of North Carolina's soldiers deserted, some no doubt encouraged by rulings of state courts. (Document 12.5) Nearly 15,000 men of military age were kept out of service by their governor, who designated them as essential officers of the state. Beginning in 1863, many North Carolinians began to call publicly for peace and demand that politicians initiate negotiations to end the bloodshed. This peace movement made great gains among Tar Heel voters and gave rise to persistent rumors in Richmond and elsewhere that the Old North State was going to leave the Confederacy. Disaffection was rampant in several parts of the state. (Document 12.6) Confederate authority disappeared in some mountain counties, where the tax collectors and conscription officers could not appear in safety. In sections of the piedmont bitter conflict raged between supporters of the Union and of the Confederacy. (Document 12.7)

In these troubled times the citizens of the state expressed their feelings in different ways, all representing variations on the theme of reluctant participation. Many North Carolinians emphasized the needs of local defense over the exigencies of the Confederacy and demanded that the Richmond government do more for them. Others, especially political leaders, reacted to undesirable, unpalatable (but necessary) war measures by resorting to states' rights theory. Confederate laws on conscription, impressment, and suspension of the writ of habeas corpus, they objected, were unconstitutional expansions of power by the central government at the expense of state authority and individual freedom. Their protests contained a large element of sincerity, but such opposition would not have appeared as early or been as strong if their commitment to the Confederacy had been intense. Men of slender means often felt compelled to put the needs of their families first, leaving the armies or resisting taxation and impressment. Surrounded by suffering and military defeat, some decided to face reality and work for peace. These Tar Heels felt sincerely that their situation was intolerable and sure to worsen if the Confederacy continued to struggle. Still others recognized that they were acting out a tragedy but concluded that honor required them to go on to the final curtain. All of these reactions evidenced a suffering people trying to deal with problems they never sought under burdens that few could carry. It was a painful experience for North Carolinians.

Fortunately for the state, the political process had identified a leader who could express the tortured feelings of the people and find for them some relief. Governor Zebulon Vance voiced the frustrations and anxieties of North Carolinians with considerable skill and some practical results. Although Vance personally felt duty-bound to support the Confederate cause, his actions reveal that often the cause of North Carolina was paramount. To Vance, the needs of the state took precedence over those of the Confederacy.

Elected in 1862, Vance took office at a time when demands upon the central government at Richmond increasingly taxed the resources of Confederate officials. As the Confederacy turned to the states and citizens for ever-greater levels of support, Vance soon found himself in the position of pleading for North Carolina's interests and trying to defend them by use of state authority. There is no question that Vance was loyal to the Confederacy and basically determined to support its cause. When the Richmond administration rejected his arguments or won disputed points in Confederate courts, Vance capitulated or found ways to go along. Without his cooperation the Confederacy would not have received the aid that did derive from North Carolina. But many of Vance's actions are inexplicable unless one considers the situation and feelings prevailing in the state.

For example, Vance raised numerous objections to conscription, in part because it exemplified the undesirable measures that war forced upon a people who had not wanted to secede. Political leaders throughout the state objected to the "military rule" or "despotism" that was involved in conscription, suspension of habeas corpus, and other policies. But Vance also spoke out because the drain of men caused real suffering in the state. In March 1863, Vance reminded Jefferson Davis that many areas of North Carolina had few slaves and frankly told him that conscription had taken off "a large class whose labor was, I fear, absolutely necessary to the existence of the women and children left behind." Vance tried to get these men back by suggesting that detailed soldiers be sent home to help with the harvest and requested that non-slaveholding areas be exempted from further calls for troops. Occasionally the Confederate government agreed to his requests, but Vance also used his own powers to keep men in the state. Declaring that 14,675 employees were essential to state government, he exempted more men from conscription than any other governor.

Vance also opposed Confederate supply operations in North Carolina because the government's measures brought real suffering to local citizens. The tax-in-kind, which imposed on farmers a tax of one-tenth of most food crops, was an unprecedented burden. (Document 12.8) Impressment—the confiscation of private property with promise of later repayment—was another primary source of supply for the Confederate army. This method was inherently unequal and open to abuse. No governor protested more eloquently against impressment than did Vance, when he declared to Confederate Secretary of War James Seddon, "If God Almighty had yet in store another plague worse than all others which he intended to have let loose on the Egyptians . . . I am sure it must have been a regiment or so of half-armed, half-disciplined Confederate cavalry." Confederate distilleries also aroused the governor's ire.

With hunger stalking the land and foodstuffs in short supply, Tar Heels were enraged to learn that the War Department was furnishing grain to run distilleries in North Carolina. Vance promptly invoked a state law against the operation and did his best to stop it.

In addition to his effort to ameliorate the effects of conscription and taxation, Vanced helped to lead a constitutional challenge to Confederate control of international shipping. In theory, foreign trade would seem to fall under national rather than state control. But, again, in practice, this was an area holding direct consequences for the health and welfare of North Carolinians. Governor Vance had built up an extensive, state-run import-export system. He used state-chartered blockade-runners to exchange cotton for blankets, shoes, uniforms, and other clothing for the suffering soldiers of North Carolina. When the Richmond administration tightened its control over shipping, Vance protested. The Confederacy was trying to ensure that scarce cargo space would be used to further the war effort, but North Carolinians wanted to ensure the supplies necessary for their own soldiers. The central government, with its constant demands for sacrifice, had become a threat to their welfare, and the state government became their protector. Tar Heels relied on state officials to help them because the Richmond government would not or could not. Given these feelings, it was not surprising that Vance's government hoarded huge quantities of food and clothing while Lee's army fought in tatters. By the time of Lee's surrender Vance was holding back 40,000 blankets, 150,000 pounds of bacon, cloth for 100,000 uniforms, leather for 10,000 pairs of shoes, and many other supplies. These items would have aided the Confederacy, but it was impolitic to transfer them to unpopular Confederate authorities as long as there was a chance that they could be used to help North Carolinians.

The character of public sentiment in North Carolina is best illustrated by Vance's clever response to William W. Holden's candidacy in the 1864 gubernatorial election. Holden, editor of the *Raleigh Standard* and an established political leader, had staked out a strong position as the candidate who most desired peace. (Document 12.9) Scores of public meetings had been held throughout the state during the summer of 1863 to endorse Holden and demand negotiations. (Documents 12.10 and 12.11) Jefferson Davis was horrified and urged Vance to deal harshly with "traitors." Vance determined to resist the peace movement, but he recognized the depth of the malaise affecting his state. He had seen the people's sufferings, and he could sympathize with their despair. No heavy-handed, pro-war approach, he knew, could be viable politically.

Accordingly, Vance determined to outmaneuver Holden by drawing his sting. The governor set out to appropriate the mantle of peacemaker for himself and demonstrate to the people that their best hopes for peace rested with him. Writing to Jefferson Davis on 30 December 1863, Vance argued that discontent was so advanced in North Carolina "that it will be perhaps impossible to remove it, except by making some effort at negotiation with the enemy." Asserting that rejection by the United States of such an effort would draw southerners together, Vance urged the administration to show "the humblest of our citizens . . . that the government is tender of their lives and happiness, and would not prolong their sufferings unnecessarily one moment." This letter became evidence during the campaign that Vance had proposed negotiations and sincerely desired an honorable peace. In addition, the incumbent charged that Holden was "the *war* candidate" and declared that the editor's plan to take North Carolina out of the Confederacy would bring "a new war [with neighboring states], a bloodier conflict than that you now deplore." Vance called on the legislature to define fair terms for peace and urged that the state's congressmen be charged with the responsibility of pressing for peace and independence after the next Confederate victory.

Vance found the responsive chord in the hearts of the voters. He knew that they fervently desired peace and convinced them that he did also. But his special achievement was to persuade them that the surest and safest road to peace lay through the Confederacy. In essence he had argued that all other routes were worse. Despite the war-weariness of North Carolina's citizens, Vance won a smashing victory in the 1864 gubernatorial election. His reelection removed any danger that North Carolina would desert the Confederacy and ensured that the state would provide the southern nation with major support through the end of the war in 1865.

North Carolinians undoubtedly took little pleasure in deciding to continue a war effort that had brought them to despair, but most saw no other choice. The Civil War had trapped North Carolina in a profound irony. A state that had not favored secession became the bulwark for secession's cause. A state that was a center of disaffection became a pillar of strength for the Confederacy. The people of this state bore their burdens grimly, impatiently, and painfully, for North Carolina was the unwilling Hercules of the Confederacy. (Document 12.12)

DOCUMENT 12.1

Zebulon Vance to Jefferson Davis, 25 October 1862

The people of this State have ever been eminently conservative and jealous of their political rights. The transition from their former opinions, anterior to our troubles, to a state of revolution and war was a very sudden and extra-ordinary one. Prior to Lincoln's proclamation [calling for troops] the election for delegates to our proposed convention exhibited a popular majority of upward of 30,000 against secession for existing causes. The late elections, after sixteen months of war and membership with the Confederacy, show conclusively that the original advocates of secession no longer hold the ear of our people. Without the warm and ardent support of the old Union men North Carolina could not so promptly and generously have been brought to the support of the seceding States, and without that same influence constantly and unremittingly given the present status could not be maintained forty-eight hours. These are facts. . . .

The corollary to be deduced is briefly this: That the opinions and advice of the old Union leaders must be heeded with regard to the government of affairs in North Carolina or the worst consequences may ensue. I am candid with you for the cause's sake. I believe, sir, most sincerely that the conscript law could not have been executed by a man of different antecedents without outbreaks among our people; and now, with all the popularity with which I came into office, it will be exceedingly difficult for me to execute it under your recent call with all the assistance you can afford me. If, on the contrary, West Point generals . . . are to ride roughshod over the people . . . I shall be compelled to decline undertaking a task which must certainly fail.

The War of the Rebellion: A Compilation of the Official Records of the Union and Confederate Armies, *130 vols. (Washington, D.C.: Government Printing Office, 1880–1901), 4th ser., 2:146–47.*

DOCUMENT 12.2

Zebulon Vance to Weldon N. Edwards, 18 September 1862

Extortion and speculation have attained such proportions that I find on investigation it will be impossible to clothe or shoe our troops this winter without incurring a most enormous outlay and submitting to most outrageous prices. . . .

The cry of distress comes up from the poor wives and children of our soldiers, also, from all parts of the State. If those prices bear so hard upon the Government, what will become of them when in addition we consider the enormous rates at which provisions are selling. . . . [An] ungodly and inhuman spirit of avarice . . . is rampant in the land.

The War of the Rebellion, *4th ser., 2:85–86.*

DOCUMENT 12.3

Former Governor Thomas Bragg on Wartime Conditions

Friday, February 14, 1862

[Federal troops have captured Roanoke Island.] There is great excitement in No. Ca. and the Gov't is blamed—the Sec'y of War is censured and the Sec'y of the Navy denounced for not having a fleet of Gun boats large enough to cope with the enemy. Judge Saunders of Raleigh writes a characteristic letter on the subject—says the Island, as the people believe, was defensible if more men and powder had been there &c, and that the opinion is that our men were sacraficed, and that volunteering will stop. Another portion say No. Ca. has been neglected, her troops sent to other points, while she is left to the tender mercies of the enemy. Many of our people I fear, influenced by these and considerations of safety for themselves & property will yield and make no resistance. . . .

A letter tonight from Walter F. Leake, of the N. Ca. Convention says that he fears that our people will not bear a draft for the war or 3 years to fill up the quota of troops required of that State, and suggests whether it will not be well for the new Congress to modify the law. Our public men want more and our people, I fear, also—

Saturday, February 15, 1862

Before the Cabinet met the No. Ca. delegation in Congress called to see the President & made known the wish of the Convention of that State, that our troops in So. Carolina should be sent back to Wilmington. The President . . . spoke feelingly as to the condition of the State and the disaster at Ro. Island . . . [but] said that he could not recall the troops from So. Ca. without greatly endangering and probably losing Charleston and Savannah, upon which an attack was threatened. . . .

Sunday, February 16, 1862

There is much discontent it seems in No. Ca. The Raleigh *Standard* is doing what it can to fan the flame, and excite public indignation against the authorities here.

Monday, February 17, 1862

The provisional Congress expired today—. . . The new Congress meets tomorrow. Will the Gov't endure? Can we repel the enemy? Dangers surround us & it commences at our darkest point since the war began. Time only can determine—I am by no means confident as to the issue.

Wednesday, February 19, 1862

Col. Wheeler tells me there is a general panic among our people. He moreover says that there is a good deal of disloyalty—and a parcel of them had the boldness to hold a meeting at [R]oxobel, Bertie Co. and that the people are afraid to interfere with them, as they threaten to burn and destroy the property of any one doing so.

Thursday, February 20, 1862

I have thought tonight what I shall do with this Journal in case the worst comes to the worst. It will not be safe to keep it and yet I dislike to destroy it. I fear I shall have it to do. I must confess that taking a survey of our whole field of operations it seems to me that our cause is hopeless—God grant that I may be mistaken.

Friday, March 7, 1862

I hear bad accounts from No. Ca. Disloyalty has boldly shown itself in Randolph, Chatham, and some adjoining Counties—and they openly declare they will not submit to a draft of troops. I hear that some 400 men had been sent up from Raleigh to check them. But the Convention had weakly refused to pass a law to punish such people, and thus it will go on. In the mean time the State is Bankrupt—What are we to do—. . . . The *Standard* . . . is already denouncing those who made the war. The Ro. Island disaster has had the worst possible effect. All, I fear, believe that after all our sacrafices No. Ca. is ill treated and abandoned to her fate.

Diary of Thomas Bragg, Southern Historical Collection, University of North Carolina, Chapel Hill.

DOCUMENT 12.4

Private O. Goddin to Governor Zebulon Vance, 27 February 1863

Please pardon the liberty which a poor soldier takes in thus addressing you as when he *volunteered* he left a wife with four children to go to fight for his country. He cheerfully made the sacrifices thinking that the Govt. would protect his family, and keep them from starvation. In this he has been disappointed for the Govt. has made a distinction between the rich man (who had something to fight for) and the poor man who fights for that he never will have. The [Confederacy's] exemption of the owners of 20 negroes & the allowing of substitutes clearly proves it. Healthy and active men who have furnished substitutes are grinding the poor by speculation while their substitutes have been discharged after a month's service as being too old or as invalids. By taking too many men from their farms they have not left enough to cultivate the land thus making a scarcity of provisions. . . .

Now Govr. do tell me how we poor soldiers who are fighting for the "rich mans negro" can support our families at $11 per month? How can the poor live? I dread to see summer as I am fearful there will be much suffering and probably many deaths from starvation. They are suffering now. . . .

I am fearful we will have a revolution unless something is done as the majority of our soldiers are poor men with families who say they are tired of the rich mans war & poor mans fight, they wish to get to their families & fully believe some settlement could be made were it not that our authorities have made up their minds to prosecute the war regardless of all suffering. . . . A mans first duty is to provide for his own household the soldiers wont be imposed upon much longer.

Governors' Papers, Zebulon B. Vance, North Carolina Archives, Raleigh.

DOCUMENT 12.5

Brigadier General W. D. Pender to Major W. H. Taylor, 23 April 1863

I would beg leave to call the attention of the commanding general to the state of affairs that exists in the North Carolina regiments of the army, and the causes which, in my opinion, have brought it about. I think I am safe in saying that at least 200 men have deserted from the Twenty-fourth North Carolina Regiment in this corps within the last thirty days. This, sir, I fear is not the worst of it, for unless some prompt measures be taken to arrest those already deserted, and severe punishment be inflicted after they shall be caught, the matter will grow from bad to worse. In my humble opinion, the whole trouble lies in the fact that they believe when they get into North Carolina they will not be molested, and their belief is based upon the dictum of Judge [R. M.] Pearson, chief justice of the State, in a recent trial of persons who killed some militia officers while in the discharge of their duties. I have not seen the judge's proceedings in the case, but our men are of the opinion that he held that the conscript law was unconstitutional, and hence they draw the conclusion that enrolled conscripts will not only be justified in resisting the law, but that those who have been held in service by the law will not be arrested when they desert. This conclusion is borne out by the facts. I have heard from a reliable gentleman that the conscripts and deserters go unmolested in Yadkin County. . . . Letters are received by the men, urging them to leave; that they will not be troubled when they get home. . . . What I have stated concerning Yadkin, I fear, holds good elsewhere, and, unless some check is put upon it, will work great and serious injury to the cause.

The War of the Rebellion, 1st ser., 25, pt. 2:746–47.

DOCUMENT 12.6

Brigadier General J. W. McElroy, North Carolina Home Guards, to Governor Zebulon Vance, 12 April 1864

A band of tories, said to be headed by Montreval Ray, numbering about seventy-five men, came into Burnsville, Yancey County, on Sunday night last, the 10th instant, surprised the guard, broke open the magazine, and took all the arms and ammunition; broke open Brayly's store and carried off the contents; attacked Captain Lyons, the local enrolling officer, in his room, shot him in the arm. . . . On the day before about fifty women assembled together, of said county, and marched in a body to a store-house . . . and pressed about sixty bushels of Government wheat and carried it off. . . . I urged on the citizens to lay to a helping hand in this hour of danger, but all done no good. The country is gone up. It has got to be impossible to get any man out there unless he is dragged out, with but very few exceptions. . . . In fact it seems to me that there is a determination of the people in the country generally to do no more service in the cause.

Swarms of men liable to conscription are gone to the tories or to the Yankees—

The War of the Rebellion, *1st ser., 53:326–27.*

DOCUMENT 12.7

Judge Thomas Settle to Governor Zebulon Vance, 4 October 1864

I wrote you that after investigating the matter I would report in full the conduct of the [loyal] officers towards [deserter leader Bill] Owens wife. . . . Col. Alfred Pike [reported], "I went with my squad to Owens spring where his wife was washing & inquired of her as to Owens where-abouts, she said he was dead & buried. I told her that she must show us the grave. She thereupon began to curse us and abuse us for every thing that was bad. Some of my men told me that if I would hand her over to them they would or could make her talk. I told her to go some twenty steps apart with them, she seized up in her arms her infant not twelve months old & swore she would not go—I slaped her jaws till she put down her baby & went with them, they tied her thumbs together behind her back & suspended her with a cord tied to her two thumbs thus fastened behind her to a limb so that her toes could just touch the ground, after remaining in this position a while she said her husband was not dead & that if they would let her down she would tell all she knew. I went up just then & I think she told some truth, but after a while I thought she commenced lying again & I with another man (one of my squad) took her off some fifty yards to a fence & put her thumbs under a corner of the fence. . . . This is all I have done Sir, and now, if I have not the right to treat Bill Owens, his wife & the like in this manner I want to know it & I will go to the Yankees or anywhere else before I will live in a country in which I cannot treat such people in this manner." . . .

Allow me Governor in this connection to call to your attention a matter in which you certainly must be misunderstood although your orders on their face bear the intrepetation which the officers gave to them. I found in Chatham, Randolph and Davidson that some fifty women in each county & some of them in delicate health and five advanced in pregnancy were rudely (in some instances) dragged from their homes & put under close guard & there left for some weeks. The consequence in some instances have been shocking. Women have been frightened into abortions almost under the eyes of the terrifiers. . . .

I know that your Excellency never has intended by any order to justify torture, & yet in many cases where the treatment has been equally as bad as it was in Owens Case, the officers boldly avow their conduct & say that they understand your orders to be a full justification—

H. L. Carson Papers, Free Library of Philadelphia, Philadelphia, Pa.

DOCUMENT 12.8

Minutes of the Sampson County Court, 16 November 1863

RESOLVED, 1st that we look forward with anxiety to the State of our county & the provisions for the poor and the destitute soldiers families for the coming year, and we do earnestly ask the attention of the Secretary of War and Secretary of the Treasury of the Confederate States to this matter, we state that our crops have been short our hogs have died up so that bacon next year must be scarce that we are not a large producing people that a great deal of labor has been taken off to fill up the army & with the tithes taken out of the county our people must suffer.

2nd RESOLVED, that we earnestly ask the Hon. Secretary of War and Secretary of the Treasury (if they have the discretion) to permit the tithes [the tax-in-kind] of Sampson County to be collected and sold to the county at Government prices for the relief of our suffering poor. As by so doing our soldiers in the field will be better satisfied knowing that ample provision had been made for their wives and children at home.

3rd RESOLVED, that we desire the collection of the tithes and approve the law as the best our Congress could have done under the circumstances. Yet we feel that it will be oppressive in its opperations upon our County & particularly upon our poor for whom we have been striving to provide both by public and private liberality.

Sampson County, Clerk of Superior Court, Minutes, County Court, North Carolina Archives, Raleigh.

DOCUMENT 12.9

Editor William W. Holden Speaks for Peace

What the great mass of our people desire is a cessation of hostilities, and negotiations. If they could reach that point they would feel that the conflict of arms would not be renewed, and that *some* settlement would be effected which would leave them in the future in the enjoyment of "life, liberty, and happiness." . . .

From the beginning of the war to the present the enemy has slowly but surely gained upon us; . . . Our recruits in the way of conscripts will scarcely keep our regiments full, and we cannot hope to add materially to our forces. Our fighting population is pretty well exhausted. Everybody knows this. . . .

It is time to consult reason and common sense, and to discard prejudice and passion. Our people must look at and act upon things as they are, and not as they would have them. They must remember *that they are sovereign*—that they are the masters of those who administer the government—that the government was established by *them*, for *their* benefit; and they must not be afraid to utter their opinions freely and boldly. If they want continued, wasting, bloody war, let them say so; if they want peace, let them say so, and let them state the terms on which they would have it. That peace cannot be attained by fighting merely is now apparent to all. In the language of a highly intelligent friend who writes us from a County bordering on the South Carolina line, (from whom we should like to hear at some length) "the people are tired of this awful war. It must end at some time, and there must be a starting point to an end. Let our next Congressional elections turn on the proposition that Congress shall appoint commissioners to meet others on the part of Lincoln, to make an honest effort to stay the effusion of blood by an honorable adjustment. Let what these commissioners may do be submitted to the people. If they approve it, peace will be the result; if they reject it, the war will be renewed and continued indefinitely." If an honorable peace were tendered by the South and rejected by the North, desperation would then nerve every Southern arm, and our people would share a common fate and fill a common grave. But, this awful result, it seems to us, may be averted. It may do much good, and can do no harm to talk—to negotiate, or to pave the way to negotiations while we fight. . . .

Must we rush to our doom? . . . Why, North American savages sometimes bury the tomahawk and meet together to smoke the pipe of peace. Are we of the North and South—Christians as we profess to be—more savage than the savages?

North Carolina Standard *(Semiweekly), 17 July 1863.*

DOCUMENT 12.10

Resolutions of a Public Meeting Held in Guilford County, 15 August 1863

WHEREAS, We have every reason to feel devoutly thankful to Almighty God for the many privileges, advantages, and blessings, we, as freemen, enjoyed under a Republican form of government; therefore be it

RESOLVED, That the decisions of the Judges of our Supreme Court, and the sovereignty and laws of North Carolina ought to be respected by the military authorities at Richmond.

RESOLVED, That the course of the Confederate government towards North Carolina, from the beginning of the war, has been any thing but fair and honorable.

RESOLVED, That the act of Congress, in secret session, without consulting with their constituents at home, taking from the hard laborers of the Confederacy, one-tenth of the people's living, instead of taking back their own currency in tax, is unjust and tyrannical, and we solemnly protest against the act.

RESOLVED, That as President Davis has called upon the Governor of North Carolina for all conscripts from the age of 18 to 45, we deem it unjust to the best interests of the State, for any more troops to be furnished.

RESOLVED, That we are in favor of a Peace Convention to be composed of delegates from all the States, elected by the people, to meet soon in Convention, to make a good and permanent peace.

RESOLVED, That we are in favor of an immediate armistice, that this bloody and desolating war which has already caused the death of so many hundreds of thousands of poor unprepared mortals, and who have left behind them so many millions of mourning widows and orphans, and which has brought upon this once happy and free people, incalculable loss, and irretrievable woes, and degraded us in the estimation of all Christian people the world over—immediately cease.

RESOLVED, That in our opinion, under present and prevailing circumstances, the best thing the people of North Carolina can do, is to go for the principles of Washington, Jefferson, Madison, Monroe, Jackson & c., and for the Constitution as it is.

RESOLVED, That W. W. Holden is the ablest and best defender of the rights of the people in this State, and we cheerfully endorse his conservative sentiments and principles.

RESOLVED, That the proceedings of this meeting be sent to the Editor of the Raleigh *Standard* with a request that he publish the same.

Destructives themselves behaving very respectfully, and even voting for some of the resolutions.

North Carolina Standard *(Semiweekly)*, 25 August 1863.

DOCUMENT 12.11

The Peace Spirit Grows

We favor peace because we believe that peace now would save slavery, while we very much fear that a prolongation of the war will obliterate the last vestige of it. We are for peace because there has been enough of blood and carnage, enough of widows and orphans, heartbroken moth-

282 · *The North Carolina Experience*

ers and sorrowing fathers. We are for peace, because, with an implicit faith in Divine teaching, we believe that the sins of nations as of individuals will overtake them, and that God will avenge himself on this American people, if this unnatural, fratricidal butchery is suffered to go on. We have nothing to advise, nothing to suggest, but we know we but express the truth when we declare that the earnest prayer of all right thinking men, everywhere, is for peace, and that our people, here, in North Carolina, now as several months ago, are in favor of any peace that does not enslave and degrade them—any peace that is honorable and that respects our rights.

Raleigh Daily Progress, 15 July 1863.

DOCUMENT 12.12

Zebulon Vance to David L. Swain, 22 September 1864

It [the lack of resistance to Sherman's army after the fall of Atlanta] shows what I have always believed [,] that the great *popular heart* is not now & never has been in this war. It was a revolution of the politicians not the people; was fought at first by the natural enthusiasm of our young men, and has been kept going by State & sectional pride assisted by that bitterness of feeling produced by the cruelties & brutalities of the enemy. . . .

Duty called me to resist to the uttermost the disruption of the Union; duty calls me to stand by the new Union "to the last gasp with truth & loyalty." This is my consolation—The beginning was bad & I had no hand in it; should the end be bad I shall with Gods help be equally blameless. They shall never shake their gory locks at me & say that I did it!

Papers of Governor Zebulon Vance, North Carolina Archives, Raleigh.

SUGGESTED READINGS

Auman, William Thomas. "Neighbor Against Neighbor: The Inner Civil War in the Randolph County Area of Confederate North Carolina." *North Carolina Historical Review* 61 (1984):59–92.
Barrett, John G. *The Civil War in North Carolina.* Chapel Hill: University of North Carolina Press, 1963.
———. *North Carolina as a Civil War Battleground, 1861–1865.* Raleigh: Division of Archives and History, 1960.
Escott, Paul D. *After Secession: Jefferson Davis and the Failure of Confederate Nationalism.* Baton Rouge: Louisiana State University Press, 1978.
———. " 'The Cry of the Sufferers': The Problem of Welfare in the Confederacy." *Civil War History* 23 (1977):228–40.
Kruman, Marc. *Parties and Politics in North Carolina, 1836–1865.* Baton Rouge: Louisiana State University Press, 1983.
Mitchell, Memory F. *Legal Aspects of Conscription and Exemption in North Carolina, 1861–1865.* Chapel Hill: University of North Carolina Press, 1965.
Moore, Albert Burton. *Conscription and Conflict in the Confederacy.* New York: Macmillan, 1924.
Reid, Richard. "A Test Case of the 'Crying Evil': Desertion among North Carolina Troops during the Civil War." *North Carolina Historical Review* 58 (1981):234–62.
Scarboro, David D. "North Carolina and the Confederacy: The Weakness of States' Rights during the Civil War." *North Carolina Historical Review* 56 (1979):133–49.
Sitterson, J. C. *The Secession Movement in North Carolina.* James Sprunt Historical Publications 23 (1939).
Tatum, Georgia Lee. *Disloyalty in the Confederacy.* Chapel Hill: University of North Carolina Press, 1934.
Yates, Richard E. *The Confederacy and Zeb Vance.* Tuscaloosa, Ala.: Confederate Publishing Company, 1958.
Yearns, W. Buck, and Barrett, John G. *North Carolina Civil War Documentary.* Chapel Hill: University of North Carolina Press, 1980.

CHAPTER 13

Reconstruction

The Halfway Revolution

Allen W. Trelease

Generals Steedman and Fullerton Conferring with Freedmen at the Trent River Settlement, Harper's Weekly, *9 June 1866 (Courtesy of the Division of Archives and History, Raleigh, N.C.)*

No period in American history has undergone a greater change in historical interpretation than the Reconstruction era. This change resulted from the civil rights movement (or Second Reconstruction) of the 1950s and 1960s. Older treatments of Reconstruction rested on white-supremacist assumptions that could no longer be accepted. Historians took a new and more appreciative look at Thaddeus Stevens, Charles Sumner, and the other Radical Republicans of the 1860s, who strove to guarantee a genuine freedom and equality for black people. Occasionally the historiographical reaction may have gone too far, idealizing men who (like their opponents) were often motivated by partisan and personal considerations as well as humanitarian ones. But the new view has endured, with successive refinements of detail and interpretation.

The Republican party not only led the Union to victory in the Civil War but also assumed almost exclusive responsibility for the abolition of slavery in the face of indecisiveness or outright opposition by northern Democrats. In 1865, therefore, Republicans had some reason to see their party as the indispensable safeguard of the Union and the blacks, and a political defeat would imperil the military victory just won at the cost of four years of death and sacrifice. A quick restoration of the South, with no conditions attached beyond an oath of future loyalty, threatened to let former Confederates resume the position they had held in 1861 when they broke their former oaths of loyalty. Who, then, would protect the black population against new forms of servility and exploitation, no longer called slavery but closely resembling it? Who would keep the men in gray from returning to Washington and taking over the federal government in alliance with northern Democrats, who had previously supported them to the verge of secession? Unless preventive measures were taken, the former rebels would actually gain power in Congress and the electoral college as a result of the Republican policy of emancipation. (Southern states had been able to count three-fifths of their slaves for purposes of representation; now five-fifths of the blacks would be counted, yet virtually no southerner proposed giving them any vote or voice in government.) Republicans were determined not to see the Civil War end that way. They differed, however, in how far they would go to prevent it.

Abraham Lincoln had offered southerners a lenient peace as a means of shortening the war; he did not live long enough to confront the postwar problems sketched above. His successor, Andrew Johnson, a states' rights Democrat and a defender of slavery before the war, was not particularly bothered by them. Beginning in May 1865 with North Carolina, he appointed leading Unionists in seven southern states as provisional governors with instructions to call elections for constitutional conventions that would organize new state governments. (Lincoln had already recognized Unionist governments in the other four Confederate states.) Anyone who could vote under prewar state laws and took an oath of allegiance could participate in this process. Johnson required the new governments to ratify the Thirteenth Amendment abolishing slavery and to repudiate secession and the Confederate war debt as the conditions of his recognition. In time all of these steps were taken. But full restoration to the Union depended on Congress, which had the power to seat or not to seat a state's prospective members and to count or not to count its electoral votes.

In fact, the Republican majority in Congress refused to recognize the legitimacy of presidential Reconstruction, either Lincoln's or Johnson's, without further safeguards. Most Republicans felt fully warranted in this policy by the course of events in the South in 1865 and 1866. The new state governments proceeded to define a second-class citizenship for blacks, much like that of free Negroes before the war. Their "black codes" varied in stringency—North Carolina's was one of the least severe—but they all denied legal or political equality to persons of African descent. Some virtually remanded them to slavery or peonage. No state enfranchised blacks or provided them with schooling. Race riots occurred in Memphis, New Orleans, and elsewhere in which white authorities sanctioned and even participated in armed violence against blacks. Prominent Confederates (though not many original secessionists) were elected to office at every level and demanded a full restoration of their prewar powers and prerogatives.

The safeguards demanded by Congress escalated from 1865 to 1867 as its early proposals were rejected by Andrew Johnson and the southern power structure he had called into being. Congress's first concern was to protect the former slaves. When it passed a bill renewing the Freedmen's Bureau, a federal agency created late in the war to care temporarily for these people, Johnson vetoed the bill as an invasion of states' rights. A civil rights bill, guaranteeing basic rights to all citizens including former slaves, was vetoed on the same ground in 1866. A disappointed and increasingly angry Congress eventually overrode both vetoes. When it sought to incorporate the civil rights guarantees into the Constitution, coupled with a compromise Reconstruction program that did not require Negro voting but denied representation and electoral votes in proportion as blacks were disenfranchised, Johnson advised the states to reject the proposed amendment.

At length, in 1867, Republicans gave up trying to cooperate with Johnson and enacted their own Reconstruction program. It was based on Negro suffrage, partly because Republicans were coming to accept that provision as just and right, partly because there seemed no other way left to create a loyal (or Republican) electorate in the South that they felt safe in readmitting to the Union, and partly because blacks apparently needed the power of the ballot to protect themselves. The only alternatives seemed to be a surrender to the rebels with their black codes or an indefinitely prolonged military occupation leaving the South in political limbo. The Reconstruction acts of 1867 also required each state to ratify the proposed Fourteenth Amendment as the price of congressional recognition. A year later Congress approved a Fifteenth Amendment extending black suffrage throughout the country and embedding it in the Constitution.

Under these laws constitutional conventions met in the southern states and initiated new governments conforming to the congressional specifications. Congress recognized most of them in 1868, all of them by 1870. They were dominated at the outset by the Republican party, which organized in 1867 for the first time in most southern states in order to implement the new policy. Southern Republicans fell into three groups. Largest by far was the black population, which all but unanimously supported the party that had given them freedom, civil rights, and the ballot. Perhaps a fifth of the native white population also joined, most prominently in the Appalachian and Ozark highlands and most often as a continuation of wartime Unionism. Democratic opponents called them scalawags. And a relatively small number of northerners, carpetbaggers to their enemies, who had settled in the region during and immediately after the war, now resumed their support of the Union party; these men were influential beyond their numbers, especially in the black belts, where experienced and educated Republicans were scarce. The remaining four-fifths of the white population, most of them wartime Confederates, joined the Conservative or Democratic party in opposition to the new regimes.

The Republican governments were untraditional and unsouthern in many ways. Their personnel were drawn in considerable measure from people and groups who had been outside the power structure heretofore, and they embarked upon policies distinctly out of keeping with southern antebellum tradition. These included equal rights for blacks and a greater measure of political and social democracy in general. More public offices were made elective. Constitutions, laws, and procedures were revised and modernized, often following the latest Yankee models. More money was appropriated for public institutions such as hospitals, asylums, and, above all, schools for both races. In most states large expenditures were also made and debts incurred for railroad building and other internal improvements that it was hoped would ultimately pay for themselves. These activities cost more than small-government southerners were used to. Moreover, they largely benefited blacks, poor whites, and the urban business community, while the taxes to pay for them came primarily from landowners who were not as direct beneficiaries. With so much money passing hands, some of it inevitably was misappropriated into private pockets. Corruption existed in every state, but less on average than in the North or Washington, where larger sums were available. The corruption was also bipartisan.

Much Conservative opposition sprang from the traditional ruling class, who felt cheated of their rightful status. They were especially outraged at the elevation of their former slaves to political equality. Their cry for a return to white supremacy had wide appeal among a population that had been raised on the pro-slavery argument. Lacking sympathy for the egalitarian thrust of Republican policy, Conservatives also resented the taxes levied to make it work. So they attacked what they regarded as profligate spending and thievery on the part of the allegedly incompetent blacks, traitorous scalawags, and rapacious Yankee carpetbaggers in power. Actually, Republican officials, black and white, were as competent and honest (though not always as experienced) as their Democratic counterparts. But the charges were widely believed at the time and generally accepted by later generations. Many whites felt that civilization itself was in jeopardy. Some were prepared to go any distance to preserve it. This attitude explains the vigilantism of the Ku Klux Klan, the intimidation by paramilitary organizations, the instigation of race riots, and the stuffing of ballot boxes that occurred throughout the period and ultimately toppled one after another of the Reconstruction governments.

The old elite managed to retain most of its economic and social standing. As a result, the Republican regimes stood on shaky ground, supported mainly by the poor and uneducated. No matter how democratically elected, they depended ultimately on the support of the federal government that had set them in motion. That support soon flagged. As fears of a Confederate resurgence passed away, northern Republicans grew tired of the seemingly perpetual southern question. Why should the federal army and judiciary forever have to intervene in the South to protect black and white Republicans? It was out of keeping with American tradition and practice. Thus as one southern state after another fell into Democratic hands, sometimes following armed coups d'etat, the federal government intervened less and less. Three states, South Carolina, Florida, and Louisiana, remained under Republican control until 1877, when Republicans tacitly sacrificed them in return for southern Democrats' acceptance of Rutherford B. Hayes as president.

North Carolina's experience with Reconstruction was in many ways typical of the South as a whole. The state had lost more than forty thousand men dead. Thousands more were maimed and crippled. Battle damage had been comparatively slight, but both armies had foraged extensively and the Confederacy maintained itself partly by requisitions in kind. Fields, fences, houses, barns, roads, bridges, railroads, stores, factories, public buildings, almost all showed the results of four years of enforced neglect and military requisitions. At least five more years of sacrifice were required to restore the state's land and economy to prewar conditions.

Although the decade of the 1870s was marked by some industrial growth, especially in tobacco and textile manufacture, North Carolina remained a rural state, dependent primarily on agriculture. (In 1870 only Wilmington exceeded ten thousand people.) Most farmers were small producers (as before the war), providing most of their own needs, sending little to market, and getting little cash income in return. Only gradually did railroad expansion introduce more farmers to a market economy. The substantial minority who had depended on slave labor had to make other arrangements. But emancipation left the vast majority of North Carolina's 350,000 freedmen where they were, landless and needing agricultural work in order to live.

The sharecrop system soon evolved as the most practical for both landowners and laborers. Plantations and farms were divided into smaller tracts, each farmed by a tenant family who took a share of the crop after harvest. They depended for supplies on the landlord or a local merchant, who deducted the cost with heavy interest from the tenant's share of the crop. Often there was little or nothing left once the creditors were paid. In fact, in a time of depressed crop prices (as was usually the case until the turn of the century) and with economic power concentrated in the hands of the landowners, merchants, and bankers, sharecropping turned into a reasonable facsimile of slavery. Most blacks, and many whites as well, were forced to endure this life with little hope of improvement well into the twentieth century. (Documents 13.1, 2, and 3)

In May 1865, President Johnson named William W. Holden as provisional governor of North Carolina, charged with calling a state convention and organizing a new government. Holden was a natural choice. A poor boy who made good (like the Raleigh-born Johnson himself) he was the longtime editor of the *Raleigh Standard* and a leading power in the prewar Democratic party. More important, Holden had opposed secession in 1861 and emerged during the war as the state's leading peace advocate. He ran a losing campaign for governor against Zebulon Vance in 1864 on that platform. The convention that was elected on Holden's call in September 1865 was an all-white body, dominated by men who had either opposed secession or acquiesced in it unwillingly. In other respects they were fairly typical of the state's political leadership in 1860; some indeed had belonged to that group. They did what the president required, repealing the secession ordinance, recognizing the abolition of slavery, repudiating the state war debt, and providing for the election of new officials in November.

In the election of 1865 Holden attempted to succeed himself as governor but was defeated by Jonathan Worth, another antisecessionist who had served as state treasurer during the war. The new legislature ratified the Thirteenth Amendment and elected two former Unionists of 1861, William A. Graham and John Pool, to the United States Senate. In company with the other southern senators and representatives-elect chosen at this time, neither man was seated, although Pool went to the Senate as a Republican after the reorganization of 1868. Blacks were systematically excluded from the political process, as voters and otherwise. The black code of 1866 granted them considerable legal and economic rights as freedmen, but they were restricted in their right to testify in court or to serve on juries and were discriminated against in other ways. The legislature rejected the Fourteenth Amendment. It also abandoned state support of public education, holding that it was a luxury the state could not afford.

Meanwhile, Congress began to assert its leadership in the Reconstruction process. The Republican party organized in North Carolina in March 1867, pledging itself to implement the new policy of Congress. As in other states, a majority of the party were blacks, most of whom lived in the eastern half of the state. White Republicans were most numerous in the western half. Northerners, always few in number, achieved their greatest influence in Wilmington and other parts of the east, filling a leadership shortage in areas where most party members were former slaves. In the tidewater and piedmont and in some mountain counties, most whites supported the Conservative or Democratic party in opposition to Reconstruction, regardless of their prewar political affiliations.

Republicans won 107 of the 120 seats in the new constitutional convention mandated by Congress. The document they drew up early in 1868 provided for universal manhood suffrage, regardless of race; there was no disfranchisement of former Confederates beyond the congressional requirement that persons who had held public office before the war and then engaged in rebellion could not vote in the first elections setting up the new government. The constitution revised local government by creating a township system and substituting elected county commissioners for the old county courts. It made many formerly appointive offices elective and required a system of public schools for both races with a minimum school year of four months. The newly expanded electorate (117,240 registered whites and 79,444 blacks) approved the constitution in April 1868 by a vote of 93,084 to 74,015 and elected Republicans to all statewide offices. They also won a majority in both houses of the legislature. William W. Holden, who had embraced congressional Reconstruction from the start, was elected governor on his third attempt. Blacks won no statewide offices, but they were elected to many local positions, especially in the east, and twenty-one of them were elected to the legislature. Statewide and in most localities, the great majority of Republican officeholders were native whites.

In office, the Republicans compiled a notable and generally positive record of achievement. The new legislature quickly ratified the Fourteenth Amendment, leading Congress to seat the state's members-elect. The two new senators were John Pool and Joseph C. Abbott, a northerner who came to the state as a Union army general. The legislature was largely controlled by native white Republicans who were at least marginally more conservative than the black and northern members. During the next two years it created (but did not adequately fund) the state's first public school system for both races; adopted a new and progressive civil code; reaffirmed the legal and political equality of the races and ratified the Fifteenth Amendment; established the state's first penitentiary; abolished whipping as a punishment for crime; took steps to alleviate economic distress; and dealt as well as it could with Democratic terrorism operating through the Ku Klux Klan. The legislature was a more democratic body than any of its predecessors and, for many years after, its successors. On the other hand, it went beyond the limits of prudence or legality in voting money for railroad construction, most of which never took place; after a year the same legislators took second thought and withdrew most of the state aid. A few members took bribes in return for pro-railroad votes, the money emanating from a pair of promoters, George W. Swepson and Milton S. Littlefield, who were performing similar operations in Florida. North Carolina saw comparatively little corruption—less than many other states in this era, North and South. (Documents 13.4 and 13.5)

The new school system, and public institutions in general, were racially segregated. Very few whites of either party favored integrated facilities. But in contrast to previous regimes, which had excluded blacks from most state institutions and services, Republicans made an effort to provide equal facilities. When Conservatives regained power later, they allowed Negro accommodations to deteriorate.

Conservative opposition to the new regime and its supporters took many forms. In addition to legitimate political activity, Democrats frequently ostracized white Republicans and threatened economic sanctions against dependent black laborers who voted Republican. Somewhat more successful were intimidation and violence against Republican officials and voters of both races; there was parading by extralegal military companies, rioting, and most spectacularly, night riding in disguise.

In North Carolina as elsewhere, the Ku Klux Klan consisted of local organizations with only occasional ties outside the county or neighborhood. It made little or no impact in most counties, but those where it did were scattered across the state from the foothills of Rutherford to the coastal plain in Sampson, Jones, and Lenoir.

Terrorism was most effective politically in areas where the two parties or races were relatively evenly matched and a well-placed effort might convert potential election losses into victories. Such was true in Alamance, Caswell, and Rutherford counties, which were among the worst-infested with terrorism in the South. In 1870, after repeated efforts to end the terror peacefully and after two spectacular political assassinations in Alamance and Caswell, of Negro leader Wyatt Outlaw and state senator John W. Stephens, respectively, Governor Holden called in militia under Colonel George W. Kirk. They made scores of arrests and obtained many confessions from frightened and repentant Klansmen in those two counties. But a federal judge ordered many of the prisoners released, and it proved impossible to try any of them in the local courts, which were dominated by their friends. (Document 13.6)

Whether in reaction to the militia campaign or the political record of the legislature or for more direct reasons such as intimidation of black voters, Democrats captured control of the legislature in the fall of 1870. Led in part by members of the Ku Klux Klan, one of them the leader in an aborted assassination effort, Democrats impeached and removed Holden from office—the first state governor in American history to be so treated. When Klan activity broke out in Rutherford in 1871, the new Republican governor, Tod R. Caldwell, Holden's lieutenant governor, found it prudent to rely on the federal government, which had been unwilling to act earlier. After federal arrests and prosecutions in this and other states, Klan activity terminated in most parts of the South by the end of 1871.

Governor Caldwell was elected in his own right in 1872, and following his death two years later Republican Lieutenant Governor Curtis H. Brogden succeeded him. But Republicans never regained control of the legislature in this period, and after 1876 Democrats had a firm hold on the state. Their domination was almost assured by a series of constitutional amendments they pushed through in 1873 and 1875, offered in the name of white supremacy and small government. The most important amendment transferred the control of county government from locally elected commissioners—who might be black as well as Republican in some counties—to justices of the peace chosen by the legislature. Democratic legislative control was enhanced by various devices, legal and extralegal, to discourage black voting.

The oft-recited horrors of Reconstruction took two main forms. Economic suffering was widespread, the result almost entirely of the war. Its injurious effects were mostly temporary, but some families or individuals were hit harder than others and recovered more slowly. Reconstruction policy had comparatively little to do with their plight, except that higher taxation may have sharpened their pain. The second form of suffering, more psychological and political in bearing, was that experienced by the master race, and especially its ruling elite, when they found themselves ejected from power and replaced by people they regarded as social and racial inferiors. They were mortified at the sight of black voters crowding to the polls and carrying elections or serving in the legislature and on county commissions. This was perhaps the supreme horror of Reconstruction, exaggerated tales of which were handed down from generation to generation as object lessons for the future. In truth, Reconstruction wrought only half a revolution. Partially deprived of political power, Conservatives retained most of their economic and social eminence. Thus they were soon permitted by an acquiescent North to vault themselves once again into political mastery. By disfranchising their opponents in the years that followed, they maintained that power, with the exception of the fusion period, for almost a century.

DOCUMENT 13.1

Sidney Andrews on the White Yeomen Farmers, 1865

Spindling of legs, round of shoulders, sunken of chest, lank of body, stooping of posture, narrow of face, retreating of forehead, thin of nose, small of chin, large of mouth,—this is the native North-Carolinian as one sees him outside the cities and large towns. There is insipidity in his face, indecision in his step, and inefficiency in his whole bearing. His house has two rooms and a loft, and is meanly furnished,—one, and possibly two, beds, three or four chairs, half a dozen stools, a cheap pine table, an old spinning-wheel, a water-bucket and drinking gourd, two tin wash-basins, half a dozen tin platters, a few cooking utensils, and a dozen odd pieces of crockery. Paint and whitewash and wall-paper and window-curtains are to him needless luxuries. His wife is leaner, more round-shouldered, more sunken of chest, and more pinched of face than her husband. He "chaws" and she "dips." The children of these two are large-eyed, tow-headed urchins, alike ignorant of the decencies and the possibilities of life. In this house there is often neither book nor newspaper; and, what is infinitely worse, no longing for either. The day begins at sunrise and ends at dark; its duties are alike devoid of dignity and mental or moral compensation. The man has a small farm, and once owned six or eight negroes. How the family now lives, the propping hands of the negroes being taken away, is a mystery, even if one remembers the simple cheapness of mere animal life.

I am not speaking either of the white resident of the cities or of the "poor white," technically so named, but of the common inhabitant of the country,—the man who pays a tax and votes, but never runs for office; who was a private in the Rebel army, but never anything more; who hates the Yankees as a matter of course, but has no personal ill-will toward them; who believes in the Divine right of slavery, but is positive that a free negro cannot be made to work. He is hospitable enough in words and manner, but expects you to pay extravagantly in greenbacks or liberally in silver for a seat at his table and the use of his odd bed. His larder is lean, and his cookery is in the last degree wretched. He tenders "apple-jack," as an evidence of good-will, and wonders in a feeble way how a man can live who don't drink it at least half a dozen times a day. He likes to talk, and rarely has any work that prevents him from hanging on the fence to chat with the chance traveller who asks the road; but his conversation runs in an everlasting circle round the negro, with an occasional pause for the relation of personal adventures in the war. He receives two or three letters per year, perhaps, and wonders why a man should take a daily newspaper. He troubles himself very little about schools or education, but likes to go to meeting, and thinks himself well informed as to matters of theology. He believes the "abolishioners" brought on the war; but he doesn't love Jeff Davis or Governor Vance. He "allers dun hansumly by his niggers," and thinks them the "most ongratefullest creeturs on the face of the yerth."

The complexion of these country residents is noticeable, and suggests many inquiries. If you say that half the men and nearly all the women are very pale, you strike at the matter, but fail to fairly hit it. Their whiteness of skin is simply the whiteness of ordinary tallow. It is sallowness, with a suggestion of clayeyness. Unquestionably soap and water and crash towels would improve the appearance, but I doubt if they would give any bloom to the cheek. The skin seems utterly without vitality, and beyond the action of any restorative stimulants: it has a pitiful and repulsive death-in-life appearance. I am told the climate is in fault, but my judgment says the root of the matter is in the diet of the people. The range of eatables is exceedingly narrow, and swine's flesh constitutes at least half the food of all classes outside the towns and cities; while the consumption of grease—of fat in one form or another—would, I am sure, astonish even an Arctic explorer. The whole economy of life seems radically wrong, and there is no inherent energy which promises reformation.

The amount of tobacco consumed by the people is beyond all calculation. I hardly exaggerate in saying that at least seven tenths of all persons above the age of twelve years use it in some form. Nearly every man and boy smokes or chews, and very many of them do both, while the country women chew and smoke to some extent, and women of most classes "dip." . . . To see a man take [a quid of tobacco] from his mouth and put it in his hat when he goes to breakfast is by no means uncommon. I have even seen men lay it under the edge of their plate at dinner; and one of the leading delegates in the [constitutional] Convention held an immense quid between the thumb and finger of the hand with which he abundantly gesticulated during a ten-minutes speech! . . .

The labor system of the State is not so badly disorganized as that of South Carolina, but it is thoroughly demoralized. One sees here more white men in trades there almost given up to negroes, but he also sees negroes in trades here from which they are excluded there. The number of grown men, middle-aged men, who have no ostensible business but lounging and whiskey-drinking, is much greater in this State than in that. It is the complaint of papers in all sections of the State, that there never before were so many idle men,—vagrants, consumers, non-producers, non-taxpayers. The chief pity of the matter, however, is that they seem to have no desire for work. "And who makes so much fuss about the negroes not working as these very white drones who hug the street-corners, lounge about dram-shops, and trust to chance for food and raiment?" asks one of the Raleigh papers, very pertinently. "We trust our law-makers will do all in their power," adds another journal, "to compel the freedmen to work for an honest living; but we consider it equally incumbent on them to take steps to reduce the amount of vagrancy among the whites." These extracts are not from papers edited by Northern or outside men, but the two writers are men who have always lived in the State.

Sidney Andrews, The South since the War, *ed. David Donald (Boston: Houghton Mifflin, Sentry Edition, 1971), pp. 180–84.*

DOCUMENT 13.2

John Richard Dennett on White Racial Attitudes, 1865

There is an Assistant Superintendent of Freedmen in Salisbury, whose office is, of course, thronged by complainants. The great majority are people who have recently been turned away from home by their former owners, who are, in most cases, compelled to pay such persons a certain amount of money, or to give them sufficient corn to feed them until February 1, 1866. During the month of August applications for redress were, on an average, twenty-one each day. For the present month the average will be higher.

Having been permitted to look over the superintendent's books, I made this digest of all cases of alleged abuse of Negroes that have been reported during the first fortnight of September: Complaint is made

By colored man, John: that G.S. whipped his wife's sister because she left him, and forced her to go back and work for him. G.S. fined.

By colored man, Norris: that E. J. struck him with a brick, and threatened him with an axe.

By colored man, Anderson: that his master whipped him because he went off the plantation to see his cousin, and threatens to whip him again when he comes back from making his complaint.

By colored man, Dick: that J.W. whipped him severely, striking him seventy-two blows.

By colored woman, Martha: That J. F. Parker overtook her while on her way to the office of the Superintendent of Freedmen, put one end of a rope round her neck, tied the other round the neck of his mule, and so dragged her more than two miles. Showed marks of rope.

By colored man, Julius: That he had been sick of a fever two months, and had not yet recovered, when his master came to his cabin and beat him severely because he was not at work.

By colored woman, Louisa: That J. T. is whipping her children continually, and when she asked him not to do it, ordered her off his place and told her not to come back.

By colored man, Robert: That his sister works for a man named A.S., who ordered her to go out and make fence; that afterwards A.S. went out, and, getting angry, cut her head with a rail.

By colored man, Elias: That some citizens took his gun away from him and told him no nigger had a right to carry a gun.

By colored man, Levi: That W.F.L. has whipped him severely with a buggy-trace. Shows his back all raw.

By colored man, Sandy: That Ch. and J.L. said he must leave the plantation, or take a hundred lashes. . . .

Riding out of Concord this morning I overtook a gentleman who was going out a few miles into the country to visit his plantation, and as long as our roads lay together we travelled in company. The conversation turned upon Negroes as laborers, and he declared that since their emancipation they were nearly useless, and the only hope of the Southern agriculturist was in getting white farm-hands. Most of his acquaintances, in making their plans for next season, had decided to do as much as possible themselves, and to employ only as many colored people as were absolutely indispensable. The worst class of all were the young people of both sexes, who made twice as much noise about their freedom as their fathers and mothers did; but none were good. In his opinion, the first duty to be performed by the Legislature, when North Carolina should be fortunate enough to get a legislature, would be to pass an apprenticeship act, to be applied to all persons of color under twenty-one years of age, who, so far as was practicable, ought to be bound out to their former masters. Enactments with reference to the older Negroes would also be necessary; they were unfit to make contracts or transact any business for themselves; some of them had got money within the last two or three months, and nine times in ten they laid it out in the most inconsiderate manner, spent it for some little notion or other. They had no ideas of economy, and were as destitute of foresight as a child. . . .

I asked . . . if the State Convention would probably declare the evidence of Negroes admissible in courts of justice.

"The right to testify for and against each other in cases where no white man is concerned," he replied, "they have always had, and of course it will be continued to them; but I don't think the Southern people are prepared to admit nigger testimony against a white man. What would be the good of putting niggers in the witness-box? You must have niggers in the jury-box, too, or nigger evidence will not be believed. I don't think you could find twelve men in the whole State who would attach any weight to the testimony of ninety-nine niggers in a hundred."

He was willing that the colored population should be educated, but not without making a proviso which, he thought, would be displeasing to Northern radicals—that white and black children should be taught in separate schools. Nothing should be done that looked towards the social equality of Negroes and whites. The only result of that would be a horrible one—miscegenation and the worst forms of immorality, and, eventually, the driving out of the white race by a wretched population made up of half-castes and mixed breeds. His opinions on these subjects are such as seem to be generally prevalent in this part of the State.

John Richard Dennett, The South as It Is, 1865–1866, *ed. Henry M. Christman (New York: Viking Press, Compass Books, 1967), pp. 124–26, 130–33.*

DOCUMENT 13.3

John Richard Dennett on Racial Attitudes and Aspirations among the Freedmen, October 1865

The following conversation, which I had this morning with a colored citizen of Fayetteville, may serve to show what are the hopes and expectations that have been formed by the most intelligent men of this class—those who deserve to have and who have the most influence with their fellows—the men who framed the recent address of the colored people to the State Convention. He is a barber by trade, a light-colored man, good-looking, and with a face expressive of good sense and good feeling. He had been a slave all his life till set free by the war, but had taught himself reading and writing, and his talk showed that he had made good use of those acquisitions. What he has read, his reflection upon it, and a careful study of events on which so much for him and his race was depending, has furnished him with a set of opinions in which there is nothing of violence, though they are very decided, and has fitted him to be a leader and counsellor among his own people. This prominence seems to affect his interests injuriously, for his white customers have withdrawn their patronage from the shop of a man who allowed himself to be sent as a delegate to the Negro convention [in Raleigh].

As to the question whether or not the South shall be re-admitted to the Union before granting the right of suffrage to the Negroes, he says that he and his people are quite indifferent. Many care little or nothing about it at all, and many are perfectly willing to wait a few years, thinking that they will not have long to wait. He himself believed Negro suffrage a necessary consequence of Negro emancipation, if emancipation was made complete. If a black man could testify in court, and in all respects enjoy equality before the law, he would soon begin to educate himself and acquire property, and otherwise make himself respectable, and so prepare the way for his admission to the polls. Both of the great parties would be waiting for them by that time, for the colored population would be an element of such power that the Democrats would try to seize it if the Republicans were not beforehand with them. The South would need them, too, so that all things considered, he expected to be a legal voter in his native State before he was five years older.

But the right of Negroes to testify was something absolutely necessary, and he hoped that Congress would admit no State which had not granted it. If the North Carolina Legislature were to meet today, it would probably exclude the evidence of colored men; hardly a man could be found at present to say a word in favor of it. A year or two would probably change the popular opinion; but he hoped that Congress, to prevent the troubles of this year or two, would declare that no State had a republican form of government if every free man in it was not equal before the law, equal so far as the witness-box was concerned; he wouldn't insist on admission to the jury-box, for it required more sense to be a juror than to be a voter. But who could think it strange if a Negro, ignorant and without friends, when he felt that he had no place to go for justice, should take the law into his own hands? Then white men would do the same, they wouldn't wait either, and there would be nothing but bloodshed and burning.

Very few of the former slave-owners would give a Negro a fair chance, and for this reason, as well as to allow time for the minds of the people to cool and to make it possible for the Legislature to be just, he wanted the Freedmen's Bureau kept in existence another year.

He laughed at the idea of a Negro insurrection, and said he wished those who talked of it could know his people as well as he knew them. The worst to be feared was the occurrence of individual cases of violence or theft, when some Negro saw no other mode of redress; but there never would be a black rebellion. The Negroes wanted nothing so much as to live in peace with the white people of the States. What they had done in this very town, in respect to calling in a garrison of Negro troops, was sufficient proof of that. When Sherman's soldiers were first taken away from Fayetteville, and the town was put into the hands of the citizens, they showed a disposition to revive the slave code, and to enforce certain city ordinances that were full of the old spirit; Negroes were not to be allowed to meet together for worship, unless a white man was present in the assembly; no Negro was to carry a walking-cane; one man, after being convicted of some offence, was publicly whipped, and two men who lay in jail, awaiting trial, were taken out and whipped by persons who had no shadow of authority. The colored people didn't think such doings looked like freedom, and some of them began to talk about petitioning for a garrison of Negro troops. The citizens were very much afraid they'd do it, but after consultation among themselves, my informant said, "it was decided not to ask for a garrison, but for an agent of the Freedmen's Bureau to come up and adjust the difficulties. We knew that if we wanted to bring about a state of bad feeling between the white folks and the darkies, the surest way to do it would be to bring Negro soldiers into town."

Dennett, South as It Is, *pp. 175–77.*

DOCUMENT 13.4

The Republicans View Their Legislative Record, 1868–1869

The Legislature has adjourned and its labors are before the people. The captions of the laws show how onerous were the duties of that body, and how well they were performed.

In the front rank of its good works was the passage of a liberal homestead law, which will hereafter be a lasting monument to its fame, and a tower of strength to the people.

The amendments to the Code of Civil Procedure are numerous and dictated by experience.

The school law is not in all respects perfect, but it is the commencement of a republican system of free education which will send the light of knowledge streaming through the minds of all the children of the old North State.

Besides the leading acts, numerous railroad charters were granted, which, by a judicious system in the collection of revenue, will open the remotest parts of our grand commonwealth to the intercourse and markets of the world.

The revenue law is as good as could be devised. Owing to the numerous restrictions of the Constitution, imposed for the benefit of the people, it was difficult to frame a new system of taxation which would answer in all particulars to the preconceived opinions of men; but we believe that as the law now stands, sufficient revenue will be raised to defray both the ordinary and extraordinary expenses of the Public Treasury.

The public charities of the State were remodeled on the liberal basis provided for in the Constitution, and sufficient means appropriated to support them for the ensuing fiscal year. In the same manner the University has been placed upon a stable foundation.

The commercial interests of the State were not neglected, while the numerous acts of incorporation for cities and associations show a reviving spirit in all ranks of society.

A general law was passed conferring the requisite corporate powers upon townships, and these corporations will soon be called upon to organize and govern themselves.

Relief was granted numerous officials and persons whom the calamities of the past had reduced to the necessity of applying to the Legislature for aid.

Altogether, we think the General Assembly did well. Day by day its good works, which live after it, will become more apparent and more appreciated. Its revilers will be hushed by the hum of wheels that its laws have called into motion, and the entire people will yet applaud its liberality and independence. In our opinion the Legislature needs no elaborate defence. A fair statement of what it has done is sufficient for the present while the future will entirely vindicate the annual session of 1868–'9.

Raleigh Daily Standard, *16 April 1869.*

DOCUMENT 13.5

The Democrats View the Republican Record, 1868–1869

The history of legislation in North Carolina would form one of the strangest books that has ever been published. It would reveal an amount of fraud, venality and recklessness perfectly unparalleled, we venture to say, in the history of legislation in any age or country. If ever before there was a time demanding the most scrupulous and watchful economy, it is the present. If there was ever a time when the most careful reform and the most jealous retrenchment were imperatively necessary it is the present. And yet, in the face of wide-spread ruin and dismay; in the face of repeated failures in crops and a disorganized system of labor; with depression and anxiety in every house-hold, the members of the present Legislature have exhibited the utmost disregard of the actual condition of our people, and have wantonly and wickedly and with malice prepense concocted a system of taxation, that not only outrages public opinion, but fastens, it may be, for all time, burdens perfectly unbearable and destructive upon the landed proprietors of the State.

These representatives of the people—these public servants "so-called"—these incapable and indifferent legislators, met in Raleigh and deliberately set to work to despoil the State and add ten fold distress to her people. They enter upon a plan of spoliation as effective in its results as was the "bumming" of Sherman's scoundrels.—They lend themselves to the wildest schemes, listen with itching ears to the rapacious demands of wild cat combinations, wink at corruption and profligacy, indulge in vice and immorality, and conspire to paralyze the best interests of the State, to drive away capital, to keep capital from coming into the State and to lay taxes that not only can not be borne, but which would require probably a sixth part of the actual wealth of the whole State to pay.

Railroad schemes, without number—a continued waste of public funds, and taxes at once oppressive, and thoroughly ruinous are the results of their six months stay in Raleigh. They have done nothing but evil, and are an offense to every just and honest man. They deserve, and they will receive the hearty execration of a long suffering, industrious and frugal people. . . .

We write not of those men in both Houses who had an eye single to the honor, prosperity and credit of the State—men who stood up defiantly and continually against fraud, peculation, corruption and bribery. There were such men and they deserve well of the people. They tried faithfully to avert the wrong. Their recorded votes show that they were friends of the people, lovers of country, men of fidelity and honor. But we refer to those harpies, some from Northland, but many "native and to the manor born," who preyed upon our people, and with cormorant appetites essayed to suck the very life blood from the emaciated form of our old Mother. Carpet-baggers who came unbidden and who have fairly battened upon the political garbage that has been thrown to them; obsequious time servers and trimmers who have played the sycophants for filthy lucre—these are the creatures who have wickedly conspired against the people of North Carolina, and have sought to ruin them by the most oppressive taxation—these are the creatures who amid the troubling of the political waters have been spawned in our Legislative halls, and who ought to be denounced and shunned as you would a leper. They *are* political lepers and taint the whole political atmosphere.

Raleigh Daily Sentinel, *16 April 1869.*

DOCUMENT 13.6

Governor William W. Holden and the Ku Klux Klan, from His Annual Message to the Legislature, 22 November 1870

The present government of North Carolina commenced its operations on the 4th day of July, 1868. This government is based on the political and civil equality of all men, and it was lawfully and constitutionally established by the whole people of the State. The State had just emerged from a protracted and desperate conflict with the government of our common country, in which many valuable lives and a vast amount of property had been sacrificed. It was hoped and expected that the government thus established, after so much suffering and so many calamities, would be allowed to move quietly forward, protecting all alike, dispensing its benefits with an equal hand, and preparing the way for a realization of that prosperity which the State had formerly enjoyed. But the validity of the reconstruction acts was questioned, and the authority of the State was represented as having been derived in such a manner as to render it binding on the people only until an opportunity should be offered to throw it off. Combinations were formed in various parts of the State, of a secret character, the object of which was to render practically null and void the reconstruction acts, and to set at naught those provisions of the Federal and State Constitutions which secure political and civil equality to the whole body of our people. . . .

These combinations were at first purely political in their character, and many good citizens were induced to join them. But gradually, under the leadership of ambitious and discontented politicians, and under the pretext that society needed to be regulated by some authority outside or above the law, their character was changed, and these secret Klans began to commit murder, to rob, whip, scourge and mutilate unoffending citizens. This organization or these combinations were called the Ku Klux Klan, and were revealed to the public, as the result of the measures which I adopted, as "*The Constitutional Union Guards*," "*The White Brotherhood*," and "*The Invisible Empire*." Unlike other secret political associations, they authorized the use of force, with deadly weapons, to influence the elections. The members were united by oaths which ignored or repudiated the ordinary oaths or obligations resting upon all other citizens to respect the laws and to uphold the government; these oaths inculcated hatred by the white race against the colored race; the members of the Klan, as above stated, were hostile to the principles on which the government of the State had been reconstructed, and, in many respects, hostile to the government of the United States. They met in secret, in disguise, with arms, in a dress of a certain kind intended to conceal their persons and their horses, and to terrify those whom they menaced or assaulted. They held their camps, and under their leaders they decreed judgment against their peaceable fellow-citizens, from mere intimidation to scourgings, mutilations, the burning of churches, school houses, mills, and in many cases to murder. This organization, under different names, but cemented by a common purpose, is believed to have embraced not less than forty thousand voters in North Carolina. It was governed by rules more or less military in their character, and it struck its victims with such secrecy, swiftness and certainty as to leave them little hope either for escape or mercy. . . . I have information of not less than twenty-five murders committed by members of this Klan, in various counties of the State, and of hundreds of cases of scourging and whipping. Very few, if any, convictions have followed in these cases. The civil law was powerless. One State Senator [John W. Stephens, of Caswell] was murdered in the open day in a County court house, and another State Senator [T. M. Shoffner, of Alamance] was driven from the State, solely on account of their political opinions. In neither case was a bill found by a Grand Jury. A respectable and unoffending colored man [Wyatt Outlaw] was taken from his bed at night, and hanged by the neck until he was dead, within a short distance of [the Alamance] County court house. Another colored man was drowned, because he spoke publicly of persons who aided in the commission of this crime. No bills were found in these cases. A crippled white man, a native of Vermont, was cruelly whipped because he was teaching a colored school. No bill was found in this case. The Sheriff of [Jones] County was waylaid, shot and killed on a public highway, and the Colonel of [Jones] County was shot and killed in the open day, while engaged in his usual business. [The Lenoir] County jail was broken open, and five men taken out and their throats cut. . . . In fine . . . there was no remedy for these evils through the civil law, and but for the use of the military arm, to which I was compelled to resort, the whole fabric of society in the State would have been undermined and destroyed, and a reign of lawlessness and anarchy would have been established. The present State government would thus have failed in the great purpose for which it was created, to-wit: the protection of life and property under equal laws; and, necessarily the national government would have interfered, and, in all probability would have placed us again and for an indefinite period under military rule.

In June, 1869 . . . I caused eighteen men, murderers and robbers, to be arrested in Lenoir and Jones [counties]. . . . Five of them turned State's evidence, and exposed the secrets of the Klan, and the crimes of their confederates. None of them have been convicted. Yet the result of these arrests was, that peace and order were almost immediately re-established in those counties.

In the early part of 1870, I employed, in Chatham, Capt. N. A. Ramsay, and in Orange, Capt. Pride Jones, both belonging to the political party opposed to my administration, to aid in repressing the Ku Klux and in composing the troubles in those Counties. They performed their duty in a manner which entitles them to the thanks of every friend of law and order.

In July, of the present year, I deemed it my duty to embody a portion of the militia, and to make a number of arrests of suspected persons in the Counties of Alamance and Caswell. . . .

I did not proceed to final action in this matter until I had consulted the President of the United States, which I did in person in July last. It will be seen, by his letter . . . that he sustained me in my action. The federal troops in the State at that time were re-inforced by his order, and every precaution was taken to prevent resistance to the steps which I deemed absolutely indispensable to the restoration of the civil law and the re-establishment of peace and order. . . .

The result of this action . . . has been in the highest degree fortunate and beneficial. The power of the State government to protect, maintain, and perpetuate itself has been tested and demonstrated. The secret organization which disturbed the peace of society, which was sapping the foundations of the government, setting the law at defiance, and inflicting manifold wrongs on a large portion of our people, has been exposed and broken up. Well meaning, honest men, who had been decoyed into this organization, have availed themselves of this opportunity to escape from it, and will henceforth bear their testimony against it as wholly evil in its principles and its modes of operation. A score or more of wicked men have been driven from the State, while those of the same character who remain have been made to tremble before the avenging hand of power. The majesty of the law has been vindicated. The poor and the humble now sleep unmolested in their houses, and are no longer scourged or murdered on account of their political opinions.

General Assembly, Executive and Legislative Documents, 1870–71 *(Raleigh: James H. Moore, State Printer, 1871), document 1, pp. 11–20.*

SUGGESTED READINGS

Alexander, Roberta Sue. "Hostility and Hope: Black Education in North Carolina during Presidential Reconstruction, 1865–1867." *North Carolina Historical Review* 53 (1976):113–32.

Balanoff, Elizabeth. "Negro Legislators in the North Carolina General Assembly, July, 1868–February, 1872." *North Carolina Historical Review* 49 (1972):22–55.

Dailey, Douglass C. "The Elections of 1872 in North Carolina." *North Carolina Historical Review* 40 (1963):338–60.

Evans, William McKee. *Ballots and Fence Rails: Reconstruction on the Lower Cape Fear.* Chapel Hill: University of North Carolina Press, 1967.

Ewing, Cortez, A. M. "Two Reconstruction Impeachments." *North Carolina Historical Review* 15 (1938):204–30.

Hamilton, J. G. de Roulhac. *Reconstruction in North Carolina.* New York: Columbia University, Longmans, Green & Co., Agents, 1914.

Olsen, Otto H. *Carpetbagger's Crusade: The Life of Albion Winegar Tourgée.* Baltimore: Johns Hopkins University Press, 1965.

Stampp, Kenneth M. *The Era of Reconstruction, 1865–1877.* New York: Alfred A. Knopf, 1965.

Tourgée, Albion Winegar. *A Fool's Errand, by One of the Fools and the Invisible Empire.* New York: Fords, Howard, and Hulbert, 1880.

Trelease, Allen W. "Republican Reconstruction in North Carolina: A Roll-Call Analysis of the State House of Representatives, 1868–1870." *Journal of Southern History* 42 (1976):319–44.

_____. *White Terror: The Ku Klux Klan Conspiracy and Southern Reconstruction.* New York: Harper & Row, 1971.

Zuber, Richard L. *Jonathan Worth: A Biography of a Southern Unionist.* Chapel Hill: University of North Carolina Press, 1965.

CHAPTER 14

North Carolina in the New South

Robert F. Durden

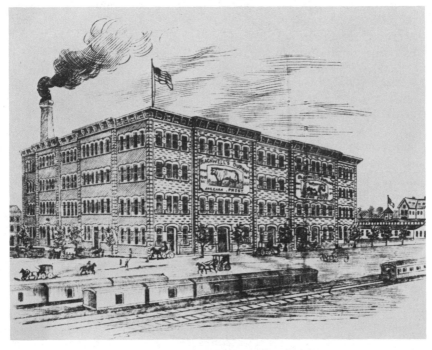

Blackwell's Durham Tobacco Company, Raleigh News and Observer, *5 April 1896 (Courtesy of the Division of Archives and History, Raleigh, N.C.)*

Long after the Civil War had ended victoriously for the Republicans, they still hailed themselves as the party that saved the Union and ended slavery. But they did not, at least for any length of time, accomplish the political remodeling of the South in the image of the North. The failure of Radical Reconstruction to achieve its long-range purposes in the South is widely recognized. Not only were the Republicans unable to build a strong wing of their party throughout the South, but by 1877 the newly gained civil and political rights of the freedmen were in jeopardy and were gradually whittled away by the dominant and largely white southern Democrats in the years that followed.

If Radical Reconstruction failed dismally at the time, some historians assert that there was, nevertheless, a "Reconstruction that took"— the acceptance of the idea of industrialization by southerners as the great hope for the future. Manufacturing replaced the agrarian life of old as the southern lodestar; and the antebellum notion that "cotton is king" was eclipsed by the belief that factories, especially cotton textile factories, would be the economic salvation of southern communities. (Document 14.1) "By the time the First World War broke out in Europe," historian Carl Degler has asserted, "the American South had been 'northernized' to a degree only hoped for by the most ambitious of Reconstructionists. Moreover, this was permanent change, for the northern industrial way had been voluntarily accepted by the South." Despite his awareness that southern industrialization had only begun by 1914 and that the vast majority of southern people remained tied to the land even after 1914, Degler still insists that the "decisive break with the agrarian tradition had been made" and that the South was at least started on the path that would lead it into the mainstream of the nation's life.

Not all observers have shared Degler's estimate of the importance of industrialization in the New South, that is, the South after the Civil War and the end of Reconstruction. Another influential view is that, despite much oratory and propagandistic writing about the desire and need for factories, southern industrialization in the late nineteenth and early twentieth centuries had made little progress. Urbanization has normally accompanied industrialization wherever it has occurred. Yet historian C. Vann Woodward has emphasized that by the time of World War I "the sum total of urbanization in the South was comparatively unimportant." The South, he argues, remained what it had been—"by far the most rural section of the Union." Certainly, manufacturing increased in the region, but it did so in the rest of the nation as well. The end result was that the South in the early twentieth century had about the same proportion of the country's factories and capital as it had in 1860.

Historians may debate the significance of industrialization in the post–Civil War South as much as they like, but the fact remains that many Tar Heels, especially in the piedmont section, rejected certain hallowed myths of the Old South and became enthusiastic converts to national American myths concerning industrialization as the pathway to progress and prosperity. A good example of this postwar belief that amounted almost to a religion was afforded by a Tar Heel orator in 1889, who hailed the completion of a railway linking the new piedmont towns of Henderson and Durham. The *Durham Recorder* (1 May 1889) reported: "The life of Durham and Henderson is Progress. . . . 'Tis this that distinguishes them from most of their sister towns, Progress, Progress, Progress." What had made this achievement possible? These towns were the homes of the "Bright Golden Tobacco of the World." Carried away by his own eloquence, in the old-fashioned southern style of oratory, the speaker spiraled into the wild-blue yonder: "Tobacco! Oh thou mighty dispeller of care, and gracious dispenser of pleasant reveries and brightest hopes. Thou Son of the American wilderness, thou hast demeaned thyself so well since Walter Raleigh first made known thy virtues, that thou has now become the Adopted Son of all nations of the earth."

Eloquence—or bombast—aside, the speaker had a valid point in spotlighting bright-leaf tobacco as a key element in the economic development of the piedmont. First grown after the late 1830s by, among others, the four Slade brothers of Caswell County in central North Carolina along the Virginia border, the new variety of tobacco flourished in relatively poor soil containing silica. The best curing process, found only after much experimentation with charcoal and other fuels, proved to be a system of flues conveying heat from a wood fire throughout a simply built tobacco barn or shed in which the tobacco leaves were hung for curing. By the time of the Civil War, the lemon-yellow and fragrant tobacco was finding an ever-increasing market, first as wrappers for plug or chewing tobacco, then for pipe smoking, and finally, starting in the 1880s, for cigarettes.

While Tar Heel farmers in an ever-widening zone of the piedmont and eastern coastal plain began to grow bright tobacco, the tobacco factories of Winston, Durham, and other fast-growing towns became dramatic symbols of a new era. In Winston, a raw new town that grew up alongside the much older Moravian town of Salem, the 1870s brought the establishment of numerous tobacco factories, but the one launched by Richard J. Reynolds grew to be the largest and by far the most important. A native of southwestern Virginia, Reynolds arrived in Winston, then a mere village of about four hundred people, in 1874, at the age of twenty-four. Familiar with the product from having grown up on a tobacco farm and as a youth peddling home-manufactured chewing tobacco in the mountains of Kentucky and Tennessee, he soon opened his first factory in Winston for the production of chewing tobacco. A small operation at first with only two regular assistants and barely a dozen seasonal helpers, the business grew steadily thanks to Reynolds's hard work, resourceful advertising, and popular product. Twenty years after the Reynolds Company was established, it began also to produce smoking tobacco, coming out with its famous, best-selling Prince Albert brand in 1908. Not until 1913 did the company begin to manufacture cigarettes, but when it did, its Camel brand quickly soared to top place.

Just as Winston grew up around its tobacco factories, so too did Durham, a hamlet of only 256 people in 1870. There the firm that was the first in the state to achieve national and even worldwide fame was W. T. Blackwell and Company, makers of the celebrated Bull Durham smoking tobacco. Blackwell and his younger partner, Julian Shakespeare Carr, pioneered in the techniques of advertising and spent vast sums of money, for that era, placing advertisements in newspapers and giving purchasers prizes and premiums, ranging from a small item such as a razor to a more costly mantel clock. Their most spectacular promotion was huge painted signs of the Durham Bull that appeared all over the United States, in Europe, and even at one time on the pyramids of Egypt.

The Bull Durham company had a head start, but a rival firm was destined to overtake and eventually absorb it. Washington Duke, a yeoman farmer in what was then Orange County, returned from the Civil War a penniless widower with four young children. In addition to resuming the farming that had always occupied most Tar Heels, he and his sons began after the war to manufacture smoking tobacco on their farm. After beating the bright-leaf tobacco with wooden flails and sifting it by hand, they packed it in small cloth bags, which Duke's young daughter helped sew and label. Then Duke loaded the bags into his mule-drawn wagon, along with spartan equipment and supplies for cooking along the roadside, and headed into the more populous eastern part of the state to peddle and barter the smoking tobacco.

In 1874, the same year Richard Reynolds launched his factory in Winston, Washington Duke and his family moved their operation from their farm into the burgeoning town of Durham. Only one of numerous small competitors of the Blackwell Company at first, W. Duke Sons and Company turned to the production of hand-rolled cigarettes in the early 1880s. Through aggressive salesmanship and advertising, the Duke Company forged ahead. Posters carried the then daring pictures of beautiful actresses who endorsed one of Duke's brands of cigarettes, such as Duke of Durham or Pin Head or Cross-Cut. In an early link to sports, the company sponsored roller-skating "polo clubs" in various parts of the nation. After 1885, when the company gambled on machine-made cigarettes and made an advantageous secret contract with the Bonsack

Machine Company of Salem, Virginia, W. Duke Sons and Company rapidly became the largest cigarette producer in the nation. (Document 14.2)

Washington Duke's youngest child, James B. Duke ("Buck" to family and intimates), emerged as the true business genius of the family. After moving to New York in the mid-1880s, he became in 1890, at the age of thirty-three, the president of the newly formed American Tobacco Company. Concentrating at first on cigarettes, this combination of tobacco manufacturers became known as the tobacco trust and, before the United States Supreme Court ordered its dissolution in 1911, dominated almost all tobacco manufacturing in the nation except that of cigars.

Just as tobacco products had been manufactured on a small scale in North Carolina before the Civil War, so, too, had textiles. The Battle family of Rocky Mount, Francis Fries of Salem, and especially Edwin M. Holt of Alamance County were among the prominent antebellum pioneers in the textile industry. Their operations were modest, however, when compared with the textile mills that sprang up in North Carolina in the last decades of the nineteenth century. (Document 14.3)

The cotton textile mill became the symbol of hope for southern communities in the lean and hungry years after the Civil War. Although towns throughout North Carolina clamored for their own mills, nearly 90 percent of them in 1900 were concentrated in the piedmont section. By that same year there were 177 cotton mills in the state employing more than thirty thousand workers and producing goods valued at $28 million. The Cone brothers of Greensboro, Daniel A. Tompkins of Charlotte, the Hanes family of Winston, and the Duke family in Durham were among the state's capitalists who invested heavily in textile manufacturing and helped make it the state's most important industry. (Document 14.4)

In good years the cotton mills, so fervently wooed by community leaders and favored by state and municipal authorities in various ways, paid handsome profits. One Tar Heel businessman, Richard H. Wright of Durham, attempting to lure a British acquaintance into investing money in a North Carolina mill venture, reported that the owners of one local mill cleared "a net profit annually of from 25% to 30% on their capital." Among the advantages were that good cotton grew nearby; rail transportation was excellent; coal could be bought from $3.15 to $3.25 per ton; and the climate was "all that can be desired." The Tar Heel entrepreneur added a final, clinching argument concerning labor for the textile mills: "Girls can be had at from $2.50 to $4.00 per week."

Cheap labor, mostly white in the case of the textile mills, was indeed one clue to their early profitability. In 1900 less than half (42 percent) of their labor was provided by adult males, and the women and children who predominated received pitifully low wages. The official state report in 1900 revealed that skilled men received average daily wages of from $1.00 to $2.50, skilled women from 40 cents to $1.00, and children from 20 to 50 cents. These operatives worked from sixty-three to seventy-five hours per week.

The mill villages that grew up around the textile factories have been compared with antebellum plantations by some historians. Though the planters had combined physical force and paternalism to keep the black slaves at their labors before the Civil War, paternalism intertwined with a wide range of economic controls as well as strong and effective opposition by management to any attempt by workers to organize themselves into labor unions characterized the mill villages of the white textile workers of North Carolina and other southern states. Long hours, low wages, and poor living conditions characterized mill life. Yet, according to labor historian Melton McLaurin, "they came, often in such large numbers that some were turned away. They came because the mills offered them the hope of a better life instead of the despair of farm life."

The "despair of farm life" points to the economically grim truth about the lives of the vast majority of Tar Heels, white and black, in the New South. The tobacco, textile, and, toward the turn of the century, furniture factories that were springing up in North Carolina clearly represented the wave of the future and were potent catalysts in bringing about a variety of changes in the state's outlook and in the lives of those who worked in or lived near the mills. But the fact remained that in 1900 the urban population of North Carolina was only 187,000 as compared with the 1,707,000 who were still rural. Farming continued to be by far the leading occupation.

Despite the losses and devastation caused by the Civil War, the volume of production of Tar Heel agriculture, like that in the rest of the South, recovered relatively quickly. Farmers specialized more than ever in two great staple crops, cotton and tobacco, and by 1900 were producing considerably more than three times as much of both as the state had produced in 1860 on the eve of the war. Yet despite such jumps in production, the farmers' incomes shrank relentlessly, and chronic economic depression haunted the agrarian majority throughout the last three decades of the nineteenth century. (Document 14.5)

Falling prices for farm crops were merely one indicator and cause of trouble. The prices of tobacco, wheat, corn, beef, and other farm products all fell steadily, but none plummeted more painfully than cotton. It sold for twenty-five cents a pound in the late 1860s and fell to twelve cents in the 1870s; when it hit rock bottom at five cents a pound during the massive depression that began in 1893, those farmers for whom it was the main means of livelihood—and they were much more numerous in North Carolina before World War I than they have been since World War II—could not make ends meet.

One result of the long agricultural depression after the Civil War was that thousands of white yeoman farmers, once proud owners of their own land, became tenants, either as cash renters or more commonly as sharecroppers. Emancipation had given blacks their freedom but not ownership of land, so it is hardly surprising that a higher percentage of black farmers than whites were tenants. By 1900 more than 40 percent of North Carolina's farms were operated by tenants.

Both black and white farmers became ensnared in the crop-lien system, a form of debt that compounded many agrarian problems and caused widespread distress. Dependent on credit and unable to obtain it from either private banks or government agencies, farmers turned to merchants, who were often landowners as well. In exchange for a first mortgage or lien on the unplanted crop of tobacco or cotton, the merchant agreed to "carry" the farmer and his family until harvest time by providing all necessary supplies, whether seed and fertilizer or essential food items and clothing. Partly to insure themselves against loss and partly because the interest they had to pay for the credit extended to them was not low, the merchants charged anywhere from 20 to 50 or 60 percent more for goods sold on credit than for those sold for cash. The result was that the farmers were habitually unable to pay off their debts to the merchants and constantly attempted to plant more and more of the principal cash crops in a vain effort to break the cycle of debt. (Document 14.6)

Illiterate though all too many North Carolina farmers were, thanks to a public school system that was so anemic it hardly existed at all, they gradually began to realize the desperateness of their plight and to search for remedial action. Just as businessmen formed trade associations or even "trusts" and industrial workers began their uphill struggle for unions, the farmers, too, turned to organization as a first step toward relief. In the 1870s the Patrons of Husbandry established local chapters or Granges, more than five hundred of them across the state. Admitting women to membership and attempting to eliminate the rancorous sectionalism that had gripped the nation for so long, the Granger movement began auspiciously but proved to be fairly short-lived. Serving primarily a social purpose, the Grange barely addressed the critical issues for agrarian America. Perhaps its influence was slight partly because in its heyday the sectional and racial issues of Reconstruction still loomed large in southern voters' minds.

Because the Farmers' Alliance did concern itself first and foremost with precisely those critical economic issues, when it entered North Carolina in the late 1880s after its formation in Texas, it traveled like wildfire across a parched and wind-swept forest. A Tar Heel agrarian leader, Leonidas Lafayette Polk, soon became national president of the Farmers' Alliance, and his weekly newspaper, the *Progressive Farmer*, became one of the major journals of the farmers' revolt. Beginning in Robeson County in the spring of 1887, the Farmers' Alliance quickly became the largest and most militant organization of farmers in the state's history. By 1890 the Alliance claimed 2,147 local chapters in the state and some ninety thousand members. Like the Grange, the Farmers' Alliance included women as full-fledged members, and although social and fraternal conviviality was an important part of the movement, the Alliance formulated a platform of political demands that dealt with matters of crucial economic importance to farmers. A national organization that grew as strong in Kansas and other western states as it did in the South, the Alliance favored neither of the two major political parties. From the first, however, it considered political action to be essential for the farmers, and it caused sleepless nights for conservative political leaders who had hoped to avoid harsh confrontations about fundamental economic issues.

The Alliancemen argued that farmers needed relief from the monetary policies of the federal government, regardless of whether the administration was a Republican one under President Ulysses S. Grant or a Democratic one under President Grover Cleveland. Some bold Alliancemen, in fact, believed the major parties had grown to look suspiciously alike in their subservience to the business interests of the country.

Fiscal conservatism won its first great triumph after the Civil War when, in a series of steps taken during the Grant administration, the federal government put a fixed ceiling on the amount of legal tender, paper money or greenbacks, in circulation and finally in 1879 made the greenbacks redeemable in gold. Thus by holding a key part of the money supply fixed even though the population and economy were growing, the conservative champions of gold and "sound money" achieved their initial monetary victory over farmers and other debtor groups.

Another major part of the country's circulating currency consisted of bank notes issued by privately owned national banks under a system launched by the United States government during the Civil War. Not only were these bank notes limited in volume and incapable of increasing with the nation's population and economic activity, but state bank notes were taxed out of existence. Tight money or deflation had also been pursued through a federal law in 1873, which eliminated silver as a basis for currency and coins, when historically in the United States silver as well as gold had been used on a basis of sixteen ounces of silver to one of gold.

The Farmers' Alliancemen believed this monetary squeeze caused the falling prices of their crops and the difficulty they faced in obtaining credit, and they responded in several ways. First, they demanded that the federal government return to issuing the legal tender paper money, the greenbacks, that it had used during the Civil War. Second, the farmers called for an end to the system whereby private bankers issued a crucial part of the nation's currency in the form of the national bank notes. And, finally, the Alliance joined other groups who, starting in the 1870s, demanded that the free and unlimited coinage of silver be resumed on the historic basis of sixteen ounces of silver to one ounce of gold. Seeking to increase the volume of the circulating currency in order to raise the prices of farm commodities and ease their debt load, the Alliancemen learned a great deal about the complexity of money and banking and resolutely moved to take political steps toward their economic goals.

In addition to their deep concern about money and credit, the embattled farmers were concerned about other issues. The nation's railway system, as vital to farmers as to manufacturers, was built with generous tax aid and tax relief by government at all levels. Yet the owners of the railways regarded them as strictly private property, even though when the railways did not enjoy a natural monopoly in a given region they usually joined with their competitors to form associations or "pools" in order to minimize competition. When federal courts ruled that state governments could not regulate the railways and early federal regulation under the Interstate Commerce Act of 1887 proved ineffective, the farmers called on the federal government either to supervise and control the railroads or to acquire ownership of them and operate them efficiently and fairly in the interest of all the people.

The farmers endorsed several reforms that they hoped would win the support of industrial workers. Among those proposals were calls for federal restrictions on the influx of immigrants, who handicapped the efforts of American workers to organize unions, and for a shorter working day in the factories. Because it was obvious that the gap between a relatively few rich Americans and the mass of poor ones was larger than ever before, the Alliance demanded a federal tax on incomes and an end to the tariff laws, which after 1861 protected American manufacturers from foreign competition yet left American farmers at the mercy of an unprotected world market for their staple crops and often forced them to pay higher prices for manufactured goods. (Documents 14.7 and 14.8)

The Alliance demands demonstrate that, in reaction to their growing economic difficulties after the Civil War and the manifest indifference of the nation's leaders to those difficulties, farmers were in no mood for a continuation of the status quo. The major focus of their economic concerns was on the federal government, but they had questions to ask of and grievances to be redressed by their state governments, too. In North

Carolina, they believed that for too long the state had wooed business and industry, neglected public education, and left a disproportionate share of the tax burden on land. The winds of change began to blow across the Old North State as the Farmers' Alliance flexed its muscles in the late 1880s.

When those agrarian winds blew, the Democrats were in power, having triumphed over the Republicans in the Reconstruction era and remained in control thereafter. Known to history as the Bourbon Democrats or sometimes as the Redeemer Democrats (because they had "redeemed" the state from Republican rule), they were not, on the whole, an inspired group of political leaders. Like their fellow Democrats in the other southern states, they had ridden to power primarily by exploiting white racism—by depicting themselves as the white man's party and their Republican opponents as the party of Negro domination and misrule.

To the dismay of the Democrats, the Republican party in North Carolina remained very much alive after Reconstruction, which was not the case in the lower South. The chief purpose of the Tar Heel Democrats, therefore, was to keep their opponents out of power, and to achieve that goal they frequently employed the philosophy of the Reconstruction era that the end justified any means. The Democrats killed local self-government, for example, by giving the state legislature the power to name local justices of the peace, who in turn named county commissioners. Ostensibly, this arrangement was to prevent black North Carolinians from holding even small, local offices in the sixteen eastern counties where blacks were in a majority of the population. In fact, however, the plan gave the Democrats control not only of the eastern counties but also of the western mountain counties, where white Republicans were numerous. Unfair election laws, fraud at the ballot box, and occasional threats or actual violence were other methods that the Democrats employed as necessary to retain power.

Staunchly committed to economy in government, the Bourbon Democrats allowed the public school system to deteriorate so badly by 1900 that it had become one of the worst in the United States. Regardless of comparative ranking, the facts that illiteracy actually increased in the 1870s and that as late as 1900 almost one-fifth of the whites and nearly half of the blacks were illiterate suggest that false economy ill served the best interests of the people of North Carolina.

Friendly to the railroads and growing manufacturing interests, the Bourbon Democrats shied away from proposals for reform or for any fundamental challenge to the status quo. Even the most popular leader among them, Governor and then United States Senator Zebulon B. Vance, deeply embarrassed as well as infuriated his supporters in the Farmers' Alliance when he agreed to introduce one of their favorite measures in the Senate only to announce subsequently that he could not vote for the bill.

Politically, therefore, North Carolina in the late nineteenth century seemed in some ways to be somnolently slipping back into its antebellum role as the "Rip Van Winkle" state. (Document 14.9) Despite the sluggish political currents, however, important developments were occurring. The "Reconstruction that took"—the acceptance and promotion of industrial growth—was gradually altering North Carolina. As a remedy for the state's economic ills, however, its slow pace and often unjust means left the long-suffering agrarian majority ripening for a revolt that would shake and help rouse the Old North State in the 1890s.

DOCUMENT 14.1

"Our Refuge and Our Strength": A Call for Industrialization, 1880

The farmers and other industrial classes of our State naturally and very properly felt deep concern in the questions involved in the late election. North Carolina naturally, and, we think, very properly took position on the national issues with what is termed the "solid South." Solid, not as against the North, not for the accomplishment of selfish designs, not against the constitution, not against any policy or measures that might best promote the interests of the entire country, but against a possible return to carpet-bag rule, against oppression and injustice, and, above all, against what we honestly conceive to be dangerous encroachments on constitutional liberty, and an evident tendency to a centralized government. Against this and all these our State will always be found "solid."

But we have been defeated in the national contest. In the administration of the national government for the next four years we need not concern ourselves, for as far as possible our councils will be ignored. What, then, is our duty? It is to go to work earnestly to build up North Carolina. Nothing is to be gained by regrets and repinings. No people or State is better able to meet emergencies. We have no fear of those social and political disruptions which so threaten and disturb the peace of Europe and of the Northern States, the outcroppings of socialism, Nihilism, Communism and labor strikes. We have no stocks and bonds in lordly monopolies to be crushed by financial convulsions. We have no great commercial centres to be ruined by fickle and treacherous speculation. We can have no horde of paupers to sap our energies.

But we have one of the finest countries in the world. And what nobler employment could enlist the energies of a people than the developing of the great resources of our God-favored State, and having it possessed and enjoyed by an enlightened, law-abiding, peaceful people? But with all its varied and splendid capabilities it is idle to talk of home independence so long if we go to the North for everything from a tooth pick to a President. We may plead in vain for a higher type of manhood and womanhood among the masses, so long as we allow the children to grow up in ignorance. We may look in vain for the dawn of an era of enterprise, progress and development, so long as thousands and millions of money are deposited in our banks on four per cent interest when its judicious investment in manufactures would more than quadruple that rate, and give profitable employment to thousands of our now idle women and children.

Out of our political defeat we must work out a glorious material and industrial triumph. We must have less politics and more work, fewer stump speakers and more stump pullers, less tinsel and show and boast, and more hard, earnest work. We must make money—it is a power in this practical business age. Teach the boys and girls to work and teach them to be proud of it. Demand a better and more liberal system of public education, and if need be, demand increased taxation to obtain it.

Infuse into that system practical, industrial education, suited to the wants of the masses and to the demands of this progressive age. Demand all legislative encouragement for manufacturing that may be consistent with true political economy. Encourage, aid, support and defend our State Department of Agriculture. Push it to the full measure of its usefulness. Uphold the hands of its officers by kind co-operation. Work for the material and educational advancement of North Carolina, and in this, and not in politics, will be found her refuge and her strength.

Raleigh News and Observer, *9 November 1880.*

DOCUMENT 14.2

The Role of Aggressive Advertising in North Carolina's Tobacco Industry

From 1884 to 1888 a craze of skating on roller skates in large rinks swept over the entire country making glad the hearts of the children and adults up to the age of 60. The game of Polo on skates was one of the exciting auxilaries of the skating rink. Perhaps more so than baseball at the present day.

Rinks of colossal proportions had been built in all the cities of the land, many of which covered as much as half a city block and accommodated from 10,000 to 12,000 spectators. Mr. [Small] in attending the first game of polo conceived the idea of securing the services of an expert polo club, equip[ping] them handsomely and play[ing] them as the Cross Cut Polo Club of Durham, N.C.

Petibaun and Co., uniform manufacturers, were consulted relative the cost of same. This decided upon, the club selected was requested by Mr. [Small] to meet him at Petibaun's the next morning to be measured for the uniforms.

Goal sticks and other paraphernalia were ordered from Spaldings and in less than 10 days the club was billed for a game in one of the leading rinks of Cincinnati. 25,000 cigarettes were sent to the rink with 125,000 cabinet photos of the leading actresses of the world.

When the game was called the local team of Cincinnati skated around the immense rink and then followed the Cross Cut team of Durham, N.C. Coming in with their handsome faces and gorgeous uniforms throwing the audience almost into a panic. Once more the South was battling against the North for the honors of the hour, while the game grew with interest and excitement until the finish.

When the audience left at the door each male visitor was presented with a 5¢ package of Cross Cut cigarettes and each lady with a set of 5 cabinet photos of the most prominent actresses in the world. (Compliment of W. Dukes Sons and Co.)

The next morning's Inquirer reported the game in detail in the sporting columns, while on the front page mentioned the game, complimenting the Cross Cuts as one of the handsomest equipped clubs in the United States. The result of the game was wired to the Sporting columns of the Press of the United States.

Unpublished memoir in the Edward F. Small Manuscripts, Duke University Library, Durham.

DOCUMENT 14.3

Tobacco Money Goes into the Textile Industry

While my associates and I have been largely engaged in the manufacture of tobacco since the war, we have for the past few years turned some attention to the Cotton Factory industry, which we are sure has a big future in the Southern States. We have recently invested in several mills and are well pleased with the result but the mills are all comparatively small and cannot meet with that degree of success that would be possible in plants of larger capacity with ample capital and I am anxious to see a very large mill established some where in the South and am satisfied that the promoters of such an enterprize would be amply repaid. Most of the mills throughout this section have struggled along with capital entirely inadequate to successfully operate even the small plants that have been erected. The Piedmont belt in North Carolina is the most healthful local-, ity in the South and there are many inducements for the location of such a mill as I would like to see erected. Splendid water power and an abundance of cheap white labor can be had and all that is needed to utilize these advantages successfully and profitably is money and men with experience in business. If you really contemplate establishing a Branch of your Lowell business in the South I would be pleased to meet and confer with you or your representative in reference to the matter, and while I do not know that it would be agreeable to you to have others join you in the enterprize, I should be very pleased to take an interest with you and believe that others of my associates would do likewise. To show you that we are people with some knowledge of large business enterprizes, it might not be out of place to enclose you the Treasurer's last report of the American Tobacco Co., of which my Brother, Mr. J. B. Duke, is President. If what I have written you is of any interest, I would be pleased to hear from you.

Benjamin N. Duke to Charles F. Lovering, Durham, N.C., 4 February 1893, B. N. Duke Papers, Duke University Library, Durham.

DOCUMENT 14.4

A Tar Heel Black Leader, Warren C. Coleman, Shares the New South Dream

Please allow me to call the attention of the public to the fact that a movement is on foot to erect a cotton mill at Concord to be operated by colored labor. The colored citizens of the United States have had no opportunity to utilize their talents along this line. Since North Carolina has fairly and justly won for herself in the Centennial at the World Fair at Chicago and at the Atlanta Exposition the honored name of being "the foremost of the States," she will further evidence the fact if she is the first to have a cotton mill to be operated principally by the colored people. We are proud of the spirit and energy of the white people in encouraging and assisting the enterprise and will our colored people not catch the spark of the new industrial life and take advantage of this unprecedented opportunity to engage in the enterprise that will prove to the world our ability as operatives in the mills thereby solving the great problem "can the Negroes be employed in cotton mills to any advantage"? And now that the opportunity is before us, experience alone will determine the question and it behooves us to better ourselves and do something, and as one man . . . [make] the effort that is to win for us a name and place us before the world as industrious and enterprising citizens.

Don't think for a moment that this desireable and enviable position can be obtained by merely a few of our people, but on the other hand, it will require the united effort of the race. Then when the people of the white race who are our friends clearly see that we are surely coming, they will "come over into Macedonia and help us." The enterprise will be just what we make of it. There is nothing to gain but everything to lose by allowing the enterprise to prove a failure.

In case of a failure, it will be due to mere neglect. If it proves a success, it will be to the honor and glory of the race. If racial weakness is set forth, it will only strengthen the sentiment already expressed about us. We can see the finger of Providence directing our cause, for we believe that God helps only those who help themselves. If we show no desire to succeed in this, and in all the enterprises designed for the industrial and financial development of the race, then it can be proven that our Liberty is a failure. We cannot afford to be idle or lukewarm in this matter. There is too much connected with it that would not let our conscience rest if we did not make the effort to carry out the plan. Can there be any among us who do not wish to see the moral, intellectual, religious and industrial character of our people elevated to a higher and broader plan[e] of civilization and true usefulness? There is no middle ground. We are either going forward or backward. The watchword is onward and upward, and if we ever expect to attain the heights of industrial usefulness, we must fall in line and march shoulder to shoulder in one solid phalanx along the road that leads to fortune and fame.

When we grasp the opportunities offered for the betterment of our condition, we are performing the great task which will at last determine our future position in the ranks of the great nations of the world. The markets of Madagascar, Zanzibar and other tropical regions where there are millions of inhabitants are open for all goods that can be produced in the mills.

Let us not be discouraged but move onward with the enterprise, with that spirit and determination that makes all things possible for those who strive in real earnest.

Allen Edward Burgess, "Tar Heel Blacks and the New South Dream: The Coleman Manufacturing Company, 1896–1904" (Ph.D. dissertation, Duke University, 1977), pp. 168–69; J. K. Rouse, The Noble Experiment of Warren C. Coleman *(Charlotte: Crabtree Press, 1972), pp. 52–54.*

DOCUMENT 14.5

"Where Is the Wrong and What Is the Remedy?" The *Progressive Farmer* Points to Agrarian Distress

There is something radically wrong in our industrial system. There is a screw loose. The wheels have dropped out of balance.

The railroads have never done a better or a more profitable business, and yet agriculture languishes. Manufacturing enterprises never made more money or were in a more flourishing condition, and yet agriculture languishes. Speculators and incorporations never accumulated fortunes more rapidly, and agriculture languishes. Towns and cities flourish and "boom" and grow and "boom," and yet agriculture languishes. Salaries and fees were never so temptingly high and desirable, and yet agriculture languishes. A city editor visits one of our flourishing towns. It is supported by "a splendid back country." The town should be a fair criterion by which to judge of the general condition of the country supporting it. He sees magnificent commercial blocks and buildings going up on the streets and corners. The merchants are busy—the farmers are rushing to and fro, trading and loading; beautiful cottages are going up in the suburbs. He is inspired by this splendid show of prosperity and writes to his home paper—"this is a magnificent country." It is on a rushing "boom" —and the town paper copies his letter without a word of comment, and with complacent satisfaction.

The city editor looked at the pleasant but delusive surface. He did not get into the "true inwardness" of the situation. He did not interview the register of deeds and find huge piles of mortgages and liens—he failed to stroll out on some leading road in the morning, and see these farmers' wagons coming into the town empty, and see them going out loaded with hay, fertilizers, and corn, meat, flour and ship stuff—he did not ascertain that the beautiful cottages were being erected by farmers who had left comfortable homes and good farms and had "come to town to educate their children."

The *Pittsboro Home* says old and young men are leaving their farms and are going to the towns. That "it is a sad fact that most of the signs of success and prosperity are confined to our towns and villages." The *News and Observer* "rejoices in the progress of various towns throughout the State." "From every quarter comes reports of city booms." Our worthy contemporary sees the languishing condition of agriculture and ascribes it largely to the robbing of the people by taxation under the form of law. This is true, but if the towns, railroads, manufactures, banks and all speculative enterprises flourish so prosperously and agriculture languishes under the same laws imposing these taxes, this is but another proof that something is radically wrong. The farmers are beginning to realize it, and they propose to institute an investigation with the view of finding a remedy. Where is the wrong and what is the remedy?

Progressive Farmer (Raleigh), 28 April 1887.

DOCUMENT 14.6

The Crop-Lien System as a Source of Agrarian Poverty

The "crop lien," as it was called, began its career soon after the war, but has grown to very large proportions. Of course it was a great convenience to be able to go to a store and buy what one wanted, or to send a servant with an order to have the thing charged. The result, however, was that wants increased, and a great deal was bought that was not really needed.

I remember reading a story about like this. One neighbor said to another, in a sort of boastful way: "I have made arrangements, with a merchant, by which I can get whatever I need on my farm, all through the year, without paying any cash." "How did you do that?" asked the other neighbor. "Why, I just gave him a 'crap lien,'" answered the first neighbor. "What is a crap lien?" asked neighbor number two. "O, its nothing but a promise to pay, at the end of the year, when the crop is gathered," said neighbor number one. "I believe," said neighbor number two, "I had rather pay the cash, for what I am obliged to have, and do without what I can't pay the cash for," said neighbor number two. "O, you are an old fogy," retorted neighbor number one. "My motto is, while we live let us live." "That's my motto, too," said neighbor number two; "and while I am living I had rather keep out of debt. That 'crap lien,' you tell me about, may be a dangerous thing after all, instead of a blessing. At any rate, I wish you would let me know at the end of the year how it worked."

As a matter of course, neighbor number one, who had given the crop lien, traded extensively—and so did the family—they got such things as they severally wanted, all the time feeling highly elated over the fact that they had such good credit.

At the winding up of the year the crap lien began to draw, and it kept on drawing. It drew all the cotton and the corn, the wheat and the oats, the shucks, the hay and the fodder, the horses and the mules, the cows, the hogs and the poultry, the farm utensils and the wagons, the carriage and the buggy; and, not being satisfied with its drawing outside, it drew the household and kitchen furniture, and as neighbor number one, in sadness explained to neighbor number two, it didn't quit drawing until it got the table, the plates and the dishes, the cups and the saucers, the knives and the forks, and when it had gotten everything else, it reached for the dish rag, and wiped up the whole concern, not leaving even a grease spot.

I think they must be using that same old "crap lien" yet; for very often I see an auction going on in front of a store, and I notice that the horses, mules, wagons, buggies, plows, hoes and rakes, baskets and buckets, and every old thing, is put up for sale. Some people don't seem to care; but it does seem to me it's paying too dear for the whistle to give "crap lien" prices for things which might be made at home, and then have to give up what has been made, at the end of the year. But, that will continue to be so, as long as farmers buy their meat in Chicago, their hay in Kentucky, and their corn and wheat from the Northwest and depend solely on cotton or tobacco to foot all the bills. A people who run in debt for meat and bread all the year can't expect to have much in the fall.

Rev. R. H. Whitaker, Whitaker's Reminiscences: Incidents and Anecdotes *(Raleigh: Edwards & Broughton, 1905), pp. 101–2.*

DOCUMENT 14.7

Farmers of Chatham County Petition the North Carolina General Assembly

To the Honorable the General Assembly of North Carolina:

Your petitioners respectfully show:

That they were appointed by the County Alliance of Chatham County, held in Pittsboro, January 4th, 1889, to memorialize your honorable body and ask for the following legislation:

I. That the state and county governments be administered on the most economical basis, and that all useless offices be abolished.

II. That our charitable and penal institutions, so far as practical, be made self-sustaining.

III. That a just and equitable equalization be established by law between the wages of the laborer and the compensations of office-holders and professional men.

IV. That sheep-husbandry, stock-raising, diversified farming and all the industries be fostered by appropriate legislation.

Your petitioners show that they are true and loyal to the best interests of North Carolina, and that they would ask nothing in conflict with the greatest good to the greatest number of their fellow-citizens.

The fact that there are seven or eight hundred lots or tracts of land now advertised to be sold for taxes in Wake County, is suggestive. This they believe to be but a fair index of the condition of things in a large part of the State; and that even this does not show the full extent of financial depression.

The failure of the crops in this county last year necessitates the buying of almost our entire supplies to make another crop, and there is very little money in the hands of the farmers. Almost every farmer is depressed; many are disheartened; labor is unremunerative; the value of land is depreciating, and there is a growing disposition to abandon the farm and seek other employment. Unless something is done to bring relief, many will be compelled to give up their farms. The boasted progress and increase of wealth in North Carolina is not shared by the farmers. They are gradually but steadily becoming poorer and poorer every year.

Relying upon your wisdom and justice, the farmers of Chatham County, for themselves and for their brother farmers throughout the State, have outlined, as above set forth, the legislation which they believe will bring contentment to the people and prosperity to the State.

The first step towards relief is to put into effect in our state and county governments something of that rigid economy which the farmers are compelled to practice, and thereby lessen the burdens of taxation.

Make the salaries of state and county officers as low as will be consistent with efficient service. Reduce, if possible, the costs and the delays of litigation, and devise some means of punishing crime and caring for criminals which will be less burdensome to the honest tax payers.

We trust that the justice of our cause and our own good intentions will be a sufficient apology for troubling your honorable body with our petition.

North Carolina Public Documents, 1889, *Document No. 25.*

DOCUMENT 14.8

The "Ocala Demands" of the National Farmers' Alliance, 1890

1. a. We demand the abolition of national banks.

b. We demand that the government shall establish sub-treasuries or depositories in the several states, which shall loan money direct to the people at a low rate of interest, not to exceed two per cent per annum, on nonperishable farm products, and also upon real estate, with proper limitations upon the quantity of land and amount of money.

c. We demand that the amount of the circulating medium be speedily increased to not less than $50 per capita.

2. We demand that Congress shall pass such laws as will effectually prevent the dealing in futures of all agricultural and mechanical productions; providing a stringent system of procedure in trials that will secure

the prompt conviction, and imposing such penalties as shall secure the most perfect compliance with the law.

3. We condemn the silver bill recently passed by Congress, and demand in lieu thereof the free and unlimited coinage of silver.

4. We demand the passage of laws prohibiting alien ownership of land, and that Congress take prompt action to devise some plan to obtain all lands now owned by aliens and foreign syndicates; and that all lands now held by railroads and other corporations in excess of such as is actually used and needed by them be reclaimed by the government and held for actual settlers only.

5. Believing in the doctrine of equal rights to all and special privileges to none, we demand—

a. That our national legislation shall be so framed in the future as not to build up one industry at the expense of another.

b. We further demand a removal of the existing heavy tariff tax from the necessities of life, that the poor of our land must have.

c. We further demand a just and equitable system of graduated tax on incomes.

d. We believe that the money of the country should be kept as much as possible in the hands of the people, and hence we demand that all national and state revenues shall be limited to the necessary expenses of the government economically and honestly administered.

6. We demand the most rigid, honest, and just state and national government control and supervision of the means of public communication and transportation, and if this control and supervision does not remove the abuse now existing, we demand the government ownership of such means of communication and transportation.

7. We demand that the Congress of the United States submit an amendment to the Constitution providing for the election of United States Senators by direct vote of the people of each state.

Proceedings of the Supreme Council of the National Farmers' Alliance and Industrial Union, 1890, *pp. 32–33.*

DOCUMENT 14.9

"Is There Intellectual Freedom in North Carolina?" Walter Hines Page Attacks the "Mummies"

[Walter Hines Page, a young journalist, left the state in the 1880s to become a distinguished editor and publisher in New York City and later to be sent by President Woodrow Wilson as the United States' ambassador to Great Britain during the First World War. Unhappy about the provincialism and complacent conservatism that he discerned in Tar Heel leaders of the 1880s, he published a scathing attack on those leaders whom he called the "mummies."]

It is an awfully discouraging business to undertake to prove to a mummy that it is a mummy. You go up to it and say, "Old fellow, the Egyptian dynasties crumbled several thousand years ago: you are a fish out of water. You have by accident or the Providence of God got a long way out of your time. This is America. The old Kings are forgotten, and this is the year 1886 in the calendar of a Christ whose people had not even gone to Egypt when you died." The old thing grins that grin which death set on its solemn features when the world was young; and your task is so pitiful that even the humor of it is gone.

Give it up. It can't be done. We all think when we are young that we can do something with the mummies. But the mummy is a solemn fact, and it differs from all other things (except stones) in this—it lasts forever. They don't want an Industrial School. That means a new idea, and a new idea is death to the supremacy of the mummies. Let 'em alone. The world must have some corner in it where men sleep and sleep and dream and dream, and North Carolina is as good a spot for that as any. There is not a man whose residence is in the State who is recognized by the world as an authority on anything. Since time began no man nor woman who lived there has ever written a book that has taken a place in the permanent literature of the country. Not a man has ever lived and worked there who fills twenty-five pages in any history of the United States. Not a scientific discovery has been made and worked out and kept its home in North Carolina that ever became famous for the good it did the world. It is the laughing stock among the States. . . .

The cause—the prime cause that is at the bottom of all this, is the organization of society, of the trades, the professions—of everything—against improvement. It is not simply because we are poor. They were poor in Georgia and Tennessee and Virginia twenty years ago, as poor as we are. Yet they are a long way ahead of us in giving every man a chance and in making intellectual and social progress. . . .

It isn't the people that are wrong.

Who is it, then?

It is the mummies. And the mummies have the directing of things. Do you want examples? If you know anything, you can name examples yourself. Count on your fingers the five men who fill the highest places or have the greatest influence on educational work in North Carolina. Not one of them is a scholar! Count the five most influential editors in the State. Not one of them could in the great centres of journalism earn $10 a week as a reporter. Go around all the leading sources of power in the same way, and you will see what is the matter. Yet when a man tells the plain truth because he loves North Carolina, the same fellows howl, 'Traitor!' . . . Men in North Carolina do not speak out what they think, but submit (as no other people ever submitted) to the guidance of the dead. I hold this to be cowardly. I think the time is come—you have made a good occasion by your recent work in the *State Chronicle*—for a getting at the truth, for independent action, for a declaration of independence from the tyranny of hindering traditions. In God's name, with such a State, filled with such people, with such opportunities, are we to sit down quietly forever and allow every enterprise that means growth, every idea that means intellectual freedom to perish, and the State to lag behind always, because a few amiable mummies will be offended? It would be cheaper to pension them all, than longer listen to them.

The utmost reverence for all men that are honest and energetic, the profoundest faith in the capabilities of our people and the sincerest affection for the old home have dictated what I have written, and I have written with soberness and with truth and for intellectual and social freedom.

Raleigh State Chronicle, *4 February 1886.*

SUGGESTED READINGS

Billings, Dwight B., Jr. *Planters and the Making of a "New South": Class, Politics, and Development in North Carolina, 1865–1900.* Chapel Hill: University of North Carolina Press, 1979.

Clay, Howard B. "Daniel Augustus Tompkins and Industrial Revival in the South." *East Carolina College Publications in History* (1965), 114–45.

Collins, Herbert. "The Idea of Cotton Textile Industry in the South, 1870–1900." *North Carolina Historical Review* 34 (1957):358–92.

Cooper, John Milton, Jr. *Walter Hines Page: The Southerner as American, 1855–1918*. Chapel Hill: University of North Carolina Press, 1977.

Degler, Carl. *Out of Our Past: The Forces That Shaped Modern America*. New York: Harper & Row, 1970.

Durden, Robert F. *The Dukes of Durham, 1865–1929*. Durham: Duke University Press, 1975.

Ebert, Charles H. V. "Furniture Making in High Point." *North Carolina Historical Review* 36 (1959):330–39.

Gaston, Paul M. *The New South Creed: A Study in Southern Mythmaking*. New York: Alfred A. Knopf, 1970.

Logan, Frenise A. *The Negro in North Carolina, 1876–1894*. Chapel Hill: University of North Carolina Press, 1964.

McLaurin, Melton A. *Paternalism and Protest: Southern Cotton Mill Workers and Organized Labor, 1876–1905*. Westport, Conn.: Greenwood Press, 1971.

Robert, Joseph C. *The Story of Tobacco in America*. 1949; repr. Chapel Hill: University of North Carolina Press, 1967.

Stover, John F. *The Railroads of the South, 1865–1900*. Chapel Hill: University of North Carolina Press, 1955.

Tilley, Nannie M. *The Bright-Tobacco Industry*. Chapel Hill: University of North Carolina Press, 1948.

Weare, Walter B. *Black Business in the New South: A Social History of the North Carolina Mutual Life Insurance Company*. Urbana: University of Illinois Press, 1973.

Woodward, C. Vann. *The Origins of the New South, 1877–1913*. Baton Rouge: Louisiana State University Press, 1951.

CHAPTER 15

Cracking the Solid South

Populism and the Fusionist Interlude

Jeffrey J. Crow

Raleigh News and Observer, *1 November 1898 (Courtesy of the Division of Archives and History, Raleigh, N.C.)*

The post–Civil War South produced a great many myths about southern society, culture, and politics. Preeminent among these myths was the idea that a "solid South" emerged following the dark years of Reconstruction. After a decade of federal occupation and political control by venal carpetbaggers, disloyal scalawags, and brutish freedmen, so the story goes, the South overturned Republican rule and turned to its planter-dominated upper class for guidance and government. With the South once again safely in the hands of men of property, wealth, family, and prestige, harmony was restored to the political system by one-party Democratic rule, prosperity promoted by industrialization, and the social order firmly fixed by rigid class and caste definitions. The solid South came to stand for the Democratic party, white supremacy, and a benign upper-class hegemony over millhands, tenant farmers, and sharecroppers, black and white alike.

Like most myths, that of the solid South had within it an element of truth. Certainly the class configurations were unmistakable. Below the tiny but powerful planter-industrialist elite stood a small but growing middle class of urban merchants, lawyers, and managers to run the factories and supply essential services to an industrializing economy. Next on the social scale came small, independent farmers, by far the most numerous of postbellum southerners. But as the agricultural depression of the 1870s dragged on into the 1890s, their numbers dwindled. They lost their farms, then their hope, and finally their social self-esteem by becoming tenants, sharecroppers, or millhands. At the bottom of the social order, kept separate by the caste of skin color, were the freedmen, only a few steps removed from bondage and often entrapped in a system of debt peonage.

For the long-suffering southern laboring classes the solid South had few allures and more than its share of disillusion. The southern social order in the decades after Reconstruction, in fact, was riddled with crisscrossing racial and class tensions that threatened the implantation of a solid South. Nowhere did these internal tensions have more persistent and destabilizing effects than in North Carolina. The challenge to the prevailing economic and political order in the Tar Heel state emanated from two distinct political forces, the Republican party, which had remained a potent force in state politics since Reconstruction, and the Populist party, the political outgrowth of a democratic reform movement that swept the South and West in the 1880s and 1890s. Together these two political counterweights to the complacent Democratic party held sway for a few brief years and sent tremors through the Tar Heel establishment, increasingly the preserve of business-oriented Bourbons. Fusion—the pragmatic, if expedient, coalition of Republicans and Populists—shook North Carolina's political, economic, and social order to its foundations.

Two-party politics had a long and venerable history in North Carolina. During the 1830s and 1840s the Whig party had controlled the state and promoted a program of internal improvements, particularly railroad building, that opened the more populous and generally nonslaveholding piedmont and west to new commercial markets. When the Democratic party, dominated by the slaveholding east, assumed power in the 1850s, it continued the policy of internal improvements, but western Whigs, even after their national party had disintegrated and the Civil War had begun, were reluctant to join their former political adversaries. After the war the Republican party found a natural constituency in these old Whigs, many of whom had been staunchly Unionist, nonslaveholding, subsistence farmers. Combined with the newly enfranchised freedmen in the east, the former Whigs made the Republican party a viable force in Tar Heel elections. Indeed, North Carolina had the most competitive two-party system in the South before 1900. Between 1880 and 1896 the Democrats never won more than 54 percent of the vote in gubernatorial elections. Though Democrats continued to prey on the bitter memories of Reconstruction, to portray themselves as the white man's party, and to court black voters locally when it suited their purposes, they were never able to stamp out Republicanism in North Carolina. When the Populist revolt added a new factor to the political equation, the fragility of Democratic control became readily apparent throughout the state.

Populism was easily the most important challenge to the southern political and economic order in the postbellum era. Its roots lay in the grinding economic hardships of the 1880s and 1890s. Economic distress grew out of financial practices at every level—federal, state, and local—that favored the creditor over the debtor and that had been zealously pursued by both Democratic and Republican administrations since the Civil War. To finance the war some $450 million in greenbacks had been issued. Bankers and bondholders, however, were quick to insist that the nation return to the gold standard by retiring the paper currency and resuming the payment of specie. In the years following the war this policy of deflation created much economic misery for the nation's laboring classes. Though the population and production of the nation continued to grow, there were fewer and fewer dollars competing for more and more goods and additional human needs. The cumulative effect of this policy was to drive prices down and interest rates up. At the same time, the federal government's tariff policy forced farmers to buy American-manufactured goods at high protected prices while they sold their crops in the world market with no protection.

Caught in this deflationary grip, southern farmers by the late 1880s were ready to listen to any organization that promised economic relief. The emergence of the Southern Farmers' Alliance seemed to offer poorer farmers a chance to escape a marketing and supply system that failed to respond to their needs and indeed victimized them. At the center of the Alliance program was the establishment of cooperative exchanges and state agencies that would enable farmers to market their crops at optimal prices and buy their farm supplies at wholesale rates. Under such a system the furnishing merchant and landlord could be bypassed.

The overall fate of the Alliance hinged on the fortunes of the cooperatives. As the Southern Farmers' Alliance steamrolled across the South, expectations swelled for cheaper supplies bought in bulk and higher prices for cotton, wheat, and tobacco. Alliance lecturers combed rural crossroads and towns preaching cooperation and building a community of true believers. Nonetheless, the cooperatives were constantly plagued by undercapitalization, lack of credit, and poor business management. In addition, Alliancemen had to contend with the mounting hostility of merchants, bankers, and eventually manufacturers, who refused to sell to the Alliance. In North Carolina a statewide exchange briefly conducted a $350,000 business, and several tobacco warehouses and a factory were established, but all these ventures experienced limited success.

The demise of cooperatives across the South forced agrarian reformers to make a crucial decision. In the South the reformers had continued to work within the Democratic party, but their strident attacks on the crop-lien system struck at the very roots of a hierarchical economic and social system presided over by Bourbon Democrats. An open break with the planter-industrialist wing of the party came when bold and visionary agrarian leaders mobilized the Alliancemen into a third-party movement. From the heart of the Alliance experience emerged the People's party. By 1892 agrarian radicals were ready to challenge the nation's political order and its monetary system, and North Carolinian Leonidas L. Polk, editor of the *Progressive Farmer*, seemed the likely choice to carry the Populists' presidential banner. Only weeks before the Populist party's national convention, however, Polk died suddenly and unexpectedly. The mantle of Populist leadership in North Carolina passed to a dynamic young Sampson County legislator, editor, and former Democrat, who soon proved a force to be reckoned with in Tar Heel politics. His name was Marion Butler.

Butler brought to the agrarian movement a hard-headed pragmatism and organizing genius that took the Populist party out of the suballiance lecture hall and raised it to the balance wheel of state politics. As early as 1892 Butler suggested a coalition of Populists and reform-minded Democrats to defeat the Bourbon-bonded Democracy, but mid-road Populists, who opposed cooperation with either major party, and rock-ribbed Democrats alike rejected such a radical proposal. Within the Republican party, however, there existed a faction that hungrily eyed the

Populists as potential allies. This Republican wing was led by perhaps the most colorful Tar Heel political figure of the period—Daniel Lindsay Russell, Jr.

Russell sprang from an old whig family in the Lower Cape Fear country. The scion of two of the wealthiest planter families in eastern North Carolina, Russell nonetheless had become a Radical Republican during Reconstruction and a proponent of various financial schemes to aid the South's struggling farmers. After several terms in the General Assembly and a six-year stint as superior court judge, Russell was elected to Congress for one term in 1878 as a Greenbacker. Though an audacious advocate of civil and political equality for blacks during Reconstruction, Russell by the 1880s had tired of the Democratic use of race to defeat such political outsiders as Republicans, Greenbackers, and Independents, who ultimately depended on the black vote for success. Emerging as a spokesman for disgruntled white Republicans who were weary of the race issue and resentful of black initiatives toward local control of the party, Russell predicted in 1892 that a coalition of Republicans and Populists would crush the Democrats, and he called for a readjustment of party lines on issues other than color. His political intuition was true, for the combined gubernatorial vote of Populists and Republicans accounted for 51.7 percent of the electorate. When the Democratic legislature of 1893 punished the Populist apostasy by severely restricting the business activities of the Alliance, the stage was set for a coalition of Populists and Republicans to overturn Democratic control of the state for the first time since Reconstruction.

A firm political friendship between Russell and Butler would not blossom for several years, but in 1894 each leader knew what his respective party had to do to win. The "fusion" of the Populist and Republican parties, as Democrats dubbed it, appealed to each side. Both parties favored electoral reforms. Since 1876 Democratic legislatures had ruthlessly maintained partisan election laws that permitted Democratic registrars to disqualify voters, especially blacks and illiterate whites, on the flimsiest pretext. The Democrats had also centralized county governments in the hands of the legislature, thereby negating home rule in various localities. Populists and Republicans also agreed on larger appropriations for public schools and a nonpartisan supreme court. For the moment, however, larger differences of economic policy between the two parties, especially currency reform, were quietly left in the background.

By combining their state and county tickets, the fusionists wrested control of the state from the Democrats in 1894. With a majority of 116 to 54 in the General Assembly of 1895, the fusionists began enacting a full slate of reforms. Home rule was returned to the counties, appropriations for public schools were increased, funds for state charitable and penal institutions were augmented, and the legal rate of interest per annum was set at 6 percent. The fusionists also showed a willingness to raise taxes on businesses and railroads, the latter being assessed at only one-third of their actual value for tax purposes. Most dramatically, the fusionists passed a new election law, perhaps the fairest and most democratic in the post-Reconstruction South, that permitted one election judge from each party to be present when the ballots were counted, that limited the registrars' power to disqualify voters capriciously, and that helped illiterates by establishing colored ballots marked with party insignia. Finally, the fusionists sent Populist Marion Butler to the United States Senate for a full six-year term and named Republican Jeter C. Pritchard to complete the two-year term left vacant by the death of Zebulon Vance.

The fusionists' bold reforms, however, made them highly vulnerable to Democratic propaganda. Populists and Republicans alike were wary of Negro participation in politics, but they understood the practical realities of winning elections. Their reform of the electoral system tended to increase black political participation both at the polls and in officeholding. For instance, an estimated 87 percent of the eligible black voters in 1896, compared to 64 percent in 1892, went to the polls. One result was the election of eleven black legislators to the General Assembly of 1897, the most since the 1880s. Similarly, the fusionists' less-than-subtle hint that they intended to regulate business and raise taxes alienated the business community, which, under the Bourbon Democrats, had come to expect favored treatment. Clearly, the political risks were great.

If the Populists and Republicans had engineered a revolution in state politics, their political alliance was by no means an easy one. With the approach of the 1896 elections and the complicating factor of presidential politics injected, cooperation once more between Populists and Republicans was uncertain. Marion Butler, who was elected national chairman of the Populist party in 1896, was reluctant to join forces with the GOP on the state and local level while contesting it nationally for the presidency and for control of the nation's economic destiny. Butler firmly believed that the Populists would soon replace the Democratic party as the second major party in the country, with the Democrats disappearing much as the Whigs had in the 1850s. Hence he perceived a greater danger from the Republicans, who remained committed to the gold standard. The Populist chieftain insisted that free silver, the most popular plank in the agrarian radicals' 1892 platform, was the issue on which to unite every reformer of every party in 1896. The free silver plank called for the unlimited coinage of silver to inflate the amount of currency in circulation and thus raise prices. Free silver, however, did not address questions more fundamental to the nation's economic structure, such as credit (still tightly controlled by the hard-money national banking system), monopolies in American corporate enterprise, and a flexible monetary system keyed to population expansion and industrial growth. On a national level Butler's plans were foredoomed, but in North Carolina his prospects for success remained undimmed. (Document 15.1)

Daniel Russell was one reason why Butler's political fortunes in North Carolina still looked bright. Russell coveted the Tar Heel governorship, and he was convinced that cooperation between the Populists and Republicans would ensure his election. First, however, he had to overcome stiff opposition within his own party from conservatives who resented the free silver policies of the Populists and who had never liked fusion anyway, and from certain Negro Republicans who were embittered by Russell's pronouncements on the Negro's fitness to hold office. Even so, Russell had staunch black allies such as James Young, a Wake County legislator and newspaper editor, who recognized the danger to black suffrage and civil rights if the Democrats regained power.

Initially, the 1896 contest for governor was a three-way race among Russell, Democrat Cyrus B. Watson, and Populist William A. Guthrie, but late in the campaign the Populists and Republicans merged their state and local tickets. Fusion enabled them to maintain control of the legislature with a majority over the Democrats of 120 to 50 and allowed Russell to capture the governorship. Populists or Republicans filled all the major statewide offices except for the supreme court.

Harmony between the two parties proved short-lived, however. In the General Assembly of 1897 a long and rancorous debate erupted between Populists and Republicans. It began with the controversy over reelection of Senator Jeter C. Pritchard, which Butler opposed because of the Republican senator's alleged waffling on free silver. The Populists in truth were determined to name their own candidate. The Republicans, on the other hand, believed a bargain had been struck in 1895 by giving Butler the long term in the Senate in return for his support of Pritchard's reelection two years later. Although the Populist caucus mandated a strict party vote for its candidate, seventeen members bolted and joined the Republicans to reelect Pritchard.

Compounding the deteriorating relations between the Populists and Republicans was newly elected Governor Russell's determination to attack J. P. Morgan's Southern Railway Company. In 1895 Democratic Governor Elias Carr had leased the state-owned North Carolina Railroad to the Southern Railway for ninety-nine years. The state railroad was a crucial link in the Southern Railway's network of lines to the lower South, and Russell, Populists, and reformist Democrats were outraged at what they considered the sale of the state's property to the Wall Street mogul. Farmers and businessmen were already chafing at the discriminatory rates Yankee-dominated railroads were charging. The leasing of the state's property to the symbol of northern finance seemed to confirm their worst fears about collusion between government and corporate enterprise. Russell, who, in his inaugural address, advocated national ownership of the railroads as public highways and conveniences, presented to the legislature a comprehensive railroad reform bill that would have annulled the ninety-nine-year lease and placed nonresident corporations under stringent state regulation. He also announced plans to increase taxation on railroads and to reduce fare and freight rates. (Document 15.2)

Russell's vigorous attack on the railroads was too much for the North Carolina GOP. Republican stalwarts deserted the governor, whom they chastised as a renegade Populist. Russell's bill provoked a vituperative debate in the legislature that pitted most of the Populists and a handful of Republican allies against the GOP and Democrats. The Russell forces even resorted to a filibuster in two marathon sessions, but they failed to pass the controversial bill.

The dual effect of these legislative encounters was to leave fusion in a shambles and to alienate the governor from his own party. Henceforth Russell and Butler pursued essentially the same course. They attempted the formation of a new party of reformers with the People's party as the nucleus. The heart of their program in the 1898 election was to be the nullification of the ninety-nine-year lease, increased taxation on railroads, and stricter state regulation of rail rates to assist farmers and small businessmen plagued by low prices for their goods and produce and high prices for shipment.

Economic issues were in fact at the core of the 1898 election in North Carolina, but the campaign was not fought openly on those terms. (Documents 15.3 and 15.4) Instead the Democrats launched a violent white supremacy campaign. Under the tactical leadership of Furnifold M. Simmons, a New Bern lawyer and former congressman, the Democrats organized White Government Unions, set up a speakers' bureau to send white supremacy spokesmen such as Charles B. Aycock across the state, and employed paramilitary units called the Red Shirts and Rough Riders to terrorize Populists, Republicans, and blacks in particular. (Document 15.5) Armed men broke up fusionist political rallies, disrupted black church meetings, whipped outspoken blacks, and drove black voters from the polls. Simmons enlisted the financial support of businessmen and manufacturers in the state by promising not to raise taxes. But the cry of "negro rule" led by Josephus Daniels's *Raleigh News and Observer* overwhelmed any public discussion of the economic issues involved in the campaign.

The pall of violence hung heaviest over Wilmington, Governor Russell's home. In August 1898, Alex Manly, black editor of the *Wilmington Record*, published an editorial defending his race against advocates of "lynch law" that was interpreted as an affront to white women. (Document 15.6) The Democratic press quickly turned the editorial into a sensational example of how fusion rule promoted black impudence. Through the broiling summer months Democratic leaders in Wilmington secretly drilled their paramilitary forces to seize control of the municipal government and stuff the ballot box if necessary to assure Democratic victory. Tensions swelled in the port city to the point that Governor Russell was persuaded by local businessmen to take down the fusionists' ticket there. His efforts to keep the peace in Wilmington and elsewhere ultimately failed, however, despite an executive proclamation demanding a cessation of all violent activities.

Two days following the election, 10 November 1898, the so-called Wilmington race riot exploded. In fact it was a coup d'etat executed by Democrats, including Alfred Moore Waddell, a former Confederate officer and congressman and member of one of the oldest and most respected families in the lower Cape Fear. Marauding white men burned the offices of the *Wilmington Record* and dragged white and black Republicans to the railroad depot, sometimes with ropes around their necks, for immediate expulsion. Gunfire crackled through black neighborhoods. Only two white men were wounded, but it has been variously estimated that eleven to thirty blacks were killed. The Democrats took control of the municipal government by forcing the Republican-dominated board of aldermen and mayor to resign, virtually at gunpoint, and by swearing in new Democratic officers on the spot.

At the state level the Democrats regained control of the General Assembly. Their first order of business in 1899 was to dismantle the fusionist reforms and to ensure that a coalition of blacks and poor whites ("low-born scum and quondam slaves," in the words of one Democratic newspaper) would never triumph again. Jim Crow segregation laws, a restrictive election statute, and a suffrage amendment to the state constitution decisively accomplished this task. The suffrage amendment instituted a poll tax and literacy test for all potential voters. Illiterate whites were to be assisted by the "grandfather clause" that permitted any lineal descendant of a citizen who voted before 1 January 1867 to register to vote by 1908. (Documents 15.7 and 15.8) Even so, the effect of the suffrage amendment, which was ratified in the 1900 white supremacy election, was to disfranchise most blacks and many whites. Whereas 85.4 percent of the North Carolina electorate voted in 1896, less than 50 percent would vote by 1904.

With the work of the 1899 legislature, the election of Charles B. Aycock to the governorship in 1900, and the replacement of Butler with

Simmons in the United States Senate in 1901 (where he remained for the next three decades), men of unquestioned Democratic pedigree once more held the reins of government and would continue to do so for many decades to come. Interparty squabbling, the antagonism of the state's business community, and the violent white supremacy campaigns of 1898 and 1900 brought the fusionist interlude to an unhappy end. (Document 15.9)

The Democrats who returned to power in 1900 were little different from the Bourbons who preceded the fusionists and were in many cases the same people. Inexorably, the loci of power continued to revolve around the same planter-industrialist elite who had prevailed in the years following Reconstruction. But for the first time since that watershed in southern life, dissenting voices had been decisively silenced and opposition to the solid South overwhelmingly crushed. With the effective removal of poor whites and blacks from the political process, the planter-industrialist elite assumed the garb of reformers and set about modernizing the state with increased government services in such areas as public health, education, and road building. Freed of the incubus of lower-class and Negro support, the so-called Progressive movement in North Carolina and throughout the South accelerated, but it was a movement that tended to enhance the interests of the business community principally and to reinforce the existing social, economic, and political order. Firmly ensconced in power, North Carolina's "progressive plutocracy," in the words of political scientist V. O. Key, Jr., would take charge of the Tar Heel state's destiny in the twentieth century.

DOCUMENT 15.1

Marion Butler on Election Strategy in 1896

Our Republican friends are trying to force us to co-operate with them on terms which would, in my opinion, mean the demoralization and disruption, if not the death, of the People's party. It is clear that this is the last year that there will be co-operation in North Carolina. Therefore, if we do not make a fight this year on such a line as will be consistent with our principles we will not gain a single vote, and will be in no position to gain any votes in the future. If we sacrifice our principles now we will not only never grow any larger, but we will lose the respect of our friends and enemies alike. We left the Democratic party because that party professed in the state to be the friends of the people, yet in each National campaign sacrificed every interest of the people and every principle of good government to support and elect a gold bug for President. Now shall we approve of the Republican party, and not only approve of but actually assist it in doing the very same things that we have condemned and repudiated the Democratic party for doing? If we do, it is an end of us, and we had as well get ready to join the Republican party outright. . . . The People's party is distinctly a party of principle; and our principles are all that we have. We are like a woman who has nothing but her chastity; when that is gone, everything is gone.

This is a golden opportunity for us to build up the People's party. We could not ask or wish for a situation more favorable to us. Both old parties have put themselves in a position where they are bound to lose votes largely, and where we are bound to get these votes if we stand squarely by the great cause of financial reform, which is now the overshadowing issue, and on which issue both of the old parties are wrong. . . . Again we will never gain votes from the Republican party as long as we co-operate with it; and if we do not draw the issue square on the money question and take a bold stand now when the people are aroused on that question, we can never hope to gain a single vote from either party in the future. Nine-tenths of the people in the state claim to be for free silver. . . . Besides, I want to say to you privately and confidentially that we are in more danger from the Republican party now than we are from the Democratic party. It is the Republican party that we will have to fight in the future in both the State and the Nation. Therefore let us ask them to join us in putting up and supporting an Independent Electoral ticket, pledged not to vote for any gold man for President. This would make the financial question the burning issue in the campaign instead of stifling it; and during the campaign we could so educate the rank and file of the Republican party on this great question that in the future when we will have to make a straight fight alone we could draw largely from the ranks of the Republican party, because we would have them educated on the great principles that we are contending for.

Marion Butler to John A. Simms, 17 February 1896, Marion Butler Papers, Southern Historical Collection, University of North Carolina, Chapel Hill.

DOCUMENT 15.2

Daniel L. Russell's Railroad Reform Bill, 1897

A BILL TO BE ENTITLED AN ACT TO PRESCRIBE THE TERMS UPON WHICH FOREIGN RAILROAD CORPORATIONS SHALL BE ALLOWED TO OPERATE RAILROADS AND TRANSACT BUSINESS WITHIN THE STATE OF NORTH CAROLINA

Sec. 1. That on and after the first day of May one thousand eight hundred and ninety-seven no railroad company or corporation organized under and [by] virtue of the laws of any government other than that of the State of North Carolina, shall hold or operate, directly or indirectly . . . any line of railway which is situate[d] within this State . . . unless said nonresident corporation shall first obtain a license. . . .

Sec. 9. The Governor of North Carolina is hereby empowered without giving bond or undertaking to bring a civil action in the name of the State of North Carolina for the purpose of having declared illegal null and void a certain contract entered into on the first day of January 1896, between the North Carolina Railroad Company and the Southern Railway Company whereby the former Company agreed to lease and demise to the last named company its franchise and property with appurtinent rights and privileges for the term of ninety-nine years. . . .

Sec. 11. That in case the said Lease . . . shall be declared illegal, null and void . . . the President and Directors of the North Carolina Railroad Company . . . shall be authorized to lease and demise the franchise and property with appurtinent rights and privileges of the said North Carolina Railroad for the term of twenty years; Provided, the capital stock owned by the State in said Company shall not in the mean time have been sold as hereinafter provided.

Sec. 12. That the Governor of the State, the Secretary of State and the Treasurer of the State or the Governor with the concurrence of either the Treasurer or the Secretary of State shall be empowered to sell all of the shares of the capital stock in the North Carolina Railroad . . . for a sum not less than two million dollars. . . . The Governor with the concurrence of the Treasurer shall be authorized to invest the money realized from the said sale in four per cent non taxable bonds of the State of North Carolina or other solvent securities, and the said fund shall constitute a part of the perminent school fund of the State, and the interest accruing thereon shall constitute a part of the fund to be expended for the maintenance of the common schools during the year when it shall be collected.

Legislative Papers, L.P. 1418 (29 January 1897), North Carolina Archives, Raleigh.

DOCUMENT 15.3

Alfred Eugene Holton, State Chairman of the Republican Party, on the Election of 1898

In the first place the Legislature of 1895 reduced the rate of interest from 8 to 6 per cent. This in the banks of the State alone amounted to a loss of 2 per cent. upon 12 or 15 millions and had the effect of depriving the banks of a large profit on rediscounts on papers that had theretofore been taken from private individuals and rediscounted in Northern banks, besides depriving the business interests of the State of a large volume of currency. This enlisted against us the interest of both the bankers who loaned, and the business men who borrowed, besides the interests of a large number of individuals who were living off the interest of their money. To these individuals this legislation meant heavy loss.

In the second place the cities and towns of the State have for many years been accumulating heavy bonded indebtedness and the spirit of repudiation, as manifested in Oxford, Stanly, Wilkes and Buncombe county bond cases, was charged to the Republicans and Populists. Therefore the people holding these bonds imagined that their interest lay in a change of administration, for they were confronted with the fact that North Carolina securities issued by cities, towns and counties could hardly be realized on. This line of securities also included mortgage bonds issued by railroads[,] and parties holding them or seeking investments feared a policy of repudiation.

In the third place the revenue act of the last Legislature enlisted the business men against us by the taxation of capital stock upon face value, this having enormously increased their taxes. Nearly every business of the State, including cotton mills, tobacco manufactories, merchants and other aggregations of capital have for several years been carrying on business almost entirely through these corporations and had their busines[s] capitalized in many instances above its actual value. Even the railroads did not feel secure from renewed attacks. In fact, every interest in the State representing capital was arrayed against us, or at least its moral support was withdrawn, all in great contrast to the campaign of 1896, when these same men, fearing Bryanism and Populism, either openly voted the Republican ticket or at heart wished Republican success and aided in bringing about the election of Senator Pritchard.

With the assurance of a legislative change of policies which the Democrats were ready to give to insure success, it was an easy matter for the Democrats to raise unlimited means with which to carry on an effective campaign. Even prominent and influential Republicans in the State made contributions.

Charlotte Observer, *19 November 1898.*

DOCUMENT 15.4

Furnifold M. Simmons on Election Issues, 1898

During the campaign I secured the services of former Governor T. J. Jarvis to visit the bankers, the railroad officials, and the manufacturers of the State, to represent to them the intolerable conditions prevailing under the Fusion domination, to persuade them that it was their duty to assist in effecting a change of régime, and to solicit funds for the campaign. Jarvis was engaged in this task for weeks, and was most successful in his appeal. From these economic leaders and from various Democrats of moderate means I obtained all the campaign funds I needed. Aid from the national organization of the party was not necessary, and we received none. . . .

I promised the various denominational colleges, which were then rather hostile to the State institutions, that I would not increase the appropriations for the latter during the session of 1898 [*sic*]. Through Jarvis, I also promised the large corporations that their taxes would not be increased during the biennium. . . . I was bitterly criticized for these promises, but I felt then, and I now feel, that they were necessary. If we were to win, every controversy which tended to divide the Democratic vote had to be held in abeyance.

J. Fred Rippy, ed., Furnifold Simmons, Statesman of the New South:

Memoirs and Addresses *(Durham: Duke University Press, 1936),*
pp. 23, 29.

DOCUMENT 15.5

Hal W. Ayer on the Red-Shirt Movement, 1899

I wish to credit you with a penetration amply sufficient to estimate
and gauge a sentiment among people when you are campaigning among
them, and I know your capacity for fighting an argumentative fight; but I
tell you that you have not begun to realize the general character of such a
fight as the democratic machine now contemplates. Their plan does not
mean argument or discussion, it means riot, slander, abuse, physical violence and general anarchy. Their plan now is to red-shirt every town in
the State, and to terrorize voters through the means of such characters as
can be hired to wear red-shirts, drink mean whiskey and raise commo-
tion generally. If we cannot succeed in effecting an organization that is
both willing and able to suppress such tyranny and terrorism by physical
force, if necessary, why then our fight will be something like that of the
billy-goat who showed enough spunk to try to but a steam-engine off the
track. You need not dismiss from your mind these things as imaginings,
etc. At this time they are real and determined upon, and to go into a
campaign in this State without taking them in consideration would show
a deplorable want of foresight and wisdom.

Hal W. Ayer to Marion Butler, 30 December 1899, Marion Butler
Papers, Southern Historical Collection.

DOCUMENT 15.6

Alex Manly on Lynching, 1898

A Mrs. Felton, from Georgia, makes a speech before the Agricultural
Society at Tybee, Ga., in which she advocates lynching as an extreme
measure. This woman makes a strong plea for womanhood, and if the

alleged crimes or rape were half so frequent as is ofttimes reported, her plea would be worthy of consideration.

Mrs. Felton, like many other so-called Christians, loses sight of the basic principle of the religion of Christ in her plea for one class of people as against another. If a missionary spirit is essential for the uplifting of the poor white girls, why is it? The morals of the poor white people are on a par with their colored neighbors of like conditions, and if any one doubts the statement let him visit among them. The whole lump needs to be leavened by those who profess so much religion and showing them that the preservation of virtue is an essential for the life of any people.

Mrs. Felton begins well, for she admits that education will better protect the girls on the farm from the assaulter. This we admit and it should not be confined to the white any more than to the colored girls. The papers are filled often with reports of rapes of white women, and the subsequent lynching of the alleged rapists. The editors pour forth volleys of aspersions against all negroes because of the few who may be guilty. If the papers and speakers of the other race would condemn the commission of crime because it is crime and not try to make it appear that the negroes were the only criminals, they would find their strongest allies in the intelligent negroes themselves, and together the whites and blacks would root the evil out of both races.

We suggest that the whites guard their women more closely, as Mrs. Felton says, thus giving no opportunity for the human fiend, be he white or black. You leave your goods out of doors and then complain because they are taken away.

Poor white men are careless in the matter of protecting their women, especially on the farms. They are careless of their conduct toward them, and our experience among poor white people in the country teaches us that women of that race are not more particular in the matter of clandestine meetings with colored men, than are the white men with colored women. Meetings of this kind go on for some time until the woman's infatuation or the man's boldness bring attention to them, and the man is lynched for rape. Every negro lynched is called a "big burley, black brute," when, in fact, many of those who have thus been dealt with had white men for their fathers, and were not only not "black" and "burley," but were sufficiently attractive for white girls of culture and refinement to fall in love with them, as is very well known to all.

Mrs. Felton must begin at the fountain head if she wishes to purify the stream.

Teach your men purity. Let virtue be something more than an excuse for them to intimidate and torture a helpless people. Tell your men that it is no worse for a black man to be intimate with a white woman, than for a white man to be intimate with a colored woman.

You set yourselves down as a lot of carping hypocrites; in fact, you cry aloud for the virtue of your women while you seek to destroy the morality of ours. Don't think ever that your women will remain pure while you are debauching ours. You sow the seed—the harvest will come in due time.

Wilmington Record, *18 August 1898, as reprinted in* Wilmington Messenger, *20 October 1898.*

DOCUMENT 15.7

Henry G. Connor on White Supremacy, 1898

I wish that you would think over and (if you have time) write down the conclusions to which you arrive, on the suffrage question. It is upon us and must be met and dealt with. The politicians have stirred the minds and feelings of the people more deeply than they intended. We must do the work and try to do it thoroughly. I find men, who would have read me out of the party in [18]94 now insisting that I must take the lead in working the problem out. I am determined that, with my consent, no law shall be passed, having for its purpose or permitting frauds. I am willing to throw every *possible constitutional* restriction around registration, but when the vote is cast it must be counted, and honestly returned. I want the final conclusion to which we arrive put in the Constitution, and I want if possible, to secure the permanent and undivided political supremacy of the white man. I think this is essential to the peace of our people. We must take the responsibility and must have the power.

Henry G. Connor to George Howard, 25 November 1898, Henry G. Connor Papers, Southern Historical Collection.

DOCUMENT 15.8

Literacy Test and Poll Tax: A Test of White Supremacy

(Sec. 4.) Every person presenting himself for registration shall be able to read and write any section of the constitution in the English language and before he shall be entitled to vote he shall have paid on or before the first day of March of the year in which he proposes to vote his poll tax as prescribed by law for the previous year. Poll taxes shall be a lien only on assessed property and no process shall issue to enforce the collection of the same except against assessed property.

(Sec. 5.) No male person who was on January one, eighteen hundred and sixty-seven, or at any time prior thereto entitled to vote under the laws of any state in the United States wherein he then resided, and no lineal descendant of any such person, shall be denied the right to register and vote at any election in this state by reason of his failure to possess the educational qualification prescribed in section four of this article: *Provided*, he shall have registered in accordance with the terms of this section prior to December one, nineteen hundred and eight. The general assembly shall provide for a permanent record of all persons who register under this section on or before November first, nineteen hundred and eight: and all such persons shall be entitled to register and vote in all elections by the people in this state unless disqualified under section two of this article: *Provided*, such persons shall have paid their poll tax as requ[i]red by law.

Public Laws of North Carolina, 1899, *chapter 218.*

DOCUMENT 15.9

Daniel L. Russell, "Republicanism in the South"

The experiment adopted by the conquering North, after the civil conflict, in reconstructing the subjugated South upon the basis of the civil and political equality of both races was startling in its radicalism, feeble in its failure to supply for its execution the element of force without which its success was plainly impossible, and disastrous to the unfortunate people whose newborn freedom it was intended to protect and preserve. True it is that this experiment was not chosen by the North of its own volition but rather was forced upon it by the attitude of the ruling classes in the South. The North offered the 13th and 14th Amendments and said "settle on this basis." Abolish slavery, secure these freed people in their civil rights and settle suffrage for yourselves, except that representation in Congress shall no longer be based on population but on the number of voters. . . . Some of us in the South believed that these terms should be accepted. But, hostility to the party which had conducted the war, saved the Government and freed the slave, was so intense that the secession States refused to accept these terms embodied in the 14th Amendment. History must record it that negro suffrage was brought about by the narrowness and spite of the Southern politicians who, instead of accepting the liberal terms offered by the North, and uniting themselves with the party of the country, went with the party of opposition and of reaction. . . .

The colored people in the cotton States, deprived of the friendly counsel of the master class who, with a few exceptions, stood as strongly against negro suffrage and against the National policy as they had stood for secession and slavery, found themselves in politics without any of the elements of safety or success except numbers. These States fell under governments that were mostly ignorant and corrupt. Those of the slaveholding class who accepted in good faith the war's results and dared to ally themselves with the Republican party were pursued, persecuted and proscribed. The intelligence of the cotton States was for secession and slavery. It was for resistance to the War Amendments. It is to-day against negro suffrage and against negro equality in any form. And yet, this intelligent and slaveholding class is, perhaps, the best friend of the negro in the South.

The opposition to negro suffrage among the whites in the slave belt of the South is almost as strong and universal, as was the devotion to the institution of slavery. The mere presence of the negro, coupled with the fact that the Federal Constitution guarantees on paper his right to vote equally with any other citizens having the same qualifications, has been sufficient to keep the whites solidly in one organization—which they call the Democratic party. Thousands of them are in their real sentiments against the Democratic party and these thousands are the property holders and business men. The manufacturers, the solvent merchants, the bankers, the prosperous planters, are mostly at war with the platform of the Democratic party and in sympathy with every tenet of the Republican party. If they resided in the free States (States that were not slaveholding), they would be outspoken Republicans. Thousands of them who themselves or whose fathers in the ante-bellum period, were anxious to go to war for States Rights, for nullification, for secession, are rounding up toward the advocacy of a strong central Federal Power with armies and navies behind it. They have abandoned secession. They have abandoned chattel slavery. They have abandoned States Rights on every question but the negro question. But as to this, they have defied the National Government by flagrant, persistent and successful nullification of its Constitution and its laws. And to this nullification, the North has submitted to an extent that looks like condonation if not approval. If your War Amendments cannot be enforced, would it not be better to repeal them?

Yet these men will go into Democratic primaries and vote this year for Bryan and pray for McKinley—not only pray for his policy but also for his reelection. . . .

This same great fact controls politics in States like North Carolina which are not in the Black Belt. But a large colored population in a few counties is sufficient to give excuse for agitation founded on race prejudice. The prejudice against these unfortunate people does not diminish as time rolls on. Nor is it necessary to go far to get at the reasons. The institution of slavery, indefensible as it was, somewhat promoted a feeling of interdependence between the master and slave—a feeling that developed into much of forbearance and friendship between them. . . . In the thirty-five years of freedom, the races have been steadily drifting apart—manners, customs, laws, sentiment, all moving toward segregation. And the colored element has year by year further and further fallen behind the white in acquisition and achievement. An impression prevails that these colored people have grown greatly in wealth, that they have acquired homesteads, have become tax-payers and given great promise along these lines. It is not true. In North Carolina they had as fair a chance as in any other Southern State,—perhaps better than any other. And there it is sad to hear their frequent boast that they own eight millions of property. This is about three per cent, according to the tax list, the total of which shows an amount much less than the actual total values of the State, but this fact does not disturb the proportion between the races. They are thirty per cent of the population. After thirty years of opportunity, they have three per cent of the property. True, they may claim that this is all net gain as they started with no property. But they did not start with nothing. They started with enormous advantages over the whites. They were accustomed to labor. The whites were not. They had been for generations the producers of the State and the whites the consumers. They were accustomed to hardship and privation and patient industry. They had the muscle. If in this thirty years they have only acquired this pittance, where will they be in another thirty years, considering that the advantages of their start are largely, if not entirely, lost?

Republicanism in the South since reconstruction, has been weakest in those sections where the colored people were numerically the strongest and it has been and is strongest where the population is substantially all white. The strongholds of Republicanism in the South are in Eastern Tennessee and Western North Carolina, in West Virginia and in Eastern Kentucky. In these regions, the institution of slavery did not flourish. There were but few slaves and, of course, but few Africans.

In North Carolina the Democratic politicians are seeking by a proposed Suffrage Amendment to our Constitution to nullify the Federal Constitution, after the manner of Louisiana. By this they hope to keep up agitation on the negro question for the pending election. They confidently hope that their opponents will permit them to force the battle and choose the ground. But if the elements opposed to them in North Carolina will refuse to accept the issue which these Democratic politicians propose, and relegate it to the judicial and political departments of the Federal Government, the Democratic party may by iniquitous election laws . . . succeed for a while. But their days of wicked triumph will be short. The colored people will see that their safety requires them to follow the men who give them employment. The colored tenant, if he votes at all, will vote with the owner of the land. The bugbear of negro supremacy being removed, the men of thought, of wealth, of enterprise and of action will take charge of the Republican party. In a few years under these conditions, the Republican party of North Carolina will be the party of property and intelligence.

Daniel L. Russell, 12 February 1900, Chicago, Illinois, Daniel L. Russell Papers, Southern Historical Collection.

SUGGESTED READINGS

Anderson, Eric. *Race and Politics in North Carolina, 1872–1901: The Black Second*. Baton Rouge: Louisiana State University Press, 1981.

Billings, Dwight B., Jr. *Planters and the Making of a "New South": Class, Politics, and Development in North Carolina, 1865–1900*. Chapel Hill: University of North Carolina Press, 1979.

Crow, Jeffrey J., and Durden, Robert F. *Maverick Republican in the Old North State: A Political Biography of Daniel L. Russell*. Baton Rouge: Louisiana State University Press, 1977.

Daniels, Josephus. *Editor in Politics*. Chapel Hill: University of North Carolina Press, 1941.

Durden, Robert F. *The Climax of Populism: The Election of 1896*. Lexington: University of Kentucky Press, 1965.

Edmonds, Helen G. *The Negro and Fusion Politics in North Carolina, 1894–1901.* Chapel Hill: University of North Carolina Press, 1951.

Gaston, Paul M. *The New South Creed: A Study in Southern Mythmaking.* New York: Alfred A. Knopf, 1970.

Goodwyn, Lawrence. *The Populist Movement: A Short History of the Agrarian Revolt in America.* New York: Oxford University Press, 1978.

Key, V. O., Jr., with the assistance of Alexander Heard. *Southern Politics in State and Nation.* New York: Alfred A. Knopf, 1949.

Morrison, Joseph L. *Josephus Daniels Says . . . : An Editor's Political Odyssey from Bryan to Wilson and F.D.R., 1894–1913.* Chapel Hill: University of North Carolina Press, 1962.

Noblin, Stuart. *Leonidas LaFayette Polk, Agrarian Crusader.* Chapel Hill: University of North Carolina Press, 1949.

Orr, Oliver H., Jr. *Charles Brantley Aycock.* Chapel Hill: University of North Carolina Press, 1961.

Woodward, C. Vann. *Origins of the New South, 1877–1913.* Baton Rouge: Louisiana State University Press, 1951.

CHAPTER 16

Professors, Fundamentalists, and the Legislature

Willard B. Gatewood, Jr.

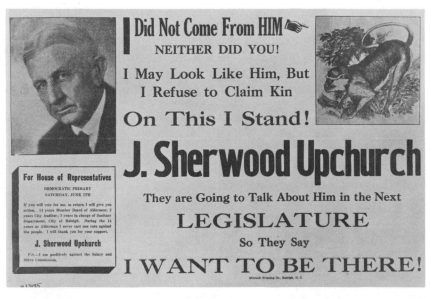

Political Broadside (Courtesy of the North Carolina Collection, Wilson Library, Chapel Hill, N.C.)

On 10 February 1925, the House Committee on Education opened hearings in Raleigh on a bill to prohibit the teaching of biological evolution in state-supported schools and colleges in North Carolina. The sponsor of the measure, David Scott Poole, a rural newspaper editor and active Presbyterian layman, set the tone of the arguments offered in its support by declaring that "the religion of the Lord Jesus is on trial." Other advocates of the bill either described evolution as an "infidel doctrine" wholly incompatible with the concept of man as a creature in God's image or dismissed it as a "mere guess" without basis in fact. A thunderous applause broke the momentary silence that followed the last speech in favor of Poole's bill when a tall, slender man with silver hair rose to address the committee. He was Harry Woodburn Chase, president of the University of North Carolina, who began with the observation: "I am not here to discuss evolution as a biologist but to speak in behalf of human liberty." After exploring at length the implications of legislation such as the Poole bill, Chase concluded: "If it be treason to oppose the bill offered in the name of tyranny over the mind . . . I wish to stand here in the name of progress and make my protest." Proponents of the measure generally agreed with Representative Zebulon V. Turlington of Iredell County, who interpreted Chase's opposition to mean that "the professors are lined up against the folks."

Through the mysterious process by which complex phenomena are simplified into a single symbolic issue, Darwin's theory of evolution became the focal point of a struggle in the post–World War I decade, filling the air with battle sounds and conjuring up images of an epic contest between fierce defenders of rival cultures. The warfare raised significant questions regarding the relationship of science and religion, intellectual freedom, separation of church and state, control of public education, and even the future of democracy and Christianity in America. Those who rallied to the antievolution standard linked Darwin's theory with secularism, relaxed standards of conduct, disintegration of the family, "godless education," communism, and a host of other sources of public concern in the postwar era. Their war against evolution symbolized their protest against the drifts of modern culture in the "New Era" following the Great War.

The decade of the 1920s witnessed the emergence of a "new America" characterized by dramatic industrial growth, a mass-consumption society, a rapid diffusion of technology, and other phenomena that accelerated alterations in traditional thought patterns, lifestyles, and moral codes. Reaction to the postwar environment was as diverse as it was complex. But the response of most Americans was one of bewilderment, prompted in large part by a desire to enjoy the material and technological fruits of modern life without abandoning traditional mores and values. A sense of uneasiness, nourished by specific events at home and abroad in the immediate postwar era, pervaded the atmosphere. Disillusioned by the failure of the war to make the world safe for democracy, Americans also viewed with alarm the postwar wave of strikes, the severe economic dislocations, the challenges posed by a foreign ideology in the form of communism, and the proliferation of radical literature pronouncing the demise of the American version of democracy and capitalism. Fearful that the nation was being wrenched from its historic moorings, many sought to relieve their anxiety by attempting to reinforce important cultural beliefs and eliminating all intrusions considered alien. Their efforts to employ the coercive powers of the state to achieve these ends invariably encountered resistance from those who viewed either their aims or tactics (or both) as threats to freedom and enlightenment. Not surprisingly, because many believed that the preservation of traditional values and the inoculation of America from the evils of a world dominated by sin would be decided on the religious front, few of these collisions generated more acrimony than the modernist-fundamentalist conflict and its most dramatic manifestation, the evolution controversy.

Although this conflict reached a climax in the new environment following World War I, its origins lay in the late nineteenth century. Especially significant in dividing Protestantism into warring factions was the impact of various intellectual currents, particularly those in science, a branch of learning that rose steadily in prestige in the half century before the war. Scientific discoveries and the application of the scientific method in diverse areas of knowledge persistently called into question traditional theological assumptions. The theories of Charles Darwin propounded in his *The Origin of Species* (1859) and *The Descent of Man* (1871) challenged the biblical account in Genesis of man's origin and development, while studies in textual criticism, comparative religion, and other areas that applied the scientific method to investigations of the Bible and religion resulted in findings that altered old concepts.

Such challenges elicited widely different responses within the Protestant community. Evangelical liberals, in an attempt to accommodate the new scientific thought without violating the essentials of their faith, described Darwinian evolution as "God's way of doing things." Evangelical conservatives opposed such a view as a threat to the authority of the Scriptures and the integrity of the Christian faith.

The emergence of radical elements within both camps frustrated efforts to maintain peace and unity. The radical movement that developed within liberal Protestantism was known as modernism. A science-oriented theology that sought the progressive revelation of God in the scientific study of man, society, and the natural world rather than in an errorless Bible, it often became confused with the larger liberal movement from which it sprang. The term *modernism* ultimately was applied to almost any attempt to reconcile the Christian faith with science, the scientific method, or the "modern way of doing things."

Opposition to modernist-liberal theology centered in fundamentalism, a movement within conservative Protestantism that emerged late in the nineteenth century. Differing from conservatives in mood and tactics, fundamentalists represented a new theological departure as well, even though they referred to theirs as the "historic faith." Although they emphasized and even exaggerated old evangelical themes, they put them together in a unique way and argued for them on grounds that would have been baffling to anyone before the late nineteenth century. From a succession of Bible and prophetic conferences beginning in the 1870s emerged various sets of statements known as "fundamentals," which served as all-purpose tests of faith. Belief in a divinely inspired, errorless Bible, including the Genesis account of creation, was the front-line defense of fundamentalist faith and its challenge to all varieties of modernism. The publication of a series of booklets between 1909 and 1914, entitled *The Fundamentals: A Testimony to Truth*, marked the transformation of fundamentalism from a movement of dissent into one intent upon wresting control of the major Protestant denominations from liberal forces.

The aftermath of World War I seemed an appropriate moment for a massive campaign to check the "journey into apostasy" blamed upon liberalism and modernism. Large segments of the American population, no longer certain of the nation's role in history and uneasy about the prevailing domestic chaos, were receptive to the fundamentalists' promise of a return to the "old time religion" and the restoration of the system of moral and social values that rested upon it. Opposition to the theory of evolution served as a symbol of their campaign to redeem America in the 1920s, and evolution became a catchall, code word signifying the totality of error in modern America.

In few localities did the social and intellectual crosscurrents of the "New Era" create more restlessness and the evolution controversy produce more ferocious combat than in North Carolina. In 1920 the state remained predominantly rural and overwhelmingly Protestant. Steeped in the individualistic piety of evangelical religion, its people boasted that theirs was "an old-fashioned Christian Commonwealth." But the "old commonwealth" had undergone substantial alteration under the aegis of early twentieth-century progressivism. By the 1920s achievements in education, industrial expansion, highway building, and race relations had won for the state the reputation of being "the Wisconsin of the South." A Tar Heel booster in 1924, for example, announced that North Carolina was progressing rapidly in every "desirable instrument of civilized life" and that much of the advancement was the result of the influence of the University of North Carolina at Chapel Hill. That vision was perhaps best articulated in 1920 by Harry W. Chase at his inauguration as university president. Chase committed the university to leadership in a movement to "hammer out a new civilization" whose goal was to liberate the mind and the spirit, "to set men free, not from responsibility but through it." During the next decade Chase, with the support of a corps of talented faculty members, remained steadfast in his commitment to this ideal.

As North Carolinians became alarmed by the unrest and irreverence of the postwar era, their sympathy for, or even tolerance of, a "new civilization" rapidly dissipated. Instead they looked frantically for a scapegoat to blame for what one clergyman described as a new age embodying "everything that hell can suggest and the devil can concoct." Their inclination was to take refuge in the evangelical faith and its moral code, which alone seemed to offer an unchanging, infallible guide. The anxiety and insecurity of North Carolinians made them susceptible to an antimodernist movement already launched by organizations such as the World's Christian Fundamentals Association. Because national fundamentalist spokesmen viewed North Carolina as a pivotal state, the war against evolution there assumed extraordinary significance.

The opening skirmish in North Carolina occurred early in 1920, when a Baptist journal in Kentucky published articles by T. T. Martin, a Mississippi evangelist, demanding the dismissal of President William Louis Poteat of Baptist-related Wake Forest College because of his espousal of the evolutionary theory. The central issue was that Poteat, a biologist, had taught evolution at the college for a generation, but he also aroused suspicion as a champion of academic freedom and various social reforms. His dogged defense of evolution in the face of Martin's accusations triggered a prolonged, noisy agitation among Baptists in North Carolina, who, like their brethren elsewhere in the South, were in the midst of major educational fund-raising campaigns. Despite threats of financial reprisals, the erudite and eloquent Poteat, supported by a host of Wake Forest alumni, refused to be coerced in matters of conscience and conviction. (Document 16.1) The college's student newspaper, edited by Wilbur J. Cash, ridiculed Baptist fundamentalists and suggested that they might replace Poteat as president with either William Jennings Bryan, the former Democratic leader who had joined the antievolution campaign, or Wilbur Glenn Voliva, the advocate of the flat earth theory. The attitude of the newspaper as well as that of the student body generally strengthened the conviction of fundamentalists that church-related, no less than state, colleges were creating doubt in the minds of their sons and daughters.

The theme of "godless education" became a favorite with a contingent of evangelists who traveled across the state in the immediate postwar era. "One-hundred percenters," who blended fundamentalist religion with fundamentalist Americanism, these men allowed neither criticism nor reservation regarding doctrines which they preached with passion and certainty. Their antipathy for modernism had clearly been heightened by the wartime anger against Germany and by the postwar Red Scare, which associated atheism with modernism. Insisting that modernist theology was atheism couched in Christian terminology, they found little difficulty in attaching the communist label to modernists.

Among the most ubiquitous revivalists who swept across the state in the early 1920s were Mordecai F. Ham, Baxter F. McLendon, (Document 16.2) and Billy Sunday. Ham sounded the alarm with his oft-repeated declaration: "The day is not distant when you will be in the grip of the Red Terror and your children will be taught free love by the damnable theory of evolution." McLendon regularly blamed the "moral leprosy" infecting modern American society upon evolutionists, whom he accused of teaching that "man was only a bankrupt monkey." By far the most famous of the trio was Billy Sunday, whose "tabernacles" reverberated with his acid denunciations of communists, flappers, wets, and modernists, all of whom he described as fruits of the same poisonous evolutionary plant. Invariably these evangelists struck a responsive chord when they lashed out at what Sunday described either as a "small group of arrogant intellectuals" who defied the will of the Christian majority, or as an "effeminate, sissified set of college professors" intent upon planting their "evolution hokum" in the plastic minds of the young. Testimonials by students from "Christian homes" whose religious faith had been wrecked by the teaching of evolution in one of North Carolina's educational institutions became standard fare in many revival services. For the evangelists, and for fundamentalists generally, the effort to stop the teaching of evolution was basically an attempt to insulate family pieties from the ravages of modern life and to save the religion of their children.

No less significant in alerting North Carolinians to the dangers of evolution were the activities of representatives of national fundamentalist organizations. In 1920, for example, the World's Christian Fundamentals Association held its first Bible conference in North Carolina at the Baptist Tabernacle in Raleigh. During the decade these annual conferences attracted fundamentalist stalwarts of national reputation, who emphasized the inerrancy of the Bible and the absurdity of the evolutionary hypothesis. Typical was Jasper C. Massee of Boston, who in 1922 asserted: "It is impossible for a man to be a Christian and believe in a theory that denies the supernatural and makes Jesus Christ the bastard son of illegitimate intercourse between Mary and Joseph." His declaration that the scientific mind could neither pray nor "approximate God" prompted a lengthy statement by members of the science faculty at North Carolina State College who sought to refute the idea that science and religion were incompatible. Arriving as Massee departed, William B. Riley challenged the college scientists to debate the question that evolution is a "demonstrated fact." Professor Zeno P. Metcalf, a well-known entomologist, accepted the challenge, and the debate took place in the crowded college auditorium on 17 May 1922. Although the debate changed the views of few, if any, in the audience, it sparked discussion of religion and science in general and aroused interest in modernism and evolution in particular.

The tempo of the struggle quickened after 1922 as laymen and preachers alike threw their support behind the antievolution cause. Laymen voiced their sentiments in letters to newspapers, articles in the religious press, and public addresses. Some judges used the bench as a platform to wage verbal warfare against evolutionists and "modernistic teachings," while the "God or Gorilla" theme emanated from pulpits throughout the state. An influential Presbyterian minister in Charlotte, for example, repeatedly warned that the teaching of evolution would "lead to carnality, sensuality, communism and the Red flag." An internationally famous fundamentalist leader, Amzi C. Dixon, returned to his native North Carolina late in 1922 to deliver a highly publicized sermon that described the theory of evolution as a "series of guesses," first propounded in the prescientific age and currently substituted for Christian truths. He further asserted that if evolution was right, then "Germany was right and Lenin and Stalin are right."

Several months after Dixon's sojourn, William Jennings Bryan, whose prestige helped transform the antievolution campaign into a popular cause, visited North Carolina to urge the Christian taxpayers of the state to drive evolutionists from their schools in order to preserve true Christianity and public morality. Those who respected his past politics but disagreed with his current religion found themselves bedeviled by divided loyalties. Such was the dilemma of Josephus Daniels, personal friend of Bryan and editor of the influential *Raleigh News and Observer*. Daniels cast his lot against the fundamentalists but to the end maintained that "half baked professors" were responsible for starting the dispute.

The impact of the controversy over evolution was nowhere more evident than in the state's major denominations. Despite efforts by some to terminate the storm that raged about Poteat, the Baptist State Convention continued to be torn by factionalism that originated in the Martin-Poteat affair. The agitation lasted until 1926, when Poteat announced his forthcoming retirement, solely because of age. But throughout the controversy North Carolina Baptists avoided the extreme actions of their brethren elsewhere in the South largely because of the moderating influence of such leaders as Poteat, Richard Vann, and Livingston Johnson.

Actually, the Presbyterians demonstrated greater tenacity than the Baptists in their efforts to eliminate evolutionary teachings from the public school curriculum. Through church papers and actions of the synod, they battled any theory that threatened to contradict the Scriptures. One result of their campaign was the establishment of an interdenominational School of Religion in Chapel Hill in 1926 to counteract the "paganism" on the university campus. The inability of the denominations that underwrote the school to agree on the contents of its curriculum and the refusal of the university to grant credit for its courses resulted in its abolition two years later. But Presbyterians could take solace in the claim that their college, Davidson, remained firmly wedded to the historic faith. Although Methodists and Episcopalians escaped the intrachurch quarrels that plagued the two other major denominations, the fundamentalist crusade garnered considerable support from individual members of both churches.

By 1924 the evolution issue had reached far beyond the church convention hall. Candidates for public office began to announce their stand in the controversy; local school boards refused to employ teachers suspected of the Darwinian heresy. Newspapers, too, aligned themselves on the issue. With few exceptions, the support for an antievolution law came from small-town and rural weeklies. Most of the city dailies characterized such a measure as a backward leap into the Middle Ages. The *Greensboro Daily News* waged the fiercest editorial fight against the fundamentalist crusade, identifying it with ignorance, bigotry, and hypocrisy. Alone among the major dailies, the *Charlotte Observer* fully endorsed the movement for an antievolution law. Described as "the city of roaring factories and snorting fundamentalists," Charlotte was the scene of the most vocal opposition to evolution in the state. Before the demise of the agitation, the Junior Order of Mechanics, the state convention of the American Federation of Labor, chambers of commerce, chapters of the Ku Klux Klan, and parent-teacher associations officially joined the fundamentalist crusade.

In January 1924, the Sub-Textbook Commission, composed of professional educators, made its recommendation regarding state-adopted textbooks to the State Board of Education. At this juncture, Governor Cameron Morrison intervened to reject two biology books on the premise that their references to evolution disqualified them for use in public schools. In rejecting the books, Morrison explained: "I don't want my daughter or anybody's daughter to have to study a book that prints pictures of a monkey and a man on the same page." A few months later Morrison publicly declared that "it was never intended that so-called scientists should so take charge of our schools as to unsettle the minds of the youth . . . and to make a monkey out of Adam." His stand naturally elicited enthusiasm among fundamentalists, but unfortunately for their cause, Morrison's term expired before the showdown in the legislature. His successor, Angus W. McLean, avoided involvement in the controversy.

Several incidents on the eve of the legislative session of 1925 strengthened the determination of antievolutionists to obliterate the Darwinian menace by statute. The first of these was the announcement that Poteat would deliver the McNair Lectures at the university in 1925. Presbyterians in particular raised objection on the grounds that the selection was tantamount to university approval of his views on evolution. This disturbance, however, was dwarfed by the furor that exploded when the university-sponsored *Journal of Social Forces* published two articles, labeled by the fundamentalists as "pagan" works written by "foreigners" and based on a "Darwinian approach to ethics." At the same time, another storm of protest focused upon Albert S. Keister, a professor of sociology at North Carolina College for Women, whose references to the mythology in Genesis during an extension class were cited as evidence of the "rank infidelity" within state schools. Armed with such proof, the antievolutionists entered the political arena to find relief from "imported theories" peddled by "highbrow professors" whose salaries came from the pockets of "God-fearing taxpayers."

Among the candidates for the legislature in 1924 who championed the movement to prohibit the teaching of evolution was David Scott Poole of Raeford. True to his campaign promises, Poole introduced such a measure in the House of Representatives in 1925. Devoid of penalty clauses, Poole's resolution simply stated that it was "injurious to the welfare of the people of North Carolina for any official or teacher paid wholly or in part by taxation to teach or permit to be taught as a fact either Darwinism or any other evolutionary hypothesis that links man in blood relationship with any lower form of life." The proponents of the Poole bill pursued three main arguments: first, the theory of evolution was scientifically unproven and therefore should not be taught as science; second, because teachers were paid with public funds, they had no right to teach anything to which a majority of the taxpayers objected; and third, if it was illegal to teach religion in public schools, it was likewise illegal to teach irreligion in the form of evolution.

An impressive array of legislators, clergymen, and rural editors rallied to the defense of Poole's bill. One of the most influential supporters in the House was Zebulon Vance Turlington (Document 16.3) of Statesville, a Presbyterian elder and veteran legislator. He not only denounced the "professors" for opposing the popular will, but also charged that they were aided by a powerful textbook lobby frightened by the possibility of a decline in the sales of evolution-oriented books. Julia Alexander of Charlotte, the lone female member of the House, proclaimed her belief in "the Bible from cover to cover," while James R. Pentuff, a Baptist minister, attempted to expose the "fallacies" of evolution. Others threatened financial reprisals upon state institutions hostile to the antievolution measure.

Opposition to the Poole bill in the legislature centered in a sizable group of alumni of Wake Forest and the University of North Carolina. Poteat's refusal to participate in a discussion that concerned only tax-supported institutions meant that the leadership of the opposition fell to Harry W. Chase, the president of the state university, who skillfully rallied the support of the university alumni. (Document 16.4) Both on the floor of the legislature and from Chapel Hill, he stated his objections to the Poole bill. He and the University of North Carolina subscribed to a theory of education that insisted upon the maintenance of an atmosphere of freedom of thought and discussion as essential to intellectual growth.

Chase disputed the validity of H. L. Mencken's reference to the South as a cultural Sahara but argued that if the region, especially North Carolina, wished to become such a place, it had only to surrender to the current agitation that was aimed at undermining the freedom of the state's educational institutions. Denying that a law against the teaching of evolution would affect only the sciences, he maintained that restricting free intellectual inquiry and teaching would create an atmosphere of evasiveness and "downright mental dishonesty" that students would retain the rest of their lives. Of immediate concern to the university president was the fear of losing some of his most distinguished faculty if the legislature enacted the Poole bill. To suggestions that his position might jeopardize the financial status of the university, Chase replied: "If this University doesn't stand for anything but appropriations, I for one don't want anything to do with it."

Among his most influential supporters were three key legislators, all university alumni, H. G. Conner, Jr., Sam Ervin, Jr., and Walter Murphy, who argued eloquently against any statute designed to limit "freedom of the mind." Of the presidents of state colleges only Chase participated in the debates; the others came down with sudden maladies or were called away on unexpected journeys. These men escaped the invective directed at Chase by antievolutionists, who capitalized on his Massachusetts ancestry to label him a "homeless liberal" and "a Damned Yankee who's ruinin' our boys."

The Poole resolution reached a vote in the House only after a series of tedious parliamentary maneuvers. Amid frayed tempers and a near riot, the measure was defeated by a vote of 67 to 46. An analysis of the vote reveals that the largest support among legislators came from the mountain districts and that only half of those who voted for the measure claimed any college education at all. But all four medical doctors in the House endorsed the bill. The vote analysis likewise discloses that legislators affiliated with Baptist and Presbyterian churches provided the greatest support for the resolution. (Document 16.5)

Aware that the fracas was not yet ended, the opponents of the antievolution legislation exerted every effort to sustain their advantage. They used the Scopes trial in Tennessee to illustrate how "monkey laws" would endanger North Carolina's recently acquired reputation for progress. Even though the trial gave the fundamentalists a martyr in Bryan and renewed their zeal to rid the state of "infidelity," press descriptions of its ludicrous aspects helped to shift public opinion against any law that might produce a similar fiasco in North Carolina, where people who were proud of its national reputation hesitated to risk being subjected to ridicule. The specter of another Dayton east of the Great Smokies encouraged more newspapers to take a clear-cut stand against the antievolutionists. The presidents of two state colleges, hitherto silent, joined Chase and Poteat. The North Carolina Academy of Science publicly denounced any effort to restrict freedom of teaching; students at the university, Wake Forest, and Duke called for the preservation of academic freedom in the state; and a host of visiting dignitaries such as Ralph Sockman and Walter Lippmann lauded North Carolina for its refusal to reintroduce the Inquisition.

Undeterred by defeat in 1925, antievolutionists stepped up their campaign against Darwinism, hoping for success in the next legislature. Antievolution literature in the form of tracts, pamphlets, and even verse appeared in profusion. Local pressure upon county boards of education resulted not only in the elimination of teachers of the evolutionist persuasion but also in the banning of books on evolution from certain public libraries. On the eve of the Democratic primary in 1926, the fundamentalists launched a new crusade for the specific purpose of promoting another antievolution bill in the legislature of the following year. Their timing was obviously designed to facilitate the election of legislators sympathetic to their cause. "Vote as you pray," they counseled the voters. In April 1926, a group dominated by Presbyterians laid plans for a new antievolution campaign and organization. On 4 May more than three hundred fundamentalists gathered in Charlotte's Second Presbyterian Church, where they organized the Committee of One Hundred to marshal antievolution sentiment in the one hundred counties of the state under the slogan, "make our schools safe for our children."

Despite its threats and promises, however, the committee's reputation was permanently injured by the intemperance and disorder of its opening session. Wild applause, inflammatory addresses, and abusive attacks upon Poteat, Chase, and Keister precluded calm deliberation. The proceedings finally broke down when a young minister shucked off his coat, doubled up his fists, and charged toward the altar to deal with a "modernist interloper." The unfavorable publicity given this extraordinary episode lent credence to the prediction that North Carolina was destined to have a Kulturkampf. Some of the original officials withdrew from the organization as a result of its demonstration of extremism. The committee, however, continued to exist and later was incorporated as the North Carolina Bible League.

At the same time that native fundamentalists revived their crusade, outside forces poured into the state to lend their aid. This phase of the antievolution campaign in North Carolina was under the direction of T. T. Martin, secretary of the Anti-Evolution League of America and director-general of campaigns of the Bible Crusaders of America. Martin's effort in North Carolina ultimately ended in abysmal failure because it alienated native fundamentalists opposed to hysteria and interference from outside. The sensationalism of his entourage and the fiasco of the original session of the Committee of One Hundred irreparably damaged the antievolution cause in North Carolina. Few antievolutionist candidates for the legislature survived the Democratic primary in 1926. (Document 16.6)

Nevertheless, the North Carolina Bible League maintained its original aim and found a legislative spokesman in David Scott Poole, who had been reelected on a one-plank platform, to sponsor another antievolution bill. Again true to his pledge, Poole introduced in the legislature of 1927 a more stringent bill providing penalties for anyone found guilty of teaching evolution in public schools. Spokesmen for the Bible League mustered considerable eloquence in an attempt to persuade the Committee on Education to give the bill a favorable report, but their pleas fell on deaf ears. A reshuffling of the committee membership in 1927 left fundamentalists hopelessly outnumbered. By a vote of 25 to 11, the committee refused to give the bill a favorable report. Although a minority report later placed the measure on the House calendar, its advocates realized the overwhelming odds against its passage and allowed the bill to die. (Document 16.7)

One of the most remarkable aspects of the evolution controversy in North Carolina was the failure of antievolutionists in a climate with so many elements favorable to their success. Failure seems to have resulted not so much from public hostility to their basic beliefs as from aversion to their tactics. Certainly the fundamentalist defeat did not signify a victory for religious modernism as the term is generally understood; in fact, modernism, even in its broadest meaning, was seldom a suitable label for the views of the opponents of the antievolution bills. For the most part, opposition came from moderates, including some fundamentalists, whose commitment to the principle of separation of church and state was greater than their fear of Darwin's theory. By no means did they regard the defeat of the Poole bills as license for radicalism; their most common reaction was that educational institutions ought to take a critical view of themselves and avoid flying in the face of orthodoxy.

The outcome of the evolution controversy has been hailed as a victory for academic freedom in North Carolina. Rarely had the question of academic freedom elicited so much public discussion in the state. But the victory in the 1920s was achieved with little support from public school-teachers or their statewide associations. The battle in which academic freedom loomed so large was waged primarily by the presidents of a Baptist college and the state university and by a few editors, politicians, and clergymen.

Finally, the failure of the antievolutionists to achieve a legislative victory in North Carolina had significant consequences far beyond the boundaries of the state. North Carolina had been considered pivotal by the national antievolutionist organizations, which reasoned that if North Carolina could be won, the nation could be won. Those entertaining such grandiose notions thought the defeat of the second Poole bill in 1927 had ominous significance for their nationwide crusade. But by that time the quickened public interest in theological polemics that emerged during the conflict over evolution had already begun to focus on another, more immediate, issue—the possibility of a Roman Catholic being elected president of the United States.

DOCUMENT 16.1

William L. Poteat on the "New Fanaticism"

Viewed thus in outline and interpreted within the scope of its purpose, the first chapter of Genesis is in remarkable accord with modern science. It gives no dates, and so allows for the antiquity of the earth demonstrated by geology. It recognized the progressive unfolding of the life of the planet through time. Its silence on the method of that unfolding is a challenge to human wit to discover it. And now, with evolution recognized at length as the method which God uses in creation, we return to this ancient work of God with a new reverence for its inspiration and a nobler view of the Divine Wisdom and Power—and find ourselves "set square with Genesis again." Finding out how God makes things does not dispense us from the necessity of having Him to make them. We are still dependent upon Divine Will and Power to initiate and energize and guide the process of evolution through to its final products. To the catechism question, "Who made you?" we may still reply, "God made me," although we now know how.

But in breaks a group insisting on verbal details and clamoring for evolutionist blood. One sympathizes with their loyalty to the truth as they see it, and weeps at the havoc they spread. Must they have details because God dictated them to an ancient amanuensis? See what follows. All the efforts which have been made to bring these primitive creation pictures into formal agreement with modern science bear the marks of unnatural forcing. They are, as a Biblical authority declares, but different modes of obliterating the characteristic features of the story. To say that the light created on the first day was cosmic light produced by collision of the molecules of the primal nebula, leaves unanswered the question: How were the first and second days marked before the creation of the sun and moon for that function? And the firmament or vault of heaven, solid and rigid enough to support an ocean of waters above it? And green plants growing on earth before the sun, on which they depend, is set in the heavens? And birds which are a higher type than reptiles and appear later in geological time precede them in the order of creation? The term "day" with evening and morning limits would never have been thought of as meaning a geological period but for the exigency of the dictation theory when men began to turn the pages of the geological record.

The men who are raising again this issue need the advice which Cromwell gave the Presbyterians of Scotland: "Pray God to teach you that it is possible for you to be mistaken." They misunderstood the doctrine of evolution and its implications. They discuss it with glaring misstatements of fact. They misrepresent the status of the doctrine in scientific opinion and appear unaware of its universal acceptance in the lay intellectual world. With Rhadamanthan pomposity and finality they consign to the eternal fires all who hold "the God-defying, soul-destroying scientific guess." The resurgence of this obscurantism in the twentieth century under the Christian name calls for protest and rebuke, not contemptuous but firm, compassionate and brotherly but uncompromising. The attitude of resistance to the enlightenment of the world exposes itself to the ridicule of the world and can hardly hope to escape it. To such an attitude in his day Erasmus spoke a bitter word: "By identifying the new learning with heresy, you make orthodoxy synonymous with ignorance." Nor can men escape the odium of their misinformation, or the crushing responsibility of causing the little ones to stumble—the little ones who have no defences against official dogmatism calling of God. There is a blazing passage about millstones and necks and the deep sea. Christianity arose in the best culture of its time and, when its teaching and spirit have been truly represented, it has been the nourishing mother of the best culture ever since. It is unfair and unjust that it should bear now the deep discredit of the new fanaticism which verily thinks it is doing God service.

William Louis Poteat, Can a Man Be a Christian To-Day? *(Chapel Hill: University of North Carolina Press, 1925), pp. 76–79.*

DOCUMENT 16.2

The Age of New Things

A revival along Bible lines is the superlative need of the Twentieth Century. There is a widespread ignorance relative to the fundamentals of our Holy Christianity. We are living in days of mental confusion, with regard to spiritual things. The very foundations are being denied, and nothing but the genuine can withstand the attack. This is the age of new things. So many new discoveries—so many inventions—so many new combinations that the people are all at sea. In this age we have new thought, new voices, new books, new theologies, new psychology, new philosophy, a new religion and everything that hell can suggest and the devil concoct. But God and salvation are the same yesterday, today and forever. We must have revivals to keep our bearings. It has gotten out that Christianity is not what it used to be. A lot of pin-whiskered mutts are telling us that the Bible is not the Word of God, in the sense that we thought it was, that the old Doctrines of the New Birth, of repentance, of the witness of the Spirit, of depravity, of judgment and hell—that our fathers believed in—are dead and buried, that the church is not worthy of any serious consideration, that Jesus Christ and His claims are not so important after all. The twentieth century is trying to forget God. They are pleasure-mad, money crazed. Earthly, sensual and devilish will describe sections of our country. It's a revival in America or revolution. If the church survives she must be revived. Judgment must begin at the house of God. It's not more members that the church needs, but the old bunch stewed over. Multitudes have the form without the power. Thousands pay no attention to their church vows. Many have never been converted. Many are backslidden. Many are doing nothing for Christ and a lost world. Where is there a Moses crying, "God save these people or blot my name off the book?" Where is there a Nehemiah who surveys a desolate Jerusalem, at night with tears? Where is there a John Knox crying, "Oh, God, save these people or I die?" Where is there a Fletcher staining the walls of his study with praying breath? Our children are growing up and they must be saved. A generation have grown up who have never seen a great revival. The overwhelming need of the hour is spirit-filled, blood-washed, fire-baptized messengers of God, with divine fire burning in their souls to unmask these devices of the devil, and to tear down the strongholds of satan, whether in high places or low. God delivered us from the effeminate, three-karat, pin-whiskered animated question marks standing up in their pulpits and oozing isms, spitting out Greek diphthongs and breathing an air of hieroglyphics and propounding pious platitudes, splitting hairs, and whittling nothing off to a point, while dance halls and low-down God-forsaken, licentious, suggestive, leg shows that pamper to lust are crowded with our young people. The majority of the people of the Twentieth Century are subjectively blind and in objective darkness, they are blind, and blind to the fact that they are blind, lost and lost to the fact that they are lost, dead and dead to the fact that they are dead; think they are going to heaven, and going straight to hell. This is no time for compromise or dodging issues. The churches are in great distress. This is a time for our preachers to stand on the wall as watchmen and describe the state of the heart, the character of life and the danger of the soul.

We need a panic in religion. My heart's cry is back to the Bible! Back to Jesus Christ! Back to Pentecost! Back to the courage of the prophets and of the apostles and forefathers! And away with this hellish, concocted, kid-glove starch that has been instituted in the place of the Holy Ghost, and give us the old-time, limb-straightening religion that puts a shine on your face, a sparkle in your eye, a shout in your soul, a victory in your life! At one time in the history of this country, the church had to go up against blatant infidels who openly assaulted the religion of Jesus Christ. Today, the devil has transformed himself into an angel of light and sits in theological seminaries in the shape of college professors and doctors of divinity, claiming to teach Christian evidences, when they are undermining the very teachings of Jesus Christ; claiming to teach Bible introduction, yet they are making the Book not worthy to be introduced; spitting out a lot of damnable heresies and false doctrines, which have just enough religion to float their fallacies.

Baxter F. McLendon, The Story of My Life and Other Sermons

(Bennettsville, S.C.: N.p., 1923), pp. 38–41, excerpt of a sermon
delivered in Greensboro, North Carolina.

DOCUMENT 16.3

The Legislators on Evolution

[Zebulon Vance] Turlington opened the debate with a denial that the Poole [antievolution] resolution was an attempt to curb free speech. "If it meant that I would be against it," he declared. He made the point that the resolution does not prevent the teaching of the truth nor prohibit the mention of evolution, but only that a theory shall not be taught as the truth.

He had been taught to love, cherish and reverence the University of North Carolina, he explained, but he had been shocked beyond expression when he had heard President [Harry] Chase of that institution reply, when asked what he would do about the teaching of atheism, that it was a matter of conscience.

"I parted company with the present management of that institution when I heard him say that," Turlington declared with earnestness.

He read sections from both the state and Federal constitutions relative to freedom of speech and of worship and submitted that they did not have reference to atheism but were bottomed upon religion.

"Who is backing the opposition to this resolution?" he asked and answering his question declared that while he could not prove it, he believed that the representatives of textbook publishers were.

"The smoothest article I have ever seen is the textbook lobbyist," he declared. "There are men who are whispering in the ears of legislators that they dare not adopt this resolution. These men do not care a snap of their finger about North Carolina."

Granting that they were not doing that which he charged, he declared that the people of North Carolina believe they are doing it and that they are attacking the sacred book of their faith in an underhanded way and argued that it is just as important that the people believe it isn't being done as it is that the book of their faith be not attacked. He argued by analogy that people must not only get justice in their courts but must believe they are getting justice and that both go together and cannot be separated.

He warned the General Assembly that if the resolution did not pass that the representatives of the people would be in Raleigh two or four years hence with a demand that appropriations for State educational institutions be reduced.

"Let us demand now that they respect our sacred book," he exclaimed.

The churches are the bulwarks of safety in North Carolina, he declared.

"Suppose somebody in our State institutions was teaching that Bolshevism had been tried and proved a success in Russia," he continued. "What would people say? Would they say that we must respect freedom of speech? No, they would rise up in their wrath and drive out such teachers."

He submitted that if professors in State institutions are not teaching things that reflect on the Bible, then they have nothing to fear from the resolution.

"It has come to the point where the professors of our great educational institutions are lined up against the great masses of the people," he urged. "It is the hardest blow that I have ever received. Don't say that it is religious bigotry. The great masses of our people are hoping that the State institutions will not be hurt and that their sacred book will not be hurt. . . ."

"Such a resolution as we now have before us serves no good purpose except to absolve monkeys from all responsibility for the human race," declared S. J. Ervin, of Burke, who declared that the only purpose that the resolution could possibly serve would be as an attempt to curb free speech.

"You can attempt it, but you can't do it by law, thank God," he explained as he pleaded with great earnestness for the Legislature not to do a foolish thing.

Anything can be proven by the Bible, if one wants to prove it, he argued, and cited as an instance the reading of a defense of human slavery based on the Bible which he found last Sunday in a book published in 1830. There is nothing in the Bible to justify woman suffrage, he declared.

He submitted that it would be an insult to the Bible, an insult to Christianity, to adopt such a resolution, he explained.

"I think the Christian religion can stand against anything and a religion that can't stand against anything can't save a man's soul," he declared. "I have more respect for the Christian religion than to think it will not stand unless we pass some weak-kneed resolution. Every minister at my home has asked me to vote against this resolution for the reasons I have named."

News and Observer *(Raleigh), 19 February 1925.*

DOCUMENT 16.4

The Vital Educational Process

February 16, 1925

The Honorable Edgar W. Pharr
House of Representatives
Raleigh, North Carolina
Dear sir:

I hope you won't take it amiss if I take just a few moments of your time in this way to tell you just what the passage of the Poole [anti-evolution] Resolution would mean to the University [of North Carolina] and to the other institutions in the state. If you take the University for example, I know you will agree with me [that] fundamentally the thing that gives it its distinction among Southern institutions and that makes it stand out as a real University is the quality of men that it is able to get and keep in its faculty. The quality of the faculty is the fundamental life-blood of an institution. Now, if any one thing is clear it is that you cannot get or keep men of the first quality under conditions that are contrary to their self-respect. The fact that the state should put on its statute books a resolution which would certainly be so construed as to harass, embarrass, and humiliate men of sincere convictions and of intellectual honesty is a blow made at the heart of the University. The question is not whether people are teaching evolution as a fact. It is the easiest thing in the world to read into utterances what was never intended. It is simply to accuse a man of things which he cannot disprove in this controversial region. The passage of the Poole Resolution would virtually set up a tribunal before which every teacher of science and related subjects would be badgered, worried, and disgraced. Good men simply will not teach in an environment of that sort. While the bill itself provides no penalty, the actual penalty is clear. It is the putting of genuine and honest men devoted to truth in the position of criminals in the eyes of the state any time that an utterance by one of these men may appear questionable . . . to any hearer. That is an intolerable position for men to find themselves in. It is an abridgement of the freedom of discussion and thought which will go a long way toward ruining the University, because it deals with the vital educational process itself, of which the appropriations and buildings are simply the means to create.

I think that you know me well enough to know that I have absolutely no sympathy with offensive and sensational statements which wound people's feelings and are destructive in character, but a net spread to catch the feet of one such man, let us say, would just as easily catch a hundred good and general servants of truth, and is a wound of the self-respect of every teacher.

So far as the situation at Chapel Hill is concerned, it is very serious, not only is the faculty discouraged by the holding up of the building programs necessitated if the Budget Commission's report prevails but right now the Dean of the graduate school . . . has an offer of a professorship of English in Johns Hopkins and the head of our extension work . . . is being approached by Wisconsin in the field of extension. One or two other men are also receiving offers from other institutions. The passage of such a bill would not only mean instantly that such men would make up their minds to go, but other men would leave just as rapidly as offers developed, and the University would be set back twenty five years in its development.

Please do not think that I am exaggerating the danger. . . . In a field of this sort misquotation is easier than anywhere else. For instance within the last week I have been accused editorially in the Charlotte *News* of having said that "the teaching of atheism was a matter of conscience," which is an absolute misquotation; and in the headlines of the Charlotte *Observer*, which furnished part of the material for Dr. Luther Little's sermon yesterday, I have been accused of talking about "Christian expediency," which is a phrase that I never used and that to my mind has no meaning, and has been distorted by Dr. Little to represent an idea which I never had remotely. . . . Suppose the Poole Bill were enacted, do you not see the possibilities of humiliation which any reputable citizen who believes in freedom of discussion is going to be subjected? These two personal experiences are simply in point which would be multiplied by a hundred under such a restrictive measure. . . .

Yours truly,
Harry W. Chase
President

Harry W. Chase to Edgar W. Pharr, 16 February 1925, University of North Carolina Papers, University Archives, University of North Carolina, Chapel Hill.

DOCUMENT 16.5

The Limits of Liberty

During the month the interest of our readers has been divided between the fate of Collins, the Kentucky mountaineer and the Poole Bill, that would forbid the teaching of evolution in our schools. The legislators have expressed their feeling on the subject and many of them have shown that whatever may be their ability as politicians, few of them are experts in logic, and few are capable of fine distinctions in thought.

The President of the University seemed to be relying upon this confusion of thought in his hearers in his remarks to the legislature. There is a charm about the word freedom that is apt to blind the judgment of nearly all men.

Men forget that there is no such thing as absolute freedom of any kind.

A man is said to be born free, yet from the time he utters the first cry, down to the time when he leaves this world, he is closely hedged about by laws which he is bound to obey.

Every man has a right to use his mind and to have his own thoughts; but he is not free to express his thoughts when they infringe upon the rights of others.

The clerk in the village grocery is free in a certain sense; but if he imagines that such freedom gives him a right to run down the value of his employers' goods, or estrange his customers, he will soon find out his mistake.

These gentlemen of the University are scholars and they are accustomed to draw close distinctions. They know that they contracted to teach, and they also know that the State can decide what they are to teach. If it is the view of the State that their teaching is injurious to the young men, then the State can put a stop to it.

No one can restrict their thought, not even the State as the employing agent; but some one can restrict expression of their thought, when such expression is undoing all the teachings of mothers and the church.

The editor of the *Charlotte Observer* puts the issue plainly when he reminds them that they do not have the liberty to undo the teachings of the Christian people of this State.

We wish it clearly understood that we are not discussing the truth or falsity of evolution. We leave that question to the scientists. The question before us is whether the Christian people of this state are going to support any institution that countenances an open attack upon our cherished beliefs, as is shown by this Committee of Ministers, in quoting from "Journal of Social Forces," a publication that is issued by "the University of North Carolina Press."

It is to the credit of Charlotte that two of her representatives are found voting on the side of the right. We regret that the other representative was found on the other side and thus represented a minority of his constituents. We hope that hereafter in selecting our representatives to the legislature, the good people of Charlotte will assert themselves and select only those in full sympathy with the moral traditions of this Christian community.

Editorial, "The Poole Bill and Our Legislators," Presbyterian Standard *66 (4 March 1925):1–2.*

DOCUMENT 16.6

Free Speech: A Red Herring

When editors of newspapers, newspaper correspondents, or anyone else make an honest mistake, it is excusable; but when anyone deliberately misrepresents an issue in any kind of contest it is not only inexcusable, but downright mean and very disgusting to fair-minded people.

If one believes he is in the right, he has nothing to lose by being fair to his opponent and certainly should not misrepresent the issue to carry his point, no matter what the issue is.

But if there has ever been a clear case of misrepresentation (yea and I make bold to say wilful misrepresentation) of an issue, it has been in the discussion now going on in North Carolina over the question of whether or not we are to continue to permit the teaching of the Darwin theory of Evolution in our State-supported schools and colleges.

Those of us who say such teaching in tax-supported schools should be prohibited have time and again stated the issue fairly and impartially, only to find, perhaps the next day, in the account of some speech, in some editorial or in the writing of some newspaper correspondent, a deliberate misrepresentation of what we are contending for.

One of their pet arguments is that we are trying to abridge the guarantee of free speech. Not one word of truth in that, and such is not the issue. Such a law as we are asking for is now on the statute books of Tennessee, and yet any man or woman inside the borders of Tennessee can teach Darwin or any such theory they please anywhere in that state without molestation, if they do so at their own charges, or if paid by those who want it taught, and our opponents know this. The same, of course, can be done here if such law is passed. Then why can't they be fair and state the case just as it is? The answer is plain, they can't win unless they fool the people, and this they seem determined to do.

Another shrewd play they make, and just as unfair, is that we want to force the teaching of "certain religious beliefs" on the people. This is another falsehood and they know it. Not one of us have asked that anything in religion be taught in our State-supported schools, not even do we ask that the Bible be taught there; and there is not a teacher in a State-supported school in North Carolina who has brains enough to hold down the job but that knows that there is not a single law in our State requiring that they teach the Bible there. Neither have we asked for such a law, and I, for one, would openly oppose such a law if it were asked for. Not because I would personally oppose the teaching of the Bible anywhere and at any time. I would glory in it for it has never been known to harm anyone; but simply because we have people in North Carolina from whom we, by law, extract taxes with which to run our State schools, who do not believe the Bible and don't want it taught to their children. Therefore, to force such people to pay taxes and use their tax money to pay teachers to teach their children a religion they do not believe would be wrong in the sight of both God and man.

God never asks that converts to the Christian religion be made by force. His message is addressed to the intelligence and the law of persuasion is the only one He asks his followers to employ.

Our State schools were established for the sole purpose of giving a literary education to the children of every family in our Commonwealth, and not for the purpose of teaching the Bible on the one hand, and most certainly not for teaching theories that contradict the Bible on the other hand.

John W. Kurfees, The Fight Is On! The Issue Is Clear Cut! (N.p., ca. 1926), pp. 1–2.

DOCUMENT 16.7

Declaration of the Committee of One Hundred

We are unalterably opposed to the union of church and state.

Inasmuch as our state supported schools are not permitted to teach the Bible we are strongly opposed to their teaching any doctrine which tends to destroy the faith of our people in the scriptures as the authoritative word of God. We want to emphasize the fact that we are not seeking to cripple any of our state schools but to strengthen them and thereby inspire our people with confidence in said institutions as safe places for our boys and girls.

We hold that it is not sufficient for a teacher to justify himself in his disbelief that the Bible is the word of God upon the ground that he does not teach this in his class, inasmuch as education is by life as well as by lip and by example as well as by precept.

This organization has nothing to do with either denominational schools or those that are privately owned, inasmuch as they are supported by voluntary contributions.

We do not question the right of freedom of thought or research. "We believe in freedom by the truth," and in freedom to search for the truth, but we challenge the right of those in charge of our state schools to employ teachers who hold views fundamentally contrary to the simple teaching of the Bible and force the taxpayer to pay the bills.

The duties of the directors will be to endeavor by conference with proper authorities and by treaty to correct the abuses complained of. In case of failure to accomplish the desired results by conference and treaty it is incumbent upon us to avail ourselves of our constitutional rights and apply to the legislature for redress of our grievances.

B. W. Wells, "Fundamentalism in North Carolina," Science 64 (2 July 1927):17.

SUGGESTED READINGS

Bailey, Kenneth K. Southern White Protestantism in the Twentieth Century. New York: Harper & Row, 1964.

Baker, James T. "The Battle of Elizabeth City: Christ and Anti-Christ in North Carolina." North Carolina Historical Review 54 (1977):393–409.

Beale, Howard K. *History of Freedom of Teaching in American Schools.* New York: Charles Scribner, 1941.

Furniss, Norma N. *The Fundamentalist Controversy, 1918–1931.* New Haven: Yale University Press, 1954.

Gatewood, Willard B., Jr. *Preachers, Pedagogues, and Politicians: The Evolution Controversy in North Carolina, 1920–1927.* Chapel Hill: University of North Carolina Press, 1966.

_____, ed. *Controversy in the Twenties: Fundamentalism, Modernism and Evolution.* Nashville: Vanderbilt University Press, 1969.

Linder, Suzanne C. "William Louis Poteat and the Evolution Controversy." *North Carolina Historical Review* 40 (1963):135–57.

_____. *William Louis Poteat: Prophet of Progress.* Chapel Hill: University of North Carolina Press, 1966.

Marsden, George M. *Fundamentalism and American Culture: The Shaping of Twentieth-Century Evangelicalism, 1870–1925.* New York: Oxford University Press, 1980.

Shipley, Maynard. *The War on Modern Science: A Short History of the Fundamentalist Attacks on Evolution and Modernism.* New York: Alfred A. Knopf, 1927.

Szasz, Ferenc Morton. *The Divided Mind of Protestant America, 1880–1930.* Tuscaloosa: University of Alabama Press, 1982.

Wilson, Louis R. *The University of North Carolina, 1900–1930: The Making of a Modern University,* Book Five. Chapel Hill: University of North Carolina Press, 1957.

CHAPTER 17

From Ordeal to New Deal

North Carolina in the Great Depression

Alexander R. Stoesen

Laurel Springs Civilian Conservation Corps Camp in Western North Carolina
(Courtesy of the Division of Archives and History, Raleigh, N.C.)

For some North Carolinians the Great Depression was a time of hunger, poverty, and general privation. Others, who had been living at the subsistence level for years, found little significant change in their lives. For the vast majority of Tar Heels the basic question was how long their office, store, or factory jobs would last or how much they would receive for the cash crops they raised. The experiences of North Carolinians during the Great Depression were myriad, but the oral history interviewer of today finds a recurring theme—dismay over the continuing expansion of the powers of the federal government, which began under Franklin D. Roosevelt and the New Deal.

If federal powers expanded during the depression decade, so, too, did the government of North Carolina. The decade of the 1930s was a time of major change in the state, and nowhere was this change more significant than in the consolidation and centralization of power in Raleigh, which began in the late 1920s with an alteration in the leadership of the Democratic party. From 1900 to 1928 the party was dominated by United States Senator Furnifold M. Simmons of New Bern. But Simmons, unwilling to support the presidential candidacy of Alfred E. Smith, a "wet" and a Roman Catholic, threw his support to Herbert Hoover in 1928. Although Hoover carried North Carolina, Simmons's support of him demolished his own political organization—the work of a lifetime. He was defeated for renomination in 1930, and the way was opened for others to take the reins of power in the Democratic party.

The most likely person to take control was O. Max Gardner of Shelby, who had been elected governor in 1928. Long active in state politics, Gardner was ambitious and well aware of the vacuum created by the removal of Simmons from the political scene. He was a strong, energetic, intelligent administrator with a successful background in the textile industry. Determined to apply the principles of sound management to state government, Gardner believed the democratic process would be enhanced by efficiency derived from centralization. Because he could not succeed himself, the long-term prospect of Gardner's changes required that he dominate the Democratic party. (Document 17.1)

Opposition to Gardner and his supporters came from Democrats who viewed consolidation and centralization as inimical to true democracy. They endorsed the view that power should be kept at the local level where the people would be able to keep it in check. Between 1928 and 1936 the struggle for control of the Democratic party paralleled the controversy over changes in the structure of government in North Carolina. The Gardner "machine" repeatedly bested the "insurgents" and successfully placed its men in the governor's chair in 1933 and 1937 and by the latter year had followers in control of every major office in state government. Gardner had replaced Simmons as the head of North Carolina's Democratic party and led in the transformation of the practice of government in North Carolina.

Changes in the government of North Carolina began modestly in 1929 with the passage of two long-sought measures—a workmen's compensation act and adoption of the secret ballot—as well as changes in the operation of some departments and commissions. But Gardner did not wait for the General Assembly to determine the next steps. Although he had many ideas of his own, he enlisted the aid of experts from the newly founded Brookings Institution in Washington, D.C., which prepared two reports during 1930. One related to state government, the other to county government, and both came complete with lists of recommendations. (Document 17.2) Although these reports were controversial and contained some proposals that would never become law, they, along with the acute financial problems facing the state, served as catalysts for reforms by the 1931 General Assembly or "Long Parliament," which sat for 141 days. In that year the state assumed control of all public roads and prisons formerly administered by the counties. Supervision of county and municipal finances, especially issuance of bonds and notes, was placed under a newly created Local Government Commission. The Consolidated University of North Carolina was created (Document 17.3), and a Division of Contract and Purchase was charged with procurement for all state agencies. In addition, the state assumed responsibility for a six-month public school term and began to search for a means to support it without the fifteen-cent statewide ad valorem property tax. Finally, in 1931, the legislature further reorganized agencies of the state government to realize greater centralized control and efficiency in Raleigh.

In 1933 the difficult issue of finding a substitute for the fifteen-cent ad valorem property tax for schools was resolved by the imposition of a 3 percent general sales tax. This revenue kept the budget balanced and made North Carolina the only state in the union without some interruption in its school system during the depression. It is an understatement to say that the fight over the sales tax was long and bitter, but the tax was reaffirmed by the 1935 legislature, and with the election of Clyde R. Hoey as governor in 1936 the tax, which had been termed an emergency measure, assumed the characteristics of permanence.

Gardner reported that in the process of enacting these reforms, North Carolina had "cleaned house" and established an efficient and modern governmental structure. Power and responsibility had shifted from the cities and counties to Raleigh, and it rested firmly on the new tax structure.

While these developments in politics and administration were taking place, the state labored under a dark financial shadow. Among the figures most familiar to Tar Heels in the early 1930s were those that demonstrated the rise in the state's debt from $13,300,000 in 1920 to $178,-264,000 in 1929. Governor J.C.B. Ehringhaus later referred to events of the 1920s as a "delirious drama of development" and said, not facetiously, that the depression began when "perhaps it was most inconvenient" for paying off the state's debt. "Never again" became the rallying cry, and, with few exceptions, development ceased until the flow of federal money began under the New Deal. Gardner was unable to balance his budgets in spite of drastic cuts in expenditures, and the state was forced to borrow at high interest. By the end of 1932 total state and local bonded indebtedness was $532,747,000, the second highest bonded debt in the nation, and half of the subunits of government were in default although the state government itself remained solvent.

When Governor Ehringhaus assumed office in early 1933, the depression was reaching its nadir. In the five months beginning in October 1932, 215 banks failed in the state, and people had almost ceased to pay the property tax. The state was burdened by a $7 million deficit, mortgages on hundreds of homes and farms were being foreclosed, and property throughout the state was being sold for taxes. The despair and gloom that affected many Tar Heels hardly relieved the prospect of the new administration of Franklin D. Roosevelt in distant Washington. (Document 17.4) Ehringhaus called for "hard self-denial" and drastically reduced expenditures. The overall budget cut amounted to 32.12 percent and included a 25 percent reduction in state employees' salaries, which had already been twice reduced by 10 percent under Gardner. Especially galling to road-conscious North Carolina was a sharp decline in gasoline tax revenues and car and truck registrations and a resulting curtailment of road construction and maintenance.

In 1933 the General Assembly passed an act to cut teachers' pay drastically. For instance, a teacher with an A-3 certificate receiving $1,000 in 1932–33 would receive $672 in 1933–34. The salary of an A-12 certificate-holder went from $1,240 to $746, while those of high school principals went from $3,900 to $1,386.72. Blacks' average pay was more than $100 less than that of whites in the same certificate classes. The only hope lay in local supplements, which were few in the early 1930s. (Document 17.5)

With reduced expenditures and the imposition of the sales tax on 1 July 1933, Ehringhaus fulfilled his promise to preserve the state's credit and "carry on essential functions." By the time he completed his term, the state enjoyed a surplus, had inaugurated the statewide eight-month school term, and transported more children in school buses than any other state in the union. Although salaries of teachers and other state employees were low, they were, at least, paid on time and in cash. The road system was being maintained by an improved central administration. Ehringhaus's fiscal policy was painful, but it enabled the state to move back to solvency. (Documents 17.6 and 17.7) When Clyde R. Hoey entered the governor's mansion in 1937, the financial shadow had begun to lift, although the fears generated by the lessons of the past continued to affect policy.

In a broad sense the burden of dealing with the depression became progressively lighter for each of the three governors of North Carolina who confronted it. Gardner essentially had to develop his own programs and could not rely on succor from Washington either in tangible or psychological forms. Many of his efforts were similar to those of Herbert Hoover, who sought voluntary action and cooperation from identifiable interest groups. Ehringhaus, although assuming office at a gloomy moment, was soon able to preside over the arrival of ever more federal money and gave his enthusiastic support to rural electrification, Blue Ridge Parkway construction, and the creation of the Social Security system. By the time Clyde R. Hoey took office in 1937, the business of facing the next day was far easier, and there were few unexpected events to disrupt the relatively smooth unfolding of his term.

One must not, however, dwell too long on politics and politicians at the expense of farmers, factory workers, and other wage earners who bore the full burden of the depression. (Documents 17.8, 17.9, 17.10, 17.11, and 17.12) Of all economic groups in the state, those who felt the impact of the depression most quickly and heavily were the farmers who produced staple crops: tobacco, cotton, peanuts, and potatoes. In a sense, the depression for the farmer arrived in North Carolina in advance of the stock market crash, and conditions merely deteriorated after 1929. For most farmers in the nation the 1920s had been lean years, and efforts to resolve their problems at the national level had been slow in coming and were generally ineffective.

Under the impact of the depression, cash income of North Carolina's farmers dropped 65.7 percent to $97 million between 1928 and 1932. Faced with a crisis of this enormity, affecting the largest single group in the state, Gardner's efforts centered on voluntary plans to reduce production and secure the cooperation of other southern states to reduce production, particularly of tobacco. Officials in Virginia and South Carolina saw the virtues of cooperation, but it soon became apparent that the problem was beyond the capabilities of individual states or groups of states and that only the federal government could bring order and stability to agriculture. Although efforts to develop a quota system among the states foundered, some success came from the "live at home" program, which since 1922 had encouraged farmers to produce enough food to provide for themselves. Such a system would break the single-crop pattern, give farmers greater independence, and keep money in the state. "Raise and save something to eat" became the rallying cry for farmers, their wives, and children. The idea was slow to take hold, but each of the depression-era governors pushed it. In the late 1930s, Hoey seemed disappointed with the slow progress toward livestock production. (Document 17.13)

The major controversy in farming derived from efforts to develop a program of crop control after the creation of the New Deal's Agricultural Adjustment Administration (AAA) in 1933. Between 1933 and 1938 a continuing struggle took place over this issue. At one point, in April 1936, after the Supreme Court had struck down the AAA, Ehringhaus had to face six thousand angry farmers at State College Stadium in Raleigh who demanded that he call a special session of the legislature to enact laws creating a compact with other states to control tobacco marketing. Ehringhaus faced them down while explaining the need for a new federal crop control program. In time, most aspects of the agricultural problem were removed from the governor's desk by the creation of compulsory quota arrangements agreed to by the farmers themselves. Given the choice of crop controls or ruinous prices, farmers did not choose the latter. The federal government in its turn vested allotments for tobacco production on the land itself rather than with the individual farmers. This program has been described as a "legal monopoly on selected acres," and it meant the end of free and open entry into tobacco production. Controls were developed for cotton, but that crop had begun its westward movement and did not have a significant long-term future in North Carolina. Finally, tenants and sharecroppers left the fields for the towns and cities, but the tenant situation did not assume crisis proportions in North Carolina as it did in Arkansas and elsewhere. The solutions for agriculture were not perfect, but they set the pattern for decades to come.

Although many factories closed or ran at reduced capacity after the 1929 depression, North Carolina produced a number of items that remained in demand despite hard times, including cigars, cigarettes, work clothing, patent medicine, and silk hosiery. Many people had the smoking habit, and they as well as new smokers found solace from nicotine. Work clothing was cheap and, after all, most relief programs required it. Home remedies replaced visits to the doctor's office and gave parents the satisfaction of doing something for a sick child. In addition, North Carolina's furniture industry expanded its hold on the middle- and low-priced market, enabling it to benefit from the depression. In the textile industry, Cone Mills had only one operating division that failed to show a profit after 1935, and a silk hosiery manufacturer in Greensboro expanded his plant in 1930, 1936, and 1938. (Document 17.14)

A crisis in manufacturing came when the National Recovery Administration (NRA) sought to reduce production and hours of work. Implementation of this program led to layoffs and to the belief by some labor leaders that the time had arrived to organize the textile mills of the South. Strikes in the textile industry had occurred in 1929 and 1931, but they gained an added dimension in 1934, when "flying squadrons" of pickets going from place to place in cars tried to shut down factories and gain the support of the workers. Law enforcement officers and the mobilization of National Guard units kept the situation under control and prevented any deaths. In the end, unionization of the textile industry in North Carolina did not occur. Scattered strikes were held in the later 1930s, but none was of major proportion or significance.

Of all groups of labor, the construction trades were hit the hardest. Building came to a virtual standstill by 1930, except for a few projects already under way or with prior appropriations. As a consequence, suppliers of building materials were affected along with workers in lumber mills and brick kilns. Residential construction revived after the mid-1930s, but most major construction involved federal aid for public buildings. With the beginning of World War II it became concentrated on military bases. Between 1930 and 1945 little major commercial construction took place, and most downtown business districts remained static, dominating retail trade until the arrival of shopping centers in the postwar era.

During the administration of Clyde R. Hoey, bond issues were again floated but only to provide matching funds for federal grants. Teachers began to receive pay increases, and North Carolinians obtained direct assistance from the federal agencies created by the New Deal. By 1939 more than 9,200 homeowners had been aided by the Home Owners Loan Corporation. Some North Carolinians also had benefited by resettlement projects. (Document 17.15) That same year North Carolina stood eighteenth in the nation in the number of farms having tractors. Although 94,711 people were unemployed in November 1937, for the era of the Great Depression as a whole, the state was 20 percent below the national ratio of the number on relief to the labor force. Also by 1937 personal income had been restored to its 1929 level. Toward the end of the decade North Carolina began to move beyond the bare essentials in education to provide free textbooks for the elementary grades and funds to advertise the state. In 1938, as Hoey put it, the "greatest building program in the history of the state" was inaugurated, and by 1940 seven years had passed without a bank failure.

In August 1940, toward the end of his term, Governor Hoey announced that the decade of the 1930s was the "most prosperous" in the history of North Carolina. (Document 17.16) He went on to give statis-

388 · *The North Carolina Experience*

tics to prove his point. In a large sense he was right; in many ways, the state in general had prospered although many individuals had not. Even in the dark years after October 1929, conditions were not so bad for everyone. A Greensboro insurance executive considered the 1929–33 period "one of the most prosperous periods" for his company and attributed that success to "faith in North Carolina, its municipalities, and its people."

Indeed, what had taken place was a transformation of the state. If the future had been "spent" in the 1920s, the new controls on local finances would keep such profligacy from ever happening again. The state had not only obtained more than half of the Blue Ridge Parkway but the beginnings of a state park system at Hanging Rock and Morrow Mountain along with the huge Great Smoky Mountains National Park, which stretched into Tennessee. One might legitimately ask whether any of these developments would have occurred as soon as they did without the depression. The reformation of the tax structure had imposed the sales tax, which, although opposed by some as regressive, had solved a financial crisis and at least placed the burden on those who purchased items. The basic issue of farm controls was resolved and removed as a major concern for state officials. And among the many New Deal programs was the lasting memory of the most popular of all, the Civilian Conservation Corps (CCC), which put thousands of young men to work on soil conservation and forestry projects but above all reinforced the work ethic. In general, the state entered the era of World War II in good shape and contained the largest number of training camps in the nation. If, as some statistics indicated, North Carolina might have received more from the New Deal, it made up for any lack during World War II.

DOCUMENT 17.1

Governor O. Max Gardner: The Lessons of the Twenties

After the war, North Carolina—traditionally conservative and stubbornly individualistic—stretched herself like a strong man after sleep. For ten years she drove ahead on a program of progress that for sheer advance matches the record of any state in the union. The 1921 General Assembly authorized the issuance of $50,000,000 in bonds for state highways, and $7,000,000 for permanent improvement at state institutions—roughly, one third of a program which contemplated the expenditure of $20,000,000 in six years. In eight years we spent $160,000,000 of state and local funds for the state highway systems, $90,000,000 for school buildings, and $32,000,000 for enlargement of state institutions. The counties, cities and districts followed the example of the state in providing permanent improvements and increasing local operating expenses. The annual tax bill of the state and local governments grew from $23,500,000 to $100,000,000. And for every dollar levied in taxes we had on the average an additional fifty cents of borrowed money to spend.

In carrying out such a sizable governmental program, mistakes and waste were inevitable. On the whole, we stepped too fast. Under a delusion of grandeur attributable in part to the fact that the Federal Government was collecting on the average more than $200,000,000 annually in revenue from and through North Carolina—last year more than from any other state except New York—we doubtless extended our spending too rapidly and made mistakes accordingly. But our mistakes were honest mistakes of judgment.

The good times stopped.

Edwin Gill, comp., Public Papers and Letters of Oliver Max Gardner: Governor of North Carolina, 1929–1933 *(Raleigh: Council of State, 1937), pp. 666–67.*

DOCUMENT 17.2

Recommendations from the Brookings Institution, 1930

A Single Integrated County Government.

In our consideration of the state government, the major recommendation made was probably that suggesting that provision be made for a unitary or integrated administrative system composed of departments corresponding to the fields of activity, each having a single major purpose or function. It is suggested that all of the arguments that can be brought forward in favor of the erection of an integrated administrative system for the state apply with equal force to the counties. It is accordingly recommended that serious consideration be given to the basic reorganization of county government along this line.

This proposal would mean that in place of the existing system, under which county administrative duties are assigned to a large number of more or less independent agencies that all powers and duties would be assigned in the first instance to a single government agency, provision being made for the actual performance of these duties by specific agencies constituting subordinate services to the general agency and acting under the latter's general direction, supervision, and control. Specifically this would mean the drafting of a new county code that would provide for the creation in each county of a board of county commissioners to which should be entrusted all county governmental authority and providing for the setting up under this board of administrative subdivisions, each having in charge the duties falling in one of the distinct fields that have been mentioned: general administration, finance, education, etc. If action were taken in this way each county would have a unitary administrative system paralleling and corresponding closely to the unitary administrative system of the state government.

Brookings Institution, Report of a Survey of the Organization and Administration of County Government in North Carolina: Submitted to Governor O. Max Gardner *(Washington, D.C.: Brookings Institution, 1930), pp. 17, 18, 21.*

DOCUMENT 17.3

Governor Gardner on Consolidation of the University, 1931

I would not for an instant minimize or assume an attitude of indifference toward, any sentimental factor which this proposal may fairly be said to involve. Still less would I deny to any institution concerned the privilege of a jealous regard for its own individual and academic integrity. As I see it, they are charged with the duty to exercise this regard. I have the deep conviction, however, that the principle and policy under consideration are so broad in their scope, and so far-reaching in their ultimate implications, that any adequate approach must presuppose that we shall forget any narrow allegiance to any institution as an institution *per se*. We must remember that we are citizens—students, if you will—of that greater institution which is the State of North Carolina, and that any move or policy which best serves its interests and welfare and progress will, in the long run best serve the University, and State College, and the North Carolina College for Women. We must see each part in its relation to the whole and broaden our perspective so as to include not only three campuses, three faculties, three traditions, and a trinity of rich opportunities, but the entire future course and future effectiveness of higher education in this State.

The provisions of the bill recognize that the objectives aimed at can be fully accomplished only over a period of time. It does enable us to make a beginning. It makes possible ultimately the united support of North Carolina behind one great, unified, coordinated and intelligently directed educational enterprise.

David A. Lockmiller, The Consolidation of the University of North Carolina *(Raleigh: University of North Carolina, 1942), pp. 119–21.*

DOCUMENT 17.4

Views of Roosevelt and the New Deal

I do think that Roosevelt is the biggest-hearted man we ever had in the White House. He undoubtedly is the most foresighted and can speak his thoughts the plainest of any man I ever heard speak. He's spoke very few words over the radio that I haven't listened to. It's the first time in my recollection that a president ever got up and said, "I'm interested in and aim to do somethin' for the workin' man." Just knowin' that for once in the time of the country there was a man to stand up and speak for him, a man that could make what he felt so plain nobody could doubt he meant it, has made a lot of us feel a sight better even when they wasn't much to eat in our homes.

Federal Writers' Project, These Are Our Lives: As Told by the People and Written by Members of the Federal Writers' Project of the Works Progress Administration in North Carolina, Tennessee and Georgia *(Chapel Hill: University of North Carolina Press, 1939) pp. 210–11.*

I thought we were goin' to starve until Roosevelt came in. Things begin to pick up a little bit then, and I was able to get hooked up on two auctioneering jobs. That was in 1935 and the first money I'd made since 1929. That was one time, and I've been through the Reconstruction of the Slave War, that a man simply couldn't make a nickel. It was the worst time I've ever seen or anybody else has that I know of for tryin' to make a dollar.

Though I'm not taking any active part in [the] union now I still have a interest in what it's doing. And I've got hopes that in not so many years the laboring man will actually have justice, he'll no longer be a pore creature that will bow his head and not open his mouth when a manufacturer says, "You'll do what we tell you, You'll shut your mind up and let us think for you, or we'll starve you to death." Labor has been stirred and it's going to think through. There might be violence; that depends altogether on the capitalist. Labor don't want to own the property, as some seem to think. It just wants a fair return of what it produces in the form of wages. I hope the labor laws passed by the New Deal administration will work out like they was intended. It's foolish to set back and say nothing could happen in our country to bring on a revolution.

Tom E. Terrill and Jerrold Hirsch, eds., Such as Us: Southern Voices of the Thirties *(Chapel Hill: University of North Carolina Press, 1978), pp. 52, 187.*

DOCUMENT 17.5

A College Graduate's View of the Teaching Profession

The minimum state salary for teachers is $520.00 per year (in fact, it is under $400; editor's note) and the maximum is $720. As you observe, there is no provision made in this budget for savings and preparation for old age. What becomes of teachers after they have become too old to work is somewhat vague. Whatever their fate, the future of the present teaching force is certainly not a brilliant one.

Neither is there an allowance made for the miscellaneous items required by everyone. This would include such necessities as tooth paste, cosmetics, stationery, literature, care of hair, etc. An amount of dental and medical care has not been included in the list. Nor is there any mention of a fund for pleasure and summer recreation.

It is safe to say that fifty per cent of the teachers are either still paying for their educations or are assisting in the support of their families. Where this additional money comes from is not known. It is shockingly clear, however, that some of these items are not on the budgets of our local teachers as their salaries make it impossible to include them. The above consists only of the necessities of life. Whether the teachers are denying themselves of new clothes and summer school or are going without as much to eat as they would like to have is undetermined. One thing is evident. They are having to deprive themselves of one or the other. The writer of this is not a teacher, and those who find these words distasteful because they savor of the truth may rest assured that not even in her most philanthropic moments would she consider entering this profession that has come to be taken for granted and practically for gratis.—WINI-FRED MARSHALL

High Point Enterprise, *13 November 1934.*

DOCUMENT 17.6

Governor J.C.B. Ehringhaus on the "Sales Tax as an Emergency Measure," March 1933

I believe in economy—drastic, rigid economy. I have preached it. I have practiced it. I shall continue to advocate it. I shall continue to stand against wastefulness and extravagance in any activity. But there is a point, even in economy, beyond which self-respecting government cannot go. For to do so means not merely an abdication of its functions but social bankruptcy, collapse of morale, and repudiation of our constitutional, social and political obligations. Government must make reasonable provisions for the activities contemplated by its constitution or it surrenders and invites the scorn and contumely of its citizens and the world at large.

We are simply facing a terrific emergency and the manifest necessity for the levy of some new taxes if the schools and the State's credit are to be saved from utter wreckage. A six months term with no chance for extension is a poor educational opportunity at best; inadequately financed, it is a delusion, a snare, and an utterly unjustifiable waste and extravagance.

You will permit me in passing to observe that I am quite sincere in saying that I loathe either form of sales tax, but I love the honor and credit of my State and the maintenance of its self-respect more even than I dislike such impositions. There are some things more odious, more undemocratic, more objectionable even, than this form of taxation. They at least have the virtue of universal application and something of relation to ability to pay, if spending has reasonable relationship to income.

David Leroy Corbitt, ed., Addresses, Letters, and Papers of John Christoph Blucher Ehringhaus, Governor of North Carolina, 1933–1937 (Raleigh: Council of State, 1950), pp. 26–27.

DOCUMENT 17.7

Governor Ehringhaus, "The Sales Tax Has Its Virtues," 24 February 1934

Today North Carolina's credit is good; its bonds are selling at par or better; its short-term notes are held largely in the state and those in New York are renewable at will and, as the bankers there advise, considered of such a high order that they are not for sale. Its interest rate has been reduced from 6 to 4 per cent, resulting in an annual saving to the State in interest alone of approximately half a million dollars: enough to pay the annual running charge of some first-class activities and institutions. We met our bond maturities and interest payments on January 1st in cash, and though they aggregated $6,103,000, we were able to do this, pay our state employees' salaries prior to Christmas and pay also our pension maturities without the necessity of resorting to temporary borrowing. This is the first time in many years in which the State has not been compelled to resort to tax anticipation borrowing along in December to meet bond maturities in January. North Carolina is today the only state in the Union in which an eight months school term is guaranteed to every child and it is a matter of pride that of the one million children throughout the Nation who have seen the schoolhouse door close in their faces during these distressful times, not one lives in North Carolina. And while the teachers' salaries are low in this state, they have also been lowered in practically every other state; and in North Carolina no teacher has failed to receive his or her pay promptly and receive it in cash, whereas in many states payments are being made in scrip which is subject to large discount. The relief in property taxes, general through the State, is manifest in Piedmont North Carolina and in your own county and neighboring counties.

The total burden of tax imposition through the State has been and still is being gradually reduced. In the midst of great distress, confronted by temptations to disastrous and destructive policies, and urged by hysterical thinking to sacrifice things saved through the years and regarded as sacred, North Carolina is fighting its way through the depression and has become, not only in the opinion of its citizens but in the eyes of the world, solvent, saving, sane, and sanguine.

Corbitt, ed., Addresses, Letters, and Papers of Ehringhaus, *pp. 127–28.*

DOCUMENT 17.8

The Dilemma of the High School Class of 1934

Most of us have homes where we can stay and get enough to eat and wear. It's the waiting that depresses us. We are young and have energy to expend. We are eager to join the fray. We, the young hopefuls of the last few graduating classes, are asking restlessly if we must sit forever watching our coat of idealism being slowly but surely rubbed off from contact with the disillusioning truth. In this great country with its forests, natural resources, countless fertile acres, and wealth untold, is there nothing we can do? We feel that we are being deprived of our just heritage. Can our patriotism stand the test of this enforced idleness?

We turn to the world and say: "Here we are; we are ready to pitch in and bear our share of the burden." But nobody seems to pay attention. The fact that we have obtained a good education apparently doesn't mean very much. Where are those opportunities of which we had been told? Where is the reward for the many years that we have spent at our books? Is it any wonder that many of us are starting our life's work in a somewhat cynical frame of mind? We were told that everybody would be ready to help us and see that we were given a good start. Where are those helpful hands now?

Willis S. Harrison, '34, "What Is There For Us To Do?," State 2 *(26 May 1934):33.*

DOCUMENT 17.9

An Appeal to the White People of North Carolina, North Carolina College Conference, 1933

(1) Crime and mob violence against the negro have been on the increase. We feel that a government as rich and strong as our own would be so jealous of its honor and good name that a lynching by white men in a caste controlled by white men, whose laws are enacted by white men, whose courts are conducted exclusively by white men, there would never be a violation of the sanctity of the law. And whenever these laws were defied or trampled upon by any group of men or mob that those who have the defense of the law would set every piece of Court machinery in motion against such crimes. Many high public officials charged with law enforcement rarely go through the formality of making inquiry into such outrages against negroes, many white people feel no shame in confessing their impotence to govern themselves. . . .

(4) Our teachers, disadvantaged by disfranchisement, by lack of the means to prepare themselves, nevertheless do meet the high and exacting standards of the best white institutions in the country, and then armed with the state's highest certificate go into the employment of a commonwealth which reduces their wages to the level of janitors and hod carriers.

We call upon the negro in every county of the state to be vigilant in the safeguarding of the rights when they are abridged or denied, the protest should be laid at the feet of those charged with the administering of local affairs and if this remedy fails, the state officials should be acquainted with the facts. There must be peace and harmony between the races in North Carolina, there must be no backward steps if there is fair play, sympathy and justice in dealing with all matters affecting the rights of every citizen regardless of race or creed.

Greensboro Daily News, 17 December 1933.

DOCUMENT 17.10

The Success of a Handicraft Industry in the Mountains

In the early days of the industry Miss Lucy and Miss Burt used to pack a cargo of weaving into the back of a Ford car and visit gift shops and resort hotels in search of a market. The problem that threatened the enterprise was not production but sales. Up to 1931 there were sixty-three weavers at work, with more women anxious to begin as soon as the demand warranted additional production. The depression crammed the big storage cupboards on either side of the fireplace in the community cabin full to overflowing with unsold coverlids, dress materials, linens, scarfs, blankets, rugs, and runners, woven in rainbow colors concocted from mountain herbs and roots. Even a sharp reduction in prices would not move them.

Miss Morgan determined to take a long chance that might set the idle looms to working again. The crowd at the Century of Progress in Chicago offered a market with ready money if she could only get the goods there to be sold. Even a little concession would cost a thousand dollars, but she was determined to get it from somewhere. Nobody believed it could be done, but it was—mostly in contributions of two, three and five dollars, collected from anybody who could be interested in the project. The purchase of the crowds at the Fair swept away the storage stock and set the business humming steadily again.

Muriel Early Shepard, Cabins in the Laurel *(Chapel Hill: University of North Carolina Press, 1935), pp. 256–57.*

DOCUMENT 17.11

Human Distress in the 1930s

Weldon, N Car.
Jan. 21—1935

My dear Mrs Roosevelt.

I am a great admirer of you and President Roosevelt. I feel we are so fortunate to have you in the white house. I have always supported you and shall in the future. I have often read your addresses + heard you speak some over the radio and I find you so much in sympathy with the (worthy needy) I know it is hard to realize how one can suffer financially when you never know what it is to want for any thing money can buy. But I am prayerfully appealing to you for a loan gift or any way we can manage it. I am desperate over my situation I cannot go on getting in debt for food milk coal and many other little necessary things. I feel I must be relieved in some way soon. I just cant stand to think I owe so much. No way at present to pay it. I will loose my credit + my good standing I so much prized. I am a Widow 57 years old. three in my family. My income is not sufficient to pay my board + household expenses. I have drawn on my insurance until I will loose it if I dont pay the interest and part premiums.

Last summer I had a critical operation. was in the hospital + bed eight weeks. I got so far behind I just cant catch up. I am not able to do my work. and cant get any one to help me because I cant pay them. Please let me have $600.00 dollars just to pay my back debts   maby I could catch up. I have a home but I dont want to mortgage my home. I am trying to rent part of it as an apt. to get something out of it. if you will just please let me have it. I will try to pay you back little at the time. I am a good honest truthful woman of a good high class family, but none are able to help me. Please dont make my name public in any way. I just feel you will help me. please *do* send me a check or money order. I feel I cant go on. So please help me I am desperate. I know you have appeals often + hard to know which is worthy but please help me. and dont let it be anything but a private affair with us if you could only know how I feel. I am most frantic with depression. Please let me hear from you. many thanks.— much Gratitude,

> (Initials omitted because of writer's request) Weldon. N. Car.

High Point N C
Dec. 15. 1935

Mr. Roosevelte   I am In nead Bad Please help me I have 7 children and is Sick all the time one of my children is Sick and has Ben for a lone time and I have No under clothes for none of the famiely we cant harly hide I Self with top cloths   I ned Milk and my Boy need milk   Please give my childrens and my Self Some under cloths or we will freze to Deth this cold wethr we can not Make it pay Rent get Something to Eat and get wood and coal no one work But my husBan he make $6.75 per week no way way I can get any under cloths for the famely please help me I have not a teeth in My head wen I Eat I nely Dieys　no way to get any please help me please.

(Anonymous)

Robert S. McElvaine, ed., Down and Out in the Great Depression: Letters from the "Forgotten Man" *(Chapel Hill: University of North Carolina Press, 1983), pp. 109–10, 158.*

DOCUMENT 17.12

A Description of Black Life in North Carolina

In North Carolina towns, as in most southern towns, there are segregated sections for Negroes, and in these sections housing and sanitation generally have been inadequate. Exploitive landlordism on the part of many white owners, and to a lesser extent, of Negro owners as well, has been an almost unregulated evil. . . .

Until recent years in North Carolina, but few recreational facilities were available for Negroes. Since 1933 some progress has been made in providing the Negroes with parks, playgrounds, and swimming pools in projects sponsored by the Federal Government in cooperation with local efforts. The races are separated in jails, prisons, and poorhouses but accommodations are generally the same.

Negroes have their own motion picture houses, restaurants, and hotels, and occupy gallery seats at some white theaters. They have had only limited use of public libraries. Separate coaches are provided on trains. Pullman tickets can be bought on some lines, but the use of the dining car is prohibited. Separate waiting rooms are the rule in train and bus stations. Buses and streetcars assign the Negroes seats in the rear.

Even educated Negroes frequently find it difficult to register and vote. Participation in civic affairs such as officeholding, policing, and jury service is practically nonexistent. As a result of the Supreme Court decision in the much-publicized Scottsboro case, Negroes are, for the first time since Reconstruction, being drawn for jury panels, though few as yet have served as jurors.

Aside from these traditional racial distinctions and discriminations, however, North Carolina bears a reputation for favorable race relations. This is perhaps partly due to the State's high educational rating. In education, social welfare, and economic advance much has been done for and by Negroes in North Carolina. It is likewise true that much more remains to be done.

Federal Writers' Project, North Carolina: A Guide to the Old North State Compiled and Written by the Federal Writers' Project of the Federal Writers' Project of the Federal Works Agency of the Works Project Administration *(Chapel Hill: University of North Carolina Press, 1939), pp. 55, 57.*

DOCUMENT 17.13

Governor Hoey on the "Needs of Agriculture," 1939

Agriculture is still the basic industry of our State since over half our people live on the farm and are engaged in farming. We have made some progress in the diversification of crops, in conserving and enriching the soil by crop rotation, lime treatment and legume crops, but we have much yet to do. We are still so thoroughly committed to the so-called money crops that it is difficult for us to get away from cotton and tobacco. This is understandable, for with all of our shortcomings in agriculture, the fact remains that North Carolina stands third among the states of the Union in the value of her cash crops—surpassed only by California and Texas.

Traveling over the State you are impressed with the scarcity of cows in the rich tobacco counties. If every family, tenant and land owner could be supplied with cows, hogs, and poultry, and then supplemented with a good garden and canning facilities to provide food for the winter season, North Carolina would increase speedily her agricultural wealth and practically eliminate pellegra, from which over 2,000 people die in this State every year, and it results from lack of proper food.

David Leroy Corbitt, ed., Addresses, Letters and Papers of Clyde Roark Hoey, Governor of North Carolina, 1937–1941 *(Raleigh: Council of State, 1944), pp. 42–43.*

DOCUMENT 17.14

A Hosiery Mill Worker Describes His Work

Knitting may look like an easy job, but it's not so easy as it looks. For one thing, it is hard on the eyes; for another it's exacting. The full-fashioned knitting machine is a delicate and highly complicated machine. A knitter must keep his wits about him constantly. It's very easy to smash a machine, doing hundreds of dollars' worth of damage and maybe putting that machine out of commission for a couple of months.

The silk threads are fine, and the needles are small and slender. Unless a man has very good eyes he will have to wear magnifying glasses soon after beginning to knit. Knitting is a young man's job. You'll see ten times as many knitters under thirty as you will over thirty. A man's eyes were not made for such fine work. The eyes of some knitters go bad after five or six years, sometimes sooner than that. In fact, unless a man has good eyes he can't learn to knit. Some learners fall down the first week on account of their eyes.

A full-fashioned knitter is considered to have a good trade hereabouts. The wage is much higher than common. A good knitter can average $40.00 a week the year round. The work is not hard except on the eyes. The light isn't always good. If a man had daylight to work under it wouldn't be so bad, but that can't always be. Most of the mills around here run three shifts, and some are naturally dark and require artificial light even at midday.

There's a boom on in the silk hosiery trade. All the mills around here are running full blast, and those that don't have third shifts are starting them. . . . Silk hosiery is a new industry in the South, but it's growing fast.

Federal Writers' Project, These Are Our Lives, *pp. 177–79.*

DOCUMENT 17.15

Planned Communities in North Carolina: A Federal "Subsistence Homestead Project" at Penderlea in Pender County

A family selected to become a part of Penderlea has much to be proud of for they must measure up to rigid requirements before the department of agriculture will grant a loan and subsequently the right to buy a farm. "A good name and reputation of the whole family, the ability to work and the will to do it, those are the things that count most here," says W. H. Robbins, community manager.

Where did the people who live there come from? They came from North Carolina. What kind of people are they? They are of the finest and purest Anglo-Saxon stock to be found anywhere. They like the farm-purchase plan; the government likes them; so they and the government have gotten together on a very fine proposition that is mutually good.

How do the growers dispose of their products? They consume a lot of it; they really practice "living at home." Right at this time, they are selling their money crops in the usual channels. Surplus truck is sold on the nearest markets to the best advantage that the individual can work out for himself. Eventually, a community marketing plan will be put into operation.

Do many families leave the project? No. In the first place, only families who are suited are accepted for settlement. They are on probation and rental plan the first year. If there is any leaving to do, the end of the first year is the time for it. At the beginning of the second year they become purchasers of their farms. In the second place, who could want to leave such a place?

To sum up, Penderlea Homestead is not an experiment; it is a successful resettlement proposition; in final analysis it will not be a government load, everything considered; the people are happy, a credit to themselves and their government.

Greensboro Daily News, *8 May 1939.*

DOCUMENT 17.16

Governor Hoey Responds to President Roosevelt's Statement on the South's Economy

A recent survey classified the South as the Nation's economic problem No. 1. With full admission of all our shortcomings and needs, I must insist that North Carolina does not fit into that classification. During the whole period of the depression, North Carolina has maintained fourth place in her total contributions by way of taxes to the Federal Government. Only New York, Pennsylvania, and Illinois exceeded this State in the sums paid annually. Of course tobacco taxes accounted for a large proportion of the total sum, but automobile purchases throughout the country help pay Michigan's, the users of all nationally sold products contribute to the home state of manufacture, and then all of us help New York pay hers by our losses on the stock exchange.

During the depression period North Carolina has received less from the Federal Government per capita than any state in the Union and we have paid more in per capita than any state save Delaware. In 1938 there were only two states whose income from cash crops was greater than North Carolina—California and Texas. We grow and manufacture more tobacco than any other state, we have attained the primacy in textiles and stand second in the manufacture of furniture. Last year the total manufactured products of North Carolina reached the grand total of one billion and three hundred million dollars. And the laborer in North Carolina received as high a percentage of the manufacturer's dollar as in any other state. There has not been a bank failure in North Carolina in more than seven years. This State stands fifth in the development of hydro-electric power. Briefly, upon this showing I regard my State as a stalwart, supporting member of the family rather than a problem child.

Corbitt, ed., Addresses, Letters and Papers of Hoey, *pp. 340–41.*

SUGGESTED READINGS

Badger, Anthony J. *North Carolina and the New Deal.* Raleigh: Department of Cultural Resources, 1981.
_____. *Prosperity Road: The New Deal, Tobacco, and North Carolina.* Chapel Hill: University of North Carolina Press, 1980.

Bell, John L., Jr. *Hard Times: Beginnings of the Great Depression in North Carolina, 1929–1933*. Raleigh: Department of Cultural Resources, 1982.

Daniel, James C. "The North Carolina Tobacco Marketing Crisis of 1933." *North Carolina Historical Review* 41 (1964):370–82.

Daniels, Jonathan. *Tar Heels: A Portrait of North Carolina*. New York: Dodd, Mead & Co., 1947.

Hunter, Robert F. "The AAA between Neighbors: Virginia, North Carolina, and the New Deal Farm Program." *Journal of Southern History* 44 (1978):537–70.

Jolley, Harley E. *The Blue Ridge Parkway*. Knoxville: University of Tennessee Press, 1969.

Marcell, Ronald E. "The Election of North Carolina's WPA Chief, 1935: A Dispute over Political Patronage." *North Carolina Historical Review* 52 (1975):59–76.

Morgan, Thomas S., Jr. "The Movement to Enact Unemployment Insurance Legislation in North Carolina, 1935–1936." *North Carolina Historical Review* 52 (1975):283–302.

Morrison, Joseph L. *Governor O. Max Gardner: A Power in North Carolina and New Deal Washington*. Chapel Hill: University of North Carolina Press, 1971.

Parker, Robert V. "The Bonus March of 1932: A Unique Experience in North Carolina Political and Social Life." *North Carolina Historical Review* 51 (1974):64–89.

Puryear, Elmer L. *Democratic Party Dissension in North Carolina, 1928–1936*. Chapel Hill: University of North Carolina Press, 1962.

Weeks, Charles J. "The Eastern Cherokee and the New Deal." *North Carolina Historical Review* 53 (1976):303–19.

CHAPTER 18

Sit-Ins and Civil Rights

Thomas C. Parramore

Civil Rights Demonstration, Chapel Hill, N.C., 1964 (Courtesy of the Division of Archives and History, Raleigh, N.C.)

During the third quarter of the twentieth century, the national and even international reputation of North Carolina as an arena of civil rights underwent a shocking change. In the first half of the century, Tar Heels generally considered themselves, and were regarded abroad, as "progressive" in the limited sense in which that adjective is applied to the southern states. The term was often used to characterize not only the enlightened partnership between business and government in the state but the tenor of race and labor-management relations, attitudes toward democracy and due process, and so on.

By the late 1950s, the luster of the state's apparent civil responsibility and racial tranquillity began to tarnish. A harshly ideological Senate campaign in 1950, followed by the prosecution of a Chapel Hill communist, was the precursor of the fall of North Carolina's image. A succession of highly publicized incidents in the 1960s and 1970s completed the state's transition from being viewed as "progressive" to being viewed as "reactionary." By 1978, North Carolina had joined South Africa and the Soviet Union on Amnesty International's list of violators of the civil and political rights of citizens.

The change in North Carolina's image raises the question of whether it paralleled a substantive change in civil rights attitudes and policies within the state. Had the progressive reputation of earlier years actually been a misperception of North Carolina's basic and traditional stance? Or is the reactionary label of recent years deserved? Is it founded, perhaps, on a few attention-getting episodes that were unfairly exploited or interpreted to North Carolina's disadvantage?

The case made by the defenders of North Carolina's progressive or, more realistically, moderate civil rights image cannot be lightly dismissed. In an age of intense regional and even national repression of blacks in the opening years of the twentieth century, Governor Charles B. Aycock launched a bold public school program that, though racially condescending, benefited blacks as well as whites. (Document 18.1) Efforts to restrict academic freedom in the state were ultimately turned back in the 1920s as they would be in the 1960s. North Carolina sent to Washington none of the vulgar racial demagogues numbered among the representatives of sister states. Moreover, gains were seen in voting rights, blacks' access to public accommodations, education, and other areas, especially after about 1940, at a rate reflective of progress in the nation as a whole.

Even so, harrowing incidents occurred well before the destructive episodes of the 1950s. The resurgence of the Ku Klux Klan after World War I, the state's sometimes vicious response to industrial strife, notably in a textile strike at Gastonia in 1929, a pattern of discrimination against black voters, and other violations of the already circumscribed civil rights of blacks and Indians were among these adverse signals. A similar spirit was displayed in calls by influential Tar Heels for the dismissal in 1903 of John Spencer Bassett, a racially conciliatory Trinity College professor and, in the 1920s, of William L. Poteat, evolutionist president of Wake Forest College. In 1920 North Carolina spurned the chance to cast the ratifying vote for women's suffrage as it later repeatedly rejected the proposed Equal Rights Amendment.

Despite this ambiguous record, at midcentury North Carolina enjoyed an enviable reputation for fair and open-minded treatment of its citizens. In large measure, this reputation can be traced to the fact that those Tar Heels with the broadest national notoriety tended to be articulate liberals. In particular, Frank Porter Graham, president of the University of North Carolina from 1931 to 1949, was widely regarded as the most effective voice of moderation and sound judgment on civil rights in the South. Under his guidance, the university was a bastion of productive liberalism and social enlightenment. Prominent liberals from the state included President Poteat of Wake Forest College from 1905 to 1927; Wilbur J. Cash, author of *The Mind of the South*; journalists Gerald W. Johnson, Walter Hines Page, and Harry Golden; playwright Paul Green; and leading newspaper editors, especially the *Raleigh News and Observer*'s Jonathan Daniels.

North Carolina's boast that it was uniquely fair and humane in its treatment of black citizens has been a theme of virtually all of its twentieth-century governors. "It is admitted," Governor R. Gregg Cherry claimed in 1945, "that North Carolina leads the South in good race relations." In 1929, Governor O. Max Gardner announced that "the relationship between the races in North Carolina is extraordinarily cordial." And Angus W. McLean observed in 1925 that "there is no longer a real race problem in the South."

This wholesome self-image won resounding endorsement in 1949 in political analyst V. O. Key's *Southern Politics in State and Nation*. Key traced the roots of North Carolina's "progressive plutocracy" as far back as Governor Aycock's educational initiatives, from which had awakened "the spirit of self-examination that still sets North Carolina apart from the South. . . . Willingness to accept new ideas, sense of community responsibility toward the Negro, feeling of common purpose, and relative prosperity have given North Carolina a more sophisticated politics than exists in most southern states." Evidence was to be found notably in industrial development and in education and race relations. (Document 18.2)

That these admirable characteristics might coexist with a marked religious fundamentalism and generally conservative notions among both rank-and-file Tar Heels and their leaders was a phenomenon requiring deeper penetration than Key could give it in a single chapter. But North Carolina was understood before 1950 to be in the vanguard of a gradual movement of the South toward the mainstream of national attitudes and practices.

The year 1950 witnessed a political contest in North Carolina that set the stage for a new and different national perception of the state and its social vision. Following the death in office of Senator J. Melville Broughton in 1949, Governor Kerr Scott named Frank Graham to fill the vacancy. Graham sought election in his own right in 1950, and the conservative wing of the Democratic party brought forward attorney Willis Smith of Raleigh to oppose him. The ensuing primary campaign is generally considered the most brutal in North Carolina's history.

During the campaign public expression was given to long-festering suspicions that the state university, under Graham's leadership, was a den of radicals. Graham was personally charged with transgressions against the traditional color line, with giving aid to radical organizations, with tolerating the presence of communists in the university student body, and with other political and social sins. In the prevailing national climate of strident McCarthyism, these were very serious allegations. Graham won the first primary but was defeated by Smith in a runoff.

The substance of the allegation that Graham was soft on communism lay largely in the activity of a small group of Chapel Hill communists headed since 1947 by Junius Scales, grand-nephew of a former North Carolina governor. Scales, a Greensboro native and veteran of World War II, was an avowed Marxist who published a pro-communist periodical and engaged in various other activities, apparently legal, in promotion of his cause.

Scales, then, had made news from time to time before his arrest in 1959 by federal authorities. He and his associates were charged, under the Smith Act of 1950, with membership in an organization dedicated to the violent overthrow of the United States government. After his trial and conviction in Greensboro, Scales received a sentence of six years in prison.

Public opinion in North Carolina, as expressed in leading newspapers, was generally favorable to Scales's conviction. But Gerald W. Johnson, writing in the *New Republic*, voiced the view of those who felt that Scales's only crime was "not thinking right." (Document 18.3) In 1962, following many appeals in Scales's behalf from Reinhold Niebuhr, Norman Thomas, the *New York Times*, and others, President John F. Kennedy commuted his sentence after fifteen months' imprisonment.

The prosecution of Junius Scales probably owed more to national hysteria over internal subversion than to any peculiar Tar Heel strain of virulence. A case with more distinctive local overtones was that of labor leader Boyd Payton. The intimate association of business and government in North Carolina was a factor in the generally unfavorable climate for labor organization and union activity. At the end of the 1950s, only 9 percent of the state's industrial workers were unionized. But the inhospitable environment became openly hostile when violence attended a strike in 1959 at Henderson.

Although there were no fatalities, the turmoil at the Harriet-Henderson Cotton Mills included rocks and bricks thrown at cars, acid poured on machines, blasts of dynamite and Molotov cocktails, and several injuries. Payton, regional director of the American Textile Workers' Union, was convicted of involvement in a conspiracy to bomb the mill's power plant. He was sentenced to seven to ten years in prison.

Critics of Payton's conviction charged that there was no evidence of his involvement in the conspiracy. That the state's key witness had a lengthy criminal record whereas Payton had none and other alleged flaws in the state's case made Payton the object of appeals for clemency by Secretary of Labor Arthur Goldberg, evangelist Billy Graham, and other prominent figures. Goldberg's role was an index of the wide tremors of labor unrest set off by Payton's conviction.

In 1965, Governor Terry Sanford commuted Payton's sentence and pardoned him. Many of those familiar with the case felt that he was found guilty partly because of public irritation over the Henderson violence. *Christian Century*, the *New Republic*, and the *Reporter* were among the national periodicals that censured the state's handling of Payton's case and the long delay in the granting of his pardon.

A common denominator, then, in the Graham-Smith campaign and the Scales and Payton cases was that they all focused national attention on North Carolina and opened the state's political and judicial systems to criticism from outsiders as well as civil rights elements within. The cumulative effect of these episodes was not sufficient seriously to damage North Carolina's progressive and moderate reputation, but it did bring the glare of national spotlights even before the integration movement began to reach crisis proportions in 1960.

Neither political nor industrial radicalism threatened to rend the South's fabric of tradition so severely as did the racial confrontation following the United States Supreme Court's *Brown* v. *Board of Education* decision in 1954. North Carolina, with other southern states, recoiled instinctively from the implications of this decision but without the threats of violence and bitter-end resistance heard elsewhere. It was ironic, then, that the specter of the ruin of North Carolina's public school system was offered as the danger justifying the state's response to federal integration initiatives. (Document 18.4)

That response was embodied in the so-called Pearsall Plan of 1956, a series of constitutional amendments allowing local school districts to close in order to avoid desegregation and providing tuition aid for white students in such districts to attend private schools. (Document 18.5) The consequence was "token integration," the acceptance of a handful of black students into formerly all-white schools in a few districts. Five years after this plan was inaugurated, only eighty-nine black children had been integrated into previously all-white schools and no whites into traditionally black schools. As late as 1966, only 6 percent of the state's black children were attending schools with whites. The aim of the federal government was effectively thwarted during these years but without the strife accompanying school integration efforts elsewhere.

Black frustration over Jim Crow restrictions widened, meanwhile, with the Montgomery, Alabama, bus boycott of 1957 and other protest demonstrations. But a distinctly new level of agitation was reached on 1 February 1960, when four black students from North Carolina Agricultural and Technical College took seats at the lunch counter of a Greensboro Woolworth store and were refused service. The quartet sat at the counter in protest against the segregated facility until closing time and returned on subsequent days, their numbers steadily enlarged by both black and white supporters. (Documents 18.6 and 18.7) Within a few days, the "sit-in" as a form of resistance to segregated accommodations had spread to fifty-four cities in nine states.

North Carolina experienced little real violence in the ensuing racial struggle. One of the most publicized episodes involved black activist Robert F. Williams of Monroe. Williams first gained public attention for his activities in 1957, but two trips to Castro's Cuba reinforced his radicalism and perhaps his insistence that blacks must arm themselves and be prepared to counter white violence with their own.

In August 1961, a Union County grand jury indicted Williams on a charge of kidnapping following an ugly racial disturbance in Monroe. He was charged with seizing a white couple and holding them briefly as hostages for the release of antisegregation demonstrators. Williams fled to Cuba and spent the next fourteen years in exile, engaged in various radical activities. He returned in 1976 to face the charges against him. By this time, one of the alleged kidnapping victims had died and the other reportedly had repudiated the kidnapping charge. Williams's claim that he had only tried to protect the couple from an angry mob went unchallenged because no one appeared in court to press charges. The case was dropped. (Document 18.8)

Despite the Williams case, North Carolina retained its moderate image as late as 1963. (Document 18.9) In 1960 the progressive wing of the Democratic party, led by Terry Sanford, turned back the gubernatorial bid of segregationist I. Beverly Lake even as other southern states yielded to the blandishments of George Wallace, Ross Barnett, and others. Amid the tumult of bombings and killings, North Carolina seemed an island of comparative calm in a sea of rage.

Mounting civil rights agitation in North Carolina in 1963 brought renewed criticism of the state university from conservative Tar Heels. In the spring of that year, elements of the student body and faculty at the University of North Carolina launched a new wave of demonstrations against segregated restaurants, theaters, and other public accommodations in Chapel Hill. Simultaneously, a member of the faculty at North Carolina State College earned notoriety for his participation in efforts to integrate facilities in Raleigh, including the Sir Walter Hotel, in-session home of many state legislators. A highlight of the latter episode was the Sir Walter coffee shop's refusal to serve a group including Angie Brooks, Liberia's ambassador to the United Nations.

On the next to last day of the legislative session in June, a bill barring radicals from speaking at state-supported facilities was hurried through the legislature and became law. The Speaker Ban Law struck at "known" communists and persons who had pled the Fifth Amendment in response to loyalty questions. For the next several years, the "Gag Law," as it was labeled by its critics, became the cause célèbre on both public and private campuses across the state. (Document 18.10)

A similar law against radical speakers had been passed and revoked in Ohio, so North Carolina was branded as the only state finding it necessary to go to such lengths to protect its university students from subversive influences. Critics of the law feared the loss of university accreditation, the flight of distinguished faculty, and a precedent for further abuses of academic freedom. Not since the controversy over teaching evolution had a public issue so divided North Carolinians or emphasized so sharply the perennial antagonisms between academicians and the general public. Liberal spokesmen across the nation denounced North Carolina for intellectual obscurantism and worse. The Speaker Ban Law was modified during the administration of Governor Dan K. Moore but, even in its milder form, was found unconstitutional by the federal courts in 1965. More than any previous episode, the Speaker Ban gave North Carolina an aura of eccentricity with respect to civil rights more bizarre than that of the "closed societies" of the Deep South.

The state, therefore, had already suffered unwelcome notoriety when a new episode—the case of the "Wilmington 10"—turned the glare of not merely national but world opinion on its civil rights climate. The trouble at Wilmington originated in the fall of 1970, when black high school students began protesting what they regarded as discriminatory policies at an integrated city school. The protests mounted to marches and classroom boycotts in January 1971. The minister of a church where the students met, Gregory Congregational United Church of Christ, called on his church's Commission on Racial Justice in Raleigh for help in organizing the students more effectively.

Organizer Ben Chavis from Granville County reached Wilmington on 1 February. In the next few days, the community was struck by a series of acts of violence, including shootings and damage to property. In one especially dangerous incident, police and firemen answering a call at a firebombed grocery store found themselves under sniper attack. Chavis and his associates were later arrested and charged with both the firebombing and sniping.

The first testimony against Chavis and nine others, including one white, was given by Allen Hall, a black man, during his own trial for assaulting a teacher and students during the protests. Jerome Mitchell and thirteen-year-old Eric Junious confirmed Hall's allegations that Chavis and the other nine had arranged and participated in the Wilmington violence.

At the trial of the Wilmington 10, civil libertarians took exception to the district attorney's use of more than forty challenges to get a jury of ten whites and two elderly blacks. Witness Allen Hall, who confessed his own involvement in the activity of the 10, received a reduced sentence of 12 years, but Chavis was convicted and sentenced to 34 years and the other nine defendants to a total of 248 years. Appeals kept the 10 out of prison until February 1976, when they began serving their terms.

Soon afterward, Allen Hall announced that he had lied at the trial after being coerced by the prosecutor. Subsequently, Junious and Mitchell also recanted amid charges of bribes and other undue influence on the part of the prosecutors of the 10. Hall reversed himself several times more, establishing at least his unreliability as a witness. But appeals to the North Carolina Court of Appeals and state supreme court were rejected, and the Federal Supreme Court remanded an appeal in 1977 to the state courts.

By late 1978, North Carolina appeared in London-based Amnesty International's list of governments believed to hold political prisoners in their jails. Political prisoners are defined by the organization as persons held for their beliefs and political activities rather than for crimes. Soviet Premier Leonid Brezhnev cited the Wilmington 10 case an an example of American injustice, and the world press maintained a lively interest in the case and its principals. President Jimmy Carter, who had made the strengthening of civil liberties globally a central thrust of his administration, found his efforts compromised by the broad negative reaction to the case. National and international concern over the fate of the 10 led

Carter to order an investigation by the Justice Department. Congress launched inquiries of its own.

Pressure built steadily on Governor James B. Hunt to pardon the 10. The governor at length responded by ordering a new investigation by the State Bureau of Investigation and concluded from its report that the trial of the 10 had been fair but the sentences excessively long. In January 1978, with only Chavis remaining in prison, Hunt announced a reduction of all the sentences by about a third. He refused to extend pardons. Chavis was soon afterward paroled.

In addition to the episodes discussed above, a long and bitter labor dispute at the J. P. Stevens Company's textile mill in Roanoke Rapids, dramatized in the film *Norma Rae*, brought still more unwelcome publicity to bear on the civil rights of minorities in North Carolina. Periodic revelations of wretched conditions at migrant labor camps, crowded and inhumane prison conditions, racial issues such as those surrounding the conviction of the "Charlotte 3," and other incidents further damaged North Carolina's deteriorating image. In 1978, Michael Myerson's book, *Nothing Could Be Finer*, unfolded a lurid catalog of the state's real and alleged violations of civil rights and liberties of its citizens during the twentieth century. The volume provided what amounted to an epitaph for V. O. Key's favorable assessment of thirty years earlier.

Analysts have not yet adequately accounted for the extreme change in the public image of North Carolina's civil rights stature. It is sometimes contended that Key was simply mistaken in 1949, that North Carolina had no just claim to the progressive and moderate traits with which she was credited in the area of race relations and social issues. The events described here indicate, however, the existence of a darker civil rights mood in the state after 1950 than before. That two of the most reactionary voices in the national Senate in 1983 were those of Senators Jesse Helms and John East of North Carolina may be taken as confirmation of an important shift in public sentiment with respect to a range of ideological issues, including civil rights.

Those who acknowledge such a shift sometimes argue that this state, unlike such others as Mississippi and Alabama, avoided a wrenching push into the twentieth century by the federal government in the 1950s and 1960s and so fell behind in its response to rapidly changing social and civil rights attitudes. The intimate association of government and business leaders in North Carolina is often credited with both a forward-looking economic spirit and a hidebound social outlook. In civil rights matters, V. O. Key's "progressive plutocracy" is held to be more of an oppressive oligarchy. (Document 18.11)

At the same time, it seems clear that the post-1950 shift in attitudes has been neither so strong nor so festering as it is sometimes portrayed in state and national media. A widely circulated story of the 1960s and 1970s, for example, repeated on the popular television show M*A*S*H, was that Dr. Charles Drew, black developer of the blood bank system, bled to death in 1950 when he was refused treatment at an Alamance County hospital following an automobile accident. The eyewitness testimony of another black physician in 1982 established that Dr. Drew received two hours of emergency treatment at the hospital before his death.

A tone of malice toward North Carolina's criminal court system has also attended commentary on the Joan Little case, in which a young black woman was tried and acquitted in the 1974 slaying of her jailer in Beaufort County. Efforts to relate North Carolina's civil rights climate to a shoot-out between communists and Ku Klux Klansmen in Greensboro in 1979 have often seemed disingenuous.

Many of North Carolina's image problems in the third quarter of the twentieth century have originated in criticism of the workings of the state's system of criminal justice. A 1975 study by Oliver Williams and Richard J. Richardson concluded that "throughout the judicial process, the data are so patterned as to suggest that elites formulate and apply policies which result, more often than not, in harshness for the average black defendant in comparison to the average white defendant." An analysis of data for the year 1979 by the North Carolina Institute of Government showed that black felons received 6 percent longer maximum sentences and 27 percent longer minimum sentences than white felons.

By the decade of the 1980s, North Carolina's image seemed to have recovered largely from the depths into which it sank in the years from 1960 to 1978. That the title "Miss North Carolina" was won by a black contestant in 1983 may have surprised many who recalled the most publicized incidents of earlier years. In the retrospect of the mid-1980s the case of the Wilmington 10 appeared to represent the climax of the series of events that generated so much bad publicity for North Carolina. Stung by that publicity, many Tar Heels had resolved to try to rehabilitate not only the image but the reality of their state and their efforts seemed to be succeeding.

DOCUMENT 18.1

Governor Aycock's Speech before the North Carolina Society, Baltimore, 18 December 1903

I am proud of my State, moreover, because there we have solved the negro problem. . . . We have taken him out of politics and have thereby secured good government under any party and laid foundations for the future development of both races. We have secured peace, and rendered prosperity a certainty.

I am inclined to give to you our solution of this problem. It is, first, as far as possible under the Fifteenth Amendment to disfranchise him; after that let him alone, quit writing about him; quit talking about him, quit making him "the white man's burden," let him "tote his own skillet"; quit coddling him, let him learn that no man, no race, ever got anything worth the having that he did not himself earn; that character is the outcome of sacrifice and worth is the result of toil; that whatever his future may be, the present has in it for him nothing that is not the product of industry, thrift, obedience to law, and uprightness; that he cannot, by resolution of council or league, accomplish anything; that he can do much by work; that violence may gratify his passions but it cannot accomplish his ambitions; that he may eat rarely of the cooking of equality, but he will always find when he does that "there is death in the pot." Let the negro learn once for all that there is unending separation of the races . . . that they cannot intermingle; let the white man determine that no man shall by act or thought or speech cross this line, and the race problem will be at an end.

These things are not said in enmity to the negro but in regard for him. He constitutes one third of the population of my State: he has always been my personal friend; as a lawyer I have often defended him, and as Governor I have frequently protected him. But there flows in my veins the blood of the dominant race; that race that has conquered the earth and seeks out the mysteries of the heights and depths. If manifest destiny leads to the seizure of Panama, it is certain that it likewise leads to the dominance of the Caucasian. When the negro recognizes this fact we shall have peace and good will between the races.

R.D.W. Connor and Clarence Poe, The Life and Speeches of Charles Brantley Aycock *(N.p.: E. R. Blanton, [1912]), pp. 161–63.*

DOCUMENT 18.2

V. O. Key's Assessment of North Carolina in 1949

The prevailing mood in North Carolina is not hard to sense: it is energetic and ambitious. The citizens are determined and confident; they are on the move. The mood is at odds with much of the rest of the South—a tenor of attitude and of action that has set the state apart from its neighbors. Many see in North Carolina a closer approximation to national norms, or national expectations of performance, than they find elsewhere in the South. . . . It enjoys a reputation for progressive outlook and action in many phases of life, especially industrial development, education, and race relations. . . . The state has a reputation for fair dealings with its Negro citizens. . . . Nowhere has co-operation between white and Negro leadership been more effective.

V. O. Key, Southern Politics in State and Nation *(New York: Alfred A. Knopf, 1949), pp. 205–6.*

DOCUMENT 18.3

Gerald W. Johnson on the Junius Scales Case, 1961

Junius Scales, the North Carolina Communist, is now doing six years in a federal prison for violating the new Alien and Sedition Law, and one of his friends sends a letter asking support of a plea for executive clemency. Since I don't believe anybody should ever have gone to jail under that law, I am of course in favor of letting Scales out, but I doubt that he has a Chinaman's chance.

If the man had murdered somebody, there would always be the chance of convincing the public that the deceased ought to have been murdered, which would set up a strong demand for Scales' release. But he, like Thoreau, is in jail not for what he did, but for what he didn't do. He was convicted of not thinking the right thoughts back in 1954, and I, for one, am persuaded that he was guilty. Furthermore, I can imagine no way of proving that he is thinking the right thoughts now, so if it is lawful to send a man to jail for wrong thinking, Scales' friends have no case at all.

What happened was that Junius Scales, a sixth-generation native, white Protestant, of Anglo-Saxon ancestry—therefore a man with no organized friends at all,—shortly after he came of voting age swallowed the Communist rumble-bumble and held it down until 1956, when Khruschev's famous speech formally admitted that Stalin had been what sensible people had all along believed he was. This was too much for Scales and he renounced the doctrine, thereby incurring the venomous hatred of the Communist Party. . . . So in 1954 he was indicted under the Smith Act and in 1958 was convicted, although he had then been out of the party for two years.

The government offered no evidence that he had advocated over-throwing the government by force and violence, and certainly he must have made no effort to do so. But it was charged that he knew the Communist Party was dedicated to violence against the government, therefore he must have approved the policy—he thought well of it, even though he did nothing about it. That was thinking wrong thoughts, so he got six years—a heavier penalty than was imposed on any other violator of the Smith Act, even those who stayed in the party after Khruschev's revelations. . . .

I wish that Scales were out of jail, not on his account, for I never laid eyes on the man, but because it seems to me that every day he stays there is a new proclamation that it is criminal to think that "whenever any Form of Government becomes destructive of these ends (life, liberty and the pursuit of happiness), it is the Right of the People to alter or to abolish it." Those words were in the document that created the United States of America.

From the New Republic, *as reprinted in the*
Raleigh News and Observer, *19 November 1961.*

DOCUMENT 18.4

Resolution of the North Carolina House of Representatives in Regard to *Brown* v. *Board of Education*

Whereas, the General Assembly of North Carolina recognizes its allegiance to the Constitution and Government of the United States and is ever mindful of its responsibility to defend the Constitution of the United

States against every attempt, foreign or domestic, to undermine the dual structure of this Union or to destroy those fundamental principles embodied in the written Constitution of the United States; and

Whereas, the founders of this great nation, fearful of the tyranny that naturally and always follows the unrestricted concentration of governmental power, secured the passage of the "Bill of Rights," consisting of the first ten amendments to the Constitution; and

Whereas, the Ninth and Tenth Amendments to the Constitution expressly and explicitly limit the Federal government to specific powers delegated to it by the terms of the Constitution and reserved to the States and their people all other powers, unless specifically prohibited by it to the States; and . . .

Whereas the methods and procedures for amending the Constitution of the United States are distinctly and plainly stated in Article V of that instrument in these words: "The congress, whenever two-thirds of both houses shall deem it necessary, shall propose amendments to this constitution, or, on the application of the legislatures of two-thirds of the several states, shall call a convention for proposing amendments, which, in either case, shall be valid to all intents and purposes, as part of this constitution, when ratified by the legislatures of three-fourths of the several states, or by conventions in three-fourths thereof, as the one or the other mode of ratification may be proposed by the congress;" and

Whereas, the Constitution of the United States may be validly amended only in the manner prescribed by the Constitution itself, and the United States Supreme Court has never had, does not now have, and should never possess, the power and authority to amend the Constitution; and . . .

Whereas, by its decision of May 17, 1954, the Supreme Court of the United States, in effect amended the Constitution by interpreting the Fourteenth Amendment in a manner clearly contrary to the well-settled construction of that Amendment; and . . .

Whereas, the General Assembly of North Carolina, mindful that powers assumed by the Supreme Court in one field today will become precedents for further assumption of power in other fields tomorrow and recognizing, as did the founders of this great nation, that tyranny naturally and always follows naked power, . . . NOW THEREFORE,

Be it resolved by the House of Representatives, the Senate concurring:

Section 1. That the United States have never granted to the United States courts, or any one of them, the power to amend the Federal Constitution, nor does the Federal Government possess any powers not delegated to it by the Constitution of the United States.

Section 2. That the disregard for established law on the part of the United States Supreme Court constitutes an unauthorized assumption of the power of the Congress and the rights of the States and the people, and a grave threat to constitutional government in these United States. . . .

Section 4. That the State of North Carolina does call upon all States and the Congress of the United States to bring to an end this unauthorized assumption of power by the United States Supreme Court and to prevent now and in the future other and further encroachments upon the reserved powers of the States and the rights of the people, to the end that constitutional government shall be preserved.

H.B. No. 15, Special Session 1956: A Joint Resolution of Concern Relating to the Assumption of Undelegated Power by the Supreme Court of the United States.

DOCUMENT 18.5

Education Expense Grants under the "Pearsall Plan"

The General Assembly of North Carolina do enact:
    Section 1. Article IX of the Constitution of North Carolina is hereby amended by adding a section which shall read as follows:
    "Education expense grants.—Notwithstanding any other provision of this Constitution, the General Assembly may provide for payment of education expense grants from any State or local public funds for the private education of any child for whom no public school is available or for the private education of a child who is assigned against the wishes of his parent or guardian to a public school attended by a child of another race. A grant shall be available only for education in a nonsectarian school, and in the case of a child assigned to a public school attended by a child of another race, a grant shall, in addition, be available only when it is not reasonable and practicable to reassign such child to a private school not attended by a child of another race."

H.B. No. 11, Special Session 1956: A Bill to be Entitled an Act to Amend Article IX of the Constitution of North Carolina so as to Authorize Education Expense Grants.

DOCUMENT 18.6

Statement by the A. and T. College Sit-in Protestors at Greensboro, February 1960

The demonstrations at the lunch counters were inspired by the desire to make known, in peaceable fashion, the fact that we are suffering a moral wrong.

Results have been twofold:

1. We have found that the law of our community and of our state does not prohibit a continuation of these conditions, yet does disapprove the method used to publicize it.

2. Our purpose of calling the attention of intelligence and goodwill to our plight has been accomplished with encouraging response.

We hope now that we can attain our goal through the peaceful channels of negotiations.

We realize that an atmosphere of ultimatum has been created, and that this is not the best condition under which favorable progress can be made.

As rational, thinking individuals, we are willing to give consideration and cooperation to those elements that are willing to turn the wheels of progress.

Our case, then, is before the reasonable local bar of public opinion, and we solicit its judgment.

Greensboro Daily News, *21 February 1960.*

DOCUMENT 18.7

The North Carolina Supreme Court on Segregated Lunch Counters, 1960

Per Curiam. McCrory-McLellan Stores (called McLellan) operated a mercantile establishment on Fayetteville Street in Raleigh where it offered for sale to the public a general line of merchandise. In this store it set apart an area for lunch counter service. This area was enclosed by a fence. McLellan pursued the policy of restricting its lunch counter service to its employees and its white patrons. This fact was known to defendants, who are Negroes. To test the right of an operator of a private mercantile establishment to select the customers he will serve in any particular portion of the store, defendants seated themselves at the lunch counter and demanded service. . . . Despite repeated requests to leave the enclosed area, they remained and persisted in their demand for services until arrested by city police and charged with violating G.S. 14-134, the trespass statute.

Defendants contend a merchant who sells his wares to one must serve all, and a refusal to do so is a violation of the rights guaranteed by the Fourteenth Amendment to the Constitution of the United States. The contention lacks merit. The operator of a private mercantile establishment has a right to select his customers, serve those he selects, and refuse service to others. The reasons which prompt him to choose do not circumscribe his right. . . .

Since defendants had no constitutional right to remain on private property over the protest of the lawful occupant, it follows that the refusal to leave when requested was a violation of the statute.

State *v.* James A. Fox and Albert Sampson, *North Carolina Supreme Court Reports, Fall Term 1960, 254 N.C. 98–99.*

DOCUMENT 18.8

Governor Sanford's Response to Robert F. Williams and the Monroe "Kidnapping"

It is well known that North Carolina had no trouble from people who seek their goals through legitimate means. It is also well known that this State will not tolerate violence from anybody for any purpose.

The band of agitators who have descended on Monroe came at the request of an outspoken advocate of violence, a self-styled "Castro" who has attempted to grow a beard, who wears a beret, and carries a loaded carbine. It is significant that he has been denounced by the respected leadership of both races.

Mayor Fred Wilson, the Sheriff, the Chief of Police and the people of Monroe and Union County have acted with utmost restraint. I can easily understand that their patience is being sorely tried.

The local enforcement officers, the State Highway Patrol and the State Bureau of Investigation are on the job.

The situation is under control and is going to be kept under control.

We are not going to allow outside agitators to promote violence in our State. We are going to put an end to it immediately.

Statement by Governor Terry Sanford, 28 August 1961, Clipping File, North Carolina Collection, University of North Carolina, Chapel Hill.

DOCUMENT 18.9

An Assessment of the Civil Rights Situation in North Carolina, 1963

As we draw to the close of this "summer of discontent" of 1963, it might be well for the people of North Carolina to take a fresh look at the subject of civil rights in our state to determine how far we have gone in a realization of our goal of equal rights and equal opportunities for all and how far we have yet to go.

Most of us in North Carolina are proud of the fact that our state is looked upon as one of the more enlightened states in the Union and that it is a state where more genuine progress has been made in working out solutions to the difficult problems of race relations than any other state in the South. We are constrained to believe that this is due in part to a genuine love for liberty which the people of this state have and a realization of the fact that if there is to be freedom at all, there must be freedom for all.

North Carolina has no cause to be ashamed of its present record concerning the right of all qualified adults to vote in free elections. This has not always been the case but today any qualified person irrespective of his color can register and vote if he is willing to make the effort to do so.

The privileges of education have been extended to all of our people. Even the restraints and handicaps which some feel go with a segregated school system are beginning to melt away for as this paper is being written many hundreds of Negro children are being admitted to formerly all-white schools in North Carolina. The prospect is that before many years have passed, such segregation in schools as will continue to exist will result from residential situations rather than from a predetermined design to keep the races separate in the schools.

The right of all of our citizens to obtain equal employment opportunities must depend primarily not upon the law itself but upon the willingness of the people who employ labor to give job opportunities to those who are best qualified irrespective of race. Because of long-standing custom and tradition, it will be many years before this goal is fully attained.

Concerning the right to a fair trial, I feel that we have practically attained that goal and that our courts will continue to mete out justice without fear or favor and without prejudice or bias.

One of the most difficult problems confronting us at this time is how we shall come to a solution of the demand of non-white people to receive equal service and consideration in those businesses and establishments which heretofore have maintained a segregated system. The difficulty here arises out of the long-prevailing custom in the South which discourages social contact between the races such as meeting and eating together. However, it may be that the ultimate answer to this problem has been discovered by the Chamber of Commerce of the City of Charlotte, which has called upon its members to abandon all segregation practices in those businesses which appeal to public patronage. It is probable that the members of the Charlotte Chamber of Commerce were actuated more by economic and moral considerations than by legal requirements in coming to this conclusion, although the City Council of Charlotte was probably more impressed with the legal futility of maintaining a segregated system when it recently repealed all of the segregation ordinances of the Charlotte City Code.

In any event, the people of North Carolina are determined as a whole to meet the problems of this changing order through which we are now passing with calmness and with determination to the end that we may find just and lasting solutions to the problems which arise when persons of different ethnic origins must live and labor together.

Paul R. Ervin, "Civil Rights in North Carolina," in George C. Cochran, ed., Civil Rights and the South: A Symposium, *reprinted from* North Carolina Law Review 42 *(1963):48–49.*

DOCUMENT 18.10

The Speaker Ban Law, 1963

No college or university which receives any state funds in support thereof shall permit any person to use the facilities of such college or university for speaking purposes who, (1) is a known member of the Communist Party, (2) is known to advocate the overthrow of the Constitution of the United States or the State of North Carolina, (3) has pleaded the fifth amendment of the Constitution in refusing to answer any question with respect to subversive connections, or activities, before any duly constituted legislative committee, any judicial tribunal, or any executive or administrative board of the United States or any state.

H.B. 1395, 1963 Session: A Bill to be Entitled an Act to Regulate Visiting Speakers at State Supported Colleges and Universities.

DOCUMENT 18.11

The Progressive Myth of Bass and DeVries, 1976

The progressive image the state projected in the late 1940s has evolved into a progressive myth that remains accepted as fact by much of the state's native leadership, despite ample evidence to the contrary. Although North Carolina has changed with the times, it is perhaps the least changed of the old Confederate states. Because of its moderation, it yielded more easily to the forces of change, but it missed the dynamic reaction to resistance that so swiftly transformed political and social development elsewhere in the South. Nor has it experienced the impact of urbanization as much as most other border South states have.

When Key wrote, the race issue was still suppressed in North Carolina as it had been for 50 years through a process in which men of some distinction ran against each other "within the accepted framework," an unspoken code which barred the arousal of racial antagonisms. The Negro was given a degree of paternalistic protection and allowed marginal political participation. But once political appeals on race were released in the 1950 U.S. Senate race against Frank Porter Graham, they proved a powerful force, and the progressive momentum slowed. . . .

Key's description of North Carolina as a "progressive plutocracy" was an apt one in the late 1940s. But when one compares indices of economic development, the level of participation and modernization of the political process, the relative neglect of long-standing social problems, the controlling oligarchy's perpetuation of "no-growth-if-it-hurts-us," two decades of a congressional delegation among the most conservative in the South, and the emergence of race as a significant political issue, what remains is a political plutocracy that lives with a progressive myth.

Jack Bass and Walter DeVries, The Transformation of Southern Politics: Social Change and Political Consequence since 1945 *(New York: Basic Books, Inc., 1976), pp. 219, 247.*

SUGGESTED READINGS

Ashby, Warren. *Frank Porter Graham: A Southern Liberal.* Winston-Salem, N.C.: John F. Blair, 1980.

Bardolph, Richard. *The Civil Rights Record: Black Americans and the Law, 1849–1970.* New York: Thomas Y. Crowell Co., 1970.

Bass, Jack, and DeVries, Walter. *The Transformation of Southern Politics: Social Change and Political Consequence since 1945.* New York: Basic Books, Inc., 1976.

Beyle, Thad L., and Black, Merle, eds. *Politics and Policy in North Carolina.* New York: MSS Information Corp., 1975.

Chafe, William H. *Civilities and Civil Rights: Greensboro, North Carolina, and the Black Struggle for Freedom.* New York: Oxford University Press, 1980.

Herzik, Eric B., and Teater, Sallye Branch, comps. *North Carolina Focus.* Zebulon, N.C.: Printed by Theo. Davis Sons, Inc., for the North Carolina Center for Public Policy Research, Inc., 1981.

Key, V. O. *Southern Politics in State and Nation.* New York: Alfred A. Knopf, 1949.

Lefler, Hugh T. *North Carolina History as Told by Contemporaries.* Chapel Hill: University of North Carolina Press, 1965.

Myerson, Michael. *Nothing Could be Finer.* New York: International Publishers, 1978.

North Carolina Advisory Committee, U.S. Commission on Civil Rights. *Equal Protection of the Laws in North Carolina.* Washington, D.C.: U.S. Government Printing Office, 1962.

CHAPTER 19

The Status of Women in North Carolina

Jane DeHart Mathews

North Carolina Suffragettes (Courtesy of the Division of Archives and History, Raleigh, N.C.)

In 1963, when Governor Terry Sanford appointed a commission to study the status of women in North Carolina, he, along with the governors of other states, tacitly acknowledged that the position of women in America has been different because their history has been different. The differing historical experience of men and women is the product of many factors. Biology, of course, is one, for until the twentieth century, when the widespread use of reliable contraceptive devices provided some measure of reproductive control, most women faced a short life expectancy and spent their entire adult lives bearing, rearing, and frequently burying children while working within the confines of home and, often, farm. Differences deriving from biology, moreover, were compounded and reinforced by other factors: inferior legal and political status, restricted educational and occupational opportunity, and cultural constraints. The latter constraints defined woman's proper place as the home and her appropriate mode of behavior as a blend of religious piety, sexual purity, and marital submissiveness. This ideal, with its origins in the nineteenth century, persisted well into the twentieth century. In the South, especially, there lingered chivalric notions about the exalted virtues of womanhood and the beneficent paternalism of manhood, which obscured even more fundamental inequalities between the sexes. The result has been not only a different history but a different status, more particularly an inferior status—a point made by the North Carolina Federation of Women's Clubs in 1914 in its report, *The Legal Status of Women in North Carolina*.

Efforts of groups such as the women's clubs to improve the position of women were part of a long and difficult quest for sexual equality punctuated at intervals by activists seeking the right of every woman to participate fully in all aspects of American life. North Carolinians were not part of the antebellum feminist movement, linked as it was with abolitionism. Turn-of-the-century activists, however, seeking new opportunities outside the home and finally the vote, were participants in a multifaceted woman's movement, which in the two decades before 1920 flourished especially as part of a broad trend toward improvement in the condition of women not only in the United States but in Europe as well. Similarly, their contemporary counterparts who recently worked in North Carolina for such measures as ratification of the Equal Rights Amendment are part of a revived feminist movement generated nationally by struggles for racial equality and social justice in the 1960s as well as by prior decades of change that eroded traditional patterns.

As important as these organized movements on behalf of female equality were, they are nonetheless only part of the story. Also part of the struggle were the private battles waged by talented, highly motivated women determined to surmount sex-related barriers in order to fulfill their full potential not only as women but as practicing professionals in such traditionally male fields as law and medicine. So, too, were the efforts of less prominent individuals, who as women and as wage workers fought for economic survival for themselves and their families with little awareness that their struggle—even when it involved public activity such as unionization—had anything to do with such concepts as women's status and women's rights.

Probing the origins of women's unequal legal and political status during the first two hundred years of our history requires returning to the seventeenth century, for English tradition and practice in both law and politics profoundly affected a royal colony and state such as North Carolina. English common law incorporated into North Carolina statutes deprived a woman upon marriage of many legal rights she had formerly enjoyed. She lost to her husband, unless there were certain technical exceptions used only by the very wealthy, her land and all other financial assets including any wages she might earn; she even forfeited her personal property. Thus with the single exception of her wedding apparel, everything she currently owned and any assets she acquired in the future were his to dispose of as he saw fit even if he chose to squander those assets. Civil rights as well as property rights were affected. A married woman was denied the right to make a binding contract except in certain rare situations—a right that was often necessary if she wished to go into business. Similarly, she had no right to sue and recover damages for bodily harm, slander, or libel. Legally, a wife's wealth was not hers but her husband's; her body was then his body, her name his name, so that any compensation for injuries to her went to him.

For a married man, acquisition of those rights also entailed certain legal responsibilities including that of supporting his wife and children. He also bore some responsibility for her behavior, as evidenced by a law on the statute books as late as 1864, which permitted a husband to "use toward his wife such degree of force as is necessary to control an unruly temper and make her behave herself." In the frontier society that was colonial North Carolina laws might be ignored. Inasmuch as a wife was considered in so many respects her husband's property, however, women in the nineteenth century as well as in the seventeenth might count themselves fortunate if wed to a kind man and a good provider. Those less fortunate had few options in an age when divorces, even for the very wealthy, were difficult to obtain. Antebellum newspapers carried notices of rewards for return of runaway wives as well as runaway slaves.

Legal status also affected political status. The right to participate in the activities of the state by serving on juries, holding office, and voting was, according to Anglo-American tradition, dependent on the holding of property. Because women were denied property rights unless single or widowed, it seemed to follow that they could not be jurors, office-holders, or voters. Although the American Revolution did much to rede-fine the relationship of men to the state, it did little to change the rela-tionship of women, despite the many contributions to independence by patriot women such as the ladies of Edenton with their famous tea party. Female support of the new nation came not through the exercise of the franchise but through the exercise of maternal influence. Republican mothers reared republican sons—youngsters trained to assume the re-sponsibilities of citizenship in a manner that would sustain the experi-ment in republican government. Although a few northern feminists be-gan agitating for the vote in the decade before the Civil War, southern patriarchs were eager to keep such radical and subversive notions out of the Cotton Kingdom—and even the backwoods of North Carolina.

Reiterating dominant cultural assumptions about the different spheres occupied by the two sexes, a writer for the *Raleigh Register* in 1850 predicted dire consequences should the female with her purer, more deli-cate spirit forsake the refinement and protection of home for the brutish-ness of the polling place. "Woman's sphere," he wrote, "is about the domestic altar and within the tranquil precincts of the social circle. When she transgresses that sphere and mingles in the miserable brawl-ings and insane agitations of the day, she descends from her lofty eleva-tion and becomes the object of disgust and contempt." There was, to be sure, a mythic quality about such rhetoric. Panegyrics on the tranquillity of the domestic sphere, the delicacy of southern womanhood, and the unbounded joys and sacred duties associated with motherhood hardly described the harsh realities of life for many women, who knew the rigors of field work as well as housework and, as was the case for the blacks among them, the further pain of the auction block and of children sold. But myths, even when they fail in many respects to correspond to reality, can still be powerful. Thus deeply held beliefs, especially about woman's nature and place, not only rationalized inequities in political status but also shaped partially the educational and occupational oppor-tunities available.

Educational opportunities for both sexes were meager indeed during most of North Carolina's history. By the revolutionary era, several free schools had been established, but in the towns where they did exist, they offered little more than the three Rs with students attending only a few months or, at most, two years. Young men from prosperous families might then be sent to one of the state's few academies, where they were introduced to the classics, mathematics, history, philosophy, and logic— subjects considered essential to a liberal education. The wealthy few might even continue on to one of the northern colleges, usually Prince-ton, or to England. Their sisters, however, were less fortunate. Most stayed home, their education ended except for the housewifely skills taught by their mothers. The small number who were sent to a boarding school in the North or in nearby Charles Town received only the training necessary to "finish" a young lady by providing her with the accomplishments necessary to acquire a suitable husband: a smattering of history, literature, and perhaps geography, lessons in music and drawing, as well as instruction in penmanship and the use of the needle. A classical education such as was offered to young men was considered not only too intellectually rigorous for the female brain and nervous system, but, if vigorously pursued, capable of "desexing" young females, thereby making them unfit for their primary roles as wives and mothers.

Such assumptions decisively shaped the educational opportunities available to women in the state in the decades following the Revolution. The University of North Carolina, established at Chapel Hill in 1795, welcomed young ladies to dances but not to classes. Denominational schools devoted exclusively to female education gradually emerged, beginning with the founding of Salem Academy by the Moravians in 1802, though the girls' school in Salem dated from 1772. St. Mary's, an Episcopal school in Raleigh, was established in 1842, followed by Greensboro Female College (Methodist, 1846), Peace Institute (Presbyterian, 1872), and the Baptist University for Women (1899)—now Meredith College.

Generally these schools, like many elsewhere, saw their primary goal as producing a well-rounded female character rather than a well-trained mind capable of engaging in the same intellectual and vocational pursuits followed by men. Graduates were praised as women of culture and refinement, who presided as "queens" over their Christian homes from which radiated "pure and bright light." Some institutions, however—Solomon Leas's Somerville Institute in Leasburg (1847) and Greensboro College in the 1840s—offered young women a full classical curriculum that included modern languages, mathematics, and the sciences.

Although the usual idealization of the home as woman's proper place was especially characteristic of the nineteenth century, when middle-class women were expected to devote themselves to motherhood and the nurture of children, the home was also a place of work. Throughout much of the state's history, women's work meant attending to house, garden, dairy, and poultry coop. When the need arose, it meant laboring in the fields or shop or, in the case of illness, childbirth, or death, serving as nurse, pharmacist, midwife, and undertaker (dressing the body for burial). Although widows might be found in the public sphere, having taken over their husbands' businesses or farms, the emphasis in the nineteenth century on domesticity and the simultaneous professionalization of medicine and law, combined with the exclusion of women from the university's professional schools, meant that economically, as well as legally and politically, women were denied rights and opportunities enjoyed by men. By the turn of the century, however, there were signs of change.

The slow process of legal change began in 1864, when married women were granted control of their own property with the proviso that they secure in writing their husband's assent before selling any of it—a stipulation not removed until 1964. Protection from physical abuse began with an 1874 court decision repudiating the husband's right to whip his wife with a "switch no thicker than his thumb." But it was another fifty years before she was permitted to sue him for physical injuries, keeping any money awarded as damages. Legislation in 1911 allowing married women to make contracts not only began the restoration of civil rights to married women but also made it possible for them to enter the business world. With the simultaneous crumbling of educational barriers around the turn of the century, new opportunities emerged both for further intellectual advancement and for employment options. In Durham, Trinity College, now Duke University, allowed female undergraduates to join males, studying in all departments under the same faculty; in nearby Chapel Hill, they were permitted to enroll for the junior and senior years, staying on, should they choose, for postgraduate work in a variety of fields including law, medicine, and pharmacy.

Most women, if they trained for work outside the home, chose careers as teachers, librarians, nurses, and secretaries because those jobs were considered most "appropriate" for their sex. Professional nursing, once deemed a vocation no respectable woman would enter, was believed to be especially suited to females because, as a Raleigh newspaper observed, Providence was thought to have endowed the fairer sex with the necessary compassion and patience to attend the sick. The instruction of small children was also considered ideal work for a young woman, who would presumably marry after a few years in the classroom and thenceforth devote herself exclusively to her own family. Indeed, because of the large number of needy females of "good birth" and a "pleasing," docile manner who would willingly accept teaching jobs for a fraction of the salary required to hire their male counterparts, teaching was transformed into an almost exclusively female profession throughout the nation and especially in the impoverished South. In this state, many such women flocked to the new Normal and Industrial College (now the University of North Carolina at Greensboro), whose graduates, within only a decade after its establishment by the legislature in 1891, were said to be teaching one-tenth of the white children in the state. (Document 19.1)

Most women working outside the home found job training not in the university or a college or even in a business school but in mills and factories. The growth of the textile industry throughout the piedmont brought entire families off the farm and into the mill, where women and children became part of the paid labor force. But although wives might work alongside husbands in the noisy, dusty, lint-filled atmosphere of the mills, jobs were segregated by sex and those assigned to women invariably carried lower wages. Wherever they worked, women in North Carolina, like their counterparts throughout an industrializing, urbanizing America, were becoming a force for change. (Document 19.2)

They were also participants in a process by which thousands emerged from the passivity, submissiveness, and domestic isolation of the middle-class Victorian home into a life of public activism that ultimately transformed the most energetic and able into politically astute suffragists committed to women's rights. To be sure, the good ladies who joined missionary societies or the Women's Christian Temperance Union did not think of themselves as a potential vanguard. Church work was, after all, an especially appropriate activity for women because they were thought by their very nature to be more pious and morally sensitive than men. Even those joining the newly organized women's clubs found it only natural that, as the sex deemed responsible for the home, they should extend their housekeeping duties to the public sphere, seeing to it that municipal ordinances providing for garbage pickup were passed, trash cans placed along the streets, sanitary drinking fountains substituted for the common cup, and playgrounds established and safely equipped. Such actions benefited both the community and the women themselves. By going to meetings, passing resolutions, appointing committees to speak with public officials, and creating agencies concerned with public issues, women acquired skills and confidence as well as a strong sense of female solidarity. Acting in ways ostensibly consistent with their traditional roles, they were not merely enlarging old roles but creating a new public one. As they did so, these "New Women," as they were called, began to discover the frustrations of second-class citizenship.

The experience of the Teachers' Assembly and the Women's Association for the Betterment of Public Schools in North Carolina was a case in point. As members moved from efforts to improve schools in their own localities to efforts to enlighten legislators about the overwhelming educational needs of the entire state, they confronted certain critical questions. Did education suffer because it was associated with women instead of men? Are we "teachers or only females," asked Edith Royster of a Teachers' Assembly in 1912. The question reflected the struggles of this enormously talented educator and her allies to change laws that kept women from serving on school committees, boards of trustees, and county boards of education, as well as commissions to select texts. It also reflected a growing feminist consciousness. Getting things done, whether in education, health, or welfare, was difficult at best; but when those engaged in the doing were regarded as "only females," the problems were compounded. Grasping the full implications of their inferior status, many of North Carolina's female activists, like their counterparts in other states, were on their way to becoming suffragists.

In May 1913, when Chief Justice Walter Clark addressed the North Carolina Federation of Women's Clubs on the legal status of the state's women, he made a forthright appeal for suffrage. Only when women voted and held office could they create a political constituency to help them improve their status both domestically and economically. Seven months later female activists and their male supporters met in Charlotte to form a state equal suffrage association. Using a network of groups such as the women's clubs, talented organizers such as Gertrude Weil of Goldsboro would, over the next few years, build a pro-suffrage constituency while other suffragist leaders lobbied legislators and publicized their cause. But in spite of the efforts of very able women and the support of influential men such as ·Clark and Josephus Daniels, publisher of the *Raleigh News and Observer* and secretary of the navy, it was an uphill fight. Women themselves were divided, some indifferent, others opposed. Male legislators, who in 1897 had referred a woman suffrage bill to the Committee on Insane Asylums, greeted a 1915 bill with the same blend of condescension, ridicule, and hostility. The level of debate, said Senator F. P. Hobgood, left him convinced that North Carolina was not just conservative, but "backward." The General Assembly's rejection of municipal suffrage in 1917 did little to change his mind.

With the outbreak of World War I, North Carolina suffragists continued their mobilization, believing that women's enormous contribution to the war effort would force lawmakers to reconsider. Although President Woodrow Wilson and Congress did indeed relent, granting women the franchise with the passage of the Nineteenth Amendment, North Carolina legislators did not. Turning back a suffrage bill in 1919 despite growing evidence of pro-suffrage sentiment, the General Assembly met in special session in 1920. Antisuffrage arguments that ratification would threaten the family, states rights, white supremacy, and those who then held power carried the day. The House not only refused to ratify, but even after Tennessee's approval made the amendment part of the Constitution, a majority refused by a vote of 71 to 41 to support a resolution ratifying a fait accompli. It was a defeat not only for North Carolina suffragists but for progressive forces in the state as well.

Despite the recalcitrance of the General Assembly, 1920 seemed to usher in an era of new options for women. For those women able to move into traditionally male domains, proving that they were indeed "the best man for the job," the challenges and rewards of professional and public life were there to be enjoyed as barriers to females continued to crumble. Three women—Ellen Winston, Susie Sharp, and Juanita Kreps—enjoyed just such careers. Winston, after working in Washington as part of Roosevelt's New Deal, was named commissioner of public welfare for North Carolina in 1944. Later appointed commissioner of public welfare in the U.S. Department of Welfare in 1963, she extended her work abroad under the auspices of the United Nations before retiring. Susie Sharp became the first woman superior court judge in North Carolina (1949), the first woman to serve on the state supreme court (1962), and the first elected woman chief justice (1974) of any state's supreme court in the nation's history. Kreps came to Duke University from Kentucky to obtain a Ph.D. in economics. Staying on at Duke to teach and write, by 1977 she was vice-president of the university and, when President Carter named her secretary of commerce that year, she became the fourth woman to fill a cabinet post in the nation's history.

For most women, however talented and well educated, the prospect of combining a high-level business or professional career with family responsibilities seemed overwhelming, especially in a society that regarded parenting as a full-time occupation for the mother. In North Carolina, as elsewhere, most middle-class women, especially those who were white, chose a different option. Forgoing the demands of regular paid employment, they devoted themselves instead to family, church, and community responsibilities, working often in voluntary organizations engaged in projects traditionally related to women's interests. Thus thousands of women across the state worked through local Parent-Teacher Association (PTA) groups for expanded school libraries, adequate food, clothing, and health care for needy children, better pay for teachers, and a variety of other improvements in the public schools. Members of the North Carolina Federation of Women's Clubs and of the Junior League also devoted countless hours to child welfare and other deserving causes. Women affiliated with local garden clubs concentrated on the beautification of public spaces across the state, and those interested in the arts worked on behalf of the state's symphony, museums, and local arts organizations. Members of local chapters of the League of Women Voters concentrated on local and state government, focusing not only on child-related issues such as schools, recreation, and juvenile justice but also on issues such as legislative apportionment, taxation, and urban renewal.

Black women, though on the whole less affluent and less educated than their white counterparts, were more dedicated, working within their own communities in local units of the state Congress of Colored Parents and Teachers, the Federation of Colored Women's Clubs, and the National Association of Colored Women. Few clubwomen, black or white, were more remarkable than Charlotte Hawkins Brown. Born in Henderson in 1882, Brown moved to Boston with her mother. Befriended by the president of Wellesley College, she took courses there and at Harvard before returning to North Carolina, where in 1904 she founded Palmer Memorial Institute for the education of black women in the little town of Sedalia in Guilford County. A suffragist, a pioneer in interracial work among clubwomen, the founder of this state's Home for Delinquent Colored Girls, an ardent spokesperson for the creation of an interracial women's campaign against lynching, and, in World War II, a consultant to the secretary of war, Brown was chosen as an American delegate to the International Congress of Women in 1946. Although Charlotte Hawkins Brown's talent and commitment were exceptional, the efforts of clubwomen of both races significantly improved the quality of life of the people in this state. Moreover, women themselves, especially the leaders among them, acquired skills and knowledge of how various institutions in the state worked, which some would subsequently devote to efforts to improve the status of that one-half of the people who happen to be female.

That women's status still needs improving nearly half a century after suffrage came as a surprise to many North Carolinians, including a good many women. But for those studying the 1969 report presented to Governor Sanford by the panel of experts (including Kreps and Winston) charged with investigating the matter, there could be no other conclusion.

Discrepancies in educational status were subtle and complex. Although adult women on the average had about a year more education than did men, women still comprised only a tiny fraction of the students enrolled in professional schools providing advanced training for doctors, lawyers, engineers, architects, and university professors. Whatever their educational level, most North Carolina women, the commission concluded, lacked access to diversified vocational training, enlightened career guidance, a role model provided by women holding important nontraditional jobs, or even the expectation of equal pay for equal work. Perhaps more important, those with small children lacked expert, readily available child care: licensed day-care facilities had only one space available for every seventeen preschool children of working mothers. Political status was also inferior in that women were far less likely to hold elective office or policy-making appointive jobs. Indeed, in 1960, the total number of women holding elective office—state, county, and local—was only 125. (Document 19.3)

Such reports, coinciding with other movements in the 1960s on behalf of equality and social justice, contributed nationally to an awareness of what those writing the North Carolina report called "the enormity of our problem." The result was the birth of a new feminist movement as former suffragists and women young enough to be their great-grand-daughters embarked on a new quest for equality, determined this time to change not only laws and institutions but values, mores, personal relationships, and ultimately themselves. As part of that quest, new feminist organizations such as the National Organization for Women (NOW) and the National Women's Political Caucus (NWPC) soon developed, generating state and local groups, especially in major urban areas. Whereas the NWPC focused on getting more women—especially feminists—into political office at every level of government, NOW and other groups concentrated initially on legal and institutional changes. Among other reforms they called on Congress to pass the Equal Rights Amendment (ERA). (Document 19.4) Although both NOW and the NWPC, as well as other feminist groups, were active in a few North Carolina cities in the early 1970s, the effort to ratify the ERA, more than any other issue, mobilized North Carolinians, especially women, in the struggle for female equality.

Ratified by many states immediately after congressional passage in 1972, the proposed Twenty-seventh Amendment would remove sex as a discriminatory classification in law, extend legal protection already provided one sex to both, and establish the principle—against the traditional bias of the common law—that women ought to be understood as individuals before the law rather than as representatives of a group. This last goal is especially important in view of changes wrought by technology in women's work over the past one hundred years. (Document 19.5)

Efforts to ratify the ERA were made at every session of the North Carolina General Assembly from 1973 until the deadline for ratification in 1982. Despite impressive support, the ERA was narrowly defeated by legislators, many of whom represented conservative, rural areas of the state and whose constituency with respect to this particular issue included the increasingly politically active fundamentalist churches. To understand why women themselves joined with these opponents of the ERA, it is important to recognize that in the course of ratification efforts, the amendment came increasingly to be seen as much more than a simple guarantee of equality under law. Indeed, it became a symbol—for supporters and opponents alike—of a feminist commitment to equality that seeks to remove not only legal forms of discrimination but also behavioral and attitudinal barriers associated with culturally defined notions about how men and women are supposed to think, feel, and act regardless of their individual needs and talents. This challenge to traditional sex roles was seen by some not as an effort to remove discrimination based solely on gender and to expand options for men and women alike but rather as a rejection of cherished norms and values—a way of life some women believed they had perfected. Thus efforts to ratify the ERA not only mobilized women against the amendment but also elicited arguments reminiscent of antisuffrage ideology, which claimed that the Nineteenth Amendment would destroy American institutions by weakening the family. (Document 19.6)

ERA supporters ultimately failed to make North Carolina one of the remaining three states whose approval was necessary for ratification. Nevertheless, the prolonged struggle for ratification in this state sensitized thousands of women to inequities of status, raised their organizational and political skills to new levels of sophistication and effectiveness, and heightened their commitment to new possibilities within their own lives as well as in the larger society. A decade of conflict over the amendment also stimulated legislators to revise discriminatory statutes and enact new laws to protect victims of domestic violence and to provide for more equitable distribution of property in the event of divorce—both measures of especial importance to women.

The debate over equal rights also prompted officials in state government to apply to themselves affirmative action measures designed to combat the effect of decades of discrimination and to seek new ways to improve the economic well-being of North Carolina's working women and their families. (Document 19.7) Although the gains of the 1970s and early 1980s have been encouraging, the forces of resistance to change are such that true equality between the sexes, as between the races, remains in North Carolina—as in America—a goal yet to be celebrated because it is still to be won.

DOCUMENT 19.1

"Reminiscences" of Mary Blanche Blackwell Smith

None of my people saw me graduate [from Greensboro Female College in 1890] for they were not able to go financially. My mother wrote she would pray for me and be with me in spirit at that time and I am sure I felt her presence. I went home and as I left the old college my trip was almost as sad going home as it was when I left. I knew there was no prospects for me in that neighborhood for I intented and had promised Dr. Dixon to teach school. The public schools in our district were a farce, only three months and only $30.00 per month for a first class teacher. . . .

I joined the Teachers Exchange of Raleigh, N.C. and soon got into communication with various schools. I wrote to Supt. J. E. Smith of the Mount Olive, N.C. Schools and inquired further into his proposition offered me. He wrote me and said he was very much impressed with my candor, handwriting, etc., and that he would like a photograph of myself. Of course I sent it and almost by return mail I was employed and urged to come as soon as possible. Before I left college I went down to Dr. Dixon's office and he talked to me like a father, I promised to teach and pay the balance of $250.00 which I owed the college and when this opportunity came, I was delighted for I felt that I could pay my debt. Without very much preparation I started to Mount Olive, N.C., alone to make a living for myself. My father took me through the country to Henderson so that I might take the train there. . . . He seemed very serious and sad as we rode along and my heart was just about breaking; for I always was a homebody. He took out $10.00 just before I got to the station and gave it to me. I knew that was all the ready money he had in the world and it hurt me to take it. He said: "Blanche, if you don't like it down there just write me and I'll get up the money someway to get you back," and I promised I'd write. It took $7.00 to pay my car fare and I only had the $3.00 left and was going into a new and strange community. . . . When the negro porter called out "All aboard for Mt. Olive" and then "let me have your valises ladies" I certainly hurried to give him mine among the first. He preceded me and when the conductor helped me get down the steps a fine looking young man like my Edwin, almost his double, stepped up to me and asked if I was not Miss Blackwell? He introduced himself as Prof. Smith and I was shocked for I thought the Principal of the school was an old gentleman with a beard and here a young man instead. . . .

Prof. Smith took me on a long trip about 40 miles, to Seven Springs, where the Mount Olive young people were putting on an entertainment play, "Ben Bolt." On that trip, about three weeks after my arrival, he declared his love for me (your's truly) and I told him that I cared for him but could not marry any one until I paid G.F.C. what I owed. I insisted on teaching until this was paid and then I would consider marriage. He insisted that he would help me pay my debt and that I must marry him in the vacation time that summer.

Mary Blanche Blackwell Smith's diaries are currently in the possession of her great-granddaughter, Cindy Lynn, who transcribed them as a student at Ohio University in 1977. The spelling conforms to the original typed script.

Union Women and the Hazards of Leadership: The Loray Mill Strike, Gastonia, 1929

Six Loray Workers and Truck Drivers are Held in Gaston Mob Murder

During recent anti-Communist disturbances in Gastonia, [Troy] Jones has been charged with threatening to dynamite union headquarters. He is the man who filed suit against the National Textile Workers of America for alienation of his wife's affection. His wife joined the organization and went north to take part in a fund-raising campaign.

Body of Victim of Mob is Buried in Bessemer City

"She was only making $9 a week," [A. W.] Williams, [secretary of the National Textile Workers Union] said, reciting the life history of the woman [Ella May Wiggins]. "On the money she made at the mill she had to support her five children. She joined the union and worked to better the conditions of working people. She was shot down without cause and has given her life to the betterment of . . . fellow workers."

(Song by Ella May Wiggins which was sung at her funeral)

We leave our home in the morning,
We kiss our children goodby,
While we slave for the bosses
Our children scream and cry.

And when we draw our money
Our grocery bills to pay,
Not a cent to spend for clothing
Not a cent to lay away.

And on that very evening,
Our little son will say:
"I need some shoes, dear mother,
And so does sister May".

How it grieves the heart of a mother,
You every one must know,
But we can't buy for our children,
Our wages are too low.

It is for our little children

That seems to us so dear,
But for us nor them, dear workers,
The bosses do not care.

But understand, all workers,
Our union, they do fear,
Let's stand together, workers,
And have a union here.

Ella May Wiggins Day: Woman Slain in Union Protest Honored (September 16, 1979)

A tribute to Ella May Wiggins and women textile workers Saturday drew 125 labor and women's rights activists to criticize low mill wages and sing labor songs inside the Bessemer City American Legion post.

For Mrs. Wiggins' three surviving children, the day was a reminder of the 50 bitter years since their mother, an outspoken 29 year-old textile worker and union organizer, was murdered during the violent Loray mill strike in Gastonia.

"You've got five children (two now dead) that grew up to be very bitter. We didn't know what a mother's love was," said Charlotte Payne, 50, of Roanoke, Va.

Mrs. Payne was one year old when her mother was shot while traveling to a union meeting. She spent her childhood in an orphanage along with four brothers and sisters, including brother Albert, now 54, and sister Millie Wandell, now 56.

Albert Wiggins, who lives in Gastonia, remembers seeing his dead mother in her coffin before her funeral. He was only 4 years old. His nerves have been fragile ever since, he said.

Mrs. Wandell, who was 6 when her mother died, remembers her mother telling her, "Always stick up for your rights because if you don't no one else will."

Mrs. Wandell, who now lives in Waverly, N.Y. said she refused to let her late husband, Merritt, join the union. "I didn't want to lose him like I lost my mamma," she said.

But she cannot stop some of her 12 children from joining picket lines. "It just tears me up. I can't stand it. I'm always expecting the worst."

At the close of Saturday's ceremony, a marble cross was unveiled at Mrs. Wiggins' grave in the Bessemer City Cemetery. The . . . [inscription] reads in part: "She was killed carrying the torch of social justice September 14, 1929." A rock without any inscription had been the only marker at the grave.

Among the groups sponsoring the tribute were the Metrolina chapter of the National Organization for Women and the Central Labor Councils of Charlotte and Hickory.

The strike at the Loray tire cord mill began in April 1929 with strikers demanding, in part, improved mill housing; at least $20 a week; 40-hour, five-day week; and equal pay for women and children.

Mrs. Wiggins was shot when a mob confronted a truckload of workers headed to a union gathering. Five mill workers were charged with the killing but were acquitted. Mrs. Wiggins' relatives and friends say an unidentified textile worker confessed to the murder on his death bed years ago.

Raleigh News and Observer, *16, 18 September 1929 and 17 September 1979; Margaret Larkin, "Ella May's Songs," Nation 129 (October 1929):382–83.*

DOCUMENT 19.3

Women Workers: The Persistence of Inequalities in the 1970s

More Women are Working

Women are the fastest growing sector of the labor force. In the last 25 years, the number of working women has nearly doubled. By 1978, about 42 million women were in the U.S. labor force, representing more than 40 percent of all workers. In 1979, for the first time, more than 50% of all American women were employed outside the home.

In North Carolina, the figures are even higher. Approximately 116,-000 women were in the labor force in 1978, or 55% of all women 16 and older. This compares with female participation rates of 37% in 1960 and 46% in 1970. By 1978, women constituted 43% of all workers in North Carolina. In High Point, 1979 figures showed more women working (20,489) than men (18,494). . . .

Women Work Due to Economic Need

Women work for the same reasons as men: to support themselves and their families. Thirty-five percent of North Carolina women in the labor force are single, widowed, divorced, or separated, and a large proportion of this group has young children. In fact, one in eight families is now headed by a woman, double the figures in 1940. Clearly, these women must work to support themselves and their children.

North Carolina has one of the highest percentages of married women in the labor force, up to 65 percent in 1978. In 1978, 68 percent of all married women were in the labor force, working or actively seeking work. The effect of inflation on family budgets has meant that these women also work out of pressing economic need. . . .

Women are Earning Less

In North Carolina and nationally, nearly 80 percent of all working women are concentrated in the four job categories: clerical, service, sales, and factory jobs. These jobs are at the low end of the pay scale, and offer little or no opportunity for advancement.

As a result, women earn significantly less than men, even when both work full-time, year round. In 1978, the median incomes in North Carolina were $7,900 for women and $11,100 for men.

This means that over one-half of full-time working women earn less than $8,000 a year, while fewer than one quarter of North Carolina men earn this little. And while 54 percent of full-time male workers earn $12,000 or more, only 14% of employed women earn this much. For persons with dependents to support, the wage gap is even more disparate. The median income of a male head of household was $12,300 in 1978, whereas a female head of household earned only $8,900. And minority women earn even less, in each category.

Women in North Carolina do not earn as much as men with comparable educational backgrounds. A woman with a high school diploma makes little more ($7,832) than a man who has not completed elementary school (7,305). And a woman with some college training makes significantly less (9,531) than a man with a high school degree ($11,720).

Finally, the unemployment rate is almost twice as high for women within each racial group as for men. Thus, unemployment in North Carolina in 1978 was: white males, 2.4%; white females, 4.1%; non-white males, 6.6%; non-white females, 11.8%.

Women in Education

In North Carolina, there is only one woman superintendent and only 195 of the state's 1,990 principals, or 9.8 percent are women. Although women make up 79 percent of elementary and secondary teachers, men hold 91 percent of the key leadership positions. Even with these disturbing figures, North Carolina fares better than many other states. A comparison study showed North Carolina ranked tenth in the nation in

1979, with women making up 14.85 percent of the state's superintendents, principals, and assistant principals. . . .

Report prepared by the North Carolina Council on the Status of Women, Raleigh.

DOCUMENT 19.4

The Equal Rights Amendment

Proposed Amendment XXVII
(Proposed by Congress on March 22, 1972)

Section 1. Equality of rights under the law shall not be denied or abridged by the United States or by any State on account of sex.

Section 2. The Congress shall have the power to enforce, by appropriate legislation, the provision of this article.

Section 3. This amendment shall take effect two years after the date of ratification.

DOCUMENT 19.5

The American Bar Association's Statement in Support of ERA

Why is the ERA Needed?

Our Constitution clearly prohibits discrimination by government on account of race, religion, and national origin. It does not clearly prohibit discrimination on account of sex. The men who drafted the Constitution two centuries ago and the men who amended it after the Civil War lived in a society that treated women as less than full citizens. A century ago, the 13th, 14th, and 15th Amendments were added to the Constitution to end black slavery and to guarantee black men the right to vote and the equal protection of the law. At that time, women were denied the vote and married women saw their property, their right to contract, their right to sue, and even the money they earned through their own labors taken from them and placed in the hands of their husbands. Eighteenth and nineteenth century authors of the Constitution did not intend to change the rule that women stand behind, not next, to men.

The ERA would change that rule. It would provide a durable guarantee that women and men will be treated by the law according to their needs, abilities, and aspirations as individuals. No ordinary statute can provide the bedrock protection assured by a Constitutional Amendment. No court decision can provide that protection, for the courts may interpret, but they may not amend, the Constitution. . . .

What Will the ERA Do?

The ERA will outlaw gender discrimination by government in much the same way the Constitution now outlaws discrimination by government because of race, religion, and national origin. For example, the ERA would outlaw securely and permanently:

—legal presumptions about the family's property, including presumptions that all household goods or farm land and equipment belong to the husband.

—unequal opportunities for males and females in public school academic and vocational programs.

—denial of social security or workers' compensation benefits to families of gainfully-employed women when such benefits are available to families of gainfully-employed men.

—unequal treatment of male and female juvenile offenders and prisoners.

—discrimination at all levels of public employment.

The ERA tells the lawmakers to classify on the basis of what people do, not who they are. Law conforming to the ERA would recognize the dignity and economic value of the homemaker's work, but it would not label the person who does the work "only a housewife." Favorable treatment due many women (and some men) because of the vital job they do at home should be assured under the ERA. The assurance would come from law that does not pigeonhole by gender. Instead of using a sex label, the law would stress the very real support the homemaker gives the family.

Will the ERA Deprive Homemakers and Children of Support in the Event of Separation or Divorce?

No. Support law conforming to the ERA would respect the division of labor that existed in the family. Ability to pay would determine who has the obligation to provide financial support. Need and family role would determine who has the right to receive payment. The full-time homemaker or the spouse who holds the lower-paid outside job would have a right to maintenance. Similarly, the child's right to support from his or her father will not be diminished by the ERA.

Will the ERA Force Wives and Mothers to Find Work Outside the Home?
No. The ERA limits what government can do. It would not apply to private relationships. A husband and wife will continue to be free to arrange their personal lives and family responsibilities as the couple sees fit.

Will Separate Restrooms Remain Under the ERA?
Yes. The Senate Judiciary Committee report explains that the ERA does not call for "unisex" public facilities. Rather, in keeping with the respect the Constitution accords personal privacy, the ERA permits sex-separated dormitories, restrooms, locker rooms, baths, showers, and sleeping facilities for prisoners, hospital patients, and military personnel.

Does the ERA Authorize Same Sex Marriages?
No. The ERA deals with government discrimination because of gender, not with discrimination based on homosexuality. The ERA calls for no change in laws defining marriage as the union of a man and a woman.

Does the ERA Deal with Abortion?
No. The Supreme Court's 1973 abortion decisions rest solely on the Due Process Clause now in the Constitution. The ERA bears no relationship to the Supreme Court's pronouncement against laws that bar abortion.

Will the ERA Eliminate Laws Assuring Women Safe, Healthy Working Conditions?
No. Federal law already prohibits different working conditions for men and women. Responsible legislators and unions now insist on genuinely protective labor legislation—laws that assure reasonable hours, adequate pay, and good working conditions for all workers.

Will the ERA Require Women's Social Organizations to Accept Men and Vice-Versa?
No. The ERA applies to government only. It does not apply to private organizations.

How Will the ERA Affect Women's Rights and Responsibilities to Serve in the Military?

If Congress reinstates a draft, all women would not be excluded, but many should be exempt for such reasons as child or other dependent care responsibilities, physical incapacity, or hardship. Women would be assigned to combat units only in the event they met standards of physical fitness and strength as stringent as those applicable to men. More significantly, the ERA will widen opportunities for women who seek the valuable job training, educational, medical, retirement, and veterans benefits associated with military service.

Does the ERA Take Away States' Rights?
No. The right of the states to legislate on matters of state concern is guaranteed by the 10th Amendment and is not affected by the ERA except that after ratification, state discrimination on account of sex, like state discrimination on account of race, religion, or national origin, will violate the Constitution.

Division of Public Service Activities, American Bar Association, 1800 M Street, NW, Washington, DC 20036.

DOCUMENT 19.6

North Carolina Women Opposing ERA Speak out against Ratification in Pamphlet Entitled "The ERA Fraud"

"My view that the ERA is the most destructive piece of legislation to ever pass Congress still stands. . . ."
—Former U.S. Senator, Sam J. Ervin, Jr.

ERA Will Hurt the Family:
ERA will invalidate all state laws which require a husband to support his wife. ERA will impose on Women the equal (50%) financial obligation to support their spouses (under criminal penalties, just like husbands).
ERA will impose on mothers the equal (50%) financial obligation for the financial support of their infant and minor children.
ERA will deprive senior women, who have spent many years in the home as wife and mother, of their present right to be supported by their husbands, and to be provided with a home.
ERA will eliminate the present right of a wife to draw Social Security

benefits based on her husband's earnings. For a homemaker to receive benefits, her husband would be forced to pay double Social Security taxes on the assumed value of her services in the home.

ERA will compel the states to set up taxpayer-financed child-care centers for all children regardless of need. (See Ohio Task Force Report)

"Not only would women, including mothers, be subject to the draft, but the military would be compelled to place them in combat units alongside of men."

U.S. House Judiciary Committee Report, No. 92-359

ERA will deprive state legislatures of all power to stop or regulate abortions at any time during pregnancy. ERA will give women a "constitutional" right to abortion on demand.

ERA will legalize homosexual "marriages" and permit such "couples" to adopt children and to get tax and homestead benefits now given to husbands and wives.

ERA is a big power-grab by the Federal Government. It will transfer jurisdiction over marriage, property rights, divorce, alimony, child custody, and inheritance rights out of the hands of the individual states and into the Federal bureaucrats and the Federal courts.

ERA will make women subject to the draft on an equal basis with men in all our future wars. ERA will make women and mothers subject to military combat and warship duty.

"I call the Equal Rights Amendment the liftin' and totin' bill. More than half of the black women with jobs work in service occupations; if the Amendment becomes law, we will be the ones liftin' and totin'."

—Jean Noble, National Council of Negro Women

ERA will eliminate all-girls' and all-boys' schools and colleges. ERA will eliminate single-sex fraternities and sororities in high schools and on college campuses.

ERA may give the Federal Government the power to force the admission of women to seminaries equally with men, and possibly force the churches to ordain women.

ERA will deprive women in industry of their legal protections against being involuntarily assigned to heavy-lifting, strenuous, and dangerous men's jobs, and compulsory overtime.

ERA will require police departments to eliminate physical tests and to pass over qualified men so that women will be hired and assigned on a one-to-one basis.

ERA will eliminate present lower life insurance and automobile accident insurance rates for women.

What ERA Will Not Do:

ERA will not give women "equal pay for equal work," better paying jobs, promotions, or better working conditions. ERA can add nothing whatsoever to the Equal Employment Opportunity Act of 1972.

ERA will not help women in the field of credit. This has already been mandated by the Equal Credit Opportunity Act of 1974. On the other hand, ERA will take away from wives their present right to get credit in their husband's name.

ERA will not give women better educational opportunities. This has already been mandated by the Education Amendments of 1972.

ERA will not help women in athletics, but will require sex-integrated coed nonsense such as the recent order by the Pennsylvania courts that all high schools must permit girls and boys to compete and practice together in all sports including football and wrestling.

ERA will not protect privacy, but instead will prohibit privacy based on sex in public school restrooms, hospitals, public accommodations, prisons and reform schools.

Women of North Carolina Against the Equal Rights Amendment, Box 30365, Raleigh, NC 27612.

DOCUMENT 19.7

Women Workers: Persistence of Inequalities in North Carolina in the 1980s

1982 Year-Round Full-Time Workers

Men:			Women		
	All men	$16,913		All women	$10,427
	White	$17,757		White	$10,672
	Minority	$12,245		Minority	$ 9,332

1982 Wages by Occupation Category by Sex
Year-Round Full-Time Wage Earners

Occupation	Male	Female
Professional, Technical	$12,615	$14,499
Managers, Administrators	21,947	17,297

Sales Workers	28,089	6,268
Craft Workers	18,529	11,202
Operatives (i.e. machine operators)	16,000	12,300
Private Household	13,177	9,590
Other Service Workers	N/A	4,712

1982 Earnings by Educational Attainment (Full-Time Workers)

School	Male	Female
Elementary	$12,154	$ 6,307
Some High School (1–3 years)	12,275	7,683
High School Graduate	16,329	10,011
Some College (1–3 years)	17,147	9,572
College Graduate	21,046	13,366
Advanced Degree	27,578	17,592

U.S. Department of Commerce, Bureau of the Census; U.S. Department of Labor; North Carolina Department of Labor; North Carolina Office of State Budget.

SUGGESTED READINGS

Banner, Lois. *Women in Modern America: A Brief History.* New York: Harcourt Brace Jovanovich, 1974.

Bird, Caroline, and U.S. Members and Staff of the National Commission on the Observance of International Women's Year. *What Women Want: From the Official Report to the President, the Congress and the People of the United States.* New York: Simon & Schuster, 1978.

Chafe, William H. *The American Woman: Her Changing Social, Economic, and Political Role, 1920–1970.* New York: Oxford University Press, 1972.

_____. *Women and Equality: Changing Patterns in American Culture.* New York: Oxford University Press, 1977.

Coates, Albert. *By Her Own Bootstraps: A Saga of Women in North Carolina.* N.p., 1975.

Evans, Sara. *Personal Politics: The Roots of Women's Liberation in the Civil Rights Movement and the New Left.* New York: Alfred A. Knopf, 1979.

Hagood, Margaret Jarman. *Mothers of the South: Portraiture of the White Ten-*

ant Farm Woman. New York: W. W. Norton, 1979. (Reprint of the 1939 edition published by University of North Carolina Press.)

Hall, Jacquelyn Dowd. *Revolt against Chivalry: Jessie Daniel Ames and the Women's Campaign against Lynching*. New York: Columbia University Press, 1979.

Kerber, Linda K., and Mathews, Jane DeHart, eds. *Woman's America: Refocusing the Past*. New York: Oxford University Press, 1982.

Lerner, Gerda, ed. *Black Women in White America*. New York: Random House, 1972.

Mathews, Donald G., and Mathews, Jane DeHart. *The Equal Rights Amendment and the Politics of Cultural Conflict: Feminists and Traditionalists in North Carolina*. New York: Oxford University Press, 1984.

North Carolina Governor's Commission on the Status of Women. *The Many Lives of North Carolina Women*. N.p., 1964.

Scott, Anne Firor. *The Southern Lady: From Pedestal to Politics, 1830–1930*. Chicago: University of Chicago Press, 1970.

Spruill, Julia Cherry. *Women's Life and Work in the Southern Colonies*. New York: W. W. Norton, 1972. (Reprint of the 1938 edition published by the University of North Carolina Press.)

Contributors

LINDLEY S. BUTLER, historian-in-residence at Rockingham Community College, is author of *Rockingham County: A Brief History* and editor of *The Narrative of Col. David Fanning.*

ROBERT M. CALHOON, professor of history at the University of North Carolina at Greensboro, is author of *Religion and the American Revolution in North Carolina* and "A Troubled Culture: North Carolina in the New Nation, 1790–1834," in *Writing North Carolina History,* edited by Jeffrey J. Crow and Larry E. Tise.

JEFFREY J. CROW, administrator of the Historical Publications Section, North Carolina Division of Archives and History, is editor-in-chief of the *North Carolina Historical Review* and coeditor, with Flora J. Hatley, of *Black Americans in North Carolina and the South.*

ROBERT F. DURDEN, professor of history at Duke University and chairman of the department 1974–80, is author of *The Dukes of Durham, 1865–1929* and, with Jeffrey J. Crow, *Maverick Republican in the Old South State: A Political Biography of Daniel L. Russell.*

PAUL D. ESCOTT, professor of history at the University of North Carolina at Charlotte, is author of *After Secession: Jefferson Davis and the Failure of Confederate Nationalism;*

Slavery Remembered: A Record of Twentieth-Century Slave Narratives; and, with others, *A People and a Nation.*

WILLARD B. GATEWOOD, JR., Alumni Distinguished Professor of History at the University of Arkansas, is author of *Science and Religion: The Controversy over Evolution; Slave and Freeman: Autobiography of George L. Knox;* and *Free Men of Color: Autobiography of Willis Augustus Hodges.*

J. EDWIN HENDRICKS, professor of history and director of the Historic Preservation Program at Wake Forest University, is author of *Charles Thomson and the Making of a New Nation, 1729–1824;* coauthor, with C. C. Pearson, of *Liquor and Anti-Liquor in Virginia, 1619–1919;* and editor of *Forsyth: The History of a County on the March.*

DON HIGGINBOTHAM, professor of history at the University of North Carolina at Chapel Hill and chairman of the department 1978–1983, is the author of *George Washington and George Marshall* and editor of the *Papers of James Iredell* and *Reconsiderations of the Revolutionary War.*

JANE DE HART MATHEWS, professor of history and American studies and director of women's studies at the University of North Carolina at Chapel Hill, is author, with Linda

Kerber, of *Women's America: Refocusing the Past.*

THOMAS C. PARRAMORE, associate professor of history and politics at Meredith College, is author of *North Carolina: The History of an American State* and *Express Lanes and Country Roads: The Way We Lived in North Carolina, 1920–1970.*

HERBERT R. PASCHAL (1927–82), professor of history at East Carolina University and chairman of the department 1963–79, was author of *A History of Colonial Bath* and numerous essays and papers on Colonial North Carolina.

WILLIAM S. POWELL, professor of history at the University of North Carolina at Chapel Hill, is author of *North Carolina: A Bicentennial History; North Carolina Gazetteer;* and editor of the *Dictionary of North Carolina Biography.*

WILLIAM S. PRICE, JR., director of the North Carolina Division of Archives and History, is editor of volumes 4 and 5 of the new series of the *Colonial Records of North Carolina* and consulting editor of the five volume series *The Way We Lived in North Carolina.*

ALEXANDER R. STOESEN, professor of history at Guilford College, is author of *A Celebration of Guilford County Since 1890.*

LARRY E. TISE, executive director of the Pennsylvania Historical and Museum Commission, is coeditor, with Jeffrey J. Crow, of *The Southern Experience in the American Revolution.*

ALLEN W. TRELEASE, professor of history at the University of North Carolina at Greensboro, is author of *White Terror: The Ku Klux Klan Conspiracy and Southern Reconstruction* and "The Civil War and Reconstruction, 1861–1876," in *Writing North Carolina History,* edited by Jeffrey J. Crow and Larry E. Tise.

ALAN D. WATSON, professor of history at the University of North Carolina at Wilmington, is author of *Society in Colonial North Carolina* and *Money and Monetary Problems in Early North Carolina.*

HARRY L. WATSON, associate professor of history at the University of North Carolina at Chapel Hill, is author of *Jacksonian Politics and Community Conflict: The Emergence of the Second American Party System in Cumberland County, North Carolina* and *An Independent People: The Way We Lived in North Carolina, 1770–1820.*

MAX R. WILLIAMS, Creighton Sossomon Professor of History at Western Carolina University, is editor of volumes 5–8 of *The Papers of William A. Graham.*

Index